ABOUT THE AUTHOR

Dorothy A. Sisk (Ed.D., UCLA) is world-renowned for her leadership in gifted education over the past twenty years. She is currently a professor at the University of South Florida, where she also directs the Gifted Children Center and The Centre for Creativity, Innovation, and Leadership, and coordinates teacher training in gifted education.

Dr. Sisk has served as the director of the U.S. Office of the Gifted and Talented, playing an instrumental role in increasing the cadre of professionally trained consultants for the gifted, thereby expanding opportunities for students.

Editor of *Gifted International* and a member of the advisory boards of *Gifted Children Monthly* and *International Journal for Gifted*, Dr. Sisk is the current Executive Administrator of the World Council for Gifted and Talented Children, a member of the National Association for Gifted Children executive board and past president of the Association for Gifted. She has also authored or coauthored numerous articles and papers, and has coauthored two recent textbooks in education.

CREATIVE TEACHING OF THE GIFTED

Other McGraw-Hill Titles for Special Education

Axelrod, Saul: Behavior Modification for the Classroom Teacher
DeLoach, C., and Greer, B. G.: Adjustment to Severe Physical Disability: A
   Metamorphosis
Robinson, Nancy M., and Robinson, Halbert B.: The Mentally Retarded Child
Ross, Alan O.: Psychological Aspects of Learning Disabilities and Reading Disorders
Ross, Alan O.: Psychological Disorders of Children
Schmid, R. E., and Nagata, L.: Contemporary Issues in Special Education
Wehman, Paul, and McLaughlin, Philip J.: Program Development in Special
   Education

CREATIVE TEACHING OF THE GIFTED

Dorothy Sisk

College of Education
University of South Florida

McGRAW-HILL BOOK COMPANY

New York St. Louis San Francisco Auckland Bogotá
Hamburg Johannesburg London Madrid Mexico Milan Montreal
New Delhi Panama Paris São Paulo Singapore Sydney Tokyo Toronto

This book was set in Optima by Harper Graphics.
The editor was Barbara L. Raab;
the cover was designed by Suzanne Haldane;
the production supervisor was Leroy A. Young.
Project supervision was done by The Total Book.
R. R. Donnelley & Sons Company was printer and binder.
Cover photo was taken by Thomas S. England, Photo Researchers, Inc.

CREATIVE TEACHING OF THE GIFTED

1 2 3 4 5 6 7 8 9 0   DOCDOC   8 9 4 3 2 1 0 9 8 7

ISBN 0-07-057701-3

Library of Congress Cataloging-in-Publication Data

Sisk, Dorothy
    Creative teaching of the gifted.

    Includes bibliographies.
    1. Gifted children—Education—United States.
2. Gifted Children—Education—Curricula.   3. Creative
thinking (Education)   4. Activity programs in education.
I. Title.
LC3993.9.S57   1987   371.95'3   86-10678
ISBN 0-07-057701-3

CONTENTS

SECTION 2 EDUCATIONAL PROGRAMS AND PRACTICES

PREFACE

Recent political and economic developments have caused educators to think with renewed vigor about the education of gifted students in our society. New developments in the field of educational psychology, sociology, biology, and mind/brain research have generated an intellectual revolution. Educators find that they cannot avoid the issue of providing appropriate education for the gifted.

The ideas in this book grew out of my association with numerous gifted students and educators at all levels. Through discussions, courses, workshops, and day-to-day contact, my appreciation and knowledge of the gifted were developed and continue to develop. I am particularly indebted to my early teachers, Jeanne Delp, Ruth Martinson, Juliana Genseley, and May Seagoe, and to my numerous colleagues in professional organizations. They are listed in the order in which we worked and planned together in gifted education: John Gowan, Bill Vassar, Joe Renzulli, James Gallagher, Marvin Gold, Kay Bruch, Irving Sato, Alexinia Baldwin, Sandra Kaplan, John Feldhusen, Joyce VanTassell-Baska, Ken Seeley, June Maker, Barbara Clark, June Cox, Jacob Getzels, Dick Benjamin, Charles Patterson, Ann Shaw, Val Wilkie, and countless others. I extend my gratitude and hope that this book passes along knowledge and encouragement to educators to creatively teach the gifted.

Creative Teaching of the Gifted is an expository text and a practical guide for those interested in teaching the gifted. Many of the ideas grew out of my varied experiences as teacher and counselor of the gifted; school administrator of gifted programs; teacher; trainer; local, state, national, and international advocate for gifted education; federal administrator of gifted programs, and, most important, parent of a gifted child. As a consequence, this book will have special appeal to counselors, teachers, school and college administrators, and all who are interested in or responsible for gifted programs. It is intended for a wide range of readers: for students preparing either to teach or to administer programs, for teachers and others actively engaged in gifted programs, and for parents and citizens—in other words for all who are, or should be, consciously concerned with effective education for gifted students.

This book is written at a time when there is considerable concern about the quality of American education and a renewed interest in gifted education. The definition of gifted used in *Creative Teaching of the Gifted* is multidimensional and includes a number of talents: intellectual talent, specific academic aptitude or talent, leadership, creative talent, including the visual and performing arts, and kinesthetics. These talents exist singly and/or in combination. There is growing evidence that school districts are broadening their efforts to identify and serve a variety of talents, notably in the visual and performing arts, in leadership, and in specific areas such as aptitude or talent in mathematics and science.

Creative Teaching of the Gifted is divided into three sections. The first, "Perspective on Education of the Gifted" provides a foundation for planning and developing programs for the gifted. Section Two focuses on educational programs and practices. Section Three covers unique problems and needs such as the special subpopulations of the gifted, counseling and guidance needs, expanding dimensions of learning, and current trends and issues in gifted education.

The Appendices include a sample list of competencies for teachers of the gifted, a sample simulation game, and a list of state directors and leaders of educational programs for gifted students.

This book can have true value only if it stimulates educators to examine, define, and extend their provisions for gifted students. During the past decade, schools have made great progress in locating and providing for gifted students. Now it is necessary to build upon the foundations of our previous experiences and to broaden the provisions so that no gifted student will be neglected.

Dorothy Sisk

ACKNOWLEDGEMENTS

I wish to entend my thanks for the skillful and dedicated assistance of Jean Peterson and Pauline Atkinson through the many revisions of the current text. In addition, the continued support of Bettina Anderson as editor was immeasurable. Lastly, I acknowledge my gratitude to the following individuals' editorial assistance which added considerably to the quality and form of the content: Percy Bates, Professor, University of Michigan; Kay Bull, University of Oklahoma; Eleanor Hall, Coordinator for Gifted and Talented, Auburn University; Julie Long, Coordinator, Programs for Gifted and Talented, Lexington, South Carolina; Sandra Kaplan, Associate Director, National/State Leadership Training Institute on the Gifted/Talented; Doris Shallcross, Professor, University of Massachusetts/Amherst; and Joseph Walker, Professor, Georgia State University.

CREATIVE
TEACHING
OF THE GIFTED

SECTION ONE

PERSPECTIVE ON EDUCATION OF THE GIFTED

A major theme of *Creative Teaching of the Gifted* is the multifaceted or multidimensional concept of giftedness. A second major theme is the individual differences of gifted students and how these unique needs and characteristics cause specific behaviors which provide insight and direction for organizing appropriate educational activities. Section One provides the necessary foundation for effective program planning and development.

The first three chapters of *Creative Teaching of the Gifted* offer a perspective on the concept of giftedness. Chapter 1 presents a brief historical summary of the growing educational and societal awareness and concern for gifted students. In addition, the differing roles and contributions of the federal, state, and local governments are introduced. Chapter 2 describes the needs and characteristics of gifted students, using a multifaceted definition and identification process. Also, the case study technique is offered as an example of multifaceted identification and planning. Chapter 3 presents a rationale for the use of individualized educational plans (IEP) and the preparation of goals and objectives.

1

CHAPTER 1

EMERGING CONCEPT OF GIFTEDNESS

What lies behind us and lies before us are small matters compared to what lies within us.

Ralph Waldo Emerson

During difficult and pressing times, armies use their best officers, athletic teams put forward their best players, and business and industry call on their most talented managers. In times of stress, the gifted and talented are valued. In an increasingly complex world, we become more dependent on technology and creative efforts and more interdependent as nations. As a result, we depend on people with broadened perspectives and international understanding. We need intelligent and creative leaders; we need the gifted and talented.

Egalitarian societies like the United States have the unique challenge to develop a reservoir of human potential and talent to its highest functioning level and still meet the needs of all children. Few people argue with the notion that a democracy respects individual differences and that the ultimate educational goal is self-realization. Yet in actual practice, two groups fare the worst in the school system: (1) the very bright and talented—the gifted; and (2) the handicapped. In attempting to meet the needs of all children, education aims for the middle and the extremes suffer.

Gallagher (1985) states the dilemma:

> Failure to help the handicapped child reach his potential is a personal tragedy for him and his family; failure to help the gifted child reach his potential is a societal tragedy. (page 4)

Photograph on facing page courtesy of Charles Harbutt/ARCHIVE Pictures Inc.

In a society that places high value on the individual, it must be recognized that progress comes through the efforts of all, but only a few will provide the ideas and plans. Society depends on the insight and foresight of its most able members, and the neglect of their total development is a loss that cannot be calculated.

AN HISTORICAL PERSPECTIVE

In exploring the roots of the gifted movement, the contribution of ancient philosophers, notably Socrates and Plato, cannot be ignored (Nettleship, 1966). Socrates observed varying stages of development at varying speeds. His concept of giftedness developed from this interaction. Socrates recognized the need for more gifted people and considered how giftedness could be nurtured. He suggested early identification and development of individual intellectual gifts. Plato stated that a more perfect social order could be achieved by identifying gifted children and educating them to become the rulers of the state. Both philosophers viewed giftedness as the ability to quickly pass through the levels of knowledge and achieve a high level of understanding at each level.

From this philosophical and rationalistic concept of giftedness posed by the ancient philosophers, scientific inquiry transformed the concept to that of intelligence as a fixed human characteristic. Over 100 years ago, Charles Darwin's (1868) investigation of the origin of species had a profound effect on the thinking of an English biologist, Francis Galton. Galton (1869), intrigued with the concept of individual differences, began researching the inheritability of human intelligence. He was the first to construct an intelligence test derived from scientific data. He based the test on the theory that sensory acuity and general intelligence at infancy are related (Howley et al., 1986).

In France, Alfred Binet developed a test to identify slow school children in order to better meet their needs. Binet (1905) questioned the concept of fixed intelligence and stated that much of intelligence was developmental and educable. In the United States, Binet's ideas were translated into a revised version of the original test by Lewis Terman in 1916 (Binet, 1916). Because Terman was employed at Stanford and because the copyright was assigned to the foundation, the test is called the Stanford-Binet.

Binet and Terman advanced the concept of intellect or giftedness from philosophical and rational inquiry into scientific inquiry of the differences of the human intellect. Yet, within the domain of scientific inquiry, the intelligence of an individual was seen as a global construct, with the intelligence quotient (IQ) indicating a fixed amount of intelligence.

From this fixed point of view, subsequent researchers explored the idea that intelligence could be defined in terms of factors or aptitudes. Spearman (1904) was one of the first to define intelligence factors. He delineated two types of aptitudes or factors: general aptitude and specific factors unique to a particular task. Each individual was thought to have so much "g" factor and then to bring to bear specific "s" factors to carry out tasks. Thurstone (1938) later delineated the "s" factors into seven primary mental abilities: number factor, verbal factor, space relations, memory, reasoning, word fluency, and perceptual speed.

Guilford (1959) continued to expand the multiple-factor theory in a factor-analytic model of intelligence. He identified and classified cognitive abilities along three dimensions: operations, contents, and products. According to Guilford's definition, the operations are intellectual activities which involve the processing of information. Contents are the types of information on which operations are performed, and products are the outcomes of the different kinds of mental ability. Guilford's work marks a turning point in conceptualizing giftedness, directing psychologists and educators away from a single measure of giftedness.

One last contribution to this brief historical background on the concept of giftedness is the monumental work of Piaget. Piaget (1952) claimed the individual plays an active role in her/his cognitive development. In order to progress through the stages of cognitive development—sensorimotor, preoperational, concrete operational, and formal operations—the individual submits to the pressure of the environment. As the individual interacts with the environment, he/she assimilates and accommodates information. Alexander and Muia (1982) illustrate these complex ideas in Figure 1-1, a simple diagram of inputs from the environment.

Life experiences interact with the individual's intellectual structure and are expressed in outputs. Alexander and Muia (1982) state:

> . . . stimulations that arise from the environment are experienced by the individual as inputs into the intellectual system, interact with that system, and are manifested in outputs unique to the individual. . . . (page 9)

At the same time these developments were taking place in the realm of scientific inquiry, schools were being established and efforts were being made to educate children.

FIGURE 1-1
Integrated view of cognitive development.
(*P. A. Alexander and J. A. Muia,* Gifted Education, *Aspen Publications, Rockville, Maryland, 1982. Reprinted by permission.*)

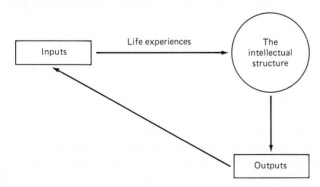

Early Education Efforts on Behalf of Gifted

Education for the gifted began in the early American colonies in 1635 with the establishment of the Boston Latin Grammar School (Gold, 1965). Soon after, Harvard College was established in 1636 and both have continued. Latin Grammar schools primarily served the gifted in the first 200 years of our country, training students as lawyers, ministers, and teachers. The rest of society was provided with a basic education by the village church schools and dame schools. Two separate educations existed in the colonies; one for the gifted, another for the masses. This system of separate education was the rule until the nineteenth century when the notion of universal public school systems was introduced.

The irony is that if separate education had continued, there might not be the present need and interest in educating the gifted. Yet democracy as we know it in the United States, with the emphasis on equality and free opportunity for development, might not have evolved.

One of the more fascinating aspects of American history is the ongoing conflict between various ideas of democracy held by both leaders and citizens. Thomas Jefferson's early ideas about the development of an intellectual class were elitist. Jefferson suggested surveying the country to identify individuals with talent and nurturing these talents. Jefferson believed the country would prosper and attain its goals if talented young people were given opportunities to become leaders. He urged that the talented be identified from various segments of society and that they be provided with scholarships to college. While he wanted to structure society to provide all citizens with an equal starting point in their lives' journeys, talent and industriousness were to be the basic sorting mechanisms.

Andrew Jackson, in contrast, thought that all men regardless of experience or education, could participate and share in the leadership of the country. Jackson hoped men with ordinary common sense would keep the intellectuals and the aristocrats in tune with reality and out of mischief. He thought that one of the functions of government in a democratic society was to assure that no person's inherent advantage (e.g., inherited wealth, social standing, and, by extension, intelligence and ability) would be translated into inordinate power or position.

The basic difference between Jeffersonian and Jacksonian education was the fundamental belief that all men should be given equal opportunity (Jefferson) and that all men should be treated equally (Jackson).

This ongoing Jeffersonian–Jacksonian ideological debate still stimulates heated discussions. The terms "Jeffersonian" or "Jacksonian" may not be used, but there is a controversy concerning the question of equal opportunity and equal treatment. If the concept of equal opportunity were enforced in today's schools, there would be no need for special program development for the gifted, for all students would develop their full potential. However, many educators view equal opportunity for all, including education for the gifted, as a form of elitism. Yet, the most undemocratic act any nation can perpetrate upon its students is to offer equal education for all and equal standards for all, with the definition of equal being "the same."

Schools' efforts to provide opportunity for all students show wide discrepancies.

Yet, as long as the public school system tries to provide for its diverse school population there is continued interest in meeting the needs of gifted students.

In reviewing the early educational efforts on behalf of the gifted, the genius of Terman cannot be ignored. He was a major catalyst for education for the gifted and devoted his life to bright and quick students.

Terman's life work, *Genetic Studies of Genius*, compiled between 1925 and 1959, is a remarkable and valuable collection of information on gifted students. Terman's project to study gifted students was funded in 1921 for $20,000. For 34 years, more than a quarter of a million dollars was raised to fund the study. As students were added, the size of the group studied grew to 1528 children. After Terman's death in 1956, the study was continued by his associate Melita Oden, who conducted follow-up testing every 5 years. It is scheduled to continue until the death of the last Terman project participant in the 21st century, and is financed primarily from Stanford-Binet test royalties.

Terman spent considerable time studying mental tests, particularly those of Galton and Binet, which led him to study gifted and precocious children. As a graduate student at Clark University, Terman studied the differences between the mentally backward and the precocious. During his doctoral work, he conceptualized his life study. He used the Stanford-Binet intelligence test to identify his subjects, with his California sample having IQs of 140 or higher. His major findings are:

- The gifted differ among themselves in many ways and are not homogenous.
- The stereotypes of the gifted child as puny, asocial, or prepsychotic, and of high intelligence as akin to insanity, are discounted.
- To identify the most intelligent child in a class, one should consult the record book for the youngest.

- Superiority in intelligence is maintained through adulthood.
- Instructional acceleration at all levels is beneficial.
- Gifted students who did not attend college had the same intellectual level as Ph.D. candidates.
- Research on the differences between the most and least successful men in the gifted group indicate socioeconomic status and college education of the father as influencing factors, as well as force of character.
- Mental age continues to increase into middle age.
- There were many more very high IQ persons than predicted by the normal curve of probability. (Terman & Oden, 1947; Gowan, 1977)

Gowan (1977), in *The Gifted and the Creative: A Fifty Year Perspective*, dedicated to the memory of Galton, Binet, Terman, and Hollingworth, made the following observations and criticisms concerning the Terman study:

- Intelligence was assumed to be a single-faceted phenomenon.
- Environmental factors such as socioeconomic status and environmental influences were not accounted for in assessing the abilities of minority group members.
- There was no attempt to measure or to recognize creative ability.

• Teacher nomination alone was not a reliable method of identification.

Another problem with Terman's study is that potentially gifted children, and those with serious problems, were not included. Gallagher (1985) points out that the Terman students were predominantly white, upper-middle-class, and high achieving, and the Terman data should be reviewed with that in mind.

As a result of Terman's work with the California students, many people continued to equate "gifted" with "heredity" and to rely on a single index of giftedness, in this case, the Stanford-Binet test.

DEFINING GIFTEDNESS

There is continuing interest in responding to the criticisms of Terman's work and the idea of relying on a single index of giftedness. Currently, many school systems view intelligence or giftedness as multifaceted, with a number of talents included under the general term of giftedness. This point of view is reflected in the national definition, adopted by the no longer existent U.S. Office of Gifted and Talented (Marland, 1972).

> Gifted and talented children are those identified by professionally qualified persons who, by virtue of outstanding abilities, are capable of high performance. These are children who require differentiated educational programs in order to realize their contribution to self and society. (Sec. 582)

Children capable of high performance include those with demonstrated achievement and/or potential ability in any of the following areas, singly or in combination:

1 General intellectual ability
2 Specific academic aptitude
3 Creative or productive thinking
4 Leadership ability
5 Visual and performing arts
6 Psychomotor ability

Renzulli (1978), in examining the Office of Education's definition, found the following problems:

1 It fails to include motivational factors (task commitment).
2 It attempts to separate the six aptitude areas by presenting six categories that represent process abilities and two that focus on the performance areas.
3 It is advocated by many people in theory, but the use of IQ tests or aptitude tests to identify all kinds of giftedness predominates in practice.

In general, educators know the definition of giftedness has advanced from a unitary concept of giftedness or one fixed score. However, as Renzulli (1978) states, many educators still plan and develop programs for one type of giftedness, the intellectually gifted. For this type of giftedness, intelligence scores are usually the main criteria. Two major problems with single-criterion identification are that many students are not performing to their potential and that many culturally different students will not be identified.

Steinberg and Wagner (1982) propose another definition of gifted: ". . . the purposive selection of an adaptation to real world environments relevant to one's life." They state that the key psychological basis of intellectual giftedness resides in insight skills. Insight skills include three main kinds of processes: (1) sifting relevant from irrelevant information, (2) combining isolated pieces of information with a unified whole; (3) relating newly acquired information to information acquired in the past.

Steinberg and Wagner emphasize problem-solving abilities and view the gifted student as one who processes information rapidly and uses insight abilities. Gardner (1983) (Ellison, 1984) also suggests a concept of multiple intelligence. He states that there are seven ways of viewing the world: linguistic and logical; mathematical; spatial intelligence; musical intelligence; fine motor movement, and interpersonal and intrapersonal. These ideas are similar to the early notions of giftedness as offered by Bish (1975) in which he called for a definition including four types of giftedness: academic, creative, psychosocial, and kinesthetic.

Clark (1983) suggests giftedness is biologically rooted and is a label for high-level intelligence resulting from the advanced and accelerated integration of brain functions. These functions include physical sensing, emotion, cognition, and intuition. She states that advanced intelligence can be expressed through abilities in areas such as creativity, academic aptitude, leadership, and the visual and performing arts. Issues emerging from these differing definitions and points of view on giftedness will be discussed in greater detail in Chapter 2.

Using a broadened definition of giftedness (Marland, 1972), a given school system would expect to locate a target population of 3 to 5 percent of its students as gifted.* The federal government's definition, in its entirety or with some modification, is used by most state education departments. Because of its wide use and emphasis on multitalent, this definition is used throughout this text.

A brief description of each area of giftedness or talent under the overall term "gifted" in the national definition is discussed to illustrate how school districts can operationalize the definition.

General Intellectual Ability or Talent

General intellectual ability is usually defined by laymen and educators in terms of a high IQ test score. Typically, students who score 132 on the Stanford-Binet; 130 on the Weschler Intelligence Scale for Children (WISC-R), Full Scale; or 130 on either the verbal or performance sections of the WISC-R are considered to be demonstrating superior general intellectual ability. Theoretically, students who have scores at this level are also expected to demonstrate outstanding performance. In reality, because of a number of single and interacting factors, the gifted

---

* The U.S. Department of Education did not publish official prevalence figures. However, 3 to 5 percent was reported in federal reports and legislation (Erickson et al., 1978; Sisk, 1981).

student with intellectual talent may be underachieving in the regular classroom. Students with general intellectual talent are often recognized by parents and educators by their wide-ranging general fund of information, high vocabulary level, memory, abstract word knowledge, and abstract reasoning.

Specific Academic Aptitude or Talent

Students with specific academic aptitude are located by outstanding performance on an achievement or aptitude test. This talent may be narrowly demonstrated in one area, such as mathematics or language arts. The Talent Search sponsored by Johns Hopkins University, through the Study of Mathematically Precocious Youth, and the National Talent Search at the universities of Arizona and Denver and at Duke and Northwestern universities identify students with specific academic aptitude. In the National Talent Search, students who score at the 97th percentile or higher on standard achievement tests are further tested on the Scholastic Aptitude Test (SAT). Large numbers of students achieve at remarkable levels on those tests.

Creative or Productive Thinking.   Getzels and Jackson (1962) in their classic study, *Creativity and Intelligence*, define creative or productive thinking as the ability to produce new forms by bringing together elements usually thought of as independent or dissimilar. They define creative and productive thinking as the aptitude for achieving new meanings that have social value.

Callahan (1978, 1980) lists characteristics of the creative, productive student. Williams (1970), Torrance (1977), and Parnes (1975) support Callahan's (1978, 1980) list of characteristics of the creative, productive student:

- Openness to experience
- Internal locus of evaluation
- Ability to play with ideas
- Willingness to take risks
- Preference for complexity
- Tolerance for ambiguity
- Positive self-image
- Ability to lose oneself in a task

Creative and productive students are identified through the use of creativity tests such as the Torrance Test of Creative Thinking (TTCT) or through demonstrated creative performance. The creative, productive student is a challenge to the regular classroom teacher. Such students often prefer working alone and do not take direction well. They need a sense of purpose and reject repetition for the sake of bringing the entire group to a certain level of performance. In addition, teachers and peers may view their sense of humor and playfulness as distracting behavior.

Leadership Ability.   Leadership can be defined as the ability to direct individuals or groups to a common decision or action (Sisk & Shallcross, 1986).

Students who demonstrate giftedness in leadership ability use group skills and negotiate in difficult situations. Many teachers recognize leadership in their students through their keen interest and skill in problem solving.

Maker (1982) lists the following leadership characteristics:

- Shows self-confidence with age mates and adults
- Carries responsibility well
- Seems comfortable when asked to show work to class
- Seems to be well liked by classmates
- Is cooperative with teachers and classmates
- Is generally easy to get along with
- Adapts readily to new situations
- Tends to dominate

These students can be identified with instruments, such as the Fundamental Interpersonal Relations Orientation-Behavior (FIRO-B), and by their demonstrated leadership, such as serving as captains of athletic or debate teams or as instigators of behind-the-scenes action in the classroom, which may be socially desirable or undesirable.

Visual and Performing Arts. Gifted students in the visual and performing arts demonstrate special talents in the arts, music, dance, drama, and other related studies. The visual and performing arts is one of the more neglected areas of giftedness in today's schools.

Torrance (1980) lists the following indicators for dramatics:

- Skilled in mimicry, imitations, and impressions
- Skilled in charades that rely on the use of gesture and body language
- Expresses ideas powerfully and accurately through body language

Similar lists can be developed in the other areas of the arts. Giftedness in the visual and performing arts may be identified through judgment of authorities in the arts by auditions, as well as through the use of general checklists.

Psychomotor Ability. The last area of giftedness was deleted by Congress in 1976 by Public Law 95-561. The Marland report (1972) listed this category for students gifted in the use of gross and fine motor development. It includes gymnastics, swimming, and other athletic areas, as well as minute precision areas such as crafts and surgery.

Legislators believed this last area of giftedness was being developed and served by the schools' sports programs; consequently, in 1976 Congress limited the funding of programs to five areas: (1) intellectual, (2) specific academic aptitude, (3) leadership, (4) creative and productive thinking, and (5) visual and performing arts.

Multiple Gifts. Clearly, students can be gifted in several areas. Few would deny the tri-level giftedness of Senator William Bradley, the athlete, legislator, and Rhodes scholar; the dual gifts of Leonard Bernstein, gifted in creative and productive thinking, as well as in visual and performing arts; or of Henry Kissinger, gifted in intellectual ability and leadership. The major implication of this for educators considering the use of multiple gifts is to eliminate the high IQ as the sole criterion for giftedness.

One of the more promising multiple-talent models is that of Taylor (1968). Taylor's (1985) groupings include academic talent and eight other types: creative and productive talent, evaluative or decision-making talent, planning talent, forecasting talent, communication talent, implementing talent, human relations talent, and discerning opportunities talent.

In a world that values products and performances, it is not strange that some view giftedness solely as a person–environment interaction. The most notable spokesperson for this view is Renzulli (1978). In his writing, Renzulli (1978) defines giftedness as real-world application of above-average ability, creativity, and task commitment. One problem posed by this definition as it is operationalized is that students who demonstrate sufficient ability to be defined as gifted may not be task committed or creative. The last two components of the Renzulli definition are developmental and, through skillful individual teaching, can be encouraged and drawn out. If a rigid interpretation of the Renzulli definition is enforced, many capable students may be excluded from a gifted program. An even greater affective consideration with the Renzulli definition is that it encourages classroom teachers to decline to nominate students who fail to complete regular classroom work or who are underachievers. To these classroom teachers, a gifted program is perceived as a reward for superior performance in the regular classroom. This type of thinking ignores the fact that gifted students may not be performing in the regular classroom for many reasons and that these students can greatly benefit from a gifted program which develops motivation and specific skills.

Giftedness can be noted in people's behavior. There have always been men and women who excelled to such a degree that their performance identified them as being gifted: Mozart, Picasso, Cassatt, Mill, the Brontes, Dickinson, Churchill, and Einstein. The problem with recognizing their gifted behaviors is that many of these gifted adults displayed little or no giftedness through their early schooling. Neither Churchill nor Einstein excelled as students. Their parents, specifically their mothers, nurtured and developed their giftedness.

In order to provide for education for all and education for special populations including the gifted, the United States has developed an elaborate system of education which includes three levels: the federal, the state, and the local. Each of these levels is examined to provide insight into the historical perspective on giftedness to better understand current efforts.

DIFFERING ROLES AND CONTRIBUTIONS OF GOVERNMENT

The Federal Government and Gifted Education

Only in the last two decades has interest in the gifted become a serious federal concern. Jackson (1979) reports that it was through a specific amendment offered by Congressman Erlenborn of Illinois that the Education Amendments of 1969 directed Congress to provide for the needs of the gifted and talented under Titles III and V of the Elementary and Secondary Education Act. But the most important point in Erlenborn's amendment was the call for the U.S. Commissioner of Education to launch a study pursuing five goals: (1) discover the special education efforts needed for gifted and talented; (2) discover if existing federal programs were currently meeting those needs; (3) evaluate how federal educational program assistance could best meet the needs of the gifted; (4) evaluate how federal program assistance could be most effective; and (5) recommend a program that would assist the gifted and talented.

Commissioner Marland made a summary report to Congress in 1972, including eleven recommendations to be taken under existing legislative authority (P.L. 91-230, Section 806). The recommendations called for: (1) a planning report on initiating a federal role in educating the gifted and talented; (2) establishment of a staff for gifted education in the United States Office of Education; (3) conducting a national survey of programs to find out costs, evaluation procedures, and model programs toward development of a clearinghouse for gifted/talented education; (4) using Title V of the Elementary and Secondary Education Act to strengthen capabilities for gifted/talented education; (5) providing two national summer leadership training institutes to train supervisory staff in state educational agencies; (6) funding research efforts and program support on behalf of minority gifted; (7) funding program efforts in career education for gifted; (8) giving special attention in one experimental school to the relationship between gifted and talented education and comprehensive school reform; (9) providing cooperative efforts in Title III programs; (10) locating and assigning one staff member for each of the ten regional Offices of Education to work with gifted and talented; and (11) studying current Office of Education programs relating to higher education to mobilize efforts on behalf of gifted and talented.

As a result of the second recommendation listed above, the staff in the Office of Gifted and Talented compiled and circulated the findings from the Marland report to state and local educational agencies. The main findings were:

1 Differential educational provisions for the gifted and talented at the federal level were almost nonexistent.

2 Minority and culturally different gifted and talented children were severely underrepresented in program efforts on behalf of gifted and talented.

3 Twenty-one states had legislative and regulatory provisions for gifted, but the majority of these represented mere intent. Ten states had full-time personnel in gifted education.

4 Research indicated that gifted and talented children required specialized educational programs to reach their potential.

5 Identification procedures for gifted and talented were inadequate because of lack of funds and inadequate testing procedures.

6 There was apathy and even hostility among educators, including teachers and administrators, concerning the need for gifted education.

7 Differential education for the gifted had measurable effects for the gifted and talented.

8 The Office of Gifted and Talented was viewed as a source of assistance in program development for gifted, but in actuality it had no federal role in delivering services to either state and local educational agencies or higher educational institutions.

As a result of the findings of the Marland Report (1972), Congress caused Public Law 93-380, called the Special Projects Act, to include a section on gifted.

Section 404 of the Special Project Act created categorical funds for the gifted and talented with appropriations for gifted and talented set at $2.56 million. The allocation of this exact amount proved ironic since the gifted and talented population figure projection was 2.56 million. Consequently, Public Law 93-380 provided $1 per gifted child. The original authorization had been $12.25 million, but with general cutbacks in educational funds, the Office of Gifted and Talented received $2.56 million to begin its first funding efforts for gifted and talented.

Public Law 93-380 funded grants to state education agencies, local education agencies, graduate training institutions, national training efforts, and model projects with special categories (early childhood, community-based mentor programs, visual and performing arts, exceptionally disadvantaged, creativity, and sparsely populated).

The state efforts under Public Law 93-380 were primarily to plan, develop, operate, and improve projects and programs for gifted and talented. Many of the states chose to employ a state consultant with their federal funds or to conduct special projects to develop greater awareness and advocacy for gifted students. The state education agencies also prepared and delivered pre-service and in-service education for teachers working with gifted students.

A smaller number of local grants were made as catalytic efforts and finally, the National/State Leadership Training Institute on the Gifted and Talented was used to train leaders in the field of gifted education.

In November 1978, Congress restructured Public Law 93-380 as the Gifted and Talented Children's Act (Public Law 95-561, Part A, Title IX of the Elementary and Secondary Education Act). Under this new law, 75 percent of the funds were redirected to the state education agencies and 25 percent were to be distributed directly by the Office of Gifted and Talented under a discretionary grant program. The framework of Public Law 95-561 provided opportunities for public and private agencies to seek funds to provide for gifted and talented students. In the state-administered section of the law, states that made applications according to the guidelines set down by the Office of Gifted and Talented received a direct yearly allotment of $50,000 for up to 3 years. In addition, states could seek other funds on a competitive basis.

Ninety percent of the funds the states received had to be distributed competitively to local school districts. Thus, the state education agencies were being asked to assume the role that the federal government had carried out under Public Law 93-380 for locally funded projects. In addition, the states were directed to provide assistance to those school divisions that did not have the resources to compete in preparing proposals. The local projects were for planning, developing, and operating gifted programs.

The federal Office of Gifted and Talented, under Public Law 95-561, distributed 25 percent of the federal funds on a competitive basis to public and private agencies, with annual priorities set by the commissioner.

In the 25 percent effort, there were several categories: (1) statewide activity projects to provide a state plan for meeting the needs of gifted; (2) educational service projects and model projects, in which all public and private agencies were eligible for funds, with the intent that innovative approaches for gifted and talented be developed; and (3) professional development, in which public and private agencies were eligible to provide training and development of materials.

Changing Federal Role of the Office of Gifted and Talented

On February 12, 1982, the Education Consolidation Act merged the efforts for gifted education with twenty-nine other programs, and the Office of Gifted and Talented was phased out. This was part of a general effort by the Secretary of Education, Terrell Bell, to curtail federal funding and functions. The role of the Office of Gifted and Talented was transferred to a transitional office from which funds were to be distributed through block state grants for total efforts in K-12 education for the twenty-nine programs. Educational effort on behalf of gifted shifted from the federal level to the state level. The state has the responsibility to establish priorities and to decide if federal block grant funds will be made available for gifted education. The congressional intent from the early establishment of Public Law 93-380 was to stimulate program development on behalf of gifted and talented rather than to deliver direct service efforts on a long-term basis to gifted students. More specifically, the intent was to prepare state education agencies to plan, develop, and implement programs for the gifted.

State Education Efforts on Behalf of Gifted

The bridge to the states under Public Law 93-380 and Public Law 95-561 was the National/State Leadership Training Institute for Gifted and Talented (N/S-LTI-G/T). In 1972 the N/S-LTI-G/T was funded through the fiscal agent of Ventura County, California, and directed its efforts toward decision makers at the state level. Their major effort was to plan and initiate activities to be carried out by state level planning teams. Another major function of the LTI was to develop training modules and to deliver technical assistance to the states. In its initial 3-year period, the LTI worked with a total of forty-eight state teams and helped develop comprehensive state plans, which in many cases were the first state efforts on behalf of gifted students.

Until the early 1970s, the active involvement of state education departments on behalf of gifted students was centered in California, Connecticut, Florida, Georgia, Illinois, Pennsylvania, and North Carolina. These pioneer efforts included a legislative definition of giftedness and in some cases categorical funds authorized for the education of gifted students.

The various definitions of gifted among states have encouraged much research. Zettel (1979a) reported that states define gifted and talented in four principal ways. The first and perhaps the most explicit reference was to the intellectually gifted or talented individual. Zettel (1979b) reported that nine states described the gifted in this manner.

For example, in the Delaware State Code, Article 24, Section 2162, the following definition for gifted is listed:

> Gifted children means children between the chronological ages of four and twenty-one who are endowed by nature with high intellectual attainment and scholastic achievement. (Delaware State, 1953)

Sixteen other states according to Zettel (1979b) mention gifted children under the broad, general rubric of exceptional children.

Seven states do not mention the words "gifted" and "talented," but define exceptionality so that "gifted" may be included. New Mexico is an example:

> Exceptional children means the children whose abilities render regular services of the public school to be inconsistent with their educational needs. (New Mexico Special Act, Session 77-11-3-1, 1972)

Four states described their gifted and talented children in terms of their being handicapped.

Zettel (1979a) reports that twenty states adopted the federal definition with all six performance areas, with Alaska and Iowa adopting a six-category definition that substituted manipulative skills for psychomotor. However, the majority of the states do not use the broad six-area definition of the federal definition, but choose to define giftedness to include three areas: general intellectual ability, creativity, and leadership (Sisk, 1984).

State commitment to gifted education can be viewed in the national survey results (Sisk, 1984) in which forty-seven states appointed a state consultant for the gifted, in comparison to the ten reported in the Marland (1972) report. A continued, growing awareness of the need for gifted education at the state level is essential if the block grant concept is to work effectively.

Role of Local Education in Establishing Programs for Gifted

Each local education school district operates under its own school board and school board policy. For example, the city of Philadelphia has a well-defined program for gifted students, and at one time (1976–1977) its city budget for the gifted exceeded that of the federal Office for Gifted and Talented. This clearly demonstrates Philadelphia's commitment to gifted education. New York City also has had programs for the gifted over the years, particularly at the Bronx High School of Science and the School for Performing Arts. Yet in many towns and cities in both Pennsylvania and New York, there are no school programs for gifted. Where there is no state mandate for the gifted, the local school board is autonomous and can make the decision of whether or not to provide for gifted students.

Gallagher and Weiss (1983) surveyed local program efforts, investigating variations in local program operation by comparing seven specific administrative strategies. The strategies were enrichment in the classroom, consultant teacher program in the regular classroom, resource room/pull-out program, community mentor program, independent study program, special classes, and special schools. The local school programs surveyed were selected by the state directors of gifted education as representative of one of the seven identified practices. Each state chose two representative programs for each administrative strategy. Many state consultants indicated that they did not use all of the program strategies. The ones most often reported were the resource room/pull-out program, the consultant teacher model, independent study, and enrichment in the classroom. The least used were the special schools and special classes. These findings parallel the general trend to meet the needs of exceptional children, whether they are gifted or handicapped and whether they are in the regular classroom or in resource areas with specialized personnel.

Gallagher and Weiss (1983) did not ask respondents what they would do if they had more freedom and options to operate; he only asked for actual program efforts. Future research may examine the gap between program aspirations and actual implementation.

Another national study was conducted by Cox (1985) for the Richardson Foundation in Fort Worth. This study surveyed the types of programs that existed for high-ability students, which programs were particularly effective, and offered opportunity for adaption to different school environments. Cox sent the initial survey to every public and parochial school district in the country (over 16,000). The information gathered from the initial survey was sent to the 4000 respondents to the first questionnaire. The 1572 responses to this second effort (400 schools, 1172 school districts) were then analyzed. Sixteen program types were used:

- Enrichment in the regular class-room
- Part-time special class
- Full-time special class
- Independent study
- Itinerant teacher
- Mentorships
- Resource rooms
- Special schools
- Early entrance
- Continuous progress
- Nongraded school
- Moderate acceleration
- Radical acceleration
- College Board and Advanced Placement
- Concurrent or dual enrollment

The Richardson study found that the most commonly offered program option was the part-time special class or "pull-out" model (72 percent of the districts). This offering was viewed as a part-time solution to a full-time problem. The Richardson study recommended comprehensive programming for gifted students with flexible pacing and multiple options, recognizing that highly gifted students with specific interests need different program options, that is, special schools, while other students' needs can be met through enrichment in the regular class-room. A step-by-step curriculum development plan is suggested to assist school districts in program planning efforts: (1) involvement of key individuals, (2) development of a definition, (3) conducting needs assessment, (4) development of a philosophy, (5) development of program goals, (6) selection of program types,

(7) development of objectives and strategies, and (8) development of evaluation procedures.

This proposed step-by-step local program development plan can be successful when it is followed by individualized programming for gifted students. What works for one local area may not work for another and what is appropriate for one gifted student may not be appropriate for another. Neither at the local level nor at the individual student level should a ready-made model or program be adopted.

In planning for the gifted, whether in an urban, suburban, or rural setting, local educational personnel should note that, no matter what the strategy, any local program efforts for gifted students have had positive effects on the gifted (Marland, 1972). Moreover, when gifted education is added to the local school offerings, other students benefit as well.

SUMMARY

Society needs its creative and intelligent individuals now, more than at any other time in history. As society becomes more complex, the need for education of the gifted becomes more obvious. Yet the need for gifted education is difficult for an egalitarian society to recognize, for equal opportunity is often confused with equal or same education.

Historically, we can trace our interest in the gifted to philosophers such as Socrates and Plato, who viewed giftedness as passing through stages of knowledge more quickly and achieving higher levels of understanding.

The concept of gifted moved from a philosophical and rationalistic concept to a fixed intelligence concept. Galton (1925) was one of the first to try and construct an intelligence test. His efforts were mirrored by Binet (1905), who was commissioned to develop a test to isolate and identify slow school children. Terman (1925) translated and modified the Binet test in 1916 (Stanford-Binet).

Galton (1925), Binet (1905), and Terman (1947) moved the concept of giftedness from one of philosophical and rational inquiry into a scientific inquiry into the differences of intellect. Thurstone (1938) and Guilford (1959) further developed an interaction theory between heredity and environment by postulating multiple factors of ability. Today these efforts are being continued by psychologists such as Gardner (1983), Steinberg, and Wagner (Steinberg & Wagner, 1982).

In examining early education in the United States, which was essentially a separate education, with Latin grammar schools serving gifted students and the village church schools and dame schools providing for the rest of society, it is interesting to contemplate that if we had kept this model, there might not be the current need for gifted education or today's democratic society.

The conflicting notions of Jefferson and Jackson, as they relate to education's role in providing equal opportunity for all or equal treatment for all, was noted. Jefferson viewed leaders as the gifted; Jackson viewed the common man as keeping the intellectual elite honest. These notions continue in today's thought, as educators and laymen try to understand gifted education.

Terman's work in gifted education supplies basic data on the gifted concerning their needs and characteristics. His study has been criticized for its research methodology and narrow definition of giftedness; however, Terman's work provides valuable information on the intellectually gifted.

Defining giftedness has progressed from a one-test and one-fixed-construct definition centering on intellectual giftedness to the concept of multiple talents or intelligences. This idea is reflected in the national definition, which is most often used by state educational agencies. These talents include general intellectual ability, specific aptitude or ability, leadership ability, visual and performing arts abilities, and psychomotor ability. This multidimensional definition is the definition used in this text. Another popular definition offered by Renzulli consists of above-average intelligence, task commitment, and creativity; however, this definition has narrow applicability to achieving students who demonstrate creativity, and it has encouraged educators to use pull-out programs for gifted students as a program type.

The role of the federal government was traced from the establishment of the Office of Gifted and Talented in 1972 to the current block grant concept. The growth in federal awareness of and support to gifted education, which concentrated on state capacity building, was reflected in a 1972 finding of ten state consultants for the gifted, as compared to the forty-seven state consultants for gifted reported in 1984. With the block grant concept enacted, and Public Law 95-561 as a forerunner, state education departments assume more and more responsibility. Currently, state education departments initiate program development and provide support to local educational agencies to deliver services to gifted students.

A step-by-step process was suggested by the Richardson study for local program development which would include individualized programming for gifted students. Both of these topics will be discussed in Chapter 3, which covers individualized education for the gifted.

EXTENDING ACTIVITIES

1 Discuss the notion of environment being partially responsible for giftedness. What are the implications of this notion for increasing the total number of gifted students?
2 Locate your state's definition for gifted, and select one other state definition to compare and contrast the two state definitions.
3 Select an outstanding individual from history such as John Stuart Mill, and note his/her historical contribution. Was a mentor involved in his/her development? Was there a relationship between the person and his/her time?
4 Discuss the concept of interactive intelligence.
5 Research the terms "egalitarianism," "equality," and "equal opportunity." What do these terms mean, and how have the concepts affected the education of the gifted?

REFERENCES

Alexander, P. & Muia, J. (1982). *Gifted education*. Rockville, MD: Aspen Publications.
Binet, A. (1905). *L'Annee psychologique*. France.
Binet, A. (1916). *The development of intelligence in children*. Baltimore, MD: Williams and Wilkins.

Bish, C. (1975). A broad concept of giftedness. Presentation. Great Falls, MT, November 1975.

Callahan, C. M. (1978). *Developing creativity in the gifted and talented.* Reston, VA: Council for Exceptional Children.

Callahan, C. M. (1980). The gifted girl: An anomaly? *Roeper Review, 2,* 16–20.

Clark, B. (1983). *Growing up gifted.* Columbus, OH: Charles E. Merrill.

Code of Alabama. Section I, Act 106, Laws of 1971: 375.

Cox, J. (1985). *The Richardson study: A national investigation of educational opportunities for able learners.* Fort Worth, TX: Texas Christian University Press.

Darwin, C. (1868). *On the origin of species.* New York: Appleton & Co.

Delaware State Code (1953). Article 14, Section 2162.

Ellison, J. (1984). Seven frames of mind. *Psychology Today,* June 21–26.

Erickson, D. (ed.) (1978). *The nation's commitment to the education of gifted and talented children and youth. Summary of findings from a 1977 survey of states and territories.* Reston, VA: Council for Exceptional Children.

Gallagher, J. (1985). *Teaching gifted children.* Boston: Allyn and Bacon.

Gallagher, J. & Weiss, P. (1983). Report on parents' educational preferences for their gifted children. *G/C/T,* November/December.

Galton, F. (1925). *Hereditary genius, an inquiry into its laws and consequences.* London: Macmillan and Company.

Gardner, H. (1983). *Frames of mind: The theory of multiple intelligence.* New York: Basic Books.

Getzels, J. W. & Jackson, P. W. (1962). *Creativity and intelligence: Exploration with gifted students.* New York: Wiley.

Gold, M. (1965). *Education of the intellectually gifted.* Columbus, OH: Charles E. Merrill.

Gowan, J. (1977). *The gifted and the creative: A fifty year perspective.* Ed., Julian Stanley, Baltimore, MD: Johns Hopkins University Press.

Guilford, J. P. (1959). Three faces of intellect. *American Psychology, 14,* 469–479.

Howley A. et al. (1986). *Teaching gifted children: principles and strategies.* Boston: Little, Brown.

Jackson, D. (1979). The emerging national and state concern. *The Gifted and Talented,* NSSSE Yearbook. Chicago: University of Chicago Press.

Maker, J. (1982). *Teaching models in the education of the gifted.* Rockville, MD: Aspen Publications.

Marland, S. (1972). *Education of the gifted and talented.* Report to Congress. Washington, DC: U.S. Government Printing Office.

Nettleship, R. L. (1966). The four stages of intelligence. In A. Sesonke (Ed.), *Plato's Republic.* Belmont, CA: Wadsworth.

New Mexico Special Act. (1972). Section 77-11-3-1.

Parnes, S. (1975). *Aha: Insights into creative behavior.* Buffalo, NY: D.O.K. Publishers.

Piaget, J. (1952). *The origins of intelligence of children.* New York: International University Press.

Renzulli, J. S. (1978). What makes giftedness? *Phi Delta Kappan, 60,* 180–184, 261.

Sisk, D. (1981). Annual program report for the office of gifted and talented. Washington, DC: Office of Education.

Sisk, D. (1984). *A national survey of gifted programs.* Presentation to the National Business Consortium for Gifted and Talented, Washington, DC, October.

Sisk, D. & Shallcross, D. (1986). Leadership: making things happen. New York: Bearly Limited.

Spearman, C. (1904). General intelligence—Objectively determined and measured. *American Journal of Psychology, 15,* 201–293.

Steinberg, R. & Wagner, R. (1982). A revolutionary look at intelligence. *Gifted Children Newsletter,* 3(11).

Taylor, C. W. (1968). Be talent developers as well as knowledge dispensers. *Today's Education,* 57, 67–69.

Taylor, C. W. (1985). *The simultaneous double-curriculum for developing human resources: A research based theory of education.* Personal correspondence.

Terman, L. M. (1925). *Genetic studies of genius (volume 1): Mental and physical traits of a thousand gifted children.* Palo Alto, CA: Stanford University Press.

Terman, L. M. & Oden, M. (1947). *Genetic studies of genius (volume 4): The gifted 1947 child grows up.* Palo Alto, CA: Stanford University Press.

Thurstone, E. L. (1938). Primary mental abilities. *Psychometric Monographs, 1.*

Torrance, E. P. (1977). *Discovery and nurturance of giftedness in the culturally different.* Reston, VA: The Council for Exceptional Children.

Torrance, E. P. (1980). Psychology of gifted children and youth. In *Psychology of Exceptional Children and Youth.* Englewood Cliffs, NJ: Prentice-Hall.

Williams, F. E. (1970). *Classroom ideas for encouraging thinking and feeling.* Buffalo, NY: D.O.K. Publishers.

Zettel, J. (1979a). Gifted and talented over a half decade of change. *Journal for the Education of the Gifted,* 3, 14–37.

Zettel, J. (1979b). State provisions for educating the gifted and talented. *The Gifted and Talented,* NSSSE Yearbook, 78(1). Chicago: University of Chicago Press.

CHAPTER 2

THE NATURE OF GIFTEDNESS: WHO ARE THE GIFTED AND HOW CAN WE IDENTIFY THEM?

There is no meaning to life except the meaning man gives his life by the unfolding of his powers.

Erick Fromm

Who Are These People? is a film produced by the National/State Leadership Training Institute of Gifted and Talented (N/S-LTI-G/T), which illustrates the on-going issue concerning the nature of giftedness (Sato, 1979). In the film, gifted students speak for themselves, and experts in education discuss general questions concerning giftedness. The day-to-day discussions on giftedness occurring in schools, businesses, and homes lead to similar questions concerning giftedness. However, these discussions lack the insights of gifted students and experts. Some of the questions are: What do we mean by gifted? Is being gifted similar to being a Renaissance individual? Can giftedness be identified in young children? Is every-one gifted?

Any inquiry or discussion of giftedness usually leads to history, as history represents society's record of greatness. These records include many so-called dullards who became geniuses: Newton, Darwin, Einstein, Edison, Hume, Chur-chill, and Pasteur. Some of the stories are magnified, but they imply many geniuses had learning problems and difficulties because of lack of interest and boredom in school. Many gifted students attest schools were filled with drill and repetition

Photograph on the facing page courtesy of Gus J. Blumberg.

in their childhood. Yet, in the histories of individuals who proved their genius as adults, one similarity does prevail. All of them possessed at least one parent or mentor who recognized and supported their giftedness (Cox, 1926). This finding was borne out by an examination of the McArthur fellows in the Richardson study who are current outstanding gifted individuals in a number of fields (Cox, 1985).

BEHAVIOR THAT INDICATES GIFTEDNESS

Terman (1925), in interviewing the parents of his intellectually gifted students, found early indications of their giftedness (see Table 2-1). These are listed by frequency and arranged according to sex. The early manifestations of superior ability were found in 282 boys and 237 girls.

A similar list of characteristics is reported by Witty (1955) in "A Genetic Study of Fifty Gifted Children" in the *39th Yearbook of the National Society for the Study of Education, Part II*. However, this list contains reference to creative talents as well as intellectual talents.

- The early use of large vocabulary, accurately employed
- Language proficiency using phrases and entire sentences at a very early age, and the ability to tell or reproduce a story at an early age
- Keen observation and retention of information about things observed
- Interest in or liking for books and later use of atlases, dictionaries, and encyclopedias

TABLE 2-1
EARLY MANIFESTATIONS OF SUPERIOR ABILITY AS
NOTED BY PARENTS

Behavior reported	Frequency	
	Boys	**Girls**
Grasps and understands new ideas quickly	50	40
Desire for knowledge	31	31
Retentive memory	21	21
Intelligent conversation	20	15
Rapid progress at school	16	16
Keen general interests	22	9
Range of general information	15	12
Reasoning ability	13	12
Early speech	11	14
Asking intelligent questions	14	11
Ability in accomplishing difficult things	14	11
Keen observation	13	10
Unusual vocabulary	8	12
Originality	3	12

Source: L. M. Terman et al., *The Mental and Physical Traits of a Thousand Gifted Children*, 1925, p. 20. Reprinted by permission.

- Ability to attend or concentrate for a longer period than is typical of most children
  - Demonstration of proficiency in drawing, music, and other art forms
  - Early discovery of cause-and-effect relationship
  - Early development of ability to read
  - Development of early interests

These lists of characteristics can be grouped in terms of psychological concepts, and it should be kept in mind that the variables interact. In addition, these selected parental comments from the Terman (1925) and Witty (1955) samples are not representative of a full socioeconomic range, or the total group of either researcher.

Newland (1976) groups the characteristics into five different kinds of behaviors:

1 *Pressing or pushing into the environment*—both physically and symbolically
2 *Discovering relationships* among things experienced
3 *Remembering what has been experienced*, facilitated undoubtedly by perceiving relationships within which things can be remembered
4 *Being motivated* or the rewarding effect of discovery
5 *Focusing on concentrating* upon a particular line of behavior

Newland (1976) explains that the pressing or pushing into the environment can be viewed as drive or curiosity and that this is reflected in asking questions and reading to acquire relevant information. The capacity of gifted students to perceive relationships relates to their focus of interests. Through this process, they identify other things or phenomena which are in harmony with that relationship. This type of thinking intensifies their tendency to generalize. Through the interaction of their so-called gifted characteristics, the gifted manifest behavior that indicates further giftedness. If Newland's thoughts are extended, giftedness will not burn out as was feared earlier ("Early ripe, early rot" fallacy), but giftedness will continue to develop throughout life.

IDENTIFICATION AND SCREENING OF THE GIFTED

Historically, the identification process for gifted students has been stimulated by a desire to gather more information about these students to place them in appropriate educational programs to develop their ability and, in recent years, to qualify them for special educational programs and to acquire federal, state or local funding.

In early days, children were educated at home and gifted individuals such as John Stuart Mill and Wolfgang Mozart were identified by their parents' observation of their precocious behavior and specific abilities. Since the advent of mass education, however, teachers are primarily responsible for identifying the gifted. As a group, teachers have been notorious for misidentifying the gifted. In the Pegnato and Birch study (1959), in which 1400 Pittsburgh middle school students were studied to compare the effectiveness (percentage of gifted located) and the efficiency (percentage of nominees found to be gifted) of seven screening devices or selection methods, teacher ratings missed more than half of the intellectually gifted, and almost one-third of the students nominated by teachers failed to qualify. All of the students were initially given individual IQ tests by the researchers. The different methods of screening or identifying the students were compared to a *criterion measure of giftedness*, in this incident, the individual IQ test.

In the Pegnato and Birch study (1959), students were nominated because they were student council members, outstanding in art and music, or appeared on at least two other lists. Nomination on one criterion, such as mathematics achievement, missed half of the students; and more than two-thirds of the math-achieving nominees failed to meet the established intelligence quotient of 132. The honor roll located 73.6 percent of the gifted, but it also listed large numbers of students who were not gifted. Group intelligence tests were effective when a low level criterion score (115) was used. Achievement tests were only slightly less useful. The most efficient means of locating the intellectually talented or gifted (132 IQ on Stanford-Binet) was the combination of group intelligence test and achievement scores as a screening criterion. This combination located 96.7 percent of the intellectually gifted.

Teacher inadequacy in nominating the gifted comes from the ongoing confusion over the definition of gifted. Giftedness can include any number of basic criteria: creativity, high achievement, grades, high scores on standardized tests and/or group ability tests, and high scores on an individual IQ test.

Several conclusions can be drawn from the Pegnato and Birch (1959) study: (1) Teachers and administrators need to agree on the type of giftedness being identified; (2) The measures used to screen and identify the gifted should be compatible with the student population and the design and intent of the gifted program.

In-service and graduate training in gifted education help sensitize and educate teachers to the identification procedures and needs and characteristics of gifted. With assistance in learning about the gifted, administrators find regular classroom teachers can become more effective in nominating students to the gifted program. Dettmer (1981) demonstrated that teachers can learn to identify gifted and develop a more positive attitude toward gifted in-service training. In-service for teachers and administrators appears to increase their effectiveness in identifying the gifted (Kranz, 1981).

Major Procedures Used in Identification

A number of methods have been used to identify the gifted, including many of the methods noted in the Pegnato and Birch (1959) study: teacher observation and nomination, group school achievement test scores, group intelligence test scores, demonstrated accomplishments (including grades), individual intelligence test scores, and creativity test scores.

Table 2-2 from the Marland report (1972) explains the percent of frequency with which the state of Illinois used the various methods and the percent recommended by experts. This table reflects an ongoing problem in gifted education: experts make recommendations that school officials find philosophically and fiscally untenable.

TABLE 2-2
MAJOR PROCEDURES USED AND RECOMMENDED FOR
IDENTIFICATION PURPOSES

Major identification procedures	Percent using	Percent recommending
Teacher observation and nomination	93	75
Group school achievement test scores	87	74
Group intelligence test scores	87	65
Previously demonstrated accomplishments (including school grades)	56	65
Individual intelligence test scores	23	90
Scores on tests of creativity	14	74

Source: S. P. Marland, *Education of the Gifted and Talented.* Washington D.C.: U.S. Office of Education, 1972, p. 261.

The pattern in most local programs is to use multiple instruments for screening and identification. This practice is reflected in the in-service and pre-service workshops of the N/S-LTI-G/T (1975–1986), and in most state plans submitted to the Office of Gifted and Talented in 1980. The danger, of course, is that the wide use of formal tests and instruments across the five areas of the federal definition may lead to test misuse. Alvino et al. (1981) in a survey of state consultants reported six test instruments being used across the five categories (intellectual, specific academic aptitude, creative and visual and performing arts, leadership, and kinesthetic), a use which in some cases did not conform to the intentions published in the test manuals. The tests were: (1) Biographical Inventory (BRIC); (2) Checklist of Creative Positives (Torrance); (3) Ross Test of Higher Cognitive Processes; (4) Renzulli-Hartman behavioral scales; (5) Structure of the Intellect (SOI) screening; and (6) System of Multicultural Pluralistic Assessment (SOMPA).

In any discussion on identification and screening of the gifted, the importance of the appropriateness of the tests and the definition of gifted must be stressed.

The confusion in the use of tests is reflected in Table 2-3 (Alvino et al., 1981, p. 130).

A definition of gifted provides a common basis for negotiation, discussion, planning, and development of gifted programs, and the definition should determine the identification procedure. Some school districts use the federal definition of gifted and require the nominees to the gifted program to demonstrate giftedness in four or five areas of giftedness. One large school system decided that in order to be identified for their gifted program, a student must: (1) be in the top 2 percent of ability (intellectual talent), (2) demonstrate creativity (creative and productive thinking talent), (3) indicate leadership (leadership talent), and (4) be in the top 2 percent of achievement in a particular area (specific academic aptitude). The procedure is described as using "multiple criteria." However, the concept of multiple criteria in the federal definition was an attempt to be more inclusive of students in the gifted program, rather than exclusive through the addition of multiple hurdles. Multiple hurdles exclude students, yet it is equally undesirable

TABLE 2-3
FREQUENCY OF CITATIONS OF KINDS OF TESTS/INSTRUMENTS/TECHNIQUES VIS-À-VIS
FEDERAL CATEGORIES

Psychometric division	Federal categories					
	General intellectual	Specific academic	Creativity	Arts	Leader	Total
Intelligence tests	238	40	12	7	6	303
Achievement tests	72	24	3	2	1	102
Creativity tests	18	11	50	2	6	87
Checklists, scales, etc.	27	10	21	12	24	94
Nominations, etc.	126	10	59	44	54	293
Total	481	95	145	67	91	

Source: J. Alvino, R. McDonnel & S. Richert, A National Survey of Identification Practices in Gifted and Talented Education, *Exceptional Children, 48*(2), 1981, pp. 124—132. Reprinted by permission.

for school districts to select gifted students on the basis of a single criteria, such as IQ.

Screening: In-Service for Staff

In-service workshops need to be planned for classroom teachers, administrators, and ancillary personnel, including guidance counselors and psychologists to ensure successful programs for gifted. If a district chooses to serve the five types of giftedness, then the in-service training and search should address and include all types of giftedness. The in-service training could include topics such as a brief historical summary of the gifted education effort, characteristics of the gifted, and the more prevalent misconceptions or myths of gifted. Some of these myths are: the gifted constitute a single, homogenous group; creativity is too difficult to measure; there is a single curriculum for gifted; gifted programs should be separate from the regular curriculum.

After a preliminary workshop session and an understanding of gifted characteristics and needs, teachers need to closely observe gifted students' behavior to recognize the various characteristics.

An example of a characteristic checklist is the Renzulli-Hartman (1971) scale. The learning characteristics address the area of intellectual talent and the creativity characteristics address the areas of creative and productive talent. Table 2-4 gives examples from this rating scale. Such items can also be adapted for student use in peer nomination.

TABLE 2-4

SAMPLE ITEMS FROM THE RENZULLI-HARTMAN SCALE FOR RATING BEHAVIORAL CHARACTERISTICS OF SUPERIOR STUDENTS

	Low			High
	1	2	3	4
Part I: Learning characteristics				
1. Has unusually advanced vocabulary for age or grade level; uses terms in a meaningful way; has verbal behavior characterized by "richness" of expression, elaboration, and fluency	—	—	—	—
2. Has quick mastery and recall of factual information	—	—	—	—
3. Is a keen and alert observer; usually sees more or gets more out of a story, film, etc. than others	—	—	—	—
Column total weight	—	—	—	—
Weighted column total	—	—	—	—
Total			_____	
Part II: Motivation characteristics				
1. Is easily bored with routine work	—	—	—	—
2. Prefers to work independently; requires little direction	—	—	—	—
3. Likes to organize and bring structure to things, people, and situations	—	—	—	—
Column total weight	—	—	—	—
Weighted column total	—	—	—	—
Total			_____	
Part III: Creativity characteristics				
1. Displays a great deal of curiosity about many things; is constantly asking questions about anything and everything	—	—	—	—
2. Is a high risk taker; is adventuresome and speculative	—	—	—	—
3. Displays a keen sense of humor and sees humor in situations that may not appear to be humorous to others	—	—	—	—
Column total weight	—	—	—	—
Weighted column total	—	—	—	—
Total			_____	

Note: (1) seldom or never; (2) occasionally; (3) considerably; and (4) most always.

TABLE 2-4 (*Continued*)
SAMPLE ITEMS FROM THE RENZULLI-HARTMAN SCALE FOR RATING BEHAVIORAL
CHARACTERISTICS OF SUPERIOR STUDENTS

	Low			High
	1	2	3	4
Part IV: Leadership characteristics				
1. Carries responsibility well; can be counted on to do what he has promised and usually does it well	—	—	—	—
2. Tends to dominate others when they are around; generally directs the activity in which he is involved	—	—	—	—
3. Is self-confident with children his own age as well as adults; seems comfortable when asked to show his work to the class	—	—	—	—
Column total weight	—	—	—	—
Weighted column total	—	—	—	—
Total				————

Source: J. Renzulli & R. Hartman, Scale for Rating Behavioral Characteristics of Superior Students. *Exceptional Children*, 1971, *38*(3) pp. 243–248. Reprinted by permission.

Another example of a device to help teachers screen their classes for nominees to the gifted program is called "Finding the Potentially Gifted Child," from Fort Worth, Texas. Some excerpts are listed in Table 2-5.

The advantage of this scale is its use of a wide variety of characteristics of gifted students including both negative and positive aspects of giftedness. Other characteristics include: most mature behavior; longest attention span; most task-committed; best motivated; most enthusiastic; best planner; most responsible; best group persuader; best liked by peers; ablest, but emotionally immature; ablest, but disruptive; ablest, but daydreamer; ablest, but with reading difficulty; high potential, but low grades.

Terman (1925) illustrates the importance of asking the right questions for student nomination in his volume, *Mental and Physical Traits of a Thousand Gifted Children*. To secure nominations for his intellectually gifted sample, he asked: Who was the brightest child in your room last year? Who is the most able in arithmetic? Who is the most able in reading? Who is the youngest child in the room? Terman reports that many students were listed several times, but 19.7 percent of the total sample were named as the youngest and listed in no other way. Terman's experience reminds us to be conscious of age differences in students and that a few months produces a significant difference in a young student's performance.

Once teachers, parents, and peers nominate a student to the gifted program, these students form a talent pool. Teachers and administrators can then gather past objective test data and information about a student's strengths, weaknesses, interests, and performance.

TABLE 2-5
FINDING THE POTENTIALLY GIFTED CHILD

Based on your knowledge of the children you teach this year, name those who displayed the greatest amount of ability in the areas below. You may duplicate names if a child shows ability in more than one area.

1. Greatest number of ideas _____
2. Most original ideas _____
3. Most elaborate ideas _____
4. Most points of view _____
5. Best sense of humor _____
6. Best "analyzer" _____
7. Most unusual questions _____
8. "Catches on" quickest _____
9. Most surprising knowledge _____
10. Largest vocabulary _____
11. Most independent _____

Source: Fort Worth, Texas Gifted Program Screening Device, 1982. Reprinted by permission, Pat Denton, Supervisor of Gifted.

Martinson (1974) stressed that the concepts of effectiveness and efficiency be considered prior to any consideration of the nominees in the talent pool. Effectiveness was defined as the number of gifted found in relationship to the actual number of gifted, and efficiency as the relationship between the number of gifted found and the number of persons nominated as gifted.

In terms of cost-effectiveness, school districts sometimes nominate only those students they are certain will be identified as gifted to conserve psychological services. Consequently, these school districts may be very efficient but not very effective; many gifted are missed when the screening does not sweep wide.

Martinson (1974) reported over 90 percent of the authorities she polled agreed that individual intelligence tests were the best means for identification. However, this information would be meaningful only if gifted programs are restricted to the intellectually gifted. Other types of tests and evaluations should be used for the nomination procedures if the federal definition or some modification of this definition is used which includes a number of types of giftedness.

Matching Screening Techniques with Program Plans

If the gifted program is to serve intellectually gifted, as defined by students who are capable of high performance with demonstrated achievement and/or potential ability in the general intellectual area, the search for nominees might begin by using the Renzulli-Hartman scale (1971), part I: Learning characteristics of gifted (Table 2-4).

If the program is to serve gifted in the visual and performing arts, a school system might use visual and performing artists to help screen for giftedness. An example of this procedure was initiated in New York City under the direction of Richard Levy of the Arts Connection in 1979. The Alvin Ailey dance troupe offered children the opportunity: (1) to hear about the dance program in a general school presentation; (2) to walk, run, jump, and leap, as well as do simple dance steps under the close, observant eye of the professional dancers; (3) to participate in simple instruction of basic dance movements; and (4) to compete in a final selection.

One unique aspect of this screening process in the arts was the self-selection aspect. All students had the opportunity to step forward and try. Students were not limited by not having had former dance lessons. Experts and judges save school personnel time and are usually in a better position to judge the full range of talents in the visual and performing arts. It is crucial, however, that experts understand developmental expectancies and that all the judges use the same criteria (Howley et al., 1986).

If the program is to serve gifted in creative or productive thinking, the students might be screened using such measures as the checklist in part III of the Renzulli-Hartman scale (Table 2-4); indices of creative classroom work of the children; creativity test scores on tests such as the Torrance Tests of Creative Thinking (Torrance, 1974) and the Guilford Tests (Guilford, 1975). These tests often tap assets and liabilities that are not used on standard IQ or achievement tests.

Nominees for a gifted program in leadership might be screened with teacher recommendations, observations of demonstrated leadership, and checklists such as part IV of the Renzulli-Hartman checklist, and parents and community members might also provide anecdotal information. Self-nomination can also be very valuable.

Specific academic programs in math or science for the gifted should screen nominees with achievement and aptitude test scores in mathematics or in the specific academic area in which the program is being planned. This information can be supplemented with teacher anecdotal information concerning exemplary classroom performance and interest. Information from checklists such as the Renzulli-Hartman part II (motivational characteristics) is also helpful, particularly if the proposed program is to be a fast-paced, academic one.

SPECIAL CONSIDERATION FOR SPECIAL POPULATIONS

The inefficiency and ineffectiveness of standardized instruments in identifying the culturally different gifted has been discussed in the literature (Bernal, 1975; Meeker, 1978; Maker 1982). Torrance (1971) suggests that educators concentrate on the subjective aspect of identification and screening of the culturally different. He acknowledges the positive skills of the disadvantaged, who are often culturally different:

1 High nonverbal fluency and originality
2 High creative productivity in small groups
3 Adeptness in visual art activities
4 High creativity in movement, dance, and other physical activities

5 High motivation by games, music, sport, humor, and concrete objects
6 Language rich in imagery (Torrance, 1971, p. 75)

Alexander and Muia (1982) list four problems that result from depending on standardized devices to identify the gifted from among a culturally diverse population:

1 The experiential knowledge required by those instruments
2 The standard English linguistic competency demanded by such measures
3 The reliability of those tests, which have as their norm middle-class white populations, for diverse populations
4 The nature of the testing process as a potential source of conflict

Several nontraditional tests have been suggested to enable the identification of gifted students from culturally diverse backgrounds, such as the Abbreviated Binet for the Disadvantaged (ABDA; Bruch, 1971). Bruch developed the ABDA by administering the Stanford-Binet to disadvantaged black populations, building a test bias in favor of black populations. Another test is the Black Intelligence Test of Cultural Homogeneity (Williams, 1972). This test includes specific vocabulary items and strengths from the black culture.

To locate Spanish-speaking gifted, school systems can use the SOMPA and Cartoon Conservation scales. Both these instruments have been recommended by Bernal (1975, 1978). The SOMPA, developed by Mercer and Lewis (1977), has been used often in gifted programs in the states of Florida and California, and it works best as part of a case-study approach. It includes data from the family, school, and community.

Additional tests to gather information on culturally diverse students are the Torrance Tests of Creative Thinking (Torrance, 1974) and the Structure of the Intellect Learning Abilities test (SOI-LA) (Meeker & Meeker, 1975). The SOI-LA deemphasizes verbal abilities and stresses figural abilities. Some gifted programs are using the Raven Progressive Matrices (Raven, 1952), which measure convergent thought production and requires less verbalization than any traditional tests. The Raven test is useful in locating the gifted among Asian students who relocate in the United States.

Taylor and Ellison (1968) suggest using an interview with the student who is "culturally different" and possibly gifted; they report success in building a comprehensive profile of the potentially gifted nominee by gathering information from parents, peers, teachers, and siblings, as well as from the individual. Their instrument, called the Alpha Biographical Inventory, has proved successful in locating children who are creative. The Alpha Biographical Inventory consists of 300 multiple choice items. Still another self-report instrument is the Group Inventory for Finding Interests (Rimm et al., 1982).

The Gifted Among the Handicapped

Evaluating the capabilities of the handicapped is a problem because traditional test items or directions must be modified. These modifications may invalidate the results, if the results are compared to the national norms. In addition, teachers of the handicapped often have low expectations for these students and are reluctant to nominate them for gifted programs. They also see serious problems with using group achievement and group intelligence tests because they discriminate against students with impaired sensory, manual, or speaking skills. Teachers of the handicapped can also see little opportunity for handicapped students to develop or demonstrate talents. To locate the gifted among the handicapped, a two-phase procedure is helpful: (1) lower the levels for acceptance in the initial screening for students with handicaps to create a talent pool; (2) make certain the examiners know the test instrument and understand the limitations of the handicapped students. Lastly, if at all possible, the examiner should be handicapped and should use specific instruments such as the SOI (Meeker & Meeker, 1975).

Specific Instruments for Use With Handicapped

Handicapped students with severely impaired motor ability, particularly individuals with cerebral palsy, can be screened and identified using the Columbia Mental Maturity Scale. This test uses the visual and perceptual abilities of the students and gives an indication of their ability to discriminate and classify. Another instrument, the Leiter International Performance Scale has been adapted for use with students who have cerebral palsy (Anastasi, 1976). In addition, Raven's Progressive Matrices have been used successfully with cerebral palsied children in identifying their giftedness (Raven, 1952).

For screening or identification of intellectually gifted blind or partially sighted students, the Hayes-Binet, a modification of the Stanford-Binet that uses items which do not require sight, could be used. Another useful test is the Wechsler Intelligence Scale for Children (WISC-R), which has been adapted for the blind or partially sighted by using the verbal items and omitting the performance items.

Hearing-impaired students can be successfully measured for their intellectual ability using the Nebraska Test of Learning Aptitude (Hiskey, 1966). The WISC-R also has been used for identifying the deaf intellectually gifted by using only the performance section. The Leiter International Performance Scale (Arthur, 1950) and Raven Progressive Matrices (Raven, 1952) can also be helpful in screening and identifying intellectual ability in the hearing impaired.

One test that is not frequently used, but which has potential in identifying gifted handicapped students because of its total pictorial nature, is the Pictorial Test of Intelligence (French, 1964). This test yields an intelligence score, with no verbal responses, and can assess the general population as well as the handicapped.

To ensure the identification of the gifted who are handicapped, it is essential that teacher nomination and observation of classroom behavior for outstanding performance in creativity, leadership, and intellectual aptitude be used with objective information from adaptive testing of the handicapped students.

USING THE CASE STUDY TECHNIQUE FOR IDENTIFICATION

A useful way to coordinate the information gathered on the students nominated for the gifted program is the case study approach. When the data is collected in a single document, it represents a final record of the initial referrals by teachers and the results of the screening procedures. This document can also include representative samples of the student's work, anecdotal information, a summary of past educational experiences, and methods of teaching used to meet the student's educational needs.

The case study technique has been used in a number of states to identify gifted students and to plan an individualized program for the students. Success has been most notable in states in which gifted education is placed under the auspices of special education at the state level. In these states, the programs for the gifted are required to follow the spirit of Public Law 94-142 which calls for an individualized educational plan (IEP) for all exceptional students.

The data base provided by the case study enables the educational team to study each student's unique abilities, talents, interests, accomplishments, special needs, and measured abilities. Usually, these data are supplemented by data on the student's health and home. A social worker, if available for a home or phone interview, might provide information on the educational level, financial status, parent attitudes toward school, and the general history of the child's development as seen by the family members. The teacher will find this information useful in planning the IEP. Martinson (1974), a proponent of the case study technique of identification, suggests that the case study be supplemented with a student autobiography and a list of interests.

Renzulli and Smith (1977, 1980) studied the case history or case study technique and found that the achievement tests and case history performances were useful to educational teams, particularly in the identification of minority-group pupils. They also found the case study technique did not yield an unmanageable number of students for screening, and that time and cost differences did not support the notion that the case study technique was unduly costly.

One important advantage to using the case study technique in the identification process is the opportunity to weight scores and to plot a profile for the individual child. This profile is prepared by using a table of instruments on which scores are available and listed with a system of weighting. One weighting system used percentiles with a scale of 1 to 5 or 1 to 10. Some school districts use national norms to compare their students; others utilize local norms. Local norms, or norms for a subpopulation, are more feasible for districts with a large number of culturally different students. If national norms are used, the scores can be reported in stanines.

USING THE TOTAL PICTURE OF GIFTEDNESS

The educational team working with the case study document needs to view a total picture. Young-Baldwin (1977) studied a group of twenty-four black youngsters identified for a gifted program at the fourth-grade level. These students became outstanding college students at institutions such as MIT, Tufts, Princeton, the University of Alabama, the University of Michigan, and Dillard University. They obviously were a credit to their gifted program.

However, if the individuals in charge of identification had not taken a total view of the data, the students could have been overlooked. The program required five criteria, two objective and three subjective. The objective criteria were superior achievement and an IQ of 130, and the subjective were teacher nomination, personal interview, and peer nomination. The twenty-four selected students would not have been selected if the two objective criteria had been the only criteria, for the mean achievement of the students was 4.9 in grade 4; their mean Otis Intelligence Test Form Beta EM was 112; and their mean Slosson Test score was 123.

These highly successful students were selected by teacher nomination, peer nomination, and personal interview. Clearly, educational teams need to rely on their professional expertise and their knowledge of the district educational plans for gifted programming in the identification decision. The match of the individual gifted student to the gifted program is essential. Chapter 3 covers the individualization of programs for the gifted through the use of the IEP. This is the logical culmination of the case-study technique used by a team of teachers, parents, and other professionals, all working together to plan an appropriate educational program for gifted students.

SUMMARY

The identification of the gifted was discussed by examining the life of John Stuart Mill, who had a complete breakdown at the age of 20. The importance of parental identification in young geniuses such as Mill or Mozart was noted. Early characteristics of giftedness observed by the parents of the participants of the Terman (1925) project were listed: grasping and understanding new ideas quickly, desire for knowledge, retentive memory, intelligent conversation, rapid progress at school, keen general interests, range of general information, reasoning ability, early speech, asking intelligent questions, ability in accomplishing difficult things, keen observation, unusual vocabulary, and originality.

The importance of in-service training for teachers to help locate the gifted was stressed. Dettmer's study (1980) demonstrated that in-service training about giftedness with teachers improves their attitudes toward the gifted, and provides knowledge of the characteristics of the gifted to help teachers become competent in identifying gifted students. This recent phenomenon is contrasted with the Pegnato and Birch (1959) study in which untrained teachers were inadequate in locating the gifted.

Major procedures used in identification were enumerated, such as teacher observation and nomination, group school achievement test scores, group intelligence test scores, previously demonstrated accomplishments (including grades), individual intelligence test scores, and scores on creativity. The data from the

Marland study (1972) indicated that teacher nomination and group scores were the most-often-used procedures and creativity scores the least used by school officials.

The importance of the definition as the basis for further negotiations, discussion, planning, and development of gifted programs, as well as its influence on the identification procedure, was stressed. The concepts of effectiveness and efficiency were described. Effectiveness is defined as the number of gifted found in relationship to the actual number of gifted. Efficiency is the relationship between the number of gifted found and the number of persons nominated as gifted.

The need to match screening techniques with program plans was discussed, such as using artists or experts to nominate a gifted student for the visual and performing arts program. Special consideration for special populations was covered and specific tests were suggested that might be helpful in screening and identifying children from the special populations, such as the handicapped and the culturally diverse.

The use of the case study technique for identification was reported. The case study technique has been used in a number of states to identify gifted students and to plan an individualized program for them. Renzulli and Smith reported the case study technique did not yield an unmanageable number of students for final screening, and that time and cost differences did not support the notion that the case study technique was unduly costly. In working with the case study technique, educators must use the "total picture" concept of giftedness and a team approach in identifying the gifted.

EXTENDING ACTIVITIES

1 Plan a comprehensive identification and screening procedure to locate the gifted in your district. Outline this plan, and compare it to the identification procedure being used in your district, if the information is available.
2 What would you predict to be the result of using group achievement tests and group intelligence tests as the screening instruments for an inner-city gifted program?
3 Define "efficiency" and "economy." Why do you think this is a problem for a school district?
4 Conduct a case study on a child whom you think might be gifted. Use items from a checklist, such as the Renzulli-Hartman (1971) scale, or construct your own to gather information. Gather as much data as possible on the child.
5 Discuss the adage "Early ripe, early rot." Does this adage relate in any way to the notion people hold of not "pushing" gifted children?

REFERENCES

Alexander, P. & Muia, J. (1982). *Gifted education*. Rockville, MD: Aspen Publications.
Alvino, J., McDonnel, R. & Richert, S. (1981). A national survey of identification practices in gifted and talented education. *Exceptional Children, 48*(2), 124–132.
Anastasi, A. (1976). *Psychological testing*. New York: Macmillan.
Arthur, G. (1950). *The Arthur adaptation of the Leiter International Performance Scale*. Chicago: C. H. Stoelting.

Bernal, E. M. (1975). Gifted Mexican American children: An ethnic–scientific perspective. *California Journal of Educational Record, 25,* 261–273.

Bernal, E. (1978). The identification of gifted Chicano children. In A. Baldwin, G. Gear & L. Lucito (Eds.), *Educational planning for the gifted.* Reston, VA: The Council for Exceptional Children.

Bruch, C. B. (1971). Modification of procedures for identification of the disadvantaged gifted. *The Gifted Child Quarterly, 15,* 267–272.

Cox, C. (1926). The early mental traits of three hundred geniuses. In L. H. Terman (Ed.), *Genetic studies of genius, Volume II.* Stanford, CA: Stanford University Press.

Cox, J. (1985). *The Richardson study: A national investigation of educational opportunities for able learners.* Fort Worth, TX: Texas Christian University Press.

Dettmer, P. (1981). Improving teacher attitudes toward characteristics of the creatively gifted. *Gifted Child Quarterly, 25,* 11–16.

Fort Worth Texas BPI (1982). *Finding the potentially gifted child.* Fort Worth, TX.

French, J. (1964). *Educating the gifted.* New York: Holt, Rinehart and Winston.

French, J. (1964). *Pictorial test of intelligence.* Boston: Houghton Mifflin.

Guilford, J. P. (1975). Varieties of creative giftedness, their measurement and development. *The Gifted Child Quarterly, 19,* 107–121.

Hiskey, M. (1966). *Hiskey–Nebraska test of learning aptitude.* Lincoln, NB: Union College Press.

Howley, A. et al. (1986). *Teaching gifted children: principles and strategies.* Boston: Little, Brown.

Kranz, B. (1981). *Talent identification instrument.* Moorhead, MN: Moorhead State College.

Maker, J. (1982). *Curriculum development for the gifted.* Rockville, MD: Aspen Publications.

Marland, S. (1972). *Educating of the gifted and talented.* Report to the Congress. Washington, DC: U.S. Government Printing Office.

Martinson, R. (1974). *The identification of the gifted and talented.* Ventura, CA: Office of the Ventura County Superintendent.

Meeker, M. (1978). Nondiscriminatory testing procedures to assess giftedness in black, Chicano, Navajo and anglo children. In A. Y. Baldwin, G. H. Gear & L. J. Lucito (Eds.), *Educational planning for the gifted: Overcoming cultural, geographical, and socioeconomic barriers.* Reston, VA: The Council for Exceptional Children.

Meeker, M. & Meeker, R. (1975). *SOI: Screening form for gifted.* El Segundo, CA: SOI Institute.

Mercer, J. & Lewis, J. (1977). *Parent interview manual: System of multicultural pluralistic assessment.* New York: Psychological Corporation.

Newland, T. E. (1976). *The gifted in socio-educational perspective.* Englewood Cliffs, NJ: Prentice-Hall.

Pegnato, C. & Birch, J. (1959). Locating gifted children in junior high schools. *Exceptional Children, 25,* 300–304.

Raven J. C. (1952). *Guide to using progressive matrices.* London: H. K. Lewis and Company.

Renzulli, J. & Hartman, R. (1971). Scale for rating behavioral characteristics of superior students. *Exceptional Children, 38*(3), 243–248.

Renzulli, J. & Smith, L. (1977). Two approaches to identification of gifted students. *Exceptional Children, 43,* 512–518.

Renzulli, J. & Smith, L. (1980). Revolving door: A truer turn for the gifted. *Learning, 9*(3), 91–93.

Rimm, S., Davis, G. & Bien, V. (1982). Identifying creativity: A characteristics approval. *Gifted Child Quarterly, 26*(4), 165–171.

Sato, I. (1979). *Who are these people?* (film). Los Angeles: National/State Leadership Training Institute of Gifted and Talented (N/S-LTI-G/T).

Taylor, C. & Ellison, R. (1968). *Alpha biographical inventory.* Salt Lake City: Institute for Behavioral Research in Creativity.

Terman, L. (1925). Mental and physical traits of a thousand gifted children. In L. Terman (Ed.), *Genetic studies of genius, Volume I.* Stanford, CA: Stanford University Press.

Torrance, E. P. (1971). Are the Torrance tests of creative thinking biased against or in favor of disadvantaged groups? *The Gifted Child Quarterly, 15,* 75–80.

Torrance, E. P. (1974). Torrance tests of creative thinking. *Norms-Technical Manual.* Lexington, MA: Personnel Press.

Williams, R. (1972). *Black intelligence test of cultural homogeneity.* St. Louis: Robert L. Williams and Associates.

Witty, P. A. (1955). Gifted children—Our national resource. *Nursing Education, 47,* 498-500.

Young-Baldwin, A. (1977). Tests can underpredict: A case study. *Phi Delta Kappan, 58,* 620–621.

CHAPTER 3

INDIVIDUALIZING EDUCATION FOR THE GIFTED

I am a part of all that
I have met
Yet all experience is an
arch where through
Gleams that untraveled world
whose margin faces
Forever and forever when
I move.

Tennyson, Ulysses

The importance of individualizing education for gifted students has been stressed by a number of authors (Kaplan, 1974; Maker, 1982; Clark, 1983; Gallagher, 1985); yet, when individualized learning is examined in practice, a multitude of interpretations are found, not all of which lead to effective education practices for gifted students. Individualized learning can range from independent study activities planned to supplement, extend, or substitute classroom work for the gifted student to the more formalized long-range planning involved in IEP.

Individualized education involves adaptation of the content, the process, the product, and the learning environment, if necessary, after a careful assessment of individual strengths and weaknesses of students. This assessment involves examining a number of sources of material such as achievement and intellectual aptitude scores, as well as interest surveys and creativity indices.

Individualized instruction is diagnostic and prescriptive as individual educational programs are developed for gifted students through teacher diagnosis. The prescription is cooperatively developed by both the teacher and the gifted student, and can include information from parents and other teachers. When the regular classroom teacher is primarily responsible for the individualization, the specialist in the gifted is included in the prescriptive partnership. The development of self-direction and self-selection of topics are key aspects in an individualized program.

INDEPENDENT STUDY

One form of individualized programming is the independent study (see Table 3-1) as exemplified by the independent study prepared for an elementary student (Sisk, 1975).

The gifted specialist teacher and the gifted student cooperatively assessed interests, established goals, and planned learning activities, learning materials, and instructional outcomes. The gifted student was encouraged to self-pace his/her work, self-evaluate by discussing areas for further study, and critically examine any need for adaptation. The consultant for the gifted worked with the gifted students and regular classroom teachers, helping regular classroom teachers to provide both a resource and support in the classroom. The independent study was planned in Spanish for a third-grade gifted student. His major strength was in language skills, in which he demonstrated an achievement level of 8.6 (eighth grade and 6 months). Teachers and parents described the student as shy and somewhat introverted. Consequently, the gifted specialist encouraged him to involve other students in his study, by using the Spanish corner and functioning as a Spanish tutor.

With older students, the Independent Study Worksheet is more detailed. Table 3-2 shows an independent study sheet for a ninth-grade Honors English student.

This sample independent study is planned for a middle school gifted student in a Los Angeles language arts/social studies gifted class. The study builds on his interest in creative writing, and it focuses on the broad theme of our inhumanity to one another and people in relation to their times. In examining the independent effort of this gifted student, several points are important to note in individualized instruction. The study varies the content, process, product, and learning envi-

TABLE 3-1
MY INDEPENDENT STUDY

What I want to study about	How I will go about it	What I will do with my knowledge
1 I want to learn more Spanish.	1 Schedule time to speak daily with a Spanish-speaking person (half an hour).	1 Help other kids with their vocabulary and drill sessions.
2 I want to learn more about the history of Spain and its culture.	2 Consult different Spanish history books.	2 Be a tutor for other students learning Spanish.
	3 Find books in the library about Spanish customs.	3 Set up a Spanish culture corner in the pod for others.

TABLE 3-2
INDEPENDENT STUDY WORKSHEET

Content to be studied	Resources/materials	Learning process/product
1 Charles Dickens: personality, beliefs, attitudes	1 *A Tale of Two Cities*, Charles Dickens	1 Prepare video tape discussion on findings
2 People's relationship to time	2 Interview English professor at UCLA, a specialist in Dickens	2 Conduct short session on Dickens with Pi Lambda Theta
3 Our inhumanity to one another	3 Examine history of French revolution through history text	3 Write article for school literary magazine
	4 Attend *A Tale of Two Cities* play in Los Angeles	
	5 Examine history books for history of England during Dickens' life	

ronment. The *content* is varied, as not all ninth-grade students read *A Tale of Two Cities*, nor are they specifically examining our inhumanity to one another. They do, however, work on the broad theme, people in relationship to their times, so gifted student independent study has carry-over to and continuity with the work in the regular classroom.

The *learning environment* is altered as the gifted student visits a college campus, attends a play in a community theater, and uses university and college libraries for historical research. The *process* is modified as higher levels of thinking, comparing, and contrasting are used with the theme: people in relationship to their times. Open-ended searching using guiding questions such as "What were the attitudes and beliefs of Dickens?" also varied the process. The pacing is individualized, as the gifted student established his own deadlines and timetables. The independent effort involves a discovery approach. The *product* uses a real audience with three major presentations: (1) a meeting of Pi Lambda Theta members, (2) a tape in his honors classes in language arts, and (3) an article for the school literary magazine. The project is a powerful stimulus to other gifted students and helps them solidify the themes of our inhumanity to one another and people in relationship to their times.

Individualization is a serious commitment for educators who work with gifted. Individualization is based on several assumptions, according to Clark (1983).

- Students should assume some responsibility for their own learning.
- Students should become independent learners.
- Students have a right to learn at their own pace, through their preferred learning style, and at their own level of ability.

- Students should apply their varying amounts and areas of knowledge.
- Students need to exercise judgment in selecting from a variety of materials. When everyone has the same material, learning ceases to be individualized. As the range of available materials and experiences increases, the range of learning opportunities for every individual also increases.
- Students should be graded in terms of their own achievement if grades must be given.
- School programs need to develop students' self-esteem.

The student's self-esteem is crucial to independent study. By identifying an area of interest and pursuing a project to its completion, gifted students take a significant step in the development of positive self-esteem, particularly as it demonstrates their knowledge and ability.

GOALS AND OBJECTIVES FOR THE GIFTED

Goals and objectives should be easily understood by students, parents, and teachers. Goals and objectives flow from the operational context. Bloom et al. (1971) define a goal as an aspiration or declaration of the school's mission. Goals are general statements that identify direction, tone, and quality. They also reflect a broad and long-term emphasis. An example is that each student will reach her/his potential or have the right to be a well-rounded individual contributing to society.

Objectives specifically describe the individual performance of a student and are sequenced to reach the goal. One interesting way of writing goals was developed by Mager (1972). Groups are asked to visualize the behavior to be expected when the goal is achieved. Participants then share these visualizations of behaviors orally or in writing. After discussion, a rewrite is attempted either on a blackboard or with individual cards. Each time the objective is rewritten, it becomes more precise. The new statements are grouped into common clusters to identify and support the final goal statements.

Another technique to generate goal statements uses a matrix. Bloom et al. (1971) suggest teachers select objectives from an array of objectives that match the content. Bloom et al. termed their technique the "preparation of a Table of Specification (TOS)."

A variation of a matrix technique proposed by Maker (1972) is based on a number of practices prevalent in the field of gifted education and research. Maker based her matrix on the work of Kaplan (1974), Gallagher (1985), Renzulli (1977), Ward (1961), and the U.S. Office of Education (1966) guidelines for preparing projects for gifted. Kaplan (1974) suggests that the type of input and expectancies need to be altered. She described the input appropriate for gifted as being accelerated or advanced, more complex, and beyond the regular curriculum. Gallagher (1985), suggests the regular curriculum be modified to meet the needs of the gifted by (1) changing the content, and stressing more complex and abstract concepts; (2) using the method of presentation of the discipline specialists; and (3) extending the learning environment beyond the classroom.

Renzulli (1977) suggests that gifted students become investigators of real problems or topics, use appropriate methods of inquiry, and function as active problem formulators and problem solvers.

Ward (1961) developed a comprehensive logical theory of ten propositions that take into account the superior characteristics of gifted and their societal roles. He suggests these propositions guide the design of their curriculum.

1 That the educational program for intellectually superior individuals should be derived from a balanced consideration of facts, opinions based on experience, and deduction from educational philosophy as these relate to the capacity of the individuals and to the probable social roles which they will fill. (p. 81)

2 That a program of education for the intellectually superior should be relatively unique. (p. 86)

3 That the curriculum should consist of economically chosen objectives designated to promote the civic, social, and personal adequacy of the intellectually superior individual. (p. 126)

4 That the education of the gifted individual should place considerable emphasis upon intellectual activity. (p. 126)

5 That the educative experience of the intellectually superior should be conservatively designed as generative of further development, extensively and intensively, along similar and related avenues. (p. 141)

6 That the education of the gifted child/youth should emphasize enduring methods and sources of learning, as opposed to a terminal emphasis upon present state of knowledge. (p. 156)

7 That the instruction of intellectually superior individuals should emphasize the central function of meaning in the acquisition of fact and principle, and the varieties of reflections of meaning in the development of communication devices of human beings. (p. 16)

8 That the instruction of the intellectually superior should include content pertaining to the foundations of civilization. (p. 170)

9 That scientific methods should be applied in the conception and in the execution of the education for personal, social, and character adjustments of the intellectually superior individual. (p. 195)

10 That instruction in the theoretical bases of ideal moral behavior and of personal and social adjustments should be an integral part of the intellectually gifted individual. (p. 201)

Maker summarizes the common elements among the ideas of Kaplan (1974), Gallagher (1985), Renzulli (1977), and Ward (1961):

1 Build upon the characteristics unique to gifted students.

2 Include concepts of higher levels of abstraction or greater complexity.

3 Emphasize the development of thinking skills at a higher level than acquisition and memory.

4 Provide any administration or other arrangement necessary to enable the pupils to use their full potential.

Using these similarities, Maker developed a matrix to plan goals and objectives for gifted students. A selected part of the matrix (learning) is illustrated in Table 3-3.

The characteristics are selected from the Scales for Rating the Behavioral Characteristics of Superior Students (SRBCSS)(Renzulli et al., 1976). Maker also identifies appropriate curricular changes for gifted students as content, process, product, and learning environment. The Maker matrix stresses matching the gifted student's needs and characteristics to the curriculum modification.

A modification of the Maker matrix is to list the characteristics of gifted students, the objectives or guiding questions, and the specific process/method and product (Sisk, 1966). Still another modification is to list the characteristics of the gifted, the strategies, a selected model for teaching, and a central stimulus (key concepts from content)(Sisk, 1985). A list of characteristics of gifted students is helpful to the classroom teacher. Seagoe (1974) offers a list of intellectual characteristics with concomitant problems (see Table 3-4). These problems are minimized by using the characteristics listed as a basis for developing curricula for gifted students.

The Sisk modification of the Maker matrix uses the Seagoe list of intellectual characteristics as the focal point, with the guiding questions extending or building upon the demonstrated behavior. The process and product are derived from the interaction of the characteristic and the objective. Table 3-5 provides an example of the modification using characteristics 12 and 14 from the Seagoe list.

In the above activity, the overall goal for the gifted student is to enable him/her to contribute to society as a positive member. The objective is to provide opportunities for identifying real problems, formulating hypotheses, and seeking solutions. The guiding question is "Are individual decisions relative?" The gifted student can use a number of different processes such as surveys, interviews, and individual inquiry in history to gather data and information. The eventual products which were self-selected by the gifted student, along with the topic, were an oral report, an editorial, and an article.

Another way to develop goals and objectives for gifted students is the Davis (1978) method, as cited by Sellin and Birch (1981). Davis endorses a matrix, using the existing curriculum areas (language arts, social studies, science, math, foreign language, arts/music, and physical education) as reference points and the areas of cognitive and affective education (Bloom, 1956; Krathwohl et al., 1964).

In summary, to prepare goals and objectives for the gifted student, teachers need to observe the individual gifted student, gather data on the student from a variety of sources, and match the student's interest and demonstrated needs to an area of study. Emphasis is on altering the content, process, product, and learning environment to allow the gifted student to move beyond the bounds of the regular curriculum. In addition, there should be opportunities to elaborate on the regular curriculum and to seek new explanations of concepts. This type of

TABLE 3-3
SUMMARY OF CHARACTERISTICS OF GIFTED CHILDREN AND THEIR IMPLICATION FOR CURRICULUM MODIFICATIONS

Child Characteristics and Probable Social Roles	Content							Process/Method								Product				Learning Environment					
	Abstractness	Complexity	Variety	Organization	Economy	Study of People	Methods	Higher Level Thought	Open-Endedness	Discovery	Proof/Reasoning	Freedom of Choice	Group Interaction	Pacing	Variety	Real Problems	Real Audiences	Evaluation	Transformation	Student Centered	Encourages Independence	Openness	Accepting	Complex	High Mobility
Learning																									
Has unusually advanced vocabulary for age or grade level; uses terms in a meaningful way; has verbal behavior characterized by "richness" of expression, elaboration, and fluency. (National Education Association, 1960; Terman & Oden, 1947; Witty, 1955)	X	X	X					X			X								X	X				X	X
Possesses a large storehouse of information about a variety of topics (beyond the usual interests of youngsters his age). (Terman, 1925; Ward, 1961; Witty, 1958)	X	X	X	X				X						X		X	X		X	X	X			X	X
Has quick mastery and recall of factual information. (Goodhart & Schmidt, 1940; National Education Association, 1960; Terman & Oden, 1947)	X	X	X					X						X					X	X					X

Source: J. Maker, *Curriculum Development for the Gifted.* Rockville, MD: Aspen Publications, 1982. Reprinted by permission.

TABLE 3-4
SOME LEARNING CHARACTERISTICS OF GIFTED CHILDREN

Characteristics	Concomitant problems
1 Keen power of observation; naive receptivity; sense of the significant; willingness to examine the unusual	1 Possible gullibility
2 Power of abstraction, conceptualization; synthesis, interest in inductive learning and problem solving, pleasure in intellectual activity	2 Occasional resistance to direction; rejection or omission of detail
3 Interest in cause–effect relations, ability to see relationships; interest in applying concepts; love of truth	3 Difficulty in accepting the illogical
4 Liking for structure and order; liking for consistency, as in value systems, number systems, clocks, calendars	4 Invention of own systems, sometimes conflicting
5 Retentiveness	5 Dislike for routine and drill; need for early mastery of foundation skills
6 Verbal proficiency; large vocabulary; facility in expression; interest in reading; breadth of information in advanced areas	6 Need for early specialized reading vocabulary; parent resistance to reading; escape into verbalism
7 Questioning attitude, intellectual curiosity, inquisitive mind; intrinsic motivation	7 Lack of early home or school stimulation
8 Power of critical thinking; skepticism, evaluative testing; self-criticism and self-checking	8 Critical attitude toward others; discouragement from self-criticism
9 Creativeness and inventiveness; liking for new ways of doing things; interest in creating, brainstorming, free-wheeling	9 Rejection of the known; need to invent for oneself
10 Power of concentration; intense attention that excludes all else; long attention span	10 Resistance to interruption
11 Persistent, goal-directed behavior	11 Stubborness
12 Sensitivity, intuitiveness, empathy for others; need for emotional support and sympathy	12 Need for success and recognition; sensitivity to criticism; vulnerability to peer group rejection
13 High energy, alertness, eagerness; periods of intense voluntary effort preceding invention	13 Frustration with inactivity and absence of progress
14 Independence in work and study; preference for individualized work; self-reliance.	14 Parent and peer group pressures and nonconformity; problems of rejection and rebellion
15 Versatility and virtuosity; diversity of interests and abilities; many hobbies; proficiency in art forms such as music and drawing	15 Lack of homogeneity in group work; need for flexibility and individualization; need for help in exploring and developing basic competencies in major interest
16 Friendliness and outgoingness	16 Need for peer group relations in many types of groups; problems in developing social leadership

TABLE 3-5
CHARACTERISTICS OF GIFTED AND APPROPRIATE
OBJECTIVES AND PROCESSES

Characteristics of gifted	Objectives/ guiding questions	Process/ product
12 Sensitivity and empathy for others	Are individual decisions relative?	Surveys
14 Independence in work and study		Inquiries into history

understanding and valuing of concepts helps gifted students use their full potential in challenging and rewarding experiences.

INDIVIDUALIZED EDUCATIONAL PLANNING AND DEVELOPMENT

Rationale for Individualized Educational Planning

Individualized planning for exceptional students is required by federal law (P.L. 94-142) or by state statute. In the states where gifted students are included in exceptional student education, teachers of the gifted are required to prepare an individualized educational plan, commonly called an IEP, as an extension of planning individualized education for gifted students. Some teachers and administrators resist using the IEP, with the argument that extra time is required to plan IEPs. However, an even more important issue is whether or not we are educating groups of gifted students with a set curriculum or individualizing with IEPs.

The idea of the IEP is not a new one; however, it has gained public recognition from Public Law 94-142 requiring IEPs for individual handicapped students. Public Law 95-561, the law providing program efforts for gifted education, does not require an IEP for each gifted student. The major thrust of Public Law 95-561 is to provide differentiated education for gifted students. Differentiated education as defined by the Office of Gifted and Talented is that process of instruction which can be integrated into the school program and adapted to varying levels of individual learning response for the education of gifted and talented students. It includes:

1 A differentiated curriculum embodying a high level of cognitive and affective concepts and processes beyond those normally provided in the regular curriculum of the local educational agency;

2 Instructional strategies which accommodate the unique learning styles of the gifted and talented; and

3 Flexible administrative arrangements for instruction both in and out of school, such as special classes, seminars, resource rooms, independent study, student internships, mentorships, research, field trips, library, media, research centers, and other appropriate arrangements (USOE, 1976).

Teachers who observe the IEP development process often see the emphasis as being on minimally complying with the law rather than on meeting the needs of individual gifted students. This minimum compliance is a legitimate concern and should be addressed. Several ways to combat "compliance mentality" are to encourage open and honest communication, to use in-service training on the construction of IEPs, and to provide adequate teacher release time to plan and prepare the IEPs.

Designing the Content of an IEP

The process of planning or designing an IEP includes assessing the individual gifted student's needs, developing a profile or matrix, identifying or developing objectives, planning learning experiences, and deciding on how to evaluate the progress of the gifted student. Key individuals need to be involved in each IEP, and their roles may vary. For example, some parents will want to be involved in their gifted child's program, particularly if the gifted child is underachieving or in some way is not functioning well in school. Other parents may want minimum involvement. Educators and parents need to agree, however, on their expectations and goals for the gifted students. In addition, the regular classroom teacher should be involved in the IEP development to ensure cooperation in the implementation of the IEP.

Kroth (1980) identifies four levels of parental involvement: (1) informational, (2) participational, (3) interactive, and (4) deep involvement. The informational level is general sharing of information concerning the gifted student's interests, early indications of giftedness, and strengths and weaknesses as seen by the parents or teachers. The participation level includes planning activities that teachers and parents think are worthwhile for the individual gifted student. The interactive and deep involvement levels include working with teachers regularly and closely on special concerns or problems such as underachievement.

Assessment

Several leading questions are helpful in compiling assessment information from a variety of sources: Is information available concerning the gifted student's aptitude, achievement, interest, creativity, and self-concept?

Maker (1982) suggests that the questions be grouped into three areas: (1) comprehensiveness, (2) variety, and (3) validity. To test the criteria of variety, she suggests these questions:

1 Do the data include assessment in a variety of settings?
2 Do they reflect the perceptions of a variety of individuals, including the student, parents, regular classroom teacher, a psychologist or diagnostic specialist, and the special teacher?

Objective data are very important, but many gifted students, particularly special populations, will not be identified if strict adherence to objective data is observed.

Validity is an important concern. The date tests were administered, and the test validity and reliability need to be documented. Alvino et al. (1981), concerned with validity of tests for gifted students, found that many tests were not adaptable to low income, disadvantaged, bilingual, handicapped, or other special populations of gifted. Yet school districts were continuing to use these instruments as measures of students; consequently, many special population students were penalized.

Compiling the Data or Information and Forming Goals and Objectives

The information can be displayed on a matrix to form an individual profile. Using this data, both long-term annual goals and short-term objectives are developed. These goals and objectives set the stage for program development.

Development of the Program Plan

Decisions about what materials and methods to use in reaching the objectives can be facilitated by using the Maker matrix or other compilations of matrix information. However, the primary emphasis is on content, process, product, and learning environment modifications.

Evaluation of Progress

A comprehensive evaluation of progress will reflect a number of evaluation procedures. To help gifted students evaluate their own progress, it is useful to ask questions such as: If you were to conduct this study again, how would you do it? What do you think were the strengths of your project? What weaknesses did you note? Are there new approaches you would use?

Other types of informal assessment are teacher observation, teacher rating scales, parent rating scales, and parent observation. However, informal assessment needs to be supplemented by formal assessment; both need to be congruent with the program processes and methods. Exhibit 3-1 illustrates a checklist as one type of informal assessment. This checklist is unique, as it includes positive and negative characteristics such as being bored with rote mechanics, displaying leadership toward undesirable goals, or having difficulty with reading. This checklist contradicts the stereotype that gifted students are always achievers and well behaved, and that they exhibit desirable behaviors.

An example of incongruence between assessment of progress and program is reflected by a rural county gifted program, in which a secondary gifted student program consists of field experiences on a salt flat, self-selected activities, and individual projects. However, paper-and-pencil achievement test assesses the learning. This test cannot reflect the student growth in attitudes toward learning, self-esteem, and the ability to get along with others. This growth was noted by teachers and parents in the day-to-day experiences of the gifted students but was not consistently documented. In addition, the gifted students expressed concern

EXHIBIT 3-1

INFORMAL ASSESSMENT CHECKLIST

_____

Name of School   Name of Student

_____

Name of Evaluation   Date of birth   Grade

_____
Relationship to child and/or school
(Teacher, principal, parent)

Please check those items most characteristic of this child according to your best judgment. It is unlikely that any child will have all of these attributes.

IDENTIFICATION CHECKLIST

___ Deals with abstractions
___ Is curious
___ Has desire for knowledge

___ Is highly verbal
___ Uses intelligent conversation
___ Has a variety of interests
___ Is capable of intense concentration

___ Has long attention span
___ Learns quickly
___ Has tremendous fund of knowledge
___ Asks intelligent questions
___ Has a good memory
___ Is quick to see relationships
___ Likes structure
___ Enjoys brainstorming, free-wheeling
___ Is bored with rote, mechanics; handwriting, spelling
___ Is intuitive
___ Is sensitive

___ Has a sense of humor
___ Has leadership qualities; is able to influence others toward desirable and undesirable goals
___ Has good coordination
___ Is keen observer
___ Has original, unique ideas
___ Deals with adults and peers
___ Has large vocabulary

___ Has much energy, which gets him into trouble at times
___ Is often bored with recitation and memorization of facts; prefers talking about ideas and problems
___ Likes to work alone
___ Best student in your room
___ Does the best critical thinking
___ An able student, but also the biggest nuisance
___ Outstanding in science
___ Oustanding in art
___ Outstanding in music
___ Outstanding in math
___ Has difficulty with reading, but is otherwise believed bright
___ Exhibits qualities of leadership among his peers
___ Seems unable to stick to a task
___ Reads well above the median for his class
___ Enjoys math, especially new approaches to problem solving, though may be bored with the familiar
___ Is first to see discrepancies

___ Self-motivated
___ Fools around a lot; with whatever is at hand
___ Is independent

EXHIBIT 3-1   *(Continued)*

___ Asks many questions, often challenging the teacher and the textbook
___ Is capable of self-directed learning

Source: Fort Worth School District, Fort Worth, TX. Reprinted by permission, Pat Denton, Supervisor
of Gifted.

and resentment over the inconsistency between the open-ended learning and the
traditional testing.

Information gathered all year long (formative) as well as at the end of the year
(summative) needs to provide data for purposes of comparison. Much data is lost
when evaluation occurs at the close of a project. Formative and summative data
provide information for redirection and extension of the program and objectives
for the individual gifted students; this last function is the major role of evaluation.

The steps in the provision of an IEP for gifted students are summarized (Cooley
& Lohnes, 1976; Provus, 1971; Stufflebeam, 1971) in Figure 3-1.

PITFALLS OF IEP PLANNING AND USE

One pitfall in working with the IEP is the "compliance mentality" which meets
the minimum requirements of the law, but rejects the spirit of the law. Teachers
mainly resist the IEP concept because of lack of time. To meet this concern, school
districts hire staffing specialists who often work out of the special education
department to take responsibility for writing the IEP. However in some cases,
these staffing specialists may not be well informed about the gifted program, its
philosophy, or delivery of service. This lack of program knowledge is compounded
by limited information on gifted students' needs and characteristics.

However, through in-service training, these staffing specialists and other key
persons writing the IEP for gifted students can learn about the gifted program and
the gifted students.

FIGURE 3-1
Steps in structuring an IEP.

Identification and referral

Assessment/certification of giftedness

Conference of key people and planning

Completion of IEP

Implementation of program

Evaluation

New/revised IEP

Another problem with the IEP is that it is often prepared before school begins, without sufficient data or face-to-face meetings with the individual gifted student. As a result, the IEP is constructed with incorrect or incomplete information. Educators may defend this practice in order to comply with fall deadlines, but this practice yields an IEP on paper only. The needs, characteristics, and interests of the gifted students may not coincide with the IEP.

Public Law 94-142 stipulates the use of IEPs and requires a parent signature and the offering of due process for the parents if they think that the IEP is not sufficient for their exceptional student. Many states offer these same rights to gifted students and their parents when the programs for gifted are administratively housed in special education. Infractions are noted during program audits. One program audit revealed that 10 percent of the IEPs lacked parents' signatures and in all the IEPs, the gifted teacher was responsible for 90 percent of the objectives and the other 10 percent were independent activities for the gifted student, to be supervised by the regular classroom teacher. This practice assumed that the gifted student's needs were being met primarily by the gifted specialist. Yet the gifted students were spending the majority of their time in the regular class setting. The evaluation processes were found to be standardized achievement tests; yet, when the objectives were analyzed, they called for higher level thinking skills, such as an analysis, synthesis, evaluation, and creative or divergent thinking. These skills are not measured by achievement tests; consequently, there was no congruence between the program objectives and the evaluation.

The IEP is a prescribed plan of action including individualized goals and objectives, the processes to be used, a timetable for mobilizing toward reaching the goals and objectives, and an assessment of the IEP effectiveness. To be effective, the IEP should be planned by the individual primarily responsible for educating the gifted student, either the regular classroom teacher or the teacher of the gifted. Staffing specialists who are skilled in writing objectives and goals are a welcome and a much-needed resource, but they should not usurp the role of the teacher of the gifted or the regular classroom teacher.

When individuals not directly involved with the gifted students plan an IEP it may not be appropriate for the individual gifted student. Not all gifted students possess the same learning styles. Some gifted students can handle a great deal of freedom and monitor their own behavior to work independently; other gifted students prefer working in small groups. Even when teaching methods are listed in program plans to alter the process for the gifted, the teachers may find gifted students do not possess these group or independent work skills.

Skill deficits in gifted students can be remedied through direct teaching, as many of the deficits are developmental skills. However, someone who is familiar with the individual gifted students must document this information so that it is included in the IEP.

A precise method of individualizing education which is useful in planning IEPs for the gifted students is suggested by Dunn and Dunn (1975):

1 Give students opportunities to build the skills needed for participation in individualized learning.

- to make choices (choosing wisely leaves many options; choosing less wisely leaves fewer options, and consequences determine the value of the choice)
- to self-evaluate
- to share
2 Teach students the skills of learning in small groups.
   - role playing
   - peer teaching
   - group analysis
   - discussion
3 Establish instructional areas that will support individualized learning.
   - interest centers
   - learning stations
   - media center
   - game areas
   - quiet reading and study area
   - assessment center
4 Develop student independence.
   - knowledge of resources, location, and use
   - alternative thinking in activities and in reporting
5 Carefully assess students, curriculum, and resources.
6 Help class learn skills of cooperative assessment, goal setting, and evaluation.
7 Let class assume more responsibility for planning and implementing the program.

This last step (7) provides an opportunity for the redirection of the IEP. As the gifted student and the program is reassessed, the learning experiences can continue or be altered.

A CASE STUDY EXAMPLE OF AN IEP

A hypothetical case of Mark Hampton, a middle school gifted student, illustrates the complete case-study process. Mark's Education Profile, completed by his classroom teacher, is shown in Exhibits 3-2 (p.56) and 3-3 (p.57). The profile form is considered part of the referral process in a local school district (Rouse, 1983).

Mark's teacher conducted this case study as part of a graduate-level course in gifted education, and he volunteered to be a subject to assist her with her assignments.

In addition to individual and group test scores, the total case study should include information on the observed behavior throughout the testing. The testing situation is a microcosm of the individual gifted student's approach to learning.

Mark was given the Wechsler Intelligence Scale for Children-Revised (WISC-R) at age 12, and he achieved a full-scale intelligence quotient of 152. The psychologist completed a behavior observation form following the testing (see Exhibit 3-4, p.60).

Mark's teacher gathered much useful information for her case study. As a result, she was able to formulate constructive goals, objectives, and activities for Mark.

EXHIBIT 3-2

EDUCATIONAL PROFILE CHART

Name of Student _____ Mark Hampton _____ Birthdate _____ Grade _____

Present Date _____   Date Admitted to Program _____

Name of Teacher _____   School _____

Profile	Low 1	2	Medium 3	4	High 5
1. Expresses many ideas	—	—	—	x	—
2. Gives variety of responses	—	—	—	x	—
3. Unusual, unique ideas (not always useful)	—	—	—	—	x
4. Adds to basic idea to make it more useful	—	—	—	x	—
5. Predicts causes/effects of given situations	—	—	x	—	—
6. Produces many words fitting different categories	—	—	—	x	—
7. Uses words to describe feelings	—	—	—	x	—
8. Uses words to make comparison; show relationships	—	—	x	—	—
9. Can make a judgement between alternatives	—	—	x	—	—
10. Sensitive to problems that can arise during a given project	—	—	x	—	—
11. Can analyze and interpret	—	—	x	—	—
12. Is able to transfer skills to problem-solving activities	—	—	x	—	—

SCORE 43

When her information was added to the student questionnaires and the psychologist's observations, a comprehensive picture of Mark evolved.

Mark's parents were contacted and asked to attend a staffing meeting. At that time, an IEP was planned and developed for Mark. The notification of the staffing meeting is shown in Exhibit 3-5, (p.61).

At the end of the staffing meeting, Mark's parents were asked to sign a placement form (Exhibit 3-6, p.62). He was then enrolled in a special social studies class for intellectually gifted students at his middle school.

Program offerings differ for gifted students throughout the United States, with service for gifted students ranging from one class per day as provided for Mark at his middle school to total program offerings at specialized schools such as the Bronx High School of Science in New York City or the Cincinnati School for the Performing Arts.

EXHIBIT 3-3

CASE STUDY FORMAT

Pupil's Name _____ Mark Hampton _____   Date __ 12/10/86 __

School _____ Jordan Middle School _____   Grade __ 6 __

1. Parent Background	Father	Mother
Educational level completed	High school	2 yrs. secondary school
Occupation	Salesman	Secretary/receptionist
Special interests and aptitudes	Mechanics	Piano and art

2. Description of Family Unit (check appropriate line)

Child Lives With: ___ Mother   ___ Father   _X_ Both natural parents

                       ___ Stepmother   ___ Stepfather   ___ Other (specify)

3. Any unusual family conditions which might influence school performance? _____

4. Description of early indications of superior ability, any special talents (e.g. speech, interests, physical development)

Speech therapist suggested he be tested at age 4. He walked early and as a child always had an interest in books. He has always had a good memory and remembered people he met. As a baby, he noticed things in his room and reacted to them.

5. Narrative summary

Mark is one of those rare young people who is totally involved, physically, mentally, and emotionally. Bright, attractive, and personable, Mark is a small, 13-year-old bundle of kinetic energy. He is self-motivated and directed, yet often unpredictable, immature, and irrepressible.

He stands up to complete projects, sometimes swaying slightly and humming or laughing softly to himself. During work in small groups, he sits in his chair on his legs or balances on his knees, frequently leaning over the table to make a point or to tell a joke. During class discussion, he rocks his chair precariously on two legs, listening intently for an opportunity to interject a question, comment, or idea. When he has a thought he cannot suppress, he waves his hand (or hands) impatiently.

While Mark's comments are always on topic, they are frequently "way-out" interpretations into which he rushes with excitement and enthusiasm. He enjoys arguing the merits of his contributions and appears to solidify his opinions in the process.

EXHIBIT 3-3   *(Continued)*

CASE STUDY FORMAT

Mark is unique among his peers not only because of his enthusiasm and behavior, but also because of his high level of self-direction. Computers are his hobby, interest, and recreation. He get his "kicks" from hanging around the Radio Shack and talking to salespeople and customers.

He does not participate in any clubs, organizations, or sports, and spends his spare time programming his computers and reading about electronics.

Recently, Mark asked how to go about copyrighting a computer program that "melds two languages" together. He has produced a number of computer programs, some of which he sent back to his former school to be used in an eighth-grade computer course. Last year, Mark helped win first place at the county's middle school science fair for his team's electronic project. He was also awarded his middle school's third-year-student science award.

Mark says he spends his entire $20 per week allowance on electronics books and equipment and has thus taught himself computer language and technology. Last year he purchased and assembled a micro-ace home mini-computer (6" × 8 ½" × 2") from a kit. The majority of his leisure time is consumed by experimenting on his larger, more versatile, 280A microprocessor.

Mark's parents serve as business managers of a large local restaurant and work long hours. Neither parent shares Mark's intense interest in computers or electronics. They do actively encourage him to pursue his interests and do make sure that he has the necessary materials. Occasionally, Mark's grandfather helps him on his electrical projects.

Both Mark and his parents have a very positive concept of Mark's intellectual abilities, especially in the areas of idea expression, problem solving, and reasoning.

Mark appears to have a high level of creativity and he is often daring in expressing his unique ideas and opinions.

Mark made a creative tape designed to explain the miracles of computers to the uninformed. His tape was informative and interesting, and his method of presentation was unique. He began his tape pretending that he was the conductor of a computer orchestra of "real" musicians who dared misbehave and had to be censored.

Mark is academically more mature and self-directed than his peers, but at times he is socially immature, even silly or giddy. His classmates frequently groan when he begins to talk, especially when he starts in on computers. The boys in the class treat Mark like a smaller, younger brother and occasionally resort to teasing him to get the inevitable tirade that is sure to follow.

6. Recommendations

Mark should be encouraged to broaden his interests to areas other than science and electronics. Physical activity outside of school would make it easier for him to work out his need for constant movement. Interaction with other young people in a club or organization might help him mature and develop socially. He should be encouraged to seek out a sport and an organization that might interest him, either at school or in the community.

Every opportunity should be given to develop some interests and leadership abilities in the social sciences areas. Since Mark likes to debate and discuss, timed debate situations in which he can actively participate may give him a chance to use his verbal skills within acceptable limits.

He should be given leadership activities that will allow him movement about the room and time in front of the class to compensate for his short stature and provide him the attention and movement that he needs. This approach will also help improve Mark's image among his peers who often treat Mark as a "little kid."

EXHIBIT 3-3 *(Continued)*

CASE STUDY FORMAT

The fact that Mark is secure and happy says something positive about his family life. One recommendation in this area would be to suggest that the family find an activity in which they participate as a family.

In order to give Mark some guidelines for planning his future academic studies in high school, suggestions were sought from the high school physics teacher, who is also a computer instructor for the local junior college. He recommended that Mark take as many advanced math and science courses as the high school offers and that he investigate summer courses at the local universities and colleges. After the sophomore year in a structured computer program, Mark can make contacts necessary in order to design programs for local businesses, as other high school students have done. The instructor questioned whether Mark's knowledge was as well-rounded and varied as it needed to be, and recommended that Mark take a "basic" data processing course given for college credit at the high school.

The annual goals that were planned for Mark during the staffing meeting are listed in his IEP:

The student will:

1 improve critical thinking abilities, and the ability to work in a group.

2 increase his knowledge of American life.

3 expand his knowledge of the future.

Evaluation of the three objectives were to be accomplished through teacher and self-evaluation for goal 1, pre- and post-test on goal 2, and teacher and self-evaluation for goal 3.

All parties agreed that Mark would attend a special social studies class for intellectually gifted one period a day.

The specific student objectives were listed:

I. A. The student will be able to gather, synthesize, and analyze data on a current issue of his choice on topics such as increased use of technology in today's world. SE, TO *

 B. The student will be able to reach a logical conclusion in written or oral presentation. CRT, PE *

II. A. The student will be able to demonstrate knowledge of the concepts and methods of the social studies during classroom analysis of a social problem. CRT *

 B. The student will be able to apply with 80 percent accuracy the FPSS (Functional Prerequisites for Societal Survival) sociological model in comparing and contrasting two specific cultures. CRT, ST *

---

* The notations at the end of the objectives refer to the following: CRT, criterion referenced testing; TO, teacher observation; SE, self-evaluation; ST, standardized test; PE, power evaluation.

EXHIBIT 3-4

BEHAVIOR OBSERVATION DURING TESTING

Name <u>Mark Hampton</u>
School <u>Jordan Middle</u>
Grade <u>Sixth</u>

1. Physical: <u>The student is full of energy, moving in his seat, drumming his fingers. He appears small for a 12-year-old.</u>

2. Attitude: <u>He was self-motivated and directed during the test, yet often unpredictable.</u>

3. Speed: <u>Quick to answer</u>

4. Speech: <u>He is fluent and loved the opportunity to talk. Excellent vocabulary.</u>

5. Posture: <u>He was often rocking the chair, hunched over his paper, using the chair only when he found it necessary. Stood to complete some items.</u>

6. Emotional: <u>He was impatient when the testing situation did not move as fast as he would have liked it to. Established an easy rapport with the tester.</u>

7. Facial expression: <u>Pleasant, alert, and animated</u>

8. Mannerism: <u>Mark is full of gestures. Some are adult, and these are also coupled with typical 12-year-old behaviors.</u>

III. A. The student will be able to identify and define specific areas of future concern. PE, SE, TO **

   B. The student will be able to design creative solutions to tomorrow's problems. CRT *

Many school districts are beginning to identify gifted students and plan educational activities for them. The case study process as illustrated by the work with Mark is an example of a school district's plan for individualized educational programs.

In many school districts the gifted program is administered under special education, and the IEP includes test data with headings such as "Intellectual processing." One school district utilizes the breakdown, shown in Exhibit 3-7 (p.63).

This breakdown indicates the intellectual processing instruments used and the testing information. Also some IEP forms may include sections on motor behavior (Exhibit 3-8, p.63).

Lastly, many forms for the IEP also include information items on the academic functioning of the student (Exhibit 3-9, p.63).

Another variation noted in the IEPs is the way in which the annual goals and objectives are reported. These are often accompanied by criterion for mastery (CRT) and the evaluation procedures. An example is a 9-year-old gifted boy who

EXHIBIT 3-5

NOTIFICATION OF STAFFING TEAM MEETING

Date _____January 15, 1987_____

Dear ___Mrs. Hampton___ :

Thank you for giving permission for your child, <u>Mark</u>, to be tested. The testing has been completed.

We have scheduled a team meeting to report the results of the testing on

    <u>Wednesday, January, 22, 1987</u>   <u>9:00 a.m.</u>   <u>Jordan Middle School</u>
          (Date)   (Time)   (Place)

We would like for you to attend this team meeting to help develop an educational plan for your child. If you cannot attend this meeting, the results will be discussed with you at another time. Please let us know what time during the day we can meet with you.

If you have any questions, please feel free to call me at any time.

Sincerely,

_____   _____Gifted Specialist_____
        (Signature)   (Title)

_____Jordan Middle School_____   _____532-8105_____

scored in the very superior range on the WISC and also excelled in achievement in all areas. Under behavioral/social/emotional, his teacher noted that he projected a keen sense of humor, enjoyed using the microscope, and was interested in being a professional baseball player. His program offerings, 4 hours per week in a center for the gifted, included the points in Exhibit 3-10 (p.64).

The teacher of the gifted is the key person in implementing the IEP, whether singly or in cooperation with the regular classroom teacher. The teacher guides and directs the gifted student and serves as an advisor and mentor. The teacher also helps the gifted student set realistic goals concerning his/her individualized work and evaluates whether or not the planned IEP meets his/her needs.

In particular, the teacher takes into consideration the learning style of the individual gifted pupil. Griggs and Price (1980) found, in their study of gifted middle school students, that gifted were less teacher-motivated and more self-motivated. The gifted, according to Griggs and Price, were able to work in a busy atmosphere and preferred studying alone. They also preferred tactile, visual, and kinesthetic means. In a recent study of secondary gifted students, Hahn (1982) found that the gifted students were concrete learners and abstract conceptualizers on the Kolb Learning Style Inventory. Conversely, she found that the teachers in the gifted program were identified as active experimenters.

These findings and observations emphasize the need for teachers to view each gifted student as a distinct and unique individual. The IEP process is a prescription,

EXHIBIT 3-6

PLACEMENT FORM

Date: <u>January 20, 1987</u>

Dear <u>Mr. and Mrs. Hampton</u> :

The testing for <u>Mark</u> was completed on _____ .
  (Name)   (Date)

The Staffing Team met on <u>January 22, 1987</u> to discuss your child's educational needs.

The following needs were identified by the team:

<u>The student was identified as gifted and could benefit from any specialized classes.</u>

An individualized educational plan was developed to meet these needs. A copy of the educational plan is available for your information.

In order to meet these needs, the Staffing Team recommended placement in the

_____ Gifted Program (Social Studies) _____

at <u>Jordan Middle School</u> _____

Your child's educational status will not be changed without your knowledge. To request a review, please contact

Ms. Brown
(Name)

<u>Teacher of the Gifted</u>   within 15 days.
      (Title)

Thank you for your cooperation in this matter. If you have any questions, please feel free to call me at any time. Please sign and return this form as soon as possible.

_____	Gifted Specialist
(Signature)	(Title)
Jordan Middle School	532-8105
(School)	(Phone)

I understand my rights regarding this placement.
___ Yes, I wish to have my child, _____, placed in _____ Program for instruction.

_____	_____
Parent(s) signature(s)	Date

EXHIBIT 3-7

INTELLECTUAL PROCESSING

Psychological (Most Recent) ─────────
                                              Date

Individual intelligence:

— — — Cattell
— — — Columbia
— — — Leiter
— — — McCarthy
— — — PTI
— — — Stanford-Binet
— _x_ — WISC-R/WPPSI

Intellectual range:

— — — Mentally deficient
— — — Borderline
— — — Low average
— — — Average
— — — High average
— — — Superior
— _x_ — Very superior

EXHIBIT 3-8

MOTOR BEHAVIOR

Motor/Self-Help/Physical

— Berry
— Bender

Educationally Relevant Medical Information: (none noted)

_____

BEHAVIORAL/SOCIAL/EMOTIONAL DATA

Vineland — Behavioral scales — Social history —

EXHIBIT 3-9

ACADEMIC ACHIEVEMENT

Pre-academic/academic:

Current reading level 7.0   Current math level 6.0
   High achiever in all levels
Current spelling level 6.0

WRAT: PIAT: Woodcock/Johnson:

SRA: MAT: SWAT:

EXHIBIT 3-10

INDIVIDUALIZED EDUCATIONAL PROGRAM

Annual goals/objectives	Criterion for mastery	Evaluation procedures
I. Justin will demonstrate growth in independent thinking skills.		
A. When presented with three choices he will be able to independently make an appropriate response.	80% accuracy	1.1 1.2
B. When presented with five choices he will be able to choose one topic, research it, and present it either orally or in written form.	80% accuracy	1.1
II. Justin will demonstrate growth in affective skills.		
A. He will be able to relate and get along with his age mates.	80% accuracy	1.1 1.2
B. He will be able to relate and get along with his intellectual mates in small-group situations.	80% accuracy	1.1 1.2
C. Same as B, but in large groups.	80% accuracy	1.1 1.2

Key to evaluation procedures

1.0 Teacher checklist
1.1 Teacher observation
1.2 Teacher tally
1.3 Internal assessment

2.0 Student evaluation
2.1 Student tested orally
2.2 Student tested in writing
2.3 Student project

3.0 Daily reading
3.1 Daily math
3.2 Daily spelling
3.3 Daily writing

but it is one that the teacher may revise and alter as the gifted student progresses.

In summary, the five components included in an IEP are (1) current educational status; (2) annual goals and short-term performance objectives; (3) specification of services to be provided with reference to inclusion or retention with age peers; (4) projected estimates for duration of services; and (5) identification of appropriate criteria for at least annual review of objectives, provide data to approach the gifted student as a total entity.

The objectives include emphasis on affective, as well as cognitive experiences and skills acquisition. Teachers need to remember that not all gifted students possess the necessary skills to be independent and successful learners, and these skill deficits may need to be prescribed in the IEP as objectives, along with strength and interest development objectives.

SUMMARY

A detailed process of individualizing education for gifted students was presented. Individualized education involves adaptation of the content, the process, the product, and the learning environment, if necessary, after careful assessment of the individual strengths and weaknesses. Individualized education is considered to be both diagnostic and prescriptive teaching. Cooperative teaching between the gifted student, the parent, the regular classroom teacher, and the teacher of the gifted in developing the individual program was stressed.

Goals and objectives, based on the individual gifted student's needs and characteristics, were discussed, and it was noted that they should be written in a manner to facilitate understanding by all concerned. Goals were viewed as statements that identify direction, tone, and quality, and objectives were viewed as specific descriptors of individual performance. Several matrices were discussed.

The rationale for IEP usage for gifted students was covered as it relates to meeting both state and federal mandates and to individualizing education for the gifted. Teachers and administrators identify lack of time as the primary reason for resistance to IEP use. Designing an IEP was covered in a step-by-step process involving assessment, compiling the data, forming goals and objectives, developing a program plan and evaluation.

Pitfalls in using the IEP with gifted students were discussed, such as the 'compliance mentality' versus a commitment to individualizing education for gifted students. A problem with IEP writing before the school year without knowledge or face-to-face meetings with gifted students was discussed. The most glaring problem in IEP usage is that, too often, the IEP is a paper document and seldom used by the teacher of the gifted in the day-to-day classroom interaction. These practices severely weaken the use of the IEP.

The end product of the IEP is a prescribed plan of action. Case studies, including the profiles and forms used to gather data for a hypothetical middle school student (such as Mark) and of an elementary school student (such as Justin) were presented. Several conclusions were: (1) the teacher is important in both planning and delivering the individualized program for the gifted; (2) the teacher can be viewed as a guide, mentor, and consultant to the gifted, noting learning styles and interests as they evolve in the classroom; (3) the ongoing nature of the IEP process is essential, with the teacher reviewing the plan when needed.

The IEP planning is a vital tool for meeting the needs of the gifted student, but it is limited by the availability and capability of the staff to gather assessment data, current status information, and the availability of resources. Most educators agree that one class per week for secondary school gifted or a weekly 4-hour enrichment period schedule at a learning center for elementary gifted is only a beginning. Research indicates education for gifted students takes place primarily in the regular classroom. This finding emphasizes the need for greater involvement and commitment on the part of the regular classroom teacher to more adequately meet the individualized needs of the gifted, as well as the need for administrators to provide sufficient time for planning and evaluation of individualized programs.

EXTENDING ACTIVITIES

1 Given a typical classroom, what are some ways that individualization could take place in the classroom? Consider content, process, product, and environment.
2 In analyzing the case study of Mark, what further recommendations can you make for meeting his unique needs and interests?
3 In talking with regular classroom teachers, how might you encourage them to use more individualization in the classroom?
4 Identify the steps in the IEP process, and list the areas of concern you have, in your individual school or in a school where you have taught, in using the steps for the individualization of gifted students' education.

REFERENCES

Alvino, J., McDonnel, R. & Richert, S. (1981). National survey of identification practices in gifted and talented education. *Exceptional Children, 48*(23), 124–132.

Bloom, B. (1956). *Taxonomy of educational objectives: The classification of educational goals. Handbook I: Cognitive domain.* New York: David McKay.

Bloom, B., Hastings, J. T. & Madaus, G. F. (1971). *Handbook on formative and summative evaluation of student learning.* New York: McGraw-Hill.

Clark, B. (1983). *Growing up gifted.* Columbus, OH: Charles E. Merrill.

Cooley, A. & Lohnes, N. (1976). *Evaluation research in education.* New York: Irvington Publishers, Halsted Press Division of John Wiley and Sons.

Davis, T. (1978). *IEP's for gifted schools, 1974 students.* Doylestown, PA: Bucks County Intermediate Unit 22.

Dunn, R. & Dunn, K. (1975). *Educator's self-teaching guide to individualizing instructed programs.* West Nyack, NY: Parker.

Gallagher, J. (1985). *Teaching gifted children.* Boston: Allyn and Bacon.

Griggs, S. A. & Price, E. G. (1980). Comparison between the learning styles of gifted in average suburban junior high school students. *Roeper Review, 3,* 7–9.

Hahn, K. (1982). *An investigation of learning styles of gifted students.* Unpublished thesis. Tampa: University of South Florida.

Kaplan, S. (1974). *Providing programs for the gifted and talented: A handbook.* Ventura, CA: Office of the Ventura County Superintendent of Schools.

Krathwohl, D., Bloom, B. & Masia, B. (1964). *Taxonomy of educational objectives. Handbook II: Affective domain.* New York: David McKay.

Kroth, R. (1980). The mirror models of parental involvement. *The Pointer, 25,* 18–22.

Mager, R. (1972). *Goal analysis.* Belmont, CA: Fearon.

Maker, J. (1982). *Curriculum development for the gifted.* Rockville, MD: Aspen Publications.

Provus, M. (1971). *Discrepancy evaluation.* Berkeley, CA: McCutcheon Publishers.

Renzulli, J. (1977). *The enrichment triad model: A guide for developing defensible programs for the gifted and talented.* Mansfield Center, CT: Creative Learning Press.

Renzulli, J., Smith, L., White, A., Callahan, C. & Hartman, R. (1976). *Scales for rating the behavioral characteristics of superior students SCRBCSS.* Wethersfield, CT: Creative Learning Press.

Rouse, J. (1983). *A programming report on gifted education.* Pinellas County, FL: Board of Public Instruction.

Seagoe, M. (1974). Some learning characteristics of gifted children. In R. Martinson (Ed.), *The Identification of the Gifted and Talented*. Ventura, CA: Office of County Superintendent of Schools.

Sellin, D. & Birch, J. (1981). *Psychoeducational development of gifted and talented learners*. Rockville, MD: Aspen Publications.

Sisk, D. (1966). *Programming for the gifted*. A report to the board of education, Inglewood, CA.

Sisk, D. (1975). *Teaching gifted children*. Columbia, SC: Department of Education.

Sisk, D. (Ed.) (1985). *Tomorrow's promise: How to encourage leadership in gifted students*. Atlanta, GA: Turner Broadcasting Company.

Stufflebeam, O. (1971). Evaluation and decision-making. In O. Stufflebeam, W. Foley, W. Gephart, E. Gerba, R. Hammond, H. Merriam & N. Provus (Eds.), *Educational Evaluation in Decision-Making*. Itasca, IL: Peacock.

U.S. Office of Education (1976). Programs for the gifted and talented. *The Federal Register, 41*, 18665–18666.

Ward, V. S. (1961). *Educating the gifted: An axiomatic approach*. Columbus, OH: Charles E. Merrill.

SECTION TWO

EDUCATIONAL PROGRAMS AND PRACTICES

Educational programs and practices for gifted are many and varied. Basic principles of program development have been suggested by a number of educators (Kaplan, 1974; Maker, 1982; Gallagher, 1985). Section Two covers various aspects of program development for gifted, including principles for planning programs. The need for matching theory and practice is discussed as well as the importance of developing community resources, with specific suggestions for building community involvement. The traditional administrative arrangements of acceleration, enrichment, and special grouping are examined, along with guidance provisions for the gifted. Chapter 4 covers the use of selected models as frameworks in developing curriculum for gifted students: Taylor, Williams, Bloom, Guilford, and Renzulli.

Chapter 5 identifies a number of selected curriculum strategies which alter the content, process, product, and learning environment for gifted students. These strategies include creative problem solving, simulation, group dynamics, futuristics, and inquiry. Chapters 6 and 7 offer practical suggestions for modifying the offerings for gifted in four essential content areas: language arts, social studies, science, and mathematics.

Many researchers stress that the teacher is the key individual in the educational program development for the gifted: Gallagher et al. (1967); Renzulli (1968); Iannon and Carline (1971); Aspy and Roebuck (1972); Lindsey (1980). Chapter 8 highlights the qualifications necessary for teaching gifted students and teacher preparation programs. Lastly, Chapter 9 discusses evaluation of programs for gifted students which emphasize basic concepts and key features in their evaluation procedures.

CHAPTER 4

PROGRAM PLANNING
FOR THE GIFTED

The belief that all genuine education comes about through experience does not mean that all experiences are genuinely or equally educative.

John Dewey

Differentiated curriculum for gifted students should embody a high level of cognitive and affective concepts and processes beyond that normally provided by the regular curriculum according to the United States Office of Education (1976). In addition, instructional strategies should accommodate the unique learning styles of the gifted. Flexible arrangements for instruction are suggested such as special classes, seminars, resource rooms, independent study, student internships, mentorships, research field trips, and library media research centers (U.S. Office of Education, 1976, pp. 18665–18666).

The ideas listed by the Office of Education complement Renzulli's (1977) suggestions about qualitative differences in the curriculum for gifted students. Renzulli defines enrichment as experiences that: (1) are above and beyond the regular curriculum; (2) take into account the students' specific content interests; (3) take into account the students' preferred styles of learning; and (4) allow students the opportunity to pursue topic areas where they have superior potential for performance to unlimited levels of inquiry.

Photograph on facing page courtesy of Milton Heiberg Studios, New York, New York.

To assist school districts in planning programs for gifted students and to ensure that a differentiated curriculum is developed, principles for planning programs are helpful.

PRINCIPLES FOR PLANNING PROGRAMS

The Curriculum Council of the National State Leadership Training Institute for Gifted and Talented (Curriculum Council, LTI; 1985) states that the philosophy underlying the education for all students in a democracy, that each child should be provided with educational experiences appropriate to his/her individual abilities, interests and learning styles, is also essential to gifted children.

The following statement can be considered the first principle for planning programs for the gifted: *Education for the gifted should be based on a sound philosophical, psychological, and pedagogical base.*

When the philosophy of a school district includes the concept of meeting the needs of all children, then the gifted students' needs are a part of a continuum of services. The unique needs of gifted students must be respected and accommodated with expanded efforts to modify and to adapt their learning experiences. Quality programs for the gifted student are based on sound psychological knowledge of their unique needs, learning and motivational characteristics, and individual interests. Good practices in general education are often translated or modified for gifted students. The program for the gifted does not need to be totally different; however, it should be appropriate and differentiated.

A second principle for planning programs for gifted students is: *Education for the gifted should be planned to be responsive to community needs and also to national and global needs.* A program for a Chicano student should take the student's neighborhood and community needs into consideration. At the same time, the program should sensitize the gifted student to a national point of view and extend this view to a global view. A gifted student's program begins where she/he is, and provides opportunities for the student to see things as they could be.

A third principle is: *Education for the gifted should reflect an inclusive rather than exclusive attitude.* The programs will be inclusive of potentially gifted students: underachievers, learning-disabled gifted, and students who might not be performing well because of cultural handicaps. This principle guides the selection of appropriate tests to identify gifted students. In applying this principle, programs will be matched to students rather than students to already existing programs.

A fourth principle is: *Education of the gifted must be an integral part of the total school system.* Saturday classes, after-school programs and summer workshops do not adequately meet the needs of gifted students. Gifted students are gifted all day, and special teachers need to communicate and work with the regular classroom teacher to plan a differentiated curriculum for the gifted. The ideal individualized plan for gifted students includes activities for the entire day, not just in the "gifted program."

A fifth principle is: *Education of the gifted should focus on the total child, providing curriculum and instruction adaptation as well as guidance.* Grouping gifted students and teaching them as a homogenous group with curriculum and strategies that do not meet their individual needs is neither adequate nor sufficient. Many gifted students become bored with school and desperately underachieve. A systematic attempt to help these gifted students reach their potential with emphasis on motivation and career guidance is needed.

A sixth principle is: *Education of the gifted should be a continuous effort on behalf of a school system.* Gifted programs should begin at kindergarten and continue through graduate school. Programs need to be articulated to flow in a systematic and dynamic fashion.

When these six principles are applied, school districts will develop programs for the gifted based on a sound philosophical, psychological, and pedagogical basis; they will be responsive to community, national, and global needs; reflect an inclusive rather than exclusive attitude; be an integral part of the school system; focus on the total child; and provide a continuous effort on behalf of gifted in the school system.

MATCHING THEORY AND PRACTICE

Bull (1982) stresses that a consistent philosophy of psychology and education be used in program development. He identifies several philosophies of psychology and education: (1) *theistic mental discipline* or *faculty psychology*; (2) *mechanist behaviorist, behaviorist stimulus/response*; (3) *scientific humanist, experimentalist, field psychologist*; (4) *natural unfolding,* or *self-actualization*; (5) *humanistic mental discipline,* and (6) *apperception,* or *Herbartianism*.

Table 4-1 lists the philosophies as they affect teacher role, instructional behavior, nature of the learning environment, nature of the learner, and level of teaching/learning.

A congruent philosophy of psychology and education has merit for the planning and developing of consistent programs. However, in examining the ideas of Bull (1982), an eclectic approach also has merit. For example, when the teacher role is considered, few educators would question the self-actualization role of the teacher as the facilitator, one who removes barriers that block needs gratification. Yet, in considering instructional behavior, *inquiry and discovery* have merit for gifted students, and these are listed under experimentalist as well as learner-directed and interest-based activities, which are listed under self-actualization. In some cases, a Socratic method is appropriate, which is listed under humanistic mental discipline. Using the different instructional behaviors, teachers can provide a wealth of learning activities rather than rely on one instructional behavior.

The learning environment sometimes needs to be structured, ordered, and controlled (humanistic mental discipline), for example, when gifted students are dissecting animals or working with stained glass cutting. In group dynamics, the teacher might want a partially open, manipulative, and interactive environment (experimentalist); whereas, in social studies, when lessons deal with broad con-

TABLE 4-1
PHILOSOPHIES OF PSYCHOLOGY AND EDUCATION

	Theistic mental discipline	Mechanist behaviorist	Scientific humanism experimentalist	Natural unfolding, or self-actualization	Humanistic mental discipline	Apperception, or Herbartianism
Psychological system	Faculty psychology	Behavioristic stimulus/ response; logical empiricist	Field psychology or positive relativism	Radical existentialist; romantic naturalism; psychedelic humanism; third force psychology	Classical humanism	Structuralism
Teacher role	Authority figure, dispenser of the punishment	Shaping behavior, developing appropriate responses, designer and manager of instruction	Manipulator; arouses intellectual curiosity; sets tasks at student's ability level; helps in goal setting; places some learning responsibility in the hands of the student; implements and promotes the development of serviceable insights	Facilitator; removes barriers that block needs gratification	Scholarly educator	Architect and builder of young minds; the indoctrinator

Instructional behavior	Exercise the facilities of the mind, e.g., willing, purposing, reflecting, imagining, remembering, reasoning	Transmission of facts and content; shaper directed	Inquiry/discovery manipulated by teacher through invitation	Learner directed and interest based; helps the student develop awareness, freedom, and responsibility; learner invitation	Training of intrinsic mental power; Socratic method	Addition of new mental states or ideas to a store of old ones in the subconscious mind; interest based in the sense of being willing to receive
Nature of the learning environment	Closed structure; oppressive	Structured, ordered, controlled	Partially open, manipulative; interactive	Open, unstructured, free person	Structured, ordered, controlled	
Nature of the learner	Student; innately bad, in need of discipline	Subject/organism development depends on outside forces	Learner: purposive development through interaction with psychological environment	Person: innately planned personality which will develop, through unfolding of instincts, needs, abilities, and talents	Student: rational animal	Unfilled vessel: development depends on outside forces

Source: Bull, K. (1982). *Philosophies of Psychology and Education.* Reprinted by permission.

cepts such as human interaction with the environment, the teacher might desire an open, unstructured free environment (self-actualization). When we view the nature of the learner, the gifted student often appears to be a "rational animal" (humanistic mental discipline) on the one hand, but she/he does display purposive development through interaction with the psychological environment (experimentalist), on the other.

Examination of different philosophies of education, as suggested by Bull, is helpful in clarifying a school district's position on issues such as teacher role and the nature of the learner, but a too-narrow interpretation of consistency can lead to a rigid or confining approach in working with gifted students.

DEVELOPING COMMUNITY RESOURCES

Lack of community involvement prevents gifted programs from becoming totally integrated within a community. The community represents a rich source of materials, resource people, and a vital partnership in the teaching process.

One school district equipped a van as a mobile laboratory and provided gifted students with an interdisciplinary field experience in science, geography, and social studies. Their involvement in the community helped residents of the town to become aware of the program for gifted students, and several community people volunteered to serve as lecturers and mentors (Dusan, 1979).

Another innovative program gave middle school gifted students access to business facilities, stock exchanges, professional offices, stores, hospitals, and public offices. The unit of study stressed career orientation, and, through cooperative involvement, the community members learned a great deal about the school's efforts for gifted students.

Gifted programs can be arranged around retirement centers, matching the multiple talents of the retirees to the interests and talents of the gifted students. Free materials are often available from public utility companies. In addition, public and private agencies are pleased to provide speakers to gifted programs. An innovative community project was carried out in Charlotte, North Carolina, in which gifted students studied hotels, telephone companies, bakeries, and newspapers and then simulated the development of their own companies. These simulated experiences were supplemented by field research trips to hotels, bakeries, newspapers, and telephone companies. The gifted student–community interaction was educationally and socially meaningful.

Through such contacts with the community, school districts build a talent pool of community members who can serve as resource people and mentors to gifted students.

ADMINISTRATIVE ARRANGEMENTS FOR THE GIFTED

Program services for gifted are usually grouped into three categories: (1) enrichment, (2) acceleration, and (3) special grouping. Still another arrangement is that of guidance. Under ideal circumstances, gifted students can be grouped together and receive enrichment, and they can be accelerated when appropriate and can experience counseling and guidance. However, most school districts cannot approximate the ideal situation. To better understand the nature of these administrative arrangements, each will be discussed individually.

Acceleration

Acceleration is the least-used administrative arrangement for gifted students, although there is little or no evidence from research reporting any negative effect of acceleration on gifted students. The need for acceleration has been supported by Gallagher (1985) who states that gifted students who anticipate a professional role can expect to be in school at least until the age of 29; consequently, anything that can be done to reduce this extended period of study serves to benefit gifted students and society.

Acceleration can take many forms: early entrance to school, grade skipping, telescoping of several grades, early entrance to college, and taking courses or subject matter out of sequence. Several states have instituted early entrance regulations to serve young gifted students. However, in spite of demonstrated advanced intellectual and social development, young gifted students and their parents are often advised to wait until regular admission time. Many educators fear "pushing children," and stress the gifted child's need for "enjoyment of the full benefits of school."

Braga (1969) investigated the effects of early admission on sixty-three gifted students in the first, third, and fifth grades. He compared the early admissions students to normally admitted students and late-admitted students. The students were compared by IQ and sex. Students admitted early and students who were regularly admitted had no significant differences on academic achievement and social and emotional development. However, teacher and parent questionnaires reported teachers were negative to the idea of early admission. Parents of early admission students were in favor of early admission and parents of regular admission students were not.

Many fears about acceleration are deep rooted and involve feelings of treating some children as "special." When asked about their feelings concerning acceleration, individuals often cite at least one case of someone who was strange, different, and accelerated. Yet, the point can be made that some individuals are strange and different, regardless of acceleration. Braga's study confirms the earlier work of Worcester (1956) who studied 4275 pupils in Nebraska. Early entrants were found to be superior in health, achievement, coordination, acceptance by others, leadership, attitudes toward school, and emotional development. Clearly these findings support Howley et al. (1986) in suggesting that young gifted students who are ready for school are better served by early entrance than by waiting for their age group, when their mental age will be far above that of their peers.

Telescoping grades, another form of acceleration, is used in the middle school years with gifted students who complete three years in two. Still another form of acceleration is family grouping, which allows a group of gifted students to telescope their grades; for example, gifted students in grades 1, 2, and 3 may complete these grades in 2 years together. In this manner, a given gifted student can complete elementary school in 4 years.

Acceleration most often takes the form of extra courses and seminars taken for college credit, and early entrance into college at the senior high level for some gifted students, particularly for the highly gifted, opportunities for acceleration are essential. At the Johns Hopkins University, Stanley et al. (1974, 1984) have validated the importance and feasibility of acceleration. Stanley advocates that highly gifted students in mathematics develop their ability at an accelerated pace. The Johns Hopkins Talent Search has shown great success and has evolved into a national talent search for highly gifted mathematics students by a number of universities (Northwestern, Duke, and the universities of Arizona and Denver). Acceleration helps highly gifted students use their talents; without acceleration, these gifted students have repetitious assignments and wasted school time.

Clark (1983) summarizes research on acceleration:

1 Gifted students are inclined to select older companions because their levels of maturity are similar. Neither the method nor the age of acceleration appears to be of consequence.

2 Acceleration allows capable students to enter their careers sooner, resulting in more productivity.

3 When he/she spends less time in school, the gifted student's educational costs are lowered.

4 Accelerated students do as well or often better than the older students in their classes.

5 The bright student is less bored and dissatisfied when accelerated.

6 Social and emotional adjustment are generally high, if most reports are above average when accelerated.

7 In general, teachers and administrators oppose acceleration, while parents and students, especially those who have experienced acceleration, support the concept. Some administrators have offered possible reasons for the negative attitudes: convenience of "lockstep," chronological grade placement; ignorance of research; discredited belief in social maladjustment; state laws preventing early admission.

8 To be successful, acceleration must be continuous and coordinated.

Acceleration meets the need of gifted students to learn at a rapid pace and thus greatly facilitates their education.

Enrichment

Enrichment is one of the more misused and misquoted educational terms. It is used for any number of activities, such as free reading, the addition of an independent study, a speaker for the classroom, field trips, and countless other experiences. Enrichment can be a catch-all for disjointed experiences which fill the day with "busy work" and "busy experiences."

Stanley (1976) states his opinion of enrichment:

Well meaning teachers try one of three types of enrichment: so-called busy work, irrelevant material (such as drama classes for boys whose major interests are mathematics and science), or really effective procedures that leave the student even more bored in later years (such as splendid modern mathematics programs in grades K-7 that lead only to conventional algebra in grade 8). Clearly we believe that a considerable amount of acceleration in subject matter and/or grade placement must accompany enrichment or be employed in lieu of it.

Effective enrichment is appropriate and realistic when defined as the addition of different areas of learning not normally found in the curriculum and more difficult or more in-depth material. With this definition, enrichment applies to any program adaptation for gifted. However, enrichment is most often used as a program effort in the regular classroom (Cox, 1985).

To keep the term "enrichment" in perspective, it is helpful to examine Kaplan's (1974) comments on differentiated education, for the terms are sometimes used interchangeably. Kaplan lists three areas to be considered in planning differentiated curriculum for the gifted: (1) procedures for presenting learning opportunities, (2) nature of the input, and (3) expectancies for learning outcomes. In enrichment, the teacher can vary the process, content, and product. This will lead to changes in the learning environment. She describes criteria for differentiated curriculum, using three descriptors: exposure, extension, and development.

Exposure: Students are exposed to experiences, materials, and information which is outside the bounds of the regular curriculum, does not match age/grade expectancies, and introduces something new or unusual.

Extension: Students are afforded opportunities to elaborate on the regular curriculum through additional allocation of working time, materials, and experiences and/or further self-initiated or related study.

Development: Students are provided with instruction which focuses on thorough or new explanation of a concept or a skill which is part of a general learning activity within the regular curriculum (p. 123).

Special Grouping

Many educators have consistently advocated building enrichment experiences from the individual characteristics of gifted students (Renzulli, 1978; Ward, 1981; Passow, 1981; and Maker, 1982). Gifted students have special needs, which cause them to behave in certain ways; for example, gifted students have an intense desire to know and want to devour a subject. This need causes them to resist interruption and to behave as though they didn't hear directions. A learning provision based on this observation is to vary the learning environment to plan a work-block or time of uninterrupted study, or, to use Kaplan's terms, an extension.

Maker (1982) organized a comprehensive approach to developing qualitatively different curriculum based on authorities in gifted (Kaplan, 1974; Renzulli, 1976; Ward, 1981; and Gallagher, 1985). Her plan consists of matching a gifted child's characteristics to content, process/method, product, and learning environment. A similar model was used by Sisk (1985) in planning and developing curriculum for the Turner Broadcasting Company. The variables used were the gifted students' characteristics, teaching strategies, and appropriate models matched to key concepts of selected disciplines.

Gifted students have a right to pursue learning at their own pace, to their level of capability; enrichment is a useful tool in providing challenge and ecouragement.

Special grouping has been widely used for gifted students throughout history on an informal friendship basis, in clustering groups of gifted students in the regular classroom, in a special class, in special schools, or in special seminars.

The term "least restrictive environment" (Public Law 94-142) has unique application to gifted education. For gifted students, the least restrictive environment may mean grouping gifted students to encourage maximum use of their potential. A continuum of services for gifted students ranges from the full-day program at special schools for gifted students to the 1-day resource room approach.

The continuum of services includes:

Regular classroom
Regular classroom with cluster
Regular class with pull-out
Regular class with cluster/pull-out
Individualized classroom
Individualized classroom/cluster
Individualized classroom with pull-out
Individualized classroom/cluster/pull-out
Special classes with some integrated classes
Special classes
Special schools

Few educators deny that gifted students need to work with other gifted students for part of the day to learn at their own pace and to motivate and stimulate one another. Controversy centers around the amount of time needed for such interaction.

Special Classes

Special classes for gifted students were initiated in 1920 in Cleveland's program of Major Works Classes (MWC). In the MWC, gifted students follow the regular curriculum, but it is differentiated in its depth of examination; range of supporting activities such as foreign language, debate, music, and art; emphasis on purposeful learning; and intense involvement. MWC can be found in a number of cities such as Fairfax, Virginia; Orlando and West Palm Beach, Florida; Garden Grove and San Diego, California; as well as Saskatoon, Saskatchewan; Toronto, Ontario; and Tel Aviv, Israel. The MWC concept varies the learning environment, content, and processes, and it accommodates the learning style of the individual gifted student.

Special Schools

The Bronx High School of Science in New York City is one of the older examples of a special school for gifted secondary students. Students are identified through specific aptitude tests, with scores at the 98th percentile on achievement measures in science. In 1976–1979, the Bronx High School of Science was awarded a 3-year grant as a model secondary program through the Office of Gifted and Talented. Galasso (1979) states that Bronx High School students represent all geographic areas and all socioeconomic levels in the city of New York. The teachers emphasize laboratory work and inquiry, with each gifted student presenting a scholarly paper, and competing in a variety of scientific competitions. In addition to the exemplary science program, a 4-year mathematics sequence is provided along with the regular high school curriculum.

Another example of a special school is Pineview School in Sarasota, Florida, serving elementary, middle, and senior high school intellectually gifted students (grades 2–12). Over nine hundred gifted students are housed in a single complex. Students who attend Pineview are identified as intellectually gifted, scoring a minimum IQ of 132 on individually administered intelligence measures. In addition, the gifted students must display sufficient motivation, achievement level, and emotional maturity to successfully complete the curriculum which is accelerated and enriched. The teaching staff at Pineview interviews parents and students as part of the admission process. Classes are small and extra subjects are provided through flexible scheduling and cross-age grouping.

Special Grouping in Resource Room

An approach in which gifted students receive special instruction with other gifted students in a seminar, resource room, or special class is called a "pull-out program." An obvious drawback to the pull-out approach is the gifted students' re-entry to the regular classroom. If they are held responsible for regular classroom work as well as the accelerated work in the gifted resource room, they can be overburdened. When teachers in the regular classroom are not involved in planning the resource room work, they may feel alienated and hostile to the process of enrichment. These feelings can be offset when the regular classroom teacher and the teacher of the gifted cooperatively plan the enrichment. When communication and team planning exist, resource rooms are positive influences for the regular classroom teacher, the gifted students, and other students.

Cloud (1982), an itinerant teacher of the gifted, reported success with the use of "international days," a result of cooperative planning with parents, regular classroom teachers, and the gifted students. She experienced high enthusiasm with her interdisciplinary approach, including interest reports on food, dances, music, and art work.

When resource rooms are housed in individual schools to serve the gifted students and when cooperative sharing of speakers and materials is arranged, the resource rooms enrich the entire school and can be considered a successful arrangement.

Resource Centers

The center approach is one of the more popular arrangements for working with gifted students in the United States (Cox, 1985). The Learning Center for gifted students in Tampa, Florida was exemplary as a resource center, and serves as a model for parent-initiated programs. The Hillsborough County Association for Gifted Education (HAGE), a parent group of approximately two hundred members, petitioned the Tampa City Council to use a vacant public library for a learning center. The City Council agreed and charged the program an annual fee of $1.00. In the summer of 1969 the program began with approximately one hundred gifted students, one employee from the Tampa public school system serving as director, and ten graduate trainees in gifted education from the University of South Florida serving as teachers. As the program expanded, over a thousand gifted students were involved. The students were bussed from their home schools for half a day of enrichment activities each week. Classes in computer, drama, art, Spanish, creative writing, marine biology, marketing, mysteries, heroes, and countless other topics were offered.

Another example of a resource center is the New Orleans Center for Creative Arts, which offers classes in the visual and performing arts. The gifted students work with highly qualified artists and performers as teachers in areas of art, dance, and music.

Clark (1983) summarizes the research on special grouping and reports:

1 Significant academic gains result when programs are adjusted to student abilities. Grouping alone is insufficient to show differences in achievement of grouped over nongrouped gifted students.

2 Attitudes of parents, teachers, and gifted students are generally favorable toward special groups or classes, especially if such grouping is flexible and not totally segregated.

3 Positive development in self-concept and a sense of well-being result from special group placement.

4 The amount of time spent in special groups or classes relates positively to achievement gains of gifted students.

5 Attitudes of other parents and teachers are reported as more negative toward grouped learners.

6 There is more opportunity for individual expression, in-depth study, acceleration, and freedom from regimentation in ability-grouped classes.

Ability grouping provides many answers to educating gifted students, but it is not the total solution. Modifications and adaptations, whether enriching the curriculum or accelerating it, must still be accomplished.

Guidance Measures

Schools are increasingly more aware of the impact of giftedness on the individual student as well as on the student's family. Guidance approaches have been initiated to respond to this awareness. Hackney (1981), at Purdue University, recorded the following observations by parents about their gifted children:

1 They altered the normal roles in the family.
2 They affected parents' feelings about themselves in the family.
3 They required the family to make a special adaptation.
4 They produced special family/neighborhood issues.
5 They produced special family/school issues.

The parents reported experiencing difficulty in clarifying differences between their parental role and the child's role and in determining whether the child should be treated as a child or as an adult. Hackney found that the gifted child frequently assumed the role of a third parent in the family system. This behavior was a detriment to the child's social skills, because in school the gifted student often puts equal pressure on the teacher to become a co-teacher. To counteract these problems, Hackney emphasizes the importance of a good home–school relationship and suggested that counselors serve as: (1) communicators, (2) mediators, and (3) educators to help the family and the school system meet the needs of gifted students.

A guidance approach in working with gifted students in Falls Church, Virginia, found that gifted students need counseling and have a common collection of problems resulting from their giftedness. These problems as identified by Allen and Fox (1979) are:

1 *Environmental.* The lack of a sufficiently challenging or interesting school situation leaves the gifted student resentful or "turned off."
2 *Interpersonal.* The gifted adolescent does not want to be different, and acceptance by her/his peers is crucial. Unrealistic demands may be made by parents, teachers, and counselors.
3 *Individual.* Even though the self-concept of gifted students is usually positive, they need to be encouraged to maintain belief in their own work. Self-acceptance also may need to be strengthened.

Allen and Fox (1979) compiled eight myths concerning gifted education that are useful to the counselor:

1 A gifted student will be outstanding in everything he/she does.
2 Gifted students are more prone to have emotional disturbances or adjustment problems.
3 The gifted are apt to be physically inept.
4 Gifted students can make it on their own without assistance.

5 A person's emotional maturity should be as advanced as his/her intellectual maturity.

6 Gifted underachievers need to be pushed harder.

7 The gifted are socially confident to a point of conceit.

8 The gifted are socially isolated from their peers.

The Falls Church project uses group counseling and provides opportunities for gifted students to experience a caring, open, accepting, understanding, and trusting environment. The program focuses on interpersonal communication skills such as listening to ideas and feelings, accepting the value of all contributions, and giving positive personal feedback and helpful criticism. Participation in guidance approaches helps reduce the gifted student's sense of emotional isolation.

Lastly, Safter and Bruch (1981) suggest Differential Guidance for Gifted (DGG) as a useful tool. They use several variables in planning a counseling/guidance approach for gifted students: (1) the type of giftedness, (2) the socioeconomic status, (3) the value orientation, and (4) the grade or developmental level of the gifted child. Safter and Bruch state that gifted students who come from families with a low values orientation may be classified as underachieving gifted students. They recommend an inclusive approach in which the counselor takes a major responsibility for the identification and placement process of gifted students and ensures that the program is built on the gifted students' needs.

FRAMEWORK FOR CURRICULUM DEVELOPMENT

Various theoretical models have proved successful in building curriculum and developing programs for gifted students. Many local school districts select and use a single model, but most educators find that various models of learning and intellectual functioning supplement and complement one another to provide growth in the cognitive and affective areas.

The Guilford model (Figure 4-1) is often used to plan curriculum for gifted programs. The ideas basic to the Structure of Intellect (SOI) model, formulated in the 1950s, were successfully refined until the present model was developed. The model is a three-way classification of intellectual abilities designed to encompass and organize intellectual aptitude factors. It has served to predict the existence of undiscovered factors. The three dimensions of the model specify: (a) the operation, (b) the content, and (c) the product of a given intellectual act. Guilford defines cognition as understanding, discovery, rediscovery, awareness, and comprehension. Memory is defined as the retention and recall of knowledge. Convergent thinking is defined as the reorganization of information, and divergent thinking is the imaginative, spontaneous, and fluent self-expression. Lastly, evaluation is defined as judging, assessing, and evaluating.

Another useful model is Bloom's (1956) taxonomy which began as a framework for developing test materials. The taxonomy includes three domains for educational objectives: cognitive, affective, and psychomotor. The cognitive and affective are most often used in gifted programs. The cognitive classifications are knowledge, comprehension, application, analysis, synthesis, and evaluation. The

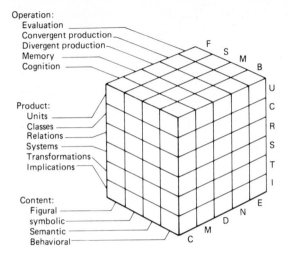

FIGURE 4-1
Guilford's structure of intellect.
(*J. P. Guilford*, Way Beyond IQ,
*Creative Education Foundation,
Bearly Limited, Buffalo, New York,
1981. Reprinted by permission.*)

affective classifications are receiving, responding, valuing, organization, and characterization (Krathwohl et al., 1964).

Teachers of the gifted can plan lessons involving the affective and cognitive levels, using the Krathwohl et al. taxonomy for the affective domain, and supplement intellectual operations as defined by Guilford (1977) in the Structure of Intellect.

A lesson for tenth-grade gifted students using a standard text, *Question and Form in Literature* (Scott, Foresman & Company, 1979), is suggested by Lauren (1983a):

The students have read "The Monkey's Paw." The questions based on the Guilford and Bloom models can be used in small group discussion. Questions using Guilford's model are:

1 *Cognition* (understanding, discovery, rediscovery, awareness and comprehension). The fact that "The Monkey's Paw" will end tragically is foreshadowed in several ways. Cite specific instances of foreshadowing that occur during the evening of the Sergeant-Major's visit.

2 *Memory* (retention and recall of knowledge). What is the first clue that the monkey's paw has evil properties?

3 *Convergent* (reorganization of information). Why does Mr. White make the third wish?

4 *Divergent* (imaginative, spontaneous, and fluent self-expression). Can you think of a third wish that might have ended the story differently?

5 *Evaluation* (judgment, assesses, and evaluates). Why doesn't the author have Mr. White make such a wish?

Planning questions to cover all levels of Guilford's intellectual operations enables the teacher to consciously lead the gifted student from the lower levels of thinking to the higher levels of thinking. Without this type of mental stretching of their thinking, gifted students may become bored, restless, disruptive, and may underachieve.

The affective domain can be tapped with questions based on the affective domain of Krathwohl et al. (1964):

1 *Receiving* (directions of attention): Did you anticipate the ending of the story?

2 *Responding* (behavior accompanied by feeling of satisfaction): What part of the story did you find most suspenseful?

3 *Valuing* (ascribing worth or emotional acceptance): What do you think is the moral of this story?

4 *Organization* (ordered relationship of complex values): What was your initial attitude toward the White family? How did your attitude change?

5 *Characterization* (generalized sets consistent with total philosophy of beliefs): If you could have made the three wishes, what would they have been?

Teachers of the gifted who plan questions in an organized fashion using models such as Bloom et al. (1956), Krathwohl et al. (1964) (cognitive and affective), and Guilford (1977) help gifted students explore insights and attitudes in a deliberate manner.

A model developed to stimulate creativity in gifted students is that of Williams' Plank presented in Figure 4-2 (Williams, 1970, p. 203).

The Williams' model consists of three dimensions. Dimension 1 (D1) is subject matter, Dimension 2 (D2) is teaching strategies, and Dimension 3 (D3) consists of pupil behaviors such as cognitive behaviors (fluent, flexible, original, and elaborative thinking) or affective behaviors (curiosity, risk taking, complexity, and imagination). Using Williams' Plank as a model, teachers develop lessons in the different areas and plan for specific levels or types of behavior.

A language arts lesson (Lauren, 1983b) based on the Williams' model is:

Objective: to encourage imagination (intuition), flexible and original thinking.

Strategies: examples of change (6) and intuitive expressions (11).

The gifted students read *The Velveteen Rabbit* by Margery Williams and discuss their feelings. They share stuffed toys they had or have, answering questions such as, "What happened to it?" "Why did you like it so much?" They discuss the importance of love and security for the very young child and how love helps us change and grow.

Following the discussion, the gifted students view the movie *Junkyard* and discuss the concept of "disposable society" and its effect.

Follow-up: The gifted students can bring in stuffed animals for a type of museum of youth; write a guided fantasy of junked objects being revitalized; or interview an elderly person to sensitize them to the notion of "junked people" and "junked relationships."

To use the model, the chosen strategy (D1) was intuitive expression, the selected subject matter (D2) was language arts, and the behaviors or objectives (D3) were to encourage imagination and flexible and original thinking.

D1⇄D2→D3

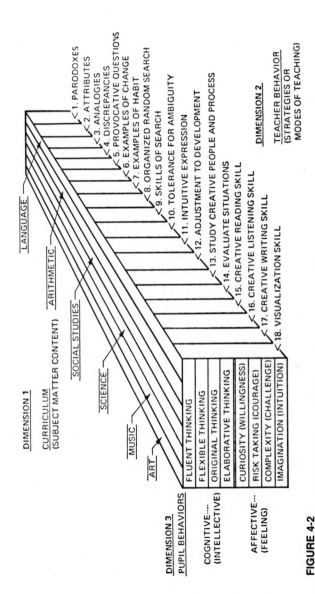

FIGURE 4-2

The Williams' model. (*F. Williams, Classroom Ideas for Encouraging Thinking and Feeling, D.O.K. Publishers, Buffalo, New York, 1970. Reprinted by permission.*)

A model specifically designed for gifted students is the Renzulli Enrichment Triad (Renzulli, 1977). The Renzulli model guides the student through awareness, the learning process, and the development of a product. The model consists of Type I Activities, or general exploratory; Type II Activities, or group training; and Type III Activities, or individual and small group investigations of real problems. The first two types of activities are considered appropriate for all learners, but Type III is the major focus of the model, which is specifically designed for gifted students. Renzulli recommends gifted students spend one-half of their time in Type III Activities working on real problems as real investigators, using the methods of scientists in the field. Type I Activities broaden the gifted student's interests and those of Type II build independent skills necessary for individual and small group investigations (Type III).

Many gifted programs have been developed using the Triad model; however, there are drawbacks as noted by Maker (1982) who states that educators may blindly adopt the Triad without considering its philosophical basis and the requirements for implementation. The advantage of the Triad is its simplicity and its use in the regular classroom. The teacher can explore activities (Type I), teach the necessary skills (Type II) and help gifted students plan activities to work on real problems (Type III). The Renzulli model requires flexible teachers who will allow students to explore real problems; undergo processes that reflect *real* processes; and engage in activities that lead to products created for a real audience.

Still another model is the multiple-talent model of Taylor (1984, 1985), represented in Figure 4-3. (Taylor has subsequently added three dimensions: discerning opportunities, social relationships, and implementing action.)

Taylor's groupings of talents specify academic talent and eight other types: creative and productive talent, evaluative or decision-making talent, planning talent, forecasting talent; communication, implementing, human relations, and discerning opportunities talents.

In Chapter 5, the Taylor model is applied to bibliotherapy as a strategy and is covered in depth. An example of a lesson based on Taylor is offered.

Unit Objectives. The gifted students will develop a basic understanding of Greek and Roman mythological characters: the gods, their powers, and their purposes for ancient man. They will also relate other cultural, folk, and modern-day myths.

Learning Objectives. The gifted students will develop an understanding of the world as Pandora saw it and of her mythological effect upon that world.

Activities
I Boundary-breaking questions, to be used in a circle.
   A Communication and decision-making. If you were Pandora and released the miseries upon the world but could catch one and bring it back so that it could never be used, which one would you catch?
   B Predicting, forecasting, and communication. How would people have had to change when misery was introduced into their lives?
   C Communication and decision-making. If you had Pandora's box filled with hope and happiness, which would you like to let out?
   D Decision-making, planning, communication, and implementation. Choose a misery and tell how the world could get rid of it today.

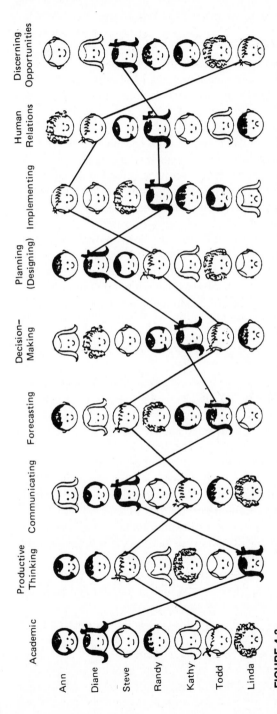

FIGURE 4-3
Taylor's talent totem poles—1984 extended version. (© 1984, Calvin W. Taylor, in "The Simultaneous Double-Curriculum for Developing Human Resources: A Research Based Theory of Education," Journal for the Education of the Gifted. Reprinted by permission.)

II Break into small groups and list all of the miseries that you can think of that afflict the world (academic, human relations, and communication). Choose those for which you are in some personal way responsible, and plan what changes you could make (decision-making, planning, and implementation).

III As a total group, the students will analyze the lists of changes and implement solutions to be charted in their journals (academic, decision-making, planning, implementation, human relations, creative and communication, and discerning opportunities).

The Taylor model helps teachers of the gifted to plan lessons that provide for various levels of thinking. Few activities will address a single level. The more levels an activity covers, the more opportunity there is for creative thinking.

Many good teachers plan lessons to encourage students to use a variety of levels of thinking, but when questioned as to their planning strategies, they reveal that much of their planning has been intuitive. Using models such as the Guilford, Bloom, Renzulli, Williams, or Taylor enables the teacher to make a deliberate plan to provide learning experiences for a specific talent or level of thinking. The learning is not left to chance. In using models to develop curriculum, teachers understand Dewey's message "that all experiences are not genuinely or equally educative." Education, to be meaningful to gifted students, needs to be a planned activity if their potential is to be developed fully.

SUMMARY

Principles of planning and developing programs for gifted students were listed. Using the six principles, school districts can develop gifted programs based on a sound philosophical, psychological, and pedagogical basis; be responsive to community, national, and global needs; reflect an inclusive rather than exclusive attitude; make the gifted program an integral part of the school system; focus on the total child; and provide a continuous effort on behalf of gifted in the school system.

The need for matching theory and practice was discussed. Bull (1982) listed six philosophies of psychology and education: (1) theistic mental discipline; (2) mechanist behaviorist; (3) scientific humanism experimentalist; (4) natural unfolding or self-actualization; (5) humanistic experimentalist; and (6) apperception, or Herbartianism. An examination of the different philosophies is useful and meaningful in clarifying a school district's position on issues such as teacher role and the nature of the learner; however, a too-narrow interpretation of consistency can lead to a rigid approach in working with gifted students.

The importance of developing community resources was noted, and the need for school officials to view the community as a source of materials, resource people, and a vital partnership in the teaching was explained.

The advantages and disadvantages of acceleration, enrichment, special grouping, and guidance were covered as traditional patterns of working with gifted students. Enrichment is most often used in resource settings; acceleration is the pattern most misunderstood and feared by educators.

Lastly, a framework for curriculum development, using a variety of theoretical models such as those of Bloom, Krathwohl et al., Williams, Taylor, Renzulli, and Guilford, was discussed. Sample lessons for gifted students showed ways to maximize learning in the classroom. The need for specific planning for specific teaching outcomes, rather than intuitive teaching, was emphasized.

EXTENDING ACTIVITIES

1 Plan a talk (45 minutes) for a local school district using the six principles for program development. Remember, your time is limited and you want the school district to build a quality program based on the principles.
2 Select one of the philosophies of psychology and education (Bull, 1982) and trace your own thinking and values on programs for gifted. Note agreements and consistency with a given point of view.
3 Choose a theoretical model, and plan a lesson for gifted students to be used in a regular classroom period.
4 Select an administrative arrangement, and research a program based on that particular pattern. For example: the MWC as an example of special grouping.
5 Design a community project for gifted in your own community. Write a two-paragraph description of the project for a local newspaper.

REFERENCES

Allen, S. D. & Fox, D. K. (1979). Group counseling for the gifted. *Journal for the Education of the Gifted, 3*(2), 86–92.

Aspy, D. & Roebuck, F. (1972). An investigation of the relationship between student levels of cognitive functioning and the teacher's classroom behavior. *Journal of Educational Research, 65*(8), 365–368.

Bloom, B. (Ed.) (1956). *Taxonomy of educational objectives. Handbook I: Cognitive domain*. New York: David McKay.

Bull, K. (1982). *Philosophies of psychology and education*. Unpublished paper. Stillwater: Oklahoma State University.

Braga, J. L. (1969). Analysis and evaluation of early admission to school for mentally advanced children. *Journal of Educational Research, 63*, 103–106.

Clark, B. (1983). *Growing up gifted*. Columbus, OH: Charles E. Merrill.

Cloud, B. (1982). *Enrichment for gifted students*. A presentation to an Elementary Gifted Institute, Washington, DC.

Cox, J. (1985). *The Richardson study: A national investigation of educational opportunities for able learners*. Fort Worth: Texas Christian University Press.

Curriculum Council: National Curriculum Council. (1985). *Programs for the gifted, colloquium and conference proceedings*, January. Arlington, VA: National Curriculum Council.

Dusan, N. (1979). *Seminole county project*. Report to the Office of Gifted and Talented, Washington, DC.

Galasso, V. (1979). *Bronx high school of science model*. Status report to Office of Gifted and Talented, Washington, DC.

Gallagher, J. (1985). *Teaching of the gifted child*. Boston: Allyn and Bacon.

Gallagher, J., Aschner, M. & Jenne, W. (1967). *Productive thinking of gifted children in classroom interaction*. CEC Research Monograph Series B, B-5, 1–103.

Guilford, J. P. (1977). *The nature of human intelligence.* New York: McGraw-Hill.

Hackney, H. (1981). Gifted child, the family, and the school. *Gifted Child Quarterly,* 25(5), 1–4.

Howley, A., Howley, C. & Pendarvis, E. (1986). *Teaching gifted children: principles and strategies.* Boston: Little, Brown and Co.

Iannon, R. V. & Carline, J. (1971). A humanistic approach to teacher education. *The Journal of Teacher Education, 22,* 429–433.

Kaplan, S. (1974). *Providing programs for the gifted and talented: A handbook.* Ventura, CA: Office of the Ventura County Superintendent of Schools.

Krathwohl, D. R., Bloom, B. S. & Masia, B. B. (1964). *Taxonomy of educational objectives: The classification of educational goals. Handbook II: Affective domain.* New York: David McKay.

Lauren, B. (1983a). *Enrichment lesson based on Guilford and Bloom.* Presentation at the Florida Association for Gifted, Tampa, FL.

Lauren, B. (1983b). *Enrichment lesson based on Williams' model.* Presentation at the Florida Association for Gifted, Tampa, FL.

Lindsey, M. (1980). *Tracing teachers of the gifted and talented.* New York: Teachers College Press.

Maker, J. (1982). *Curriculum development for the gifted.* Rockville, MD: Aspen Systems Corporation.

Passow, A. H. (1981). Nurturing giftedness: Ways and means. In A. H. Kramer (Ed.), *Gifted Children: Challenging Their Potential.* New York: World Council for Gifted and Talented Children.

Renzulli, J. (1968). Identifying key features in programs for the gifted. *Exceptional Children, 35,* 217–221.

Renzulli, J. (1976). *New directors in creativity.* New York: Harper & Row.

Renzulli, J. (1977). *The enrichment triad model: A guide for developing defensible programs for the gifted and talented.* Mansfold Center, CT: Creative Learning Press.

Renzulli, J. (1978). What makes giftedness? *Phi Delta Kappan, 60,* 180–184, 261.

Safter, H. T. & Bruch, C. B. (1981). Use of DGG model for differential guidance for the gifted. *Gifted Child Quarterly, 25,* 167–174.

Sisk, D. (1985). *Tomorrow's promise: how to encourage leadership in gifted students.* Atlanta, GA: Turner Broadcasting Company.

Stanley, J., Keating, D. & Fox, L. (1974). *Mathematical talent, discovery, description and development.* Baltimore, MD: Johns Hopkins University.

Stanley, J. C. (1976). Use of tests to discover talent. In D. P. Keating (Ed.), *Intellectual Talent Research and Development.* Baltimore, MD: Johns Hopkins University.

Stanley, J. (1984). The exceptionally talented. *The Roeper Review,* February, 16.

Taylor, C. W. (1984). Talent developers as well as knowledge dispensors. *Today's Education, 57,* 67–69.

Taylor, C. W. (1985). Multiple talents. *Journal for the Education of the Gifted. 8* (3), 187–198.

U. S. Office of Education. (1976). Programs for the gifted and talented. *The Federal Register, 41,* 18665–18666.

Ward, V. (1981). Basic concepts: The gifted student: A manual for program improvement. Southern Regional Project for Education of the Gifted. (Reprinted in W. Barbe & Renzulli (Eds.), *Education and Psychology of the Gifted.* New York: Irvington.).

Williams, F. (1970). *Classroom ideas for encouraging thinking and feeling.* Buffalo, NY: D.O.K. Publishers.

Worcester, D. (1956). *The education of children above average mentality.* Lincoln: University of Nebraska Press.

CHAPTER 5

CURRICULUM STRATEGIES
FOR THE GIFTED

CHAPTER 5

CURRICULUM STRATEGIES FOR THE GIFTED

The human mind, over-stretched to a new idea, never goes back to its original dimensions.

Oliver Wendell Holmes

Many teachers are making a conscious effort to plan meaningful educational experiences for gifted students as a result of the increased interest in "excellence" in the 1980s, prompted by national studies: the National Commission on Excellence, *A Nation at Risk* (1983); the Carnegie Foundation for the Advancement of Teaching, *High School: A Report on Secondary Education in America* (Boyer, 1983); the joint effort of the National Association of Independent Schools and the National Association of Secondary School Principals, *Horace's Compromise: The Dilemma of the American High School* (Sizer, 1984); Goodlad's, *A Place Called School* (1983); the Education Commission for the States, *Action for Excellence* (1984); and the Twentieth Century Fund Task Report (1983). These teachers need guiding principles in developing differential curriculum. To meet this need, the National Committee for Curriculum Development, sponsored by the National Leadership Training Institute on the Gifted and the Talented (NLTI/ GT), identified thirteen principles to be used in planning curriculum for the gifted (Kaplan, 1979). The committee, composed of leaders in the field of gifted education, meets annually (a) to discuss curriculum issues; (b) to create documents to be used by school administrators and teachers in planning, developing, and delivering services for gifted; and (c) to conduct training and dissemination institutes. The principles, one of the better compiled lists available for teacher use,

Photograph on facing page courtesy of Milton Heiberg Studios, New York, New York.

are concise, relevant, useful, and easy to implement in a variety of settings. The rationale behind the principles of a differentiated curriculum is that curriculum changes are mandated by the differences in learning, emotional, and social characteristics of gifted students. A differentiated curriculum responds to these needs such as the ability to see concepts and relationships more easily (Principles 1, 2, 3, and 6); a great deal of independence in thought and action (Principles 4, 5, and 8); an unusual amount of curiosity and a wide variety of interests (Principles 7, 10, and 11); an unusual degree of sensitivity (Principles 5, 6, 9, and 13).

SELECTED STRATEGIES AND THEIR APPLICATION TO PRINCIPLES OF A DIFFERENTIATED CURRICULUM

In this chapter, selected curriculum strategies and teaching techniques are illustrated. These include course compacting; research and study skills; listening skills and time management; and use of questioning, inquiry, creative problem solving, simulation, and futuristics. At the end of each subsection, the related principles are identified that complement the strategy. The principles of a differentiated curriculum developed by the Leadership Training Institute (LTI) are:

1 Present content related to broad-based issues, themes, or problems.
2 Integrate many disciplines into the area of study.
3 Present comprehensive, related, and mutually reinforcing experiences within an area of study.
4 Allow for the in-depth learning of a self-selected topic within the area of study.
5 Develop independent or self-directed study skills.
6 Develop productive, complex, abstract, and higher level thinking skills.
7 Focus on open-ended tasks.
8 Develop research skills and methods.
9 Integrate basic skills and higher level thinking skills into the curriculum.
10 Encourage students to develop products that challenge existing ideas and produce "new" ideas.
11 Encourage students to develop products that use new techniques, materials, and forms.
12 Encourage students to develop self-understanding, i.e., to recognize and use their abilities, to become self-directed, and to appreciate likenesses and differences between themselves and others.
13 Evaluate student outcomes by using appropriate and specific criteria through self-appraisal and criterion-referenced and standardized instruments.

The first strategy to be discussed is course compacting. All of the strategies selected for this chapter are applicable to gifted students from the age of approximately 4 years to 18 years, although the content may need modification.

COURSE COMPACTING

Compacting is a process in which teachers *analyze* the area of study and procedures used in teaching the material and *plan* ways to judiciously cover the area. The two essential ingredients for success in course compacting are a careful diagnosis and a synthesis of the material to be covered, including objectives and content.

With compacting, gifted students are relieved of the boredom that comes from reviewing work in areas they have mastered. Compacting identifies basic skill areas in which gifted students need additional work, and it ensures they have the standard competencies necessary for achievement. Through this assessment process and "teaching to the individual's needs," the gifted student and her/his teachers receive an extra bonus of time to be used for studies on topics which hold more interest.

Compacting is a technique for fast-paced instruction to match the rapid learning of gifted students. Stanley (1976, 1984), in his model, Study of Mathematically Precocious Youth (SMPY), makes a strong case for the use of achievement tests for specific academic abilities. Through diagnostic–prescriptive approaches, Stanley and his associates group gifted students for appropriate instruction. On the basis of SAT scores in math and expressed interest in the program, gifted students from junior high age and above are given opportunities to enroll in advanced math courses. Since 1980, the SMPY Talent Search model has expanded to include search centers at Duke, Northwestern, and the Universities of Arizona and Denver, with summer programs at Dickson College in Pennsylvania and Franklin and Marshall (Durden, 1983).

In a comprehensive presentation on course compacting, Renzulli and Smith (1980) advocate pretesting the skills of gifted students and identifying curriculum areas in which they are knowledgeable and experienced. The format they use consists of three areas: (a) curriculum areas to be considered for compacting, (b) procedures for compacting basic material, and (c) acceleration and enrichment activities.

These three areas guide the classroom teacher through a procedure of identifying the material to be covered during a unit (for a class or a year) and the assessment information that can be used to justify the need for compacting. If, for example, a gifted student has scored 2 years above grade level on the reading and language arts section of a standardized achievement test, this information, along with the observed behavior of the gifted student, could be used to consider compacting. Information from student records and previous teachers help construct a total picture of how well a particular gifted student is functioning. Once the data is collected to identify the student's standing in a given skill area, procedures for compacting the unit or course material are planned. Perhaps the student needs more work on punctuation. This can be accomplished with (1) a programmed punctuation unit, (2) completing the textbook section on punctuation through independent study, or (3) simple drill, monitored by the teacher. Specifying the activities is as important as specifying appropriate assessment procedures to gauge the gifted student's proficiency in the basic skill or curricular area.

Through techniques such as unit or course compacting, learning becomes more highly targeted and more responsive to the gifted student's need for high achievement. Once the basic skill or curriculum information is learned, the gifted student can then work on accelerated material, particularly if grouped with intellectual peers or work on in-depth study and research.

If no diagnostic instruments or tests are available for assessment, the teacher can review the main objectives of a specific unit or course of study and construct instruments that test specific competencies. This approach is a type of mastery or prescriptive learning. Compacting encourages teachers to use time wisely and efficiently and to make decisions based on such questions as: Is reading a given textbook chapter outside of class, followed by a videotape of a follow-up topic, the best way to use classroom time? Could the tape be made available for viewing by the gifted students during study hall, lunch, or after school? Could a speaker engage the gifted students' interests and cover the material as well? Can two objectives and activities be merged into one activity?

Making such decisions helps teachers of the gifted become more proficient in compacting.

Application of the Principles of Differentiated Curriculum to Compacting

Compacting enables gifted students to develop independent or self-directed study skills (Principle 5), because the gifted student is aware of the level at which he/she is functioning and the specific work he/she must do to learn the basic skill. This flow of information between student and teacher helps build a legitimate need to master a skill and stimulate more self-direction.

Through compacting, teachers integrate basic skills and higher level thinking skills (Principle 9) using broad-based learning activities. For example, an eighth-grade language arts unit on research skills can also include note taking. Note taking may be the basic skill needed to engage in independent study and to analyze broad-based themes.

Compacting encourages teachers to evaluate gifted students' work with appropriate criteria (Principle 3), for, as teachers begin to test mastery through objective measures or through teacher-made instruments based on course and content objectives, they become more sensitized to the need for an overall use of broadened types of evaluation. And, most importantly, gifted students can be clustered within a regular classroom to provide the dynamics of group instruction as the curriculum is tailored to the gifted students' need for in-depth learning (Principle 4).

RESEARCH AND STUDY SKILLS: TIME MANAGEMENT AND LISTENING SKILLS

Many gifted students want to do independent study, and most gifted programs provide some type of independent work. Yet, as many teachers know, not all gifted students are capable of the high level of commitment necessary to do independent work. Teachers and parents of the gifted often report that gifted students do not listen closely to the assignments, miss deadlines, display poor time management, and lack research and study skills.

Some gifted students do not see the purpose of independent study and have not experienced the excitement and intense involvement in high-interest projects.

The simple truth may be that they lack the prerequisite skills. To remedy this, teachers can appeal to their needs and interests. The first step in teaching research skills is to concentrate on the skills needed for individualized learning.

Dunn and Price (1980) suggest that students learn to make choices, to evaluate their own work, and to share the results of their work. The role of the classroom teacher in building these skills begins with providing choices for the gifted students and engaging them in dialogues concerning their learning and outcomes.

The use of a contract can help gifted students master independent study. The sample contract in Table 5-1 was planned for a fourth-grade student, to extend her regular classroom work in social studies. Because the class is learning about South Africa, her videotape and bulletin board enrich their studies.

Another gifted student is studying Zimbabwe, and the two students compare and contrast their findings. These students develop their ability to do independent investigations and their knowledge of resources. They discover where to locate resources and demonstrate alternative thinking in activities and reporting. The goal for independent study is lively and interesting reports.

Independent study for young gifted students can move from contracts to complex research projects with hypotheses. Learning the skills to do research and carrying out independent study helps develop skills Renzulli calls Type III Activities in his Enrichment Triad model. Renzulli (1977) sees gifted students as true inquirers in their areas of interest. The primary focus of the gifted students' time is on investigating real problems in a manner consistent with their preferred style of learning.

Dunn and Price (1980) suggest that students involved in independent study develop knowledge of resources, their locations and their use, as well as an

TABLE 5-1
CURRICULUM STRATEGIES
Independent Study Contract

What I want to study about	How I will go about it	What I will do with my new knowledge
1 I want to know more about South Africa: Who were the first settlers? Where did they come from and why?	1 I will interview Dr. Lowe, who is an historian from South Africa.	1 Create a video tape, a 15-minute presentation using information and pictures for a look at how South Africa used to be and how it is today, for the school news.
2 I want to know who lived there first, what natives?	2 *National Geographic*, June 1982, has an issue on South Africa.	2 Construct bulletin board for classroom.
3 I want to know why they decided on apartheid.	3 Study life of Rhodes (biographies).	3 Do a 5-minute morning talk.
	4 Interview South African students at UCLA.	
	5 Review history books.	

Source: Sisk, 1983.

awareness of different types of reporting. Gifted children as young as 8 years of age can successfully learn note taking and elements appropriate to written reports, including table of contents, footnoting, and bibliography. In preparing oral reports, gifted students learn the use of note cards, overhead transparencies, slides, and other aids.

Maker (1982) suggests a simulation game called "Search" which has been modified to teach library skills. In this game, students learn research and library skills in two teams. Each team develops a unique problem, using goal setting. Goal setting is defined as what each student wants to have happen. The teams exchange problems, conduct research, and share the products from the investigation.

To teach the correct investigative procedures, teachers can use the APA (American Psychological Association) *Publication Manual* (1984) for guidelines. Other useful sources are the University of Chicago's *A Manual of Style* (1969), Strunk and White's *Elements of Style* (1979), and Von Til's *Writing for Professional Publications* (1981). When gifted researchers learn a style at an early age, they move easily and smoothly into independent research efforts at the middle and secondary school level. Gifted students can become familiar with basic skills for historical, descriptive, and experimental research. These skills are essential tools for their future investigations.

Time Management

Time management is self-management. This concept is covered by Douglas and Douglas (1980) in *Manage Your Time, Manage Your Work, Manage Yourself*. Self-management is extremely important for gifted students, because they often want to do everything. They use the strategies of working faster and longer to manage time, but according to Douglas and Douglas, they should make choices. By making choices, gifted students learn to prioritize activities and to follow decisions with action. They suggest an exercise (see Figure 5-1) that is particularly useful

FIGURE 5-1
External/internal continuum.

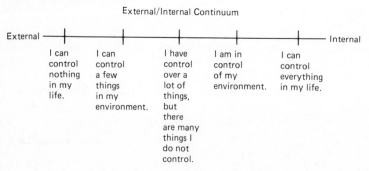

in encouraging gifted students to take control of their lives, the external/internal continuum.

Students examine their lives at school and at home and place themselves on the continuum. Following their initial assessment, they discuss their feelings about their selection and set goals for gaining more control over their lives. The idea behind the external/internal continuum is that the more you believe you can control, the more you will control. By using this continuum, gifted students learn planning and time management.

A five-step time management procedure, suggested by Douglas and Douglas (1980) was used with sixty-five gifted secondary school students. The five-step procedure included: (a) desire, (b) knowledge, (c) visualization, (d) planning, and (e) action. In the first step, the students listed areas for change in their study habits. This task emphasizes the importance of wanting to make change in changing behavior. Many of the gifted students identified time management as a problem. In the second step (knowledge), the students analyzed their use of time and clarified their specific objectives. Then they set priorities and outlined specific steps to be taken. In step three (visualization), they closed their eyes and visualized themselves accomplishing the activity. The visualization affirmed their commitment to change. This affirmation was followed by planning scheduled time for the various activities and working out alternatives. The alternatives were charted and ranked according to priority. Step five (action) was implementing the alternatives and plans. After this step, the students attended a time management lecture in which a mental process for becoming more disciplined was explained. The following words were used:

almost	planning
just about	hoping
nearly	wishing
not quite	wanting
yearning	

A lively discussion took place as the students recognized how using different words or ways of looking at tasks can limit behavior, goal setting, and attainment. The above group of words was contemplated for 5 minutes. Then the students were asked to contemplate another group of words:

strike	a winner
arrive	satisfied
success	victory
on the mark	triumph
achievement	

At the end of the project period, the sixty-five students were able to successfully complete their projects, and their classroom teachers reported considerable change in their school attitudes. In a follow-up questionnaire, the students reported attitude changes, preparedness, and willingness to take action and change (Sisk, 1982).

Listening Skills

Listening is more than just hearing and takes a considerable amount of waking time. Stevens and Nichols (1957) conducted a study in which they examined a variety of occupations. They found that 70 percent of waking time is spent in communication; writing takes 9 percent, reading absorbs 16 percent, talking accounts for 30 percent, and listening occupies 45 percent.

If for no other reason than the large amount of time spent listening, we ought to do it well. But many people are very poor when it comes to listening. Gifted students are by nature inquisitive; they are keen on taking in information and can become much better information gatherers when they learn to be better listeners. In school, gifted students have ample training in "antilistening." They learn to not listen when they already know the material, when they are bored, or when they are being criticized or rejected. Classrooms often are structured for a large ratio of listening time to talking time, and for this reason many gifted students tune out.

One simple way to encourage listening is to ask more questions. As gifted students listen less and respond or talk more, their listening efficiency increases. In Table 5-2, Bolton (1982), author of *People Skills*, lists three kinds of listening skills.

Attending is defined as giving physical attention to another person or listening with the body. When attending, the nonverbal communication indicates a posture of involvement, appropriate body action, eye contact, and a nondistracting environment. The use of good *attending skills* indicates interest to others. The effect of good attending on others was demonstrated in a study conducted by Ivey and Hinkle (1970). They trained six students in attending behavior and then asked a professor to lecture.

The skill of *infrequent questions* is asking open questions, such as "What's on your mind?," as opposed to more specific questions which can be answered quickly with "yes" or "no." Good interviewers ask open questions, such as "Can you explain it to me?" "Why?" "Why not?" "How would you have handled it?" In day-to-day interactions, most people ask far too many questions. Such frequent questioning can cut the listener's involvement with the speaker. Gifted students in particular ask too many questions in order to direct the conversation. Their controlling behavior often makes it difficult to have conversations with them. Lastly, the skill of *attentive silence* is useful in teaching gifted students how to follow. By learning and practicing the value of silence, gifted students will be surprised at how much more people talk to them and with them.

Reflecting skills are skills such as paraphrasing or giving concise responses to the speaker that restate the essence of the other's content. A good paraphrase is brief and captures the essential message. An example of good paraphrasing is this discussion between a gifted student and his teacher:

Teacher: I don't know whether to plan the field trip or not. The principal isn't sure either. I love field trips . . . they are stimulating and challenging and we will benefit from them. But sometimes, I think they take so much time and we could get the same material in class. . . .

TABLE 5-2
THREE KINDS OF LISTENING SKILLS

Skill clusters	Specific skills
Attending skills	• A posture of involvement • Appropriate body motion • Nondistracting environment • Eye contact
Following skills	• Door openers • Minimal encouragers • Infrequent questions • Attentive silence
Reflecting skills	• Paraphrasing • Reflecting feelings • Reflecting meanings • Summary reflections

Student: You enjoy the field trips, but sometimes the work involved makes you think we should stay in class.

The student restated the essence of the problem. He did it concisely and in his own words. When the paraphrase is on target, the speaker usually says "yes" and continues talking. Another listening skill is *reflecting feelings*:

Mary: I was sure I'd get an *A* on that paper. I worked so hard for it.
Sue: It is really discouraging.
Mary: Sure is. Will I ever be on target in that class?

Mary recognized that Sue understood, and continued the discussion. Sue perceived that Mary was feeling a number of emotions—frustration, anger, discouragement—but decided that discouragement was the dominant one. By acting on her assumption, Sue was perceived as a good listener and Mary felt understood. Bolton (1982) states that a lack of response to the speaker on the part of the listener, when listening does not encourage disclosure of feeling, can be a signal that the speaker's personal reaction to the events was missed. The uniqueness of the other person can be overlooked if there is a low level of awareness of the speaker's emotion. When someone is discussing a problem, reflecting feelings helps the speaker understand his/her feelings and moves the conversation toward new understanding and possible solutions to the problem.

Reflecting meanings is similar to reflecting feelings, as meanings are often attached to feelings. When feelings and facts are joined in one response, there is a reflection of meaning (Bolton, 1982). For example:

Melissa: I've been up all night writing my paper, and I look a wreck. I don't know how I'm going to complete this project. I feel like it just won't work out.
Terry: You are really concerned about the project, and you're worried that it won't work out.

By restating as a summation Melissa's feelings and ideas, Terry offers her an opportunity to continue expressing herself and possibly to move toward constructive action. When gifted students learn to use reflective listening skills, they check on the accuracy of their perceptions. They also channel their natural warmth and concern for others using this skill. By listening more closely to others, the gifted will be in a better position to communicate with others and to use their potential as thinking, caring, feeling individuals.

Application of the Principles of Differentiated Curriculum to Research, Study, Listening, and Time Management Skills

Research and study, listening, and time management skills will help gifted students develop productive, complex, and higher level thinking skills (Principle 6), but their major contribution is to the development of self-understanding (Principle 12). Through the use of skills such as listening and time management, gifted students recognize their abilities, become more self-directed, and appreciate the similarities and differences between themselves and others.

USE OF QUESTIONING

A discussion of questioning is incomplete without a discussion of the thinking process. When teachers question skillfully, they stimulate gifted students to higher levels of thinking. It is useful to approach the questioning process by examining models that are process oriented.

One of the more frequently used models for developing higher level thinking processes is Bloom's taxonomy. Many gifted programs use either the cognitive taxonomy of Bloom (1956) or the affective taxonomy of Krathwohl et al. (1964) to plan questions. Taxonomies provide structures to understand and develop questions. The teacher can present ideas and concepts in a sequential process. Because the taxonomies are behavioral descriptions, the thinking that is required is observable.

The question construction wheel (Figure 5-2), developed by a group of Garden Grove, California, teachers of the gifted, facilitates gifted students' thinking. The middle circle represents the cognitive taxonomy of Bloom et al. The pie-shaped wedges represent one level of thinking in the cognitive domain. The middle ring identifies possible process verbs, and the outer ring contains possible products. The classification of questions in the outer ring is based on the work of Sanders, *Classroom Questions, What Kinds?* (1966).

The use of the wheel is demonstrated in the following scenario:

A teacher of a gifted honors class in English is preparing a lesson; the first decision is what levels of questions to emphasize. The teacher decides to concentrate on knowledge and comprehension (Bloom) with emphasis on memory, translation and interpretive questions (Sanders). In planning the lesson, the recall section (Bloom) is identified or located in the center of the wheel and the corresponding verbs for process are examined in the second wheel. The choices are: define, describe, label, locate, recite, select, memorize, recognize, name, state, and identify. The products in the outer ring, ap-

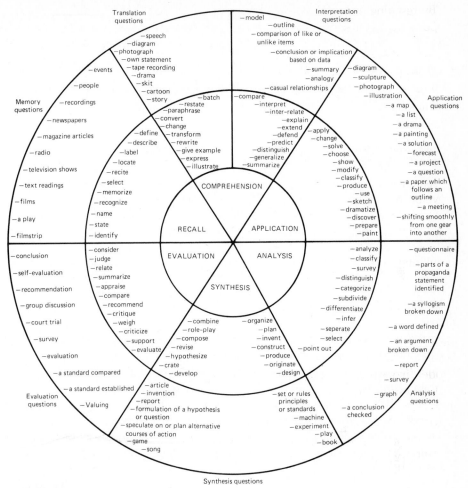

FIGURE 5-2
Question construction wheel. (*Garden Grove Unified Schools, Garden Grove, California. Reprinted by permission.*)

propriate for the memory level are: events, people, recordings, newspapers, magazine articles, radio television shows, text reading, films, a play or a filmstrip. Using the Sanders classification of questions, the type of question appropriate at the recall level is memory. The teacher asks the gifted students to *describe* (Bloom) (process) the setting for *A Midsummer Night's Dream* play-within-a-play (recall) and make a *record* of their description (product). According to Sanders, this activity is at the memory level.

At the comprehension level, the activity or question (process) is to *paraphrase* the words of Shakespeare's play-within-a-play, *translating* (Sanders) the words into *their own statement of language* (product). The gifted students will *interpret* (Bloom) (process) by comparing their translation or version of the play-within-a-play with that of Shakespeare. They will perform their version or translation, and Shakespeare's for their classmates and ask them for a preference. The students will then *make conclusions based on the data* (interpretations) (Sanders) concerning student preferences and discuss the timelessness of Shakespeare's style.

Even though the teacher of the gifted decided to concentrate on the levels of knowledge and comprehension (Bloom et al., 1956), use of the wheel encouraged higher levels of thinking. The gifted student translates and interprets (Sanders, 1966), as well as analyzes, synthesizes, and evaluates (Bloom et al., 1956; Sanders, 1966).

The Taxonomy of Cognitive Objectives

A breakdown of the levels of the cognitive domain with corresponding process verbs further clarifies the use of the wheel for constructing questions.

Knowledge

The first level, knowledge, consists of recall or recognition of specific information. Process verbs for knowledge include *define, repeat, name,* and *recall.*

The second level is comprehension or understanding information that is given. Verbs that might be used to elicit comprehension would be *restate, explain, locate,* and *express.*

At the level of application, the student uses methods, concepts, principles, and theories in new situations. Process verbs that express the idea of application include *translate, apply, practice, operate,* and *demonstrate.*

At the analysis level, the student breaks information down into its constitutent elements and is involved in *analyzing, examining, differentiating,* and *calculating.*

The synthesis level consists of putting together constituent elements to form a whole; this process requires original thought. Process verbs that describe this level are *rearrange, combine* or *recombine,* or *put together* to form a new pattern or product.

Evaluation is judging the value of issues, materials, and methods by developing and applying standards and criteria. Verbs that can be used include *judge, evaluate, appraise, rate, assess, estimate,* and *choose.*

The first step in constructing a series of questions for gifted students is to select the appropriate level in the taxonomy. However, gifted students need to experience all levels of questioning. They cannot analyze material they do not comprehend or recall. There must be free flow between the different levels. Clark (1983) states that Bloom's taxonomy is often used as a linear model, yet it can also be viewed as cyclical, with the highest level, evaluation, often creating new information that then becomes knowledge; thus the cycle begins again.

Taba's Questioning Techniques

Another process model that is useful in building questions for gifted students is that of Taba. Her series of four sequential questioning techniques grew out of a lifetime effort in researching the ways children think (Taba, 1963; Taba & Elzey, 1964; Taba et al., 1971).

The Taba strategies are: (a) concept development, (b) interpretation of data, (c) application of generalizations, and (d) resolution of conflict or interpretation of feelings, attitudes, and values.

Concept Development

In the first strategy, concept development, students are asked to clarify concepts by verbalizing their own thoughts and to extend concepts both by building on the ideas of others and having their ideas built upon.

The concept development strategy contains five steps. The first step is *listing*. It involves the process of differentiating relevant from irrelevant information. The second step is *grouping*, in which students notice common attributes of items and put them together on the basis of their commonalities. The third step, *labeling*, is an abstracting or synthesizing process in which students locate words or phrases to express the relationship or commonality among diverse items. The fourth step, *subsuming*, provides another opportunity to see different relationships and new attributes of the items. The fifth step recapitulates all of the previous steps.

Interpretation of Data

Interpreting data deals with gathering information and making inferences. It calls for *listing* as the first step in which students use their collective observations to decide what is relevant and what is not. In the second step, they *infer cause and effect*. In the third step, the students *infer prior causes and subsequent effects*. The emphasis is on probing deeply for influences that are removed from the immediate situation. In the fourth step, the students *reach conclusions*, and in the fifth, they *generalize*. Here they are asked to justify their generalizations and critically review the statements of others.

Application of Generalizations

In this strategy, students must apply previously learned generalizations and facts to other situations. The first step in this strategy is *to predict*. Students use their own creativity to *think up possible outcomes of hypothetical situations*. In the second step, *inferring conditions*, the students are urged to bring their discussion and comments to a reality base to build a logical, justifiable set of relationships. The next step, *inferring consequences and conditions*, is more or less a continuation of the first two steps. The major idea is to extend the predictions and conditions from the original situation. In the fourth step, *conclusions*, the students are asked to consider all the predictions, conditions, and reasons that have been previously discussed and to render a judgement about which conditions they think are likely to prevail. In the fifth step, they *examine generalizations* forming general statements and look critically at others' statements.

Resolution of Conflict

This strategy could be called interpretation of feelings, attitudes, and values. The students gain practice in this strategy by exploring the feelings and attitudes behind people's behavior. In the first step, *listing*, the students are again concerned with differentiating relevant from nonrelevant data. In the second step, they *infer reasons and feelings*. Generating alternatives and examining their consequences is the third step, followed by evaluation or deciding upon the most appropriate action, followed by generalizing, in which the students form an abstract statement about how people usually handle such situations.

Taba et al. (1971) lists four general types of questions: (1) Questions calling for variety, such as "What else might happen?" or "What else could we call that group?" (2) Those calling for clarification or extension, such as "What do you mean?" and "Please explain more about the idea." (3) Questions calling for reasons or support for ideas, such as "Tell us how you know that and what leads you to believe that." (4) Questions that focus thinking, such as "Which items go together because they are alike?" "What do you think prevents. . . ?" "How did . . . happen?" or "What were the results of. . . ?"

Although Taba developed her teaching strategies for the regular classroom, her inductive approach and emphasis on inquiry make them applicable to gifted students. Taba et al.'s *A Teacher's Handbook for Elementary Social Studies* (1971) is a useful resource for elementary school teachers of the gifted, yet the thinking skills and questioning processes are also appropriate for secondary school teachers to use. In addition, Kaplan (1980) cites Taba's strategies as being particularly useful for preschool children, in that they teach children to think by learning the processes of formulating concepts and generalizations through information gathering and organizing. There is active interaction with the data to be learned.

Many models can be used to teach questioning techniques, and, besides those referred to in this chapter, several others have been discussed in Chapter 4. But the major purpose in selecting a model is to provide gifted students with a sequential and orderly guide for thinking during the teaching/learning process.

Application of the Principles of A Differentiated Curriculum to the Use of Questioning

The use of questioning helps focus the gifted student's attention on open-ended tasks (Principle 7). It also helps to integrate the basic skills and higher level thinking skills (Principle 9) into the curriculum. The use of Taba's model provides ample opportunity to explore broad-based themes (Principle 1) such as "Human Beings' Inhumanity to One Another" or other broad-based issues or problems. The use of questioning also encourages gifted students to develop self-understanding and to interpret feelings, attitudes, and values (Principle 12).

Taba's approach provides a foundation of skills for gifted students, leading them to become first-hand inquirers or investigators of problems (Principle 5). Teachers can place gifted students in charge of their own learning through the use of questioning.

INQUIRY

Suchman (1961) has applied inquiry to the education of all students but particularly to the gifted. The Suchman inquiry model can be depicted as shown in Figure 5-3.

The inquiry program consists of three steps: (a) establishing the properties of objects involved in the problem, (b) finding which objects are relevant to the problem, and (c) discovering how they function in the solution. In an inquiry session, the students formulate and test their own theories in discussions with the teacher, who responds only with a "yes" or "no." During the session, students learn about the learning process itself. Inquiry sessions are lively and productive, and they lead to new and more productive questions. When students are recognized by the teacher, they may ask questions until they wish to yield the floor to someone else. This process allows the individual student to think aloud and to experiment. Students indicate their willingness to yield by saying "pass." During the inquiry session, the students are not permitted to discuss their theories among themselves, unless they call for a conference. Gifted students often call for conferences and consult resources in order to solve a problem or formulate a theory.

Suchman developed problems for discussion (dissonant events) which are available on film and tape. Teachers can also perform experiments with unexpected outcomes or dissonant events for inquiry sessions.

One example of inquiry for elementary school gifted students is based on the apparatus shown in Figure 5-4:

As the students discover the apparatus, they ask questions such as:

What keeps the paper clip up?
Will it fall if we poke it?
Would it stand up if the string were metal?
How long will it stand up?
What's between the clip and the magnet?
Will a bar magnet work?

These questions have potential for inquiry training. The lists of concepts included in the above experiment are: magnetic field, magnetic force, magnetic induction, and forces in equilibrium. A great amount of versatility is embedded in simple experiments to extend scientific thinking.

Another suitable method to stimulate inquiry for young gifted students is labeling items with provocative questions. A rock can be labeled "I am a rock, I'm

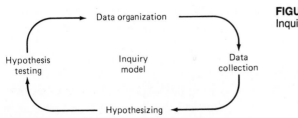

FIGURE 5-3
Inquiry model.

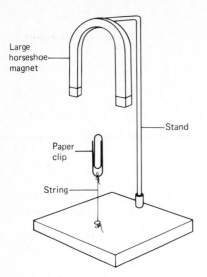

Large horseshoe magnet

Stand

Paper clip

String

FIGURE 5-4
Example of inquiry.

made of minerals." "Are there other rocks and minerals in this room?" "What is the oldest rock in this room?" "Add a difficult question to stump others about rocks!" Science "curiosity boxes" can include a variety of objects such as seeds, with questions such as "Are all of the seeds the same?" "How are they different or alike?"

Inquiry includes experimentation with many phenomena, answering questions without using the authority of a textbook or a teacher.

This experimentation requires a permissive, cooperative classroom atmosphere, in which both teacher and students examine the evidence, assess their hypotheses and assumptions, and arrive at reasonable and logical conclusions consistent with the data. In short, the students learn to think and act like scientists.

Application of the Principles of a Differentiated Curriculum for the Gifted to Inquiry

Inquiry encourages the gifted student to integrate many disciplines to solve problems (Principle 2). It also encourages productive and higher-level thinking (Principle 6), providing gifted students with the opportunity to use research skills and methods in problem solving (Principle 8). The debriefing session, in which the teacher discusses the process, meets the principle of encouraging the development of self-understanding (Principle 12). Gifted students enjoy the feedback and reinforcement provided by their "successes" as they pose questions. This aspect of inquiry encourages students to experience self-appraisal (Principle 13).

CREATIVE PROBLEM SOLVING

The use of creative problem solving as a curriculum strategy for gifted enables them to be actively involved in their own learning. As the students engage in real problems the learning environment becomes highly challenging and motivating.

Parnes (1975) in *Aha: Insights into Creative Behavior* relates his exposure to Alex Osborn's ideas. Osborn invited Parnes to work with the Creative Problem Solving Institute (CPSI) in 1956. This was a turning point in Parnes' life work. He became president of the Creative Problem Solving Foundation; the group hosts an annual problem-solving institute in Buffalo as well as regional conferences in the U.S. and overseas. The creative problem-solving process as taught by CPSI consists of five steps: fact finding, problem finding, idea finding, solution finding, and acceptance finding. Table 5-3 compares the Osborn/Parnes creative problem-solving process to the theories of intellectual functioning of Bruner and Guilford (Parnes, 1972).

In each approach, knowledge or sensory input is manipulated by some transformation, operation, or idea-finding process, for a meaningful purpose called evaluation, product, or solution finding.

The five steps in the creative problem-solving (CPS) process are briefly discussed below.

Fact finding involves listing all the known facts about the problem and securing as much new data about the problem as possible, as soon as possible. In this step, the problem is often viewed as a mess and may well be ill-defined.

Problem finding involves writing or stating the problem in a well-defined procedure, by using an "In what ways might I . . ." kind of question, and encouraging the problem solver to elaborate on the problem and seek more new ideas. During the problem-finding step, an attempt is made to identify the subproblems that make up the major problem. This may lead to a restatement or narrowing of the problem. An example: A father first stated his problem as "In what ways might I help my son with his homework?" Then, after listing several subproblems and speculating on the other possible problems, he changed the problem statement to "In what ways might I spend more time with my son?"

In *idea finding*, the major focus is to generate as many ideas as possible. In free-wheeling, brainstorming sessions no judgment is placed on ideas. The goal is simply to list as many ideas as possible, giving free reins to imagination.

Solution finding involves choosing the alternatives, generated during the idea-finding phase, with the greatest potential for solving the problem. The first step in solution finding is to establish criteria for evaluating the alternatives, followed

TABLE 5-3
COMPARISON OF THE OSBORN/PARNES CREATIVE PROBLEM-
SOLVING PROCESS TO BRUNER'S AND GUILFORD'S THEORIES
OF INTELLECTUAL FUNCTIONING

	Bruner (1962)	Guilford (1967)	Osborn (1963)
Input:	Acquisition	Contents	Fact finding
Processing:	Transformation	Operations	Idea finding
Output:	Evaluation	Products	Solution finding

by applying each criterion to each alternative in as objective a manner as possible. Sometimes this is done by weighting each criterion and then applying it to each alternative. This can be accomplished by creating a matrix listing each idea or alternative and rating it against every criterion.

The last step is *acceptance finding* or developing a plan of action. The problem solver considers the individuals who would accept or reject the plan. Brainstorming may come into play, as the creative problem solver prepares for implementation.

Figure 5-5 summarizes the creative problem-solving process. When the problem solver thinks of as many ideas as possible but defers judgment as to their validity, divergent thinking is elicited; when the emphasis is on coming to a logical or one-answer response, the problem solver is engaged in convergent thinking.

Brainstorming Osborn (1963) established four basic rules for effective brainstorming: (a) criticism must be ruled out, (b) free-wheeling is encouraged, (c) quantity is desired, and (d) combination and improvement are sought. Brainstorming is usually conducted in a group, but it can be effective with individuals if judgment is deferred. Deferring judgment is difficult because judgment and criticism are customary behaviors in social and educational settings. A list of "killer phrases" can be circulated at the beginning of a brainstorming session to help participants refrain from using comments such as "We've done that before," "It cost too much money," "That's ridiculous," or "You've got to be kidding." The free-wheeling that Osborn suggests calls for a fresh, new point of view, leading to ideas that are plausible and viable. Brainstorming emphasizes quantity, because as more and more ideas emerge, they evolve from the expected and the trivial to the unique. Ideas should be stated succinctly, with little verbalization about contributions. Verbalization slows down the process and discourages hitchhiking, or building on one another's ideas.

When classroom teachers introduce problem solving as a tool, a set of problems with time limits of 3 to 5 minutes is helpful. Some interesting problems to experiment with are:

You remember that today is your mother's birthday and you have not bought her a present. She is coming into the house this moment. How might you give her a birthday present?

Your grandmother died and left you with an attic full of clothes hangers. She was eccentric. You really want to do something with these hangers. How might you use them?

FIGURE 5-5
The creative problem-solving process.

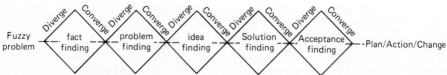

You have been asked to supervise a kindergarten class for 15 minutes while the teacher unloads her car. In what ways might you amuse the children until their teacher returns?

Young gifted students love to brainstorm; they take to it naturally because they are free about generating ideas and have not developed the strong sense of evaluation of older gifted students. They are particularly adept at free-wheeling and hitchhiking. With older gifted students, the teacher might discuss the sessions, how they feel about the constraints, and whether or not they think the session has been effective.

One way to encourage gifted students to increase their flow of ideas is to use Osborn's (1963) list of idea-spurring questions:

1 *Put to other uses?* New way to use "as is"? Other uses if modified?

2 *Adapt?* What else is like this? What other ideas does this suggest?

3 *Modify?* Change meaning, color, motion, sound, odor, taste, form, shape? Other changes?

4 *Magnify?* What to add? Greater frequency? Stronger? Larger? Plus ingredient? Multiply?

5 *Minify?* What to subtract? Eliminate? Smaller? Lighter? Slower? Split up? Less frequent?

6 *Substitute?* Who else instead? What else instead? Other place? Other time?

7 *Rearrange?* Other layout? Other sequences? Change pace?

8 *Reverse?* Opposite? Turn it backward? Turn it upside down? Turn it inside out?

9 *Combine?* How about a blend, an assortment? Continue purposes? Combine ideas?

Shallcross (1981) has simplified the creative process learning into five steps: (a) orientation, (b) preparation, (c) ideation, (d) evaluation, and (e) implementation. *Orientation* is defining the problem or setting a goal, followed by *preparation*, or pointing toward the factual or a data-gathering stage. The five classic questions such as Who? What? When? Where? and How? are helpful in this stage. In the *ideation* stage, divergent thinking is used to arrive at many possible tentative solutions. This stage is followed by *evaluation* in which a weighted-criteria matrix can be used to help choose the most possible solutions. The matrix might look like Figure 5-6.

In *implementation*, gifted students take action and draw up a plan. Shallcross (1981) lists ten helpful questions to encourage students to prepare their plan's implementation:

1 What has to happen before anything else can?

2 Who else will be involved?

3 Do I need to convince anyone else of my ideas?

4 What strategy for convincing shall I use?

5 What materials do I need to assemble?

6 What rearranging of schedules is necessary?

7 Does anything else have to be sacrificed in order to implement this idea?

Criteria								Total score
Ideas								
1.								
2.								
3.								
4.								
5.								
6.								

The numerical weighting would be: 5. Excellent
4. Good—very
3. Good
2. Fair

FIGURE 5-6
Weighted-criteria matrix insert.

8 When is the best time to start?
9 Is the place for it to happen of concern?
10 What is the best order for the various phases of the plan's implementation?

The creative problem-solving process helps gifted students handle school-related problems and can be used as a guidance tool to build more cohesive classrooms with questions such as:

- In what ways might we organize our editorial staff to function positively?
- In what ways might we handle the problem of lost and found articles?
- In what ways might we dismiss in a more orderly fashion?
- In what ways might we minimize the friction with the other fifth-grade classes?
- In what ways might we create a more positive attitude toward school?

The creative problem-solving process can be broken down into its individual components and applied to all subject areas. Shallcross (1981) suggests a matrix to do this. Several of the components have been selected to demonstrate this point in Figure 5-7.

Use of Creative Problem Solving in the Curriculum

As teachers make a concerted effort to use creative problem solving as a strategy with gifted students, they are amazed at its versatility. In art, ideation can be brought into play by having gifted students respond to simple squiggles as stimulus pictures or by creating class or school logos. In mathematics, gifted students can

Subject areas	Problem solving abilities	Problem definition	Preparation	Ideation	Criteria selection	Evaluation	Implementation
Art							
Math							
Health							
Language arts							
Music							
Social studies							
Physical education							

FIGURE 5-7
Problem-solving matrix. (*D. Shallcross,* Teaching Creative Behavior, *Bearly Limited, Buffalo, New York, 1985. Reprinted by permission.*)

use criteria selection and evaluation to select the viable solutions for social studies projects and engage in interdisciplinary work. In science, gifted students can apply the problem-solving process to social problems and environmental concerns. In social studies, gifted students can brainstorm topics such as the world's most important problem. A group of gifted eighth-grade students did brainstorm this question and selected the lack of communication among people as the most important problem.

In health, gifted students can apply the problem-solving process to combatting pollution. In music, they can create original music from simple stimuli, such as three notes. Lastly, in language arts, gifted students can view films without sound and write original dialogue. Teachers can create other applications of the creative problem-solving process based on their own students' interests and curriculum.

Application of the Principles for a Differentiated Curriculum for Gifted to Creative Problem Solving

Creative problem solving develops productive, complex, abstract, and higher level thinking skills (Principle 6), and encourages gifted students to focus on open-ended tasks (Principle 7). By working on various problems, gifted students develop products which challenge existing ideas and produce new ones (Principle 10). Another principle that creative problem solving addresses is the development of products that use new techniques, materials, and forms (Principle 11). With the heavy emphasis on evaluation in the five-step process, the gifted become more adept in using criteria to judge their own outcomes (Principle 13).

SIMULATION

Simulation is a strategy which uses high affective involvement and stimulates cognitive development. It does this because of its close resemblance to play. Simulation is used widely in business and government to approximate real-life situations; it develops forecasting and predicting skills. Maker (1982) reports the essential elements in the use of simulation to be: (1) a contrived, structured, or simulated group interaction situation; (2) honest feedback from other participants regarding one's own behavior; and (3) honest self-analysis or critique by each participant.

These characteristics describe simulation activities for gifted students. First, a simulation activity must have a clear focus on specific concepts and processes. By focusing the activity on a clear teaching purpose, it becomes a teaching strategy and not merely a game. Second, the simulation has a basis in reality and involves the essential elements of the social process depicted in the game. Third, the simulation activity involves the dramatic qualities of a game, i.e., there must be an understandable way of scoring points that ensures a process of winning and losing.

The element of winning and losing increases competitiveness in a group of gifted students. This competition motivates cooperation because most simulation activities can only be won if team members work well together.

To enable the process of winning and losing to take place, a number of types of rules exist in simulation activities. The first type is *procedural rules* which tell how the activity is to be played. *Mediational rules* specify how an impasse or conflict is to be resolved. *Rules of behavioral constraint* tell what one player can do and the role specifications for each player. Still another type are *goal rules* which clearly delineate the goals and means for achieving them. Finally, the *police rules* specify the consequences to a player's breaking the rules.

Many types of simulation activities are available commercially. One of the organizations which produces simulation activities is Project Simile at the Western Behavior Science Institute in La Jolla, California. Many simulations are also available through Science Research Associates. A particularly good source is Horn and Cleaves' (1980) *Guide to Simulations/Games for Education and Training*. This guide has over fifty games and simulations which are useful in social studies.

Most simulations can be accomplished effectively in short periods of time, while some may continue over a period of days or even weeks, as more information is gathered and more experiences are shared. One teacher of the gifted uses a simulation based on the legislative process over a period of a semester with a group of eighth-grade gifted students.

Simulation activities can be developed by teachers using a planning format such as that of Reid in *Turn to Page 84* (1961).

Reid suggests that the first step in devising an original simulation activity is to decide on a concise statement of a situation or problem, i.e., a communicable disease has broken out in a small town. The next step is to decide on the objectives of the simulation. The objectives are (1) The students will learn the process of group dynamics through reaching a consensus, (2) the students will develop insight into their own personal value system and that of others, and (3) the students will explore various methods of decision making.

Once the objectives are selected, a scenario or summary is written that includes past events, background information, the present time and setting, and the conditions that will affect the activity. For example, a scenario might state that the community is multiethnic and comparatively isolated. It is midwinter and the decision on what to do about the communicable disease must be made within 24 hours.

Next, the characters are identified such as: doctors, nurses, parents, teachers, principals, and students. Each character is given a brief role description, since one of the important elements of simulation is stimulating personal creativity in gifted students. The role descriptions give some directions—e.g., the doctor is the only one who knows how the cure must be utilized, or, the panel of citizens is made up of two nurses who are against the serum and two who are essentially unbiased—but they leave open the opportunity for the gifted student to develop the character to its fullest.

Following the establishment of the characters and their goals, an exact time is given for the beginning of the simulation. Reid suggests that resources be included to give the activity greater complexity. The resources may be physical, social, economic, political, or personal. Resources for this hypothetical simulation could be maps of the contaminated area, pads and pencils for the nurses, and bottles of colored water to simulate serum. Gifted students should be encouraged to use their imagination and ingenuity in securing needed props.

Rules and their administration are the last to be developed in a game format and include rules to govern players, the game pattern, and the scoring. In the case of the communicable disease simulation, perhaps a number of people (fifteen) have been exposed to the disease and there is serum for eight. How decisions are made to save these eight people and sacrifice the lives of seven others is a crucial dilemma. Each person is assigned a role on the advisory panel and given a certain number of points. Consensus is required to make decisions, and a time constraint of 1 hour may be added to allow the simulation to be accomplished in a class period.

The last and most important area in devising a simulation is the evaluation and feedback phase, sometimes referred to as processing. During processing, the teacher and students discuss how decisions were made and how individual members feel about these decisions. The teacher can reinforce positive social attitudes and arrange supplemental experiences to reinforce understandings gained in the simulation. The teacher can also make relationships or connections between the simulation and present, past, and future situations. The processing or debriefing should occupy at least one-fourth as much time as allotted to the simulation; it is essential to make connections between the simulation and the cognitive and affective growth of the gifted students.

Simulation motivates gifted students because it builds on their curiosity and keen sense of observation. It affords them opportunities to use their inquiry skills and their problem-solving abilities, as well using self-criticism, reflection, and value development.

Exhibit 5-1 shows the format for designing simulations according to Reid (1961).

An example of a simulation using the Reid format is "Uphill Controversy" (Table 5-4) which was developed by Gilbert (1970). This simulation is appropriate for upper elementary or middle school gifted students and represents a simulation in its initial stage of development.

From the initial stage of the development of Uphill Controversy, a simulation can be further developed as illustrated by Election of a President in Appendix B. Note this simulation has been divided into phases enabling the classroom time to be tightly planned and more efficiently used. Evaluation and feedback is provided each time the students experience the activity.

"Reality-based activity" is the crucial attribute in simulations. Gifted students who experience Election of a President learn the dynamics of selecting a president

---

EXHIBIT 5-1

DESIGN YOUR OWN

Name of the game ⎯⎯⎯⎯⎯⎯⎯⎯⎯⎯⎯⎯⎯⎯⎯⎯⎯⎯⎯⎯⎯⎯⎯⎯⎯⎯

Statement of the problem: ⎯⎯⎯⎯⎯⎯⎯⎯⎯⎯⎯⎯⎯⎯⎯⎯⎯⎯⎯⎯⎯⎯

Objectives of the game: ⎯⎯⎯⎯⎯⎯⎯⎯⎯⎯⎯⎯⎯⎯⎯⎯⎯⎯⎯⎯⎯⎯⎯

Scenario: Include past events, background information, the present time and setting, the conditions that may affect the game.

Characters and their goals: Give brief description of the physical characteristics, the personality, and the player's goals for the game.

A point in time: The exact place and time when the game begins.

Resources: Props for the game—physical, social, economic, political, or personal.

Rules and their administration: To govern players, the game pattern and scoring, and how they are implemented.

Evaluation and feedback: Were objectives reached? Can the game be improved?

TABLE 5-4
EXAMPLE OF A REID FORMAT SIMULATION

Aspect of game	Description
Name	*Uphill Controversy*
Objectives	To gain insight into how a school system is organized, why changes are made, and who makes the decisions
Scene	Elementary school built in 1920 (fine reputation, dwindling numbers). Many families have lived in neighborhood for 20 years
Characters	Board of Education members, teachers, children, county financial advisers, and parents
Point in Time	Press release: a decision concerning possible closure of Uphill school is to be made in 3 days, and a PTA meeting is called to discuss the issue
Resources	(1) Maps showing high school attendance area, (2) location of other elementary schools and the number of students in each, and (3) state and county transportation guidelines
Rules	Each group will meet to prepare arguments for or against school closure. One member of the group may go to another to try to form coalitions. Any number of group members may align themselves with another group, although the leader and the recorder must stay in original group
	Each group will present their proposal before the Board of Education. The Board will meet and vote on a decision. The Board will vote for the group whose proposal was most convincing. Group receiving most votes is declared the winner.
Evaluation and feedback	

Used by permission, Gilbert, P., 1970.

and what it entails to be a candidate. Upper elementary and secondary gifted students can profit from Election of a President.

Clark (1983) cautions teachers to remember that simulation activities may become emotion-laden experiences. For this reason, the teacher must be alert to perceive when to stop a simulation for a debriefing process, if necessary. Good judgment must be used in simulation, just as it must be used in any teaching activity. The teacher remains responsible for the pacing of the activities as well as for the decision of when to begin and end.

A resource for simulations is Stanford and Stanford (1969). They report on such classics as Lost on the Moon: A Decision Making Exercise in Survival and Murder Mystery (Murder Mystery, for short). In Murder Mystery, for example, participants simulate a crime-solving group. They solve the mystery by sharing clues, but this can only be done orally. Through Murder Mystery, much can be learned about problem-solving abilities and group dynamics by gifted students and their teachers.

Application of the Principles of A Differentiated Curriculum for the Gifted to Simulation

Simulation presents content which is related to broad-based issues or themes (Principle 7) and calls for higher level thinking skills (Principle 6) as gifted students are engaged in decision making, communication, persuasion, and critical thinking. Simulation encourages the development of self-understanding and the understanding of others as well (Principle 12), and it encourages gifted students to be involved in self-directed inquiry (Principle 5). Simulation is highly motivating, and gifted students may want to pursue the topic independently in greater depth.

FUTURISTICS

The study of futuristics is increasingly becoming a topic of interest for teachers. The reason behind this interest in futuristics has been expressed in a number of ways, but the primary reason teachers are turning toward futuristics appears to be the fact that today's students will spend most of their lives in the next century and teachers want to prepare them for the future. Kauffman (1976) states that 11,000 teachers reported teaching units on futuristics. The Center for Creativity, Innovation, and Leadership Development reports sending out more than 2000 inquiries on futuristics in 1984 (Drew, 1984). Still another way to gauge the interest in futuristics is to note the growing number of state, national, and international conferences with single presentations, workshops, or entire meetings on the theme of "the future."

The importance of teaching with a futuristic point of view is essential if gifted students are to use their ability to help create the future. Toffler (1981), one of the leading futurists in the United States, stated that students need help in relating the changes that will take place in the world to the changes in their own lives. He found that high school students could readily identify numerous changes that would take place in the future, but when asked to list seven events in their personal futures, their responses indicated an unchanged life. Furthermore, Toffler reported a gulf between students' perceptions of rapid change in the environment and their understanding that these changes also affect their personal lives.

The approach in utilizing futuristics with gifted students is somewhat different from that used by many teachers in the regular classroom, in that the teaching of futuristics is viewed as the adoption of a teaching philosophy which utilizes a futuristic point of view. This enhances the learning of all subjects. If futuristics is taught as a single unit or topic or as a one-exposure experience, it does not allow immersion in futuristic thinking. Futuristics emphasizes forecasting and seeing the world's problems in relation to long-term objectives. One way to visualize the total immersion process is to think of a time line:

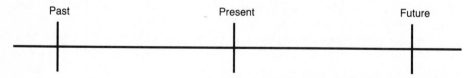

In using a time line, teachers introduce concepts such as humankind seeking immortality and challenging the gods. Information is introduced on the Egyptian practice of embalming the dead to prepare for another life and the building of pyramids to challenge the gods (past). With quick reference points, teachers can ask students to relate humankind's need for immortality and for challenging the gods today (present). As gifted students identify examples such as scientific progress in rocketry and the practice of cryogenics, teachers may add the point that Walt Disney has chosen to be encapsulated in liquid nitrogen to be revived in the future when there is a cure for his illness.

One teacher using the time line with gifted students asked them "What will humankind do to seek immortality in the future?" (future). After several thoughtful moments, the sixth-grade gifted students responded: (1) live in a spirit form, (2) use interchangable body forms, and (3) use biogenetics to live forever. In response to the question "How did man go about seeking immortality?" they replied "by creating new artificial worlds in space, and by duplicating these worlds on other planets."

Through discussions such as these, the time line becomes a vital method identifying connections between past, present, and future information.

Specific goals for teaching with a futuristic point of view are:

1 To provide students with better, more sophisticated, and more positive ways of thinking about the future

2 To provide students with skills and concepts necessary to understand complex systems

3 To help students identify and understand many of the major issues which will shape the future

4 To help students understand change and to cope with it (Sisk, 1982)

One statewide secondary school program, the Governor's Honors Summer Program used the theme "Humanity's Role in Shaping Tomorrow." The objectives for the program relate well to the previously listed goals. They are reported in the outcomes observed in students:

Generate many alternative futures

See themselves as actors with respect to their futures, rather than as passive acceptors of the future

Develop short- and long-term goals

Understand various methods of forecasting future events

Clarify personal value systems and be inclined to generate preferable futures for themselves and the world

Perceive themselves as world citizens

Recognize the forces and trends which are shaping our future

Recognize and understand the effects of accelerated change and discover ways of dealing with these effects

Appreciate and further develop skills needed by citizens of the future, which will include: fluency, open-ended thinking, divergent thinking, creative problem solving, flexibility of thought, genuineness, risk taking, originality of thought, choice discrimination decision making, and integrating information and ideas from a variety of sources (Sisk, 1982).

These objectives were modified from Kauffman's *Teaching the Future* (1976), which is available from the National Education Association.

Specific classroom assignments and activities of the gifted students were: (1) writing about utopias or descriptions of the ideal world; (2) planning a model community; (3) writing scenarios for future developments in Antarctica, Greenland, and other remote areas; (4) assessing the impact of introducing a given technology to today's world; and (5) trying to agree on the world's most urgent problems and brainstorming various possible solutions.

Specific Skills to Employ

Scenario writing is used by futurists in idea tanks or research and development institutes and can be used as a skill in teaching with a futuristic point of view. Scenario writing is both a research tool and a creative thinking skill. When introduced this way, gifted students view the tool as a legitimate device to use in thinking about the future, rather than a creative writing exercise. One way to stimulate gifted students to write scenarios is to use scenario starters. Several scenario starters are given below.

> As I was working as an auto-robot, I was assigned a new work location in AS188. I rolled into the cubicle which was to be my habitat for the 196 megatrons and my wheels became entangled in the shag carpeting. I began to probe my memory bank for ideas on how to disengage from this obstacle. By this time, the grotesque little creatures began to appear, each one with their own incredible EEG. So I quickly pushed my cinap (panic) button which projected me into the next megatron where my scanning device picked up impending doom. . . .

Students enjoy working out the next scenes either individually or in small groups. A scenario starter on future leisure time follows.

> Having a 3-day work week, I find myself in an emotional turmoil because of a lack of enjoyable, self-starting, leisure-time activities. Therefore, my task is to find and establish some productive, useful way to spend my hours. Robots have done much of the housework; computers have done most of the work, so. . . .

And lastly, a scenario starter on the future:

> Mother hooked my transporter pod to the hovercraft. I was pulled along and deposited with other pods at the Central Learning Station. All I could see, as I looked around, were the sleek, shining sides of the steel dome. Hundreds of little children were heading toward the dome. As they were donning their learning suits, they were elevated to their individuals cubicles with flashing lights and rows of colored buttons. I reached out to push a button. . . .

Future Wheels is another activity essential to a total futurist approach. Future Wheels was developed by a Washington, D.C., futurist, Jerry Glenn. The idea is to identify an existing or emerging trend and to place this trend in a hub or center, and then identify cause-and-effect relationships which may come about as a result of the trend.

For example, if the trend is biogenetic engineering, the future wheel would resemble Figure 5-8.

As students experience the future wheel, they perceive that trends interact and affect one another. Gifted students can choose aspects of the wheel to discuss and conduct individual or small group research. For example, one group of gifted students examined the idea of a super race emerging and traced that notion from the past to today using early Germanic fables and projected them to the future. Another group chose the trend of changing morality, interviewing different religious groups to note their points of view and hypothesizing what the new morality might involve.

Trending is another useful technique that complements future wheels. Trending uses questions such as the following to define and describe the trend:

1 When did this trend begin?
2 Upon whom does this trend have a positive effect?
3 Upon whom does this trend have a negative effect?
4 Does this trend interact with any other trends? If so, which ones?
5 If we were to escalate this trend, how might we do it?

FIGURE 5-8
Futures wheel.

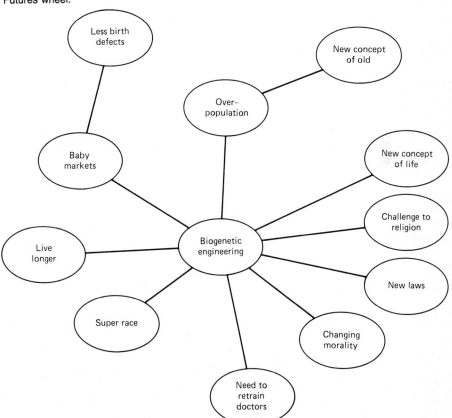

6 If we were to slow this trend down or halt it completely, how might we go about it?

7 Are there special interest groups that this trend affects?

Naisbitt's *Megatrends* (1982) makes predictions for tomorrow based on an analysis of what America is today. He lists ten directions (megatrends) that transform our lives and should be examined by gifted students.

1 *Industrial society* is moving toward *information society*.
2 *Forced technology* is moving toward *high tech/high touch*.
3 *National economy* is moving toward *world economy*.
4 *Short-term point of view* is moving toward a *long-term point of view*.
5 *Centralization* is changing toward *decentralization*.
6 *Institutional help* is moving toward *self-help*.
7 *Representative democracy* is moving toward *participatory democracy*.
8 *Hierarchies* are being replaced by *networking*.
9 North-to-south shift in population.
10 *Either/or* concept is changing to *multiple option*.

Naisbitt's trends provide gifted students opportunities to examine the restructuring of society. Most people describe the United States as an industrial society, but Naisbitt and other futurists believe that the economy has created an information society. We are, Naisbitt says, moving in a dual direction of high technology–high touch, in which there is an attempt to match technology with compensatory human responses. Naisbitt states that nations cannot continue to view themselves as isolated and self-sufficient but must view themselves as part of a global economy. Painful as it is for us to admit, the United States may not be the industrial leader in the future. This trend complements the idea of the moving from short-term considerations and rewards to long-term time frames.

In large corporations, in small organizations, and in most institutions, the ability to act innovatively and the notion of starting things from the bottom up is being rediscovered. This trend is an exciting one for gifted students to experience. It interacts with the trend of moving toward self-help and away from institutional help. It can be noted among women who want to give birth at home and among terminally ill who choose to die in their own beds. This trend in self-help is accompanied by the trend of representative democracy to become obsolete and for a new, more participatory democracy to emerge. Companion to this trend is the need to network informally and receive information on a shared basis rather than to receive it hierarchically.

Lastly, as many people leave the north and move to the south and the west and as the range of choices increases, the next decade promises to be an exciting one.

For too long educators have dwelled on the past, given little time to the present, and neglected the future. The importance of the time-line approach is verified by Naisbitt in the following observation. "The most reliable way to anticipate the future is by understanding the present." By using futuristics in the classroom, nothing is lost but boredom. In fact, there is everything to be gained as gifted students predict and forecast the future and become actively involved in planning and creating their futures. A futuristic approach provides emphasis on higher level thinking processes which are essential for gifted students.

Application of the Principles of A Differentiated Curriculum for the Gifted to Futuristics

Through futuristics, gifted students experience a number of the principles, namely, presenting content related to broad-based issues, themes, or problems (Principle 1); integrating multiple disciplines (Principle 2); allowing for in-depth learning (Principle 4); and focusing on open-ended tasks (Principle 7).

The emphasis on futuristics encourages teachers to employ two other principles as well—encouraging the development of products and ideas that challenge existing ideas (Principle 10) and encouraging the development of products that use new techniques, materials, and forms (Principle 11). Lastly, futuristics will greatly aid the encouragement of the development of self-understanding (Principle 12).

SUMMARY

With increased interest in education, teachers are in need of assistance in planning meaningful differentiated curriculum for gifted students. To meet this need, thirteen principles were developed by the LTI Curriculum Council: The rationale behind these principles for a differentiated curriculum is that changes are mandated by the differences in learning, emotional, and social characteristics of gifted students. A differentiated curriculum responds to these needs. The thirteen principles respond to the specific learning characteristics of gifted: the ability to see concepts and relationships easily; the possession of an unusual amount of curiosity and a wide variety of interests; an unusual degree of sensitivity; the ability to demonstrate task commitment, the ability to work until satisfied; and the ability to learn more quickly and easily.

Selected strategies included compacting, research study skills, listening skills, time management, use of questioning, inquiry, creative problem solving, simulation, and futuristics. These were discussed and the thirteen principles from the LTI were applied to each of the strategies or teaching techniques.

Compacting was discussed as a means of relieving gifted students from boredom resulting from review of work in basic skill areas which they have mastered. The two essential ingredients for compacting success are careful diagnosis and an overall picture of the material to be covered, including content and objectives.

Research and study skills, listening skills, and time management were covered as skills that gifted students must master to be more self-directed and to achieve their potential.

The use of questioning was also identified as a strategy for teachers to stimulate higher levels of thinking in gifted students. Two models, those of Bloom and Taba, illustrated this strategy.

Inquiry was introduced as a strategy and the work of Suchman was stressed to illustrate the inquiry session. The strategy of creative problem solving followed inquiry as another form of problem solving. The five-step method of Parnes was discussed and compared to the theories of Bruner and Guilford.

Simulation as a natural form of learning was covered and several examples of simulation games were noted, as well as a format for teachers to use in creating their own simulation games.

The last topic was futuristics. The emphasis in this section was on encouraging teachers to teach with a futuristic point of view, thus providing gifted students opportunities to experience learning in an integrated fashion. Several specific skills, such as future wheels and trending, were discussed.

EXTENDING ACTIVITIES

1 Select a unit of study and note the objectives for the particular unit. Create specific questions that can be used to measure a gifted student's performance on individual objectives.
2 Write the words given by the time management expert on a piece of paper and read the set beginning "Strike" to yourself each morning for a week. Note any differences in your attitude.
3 Set up an independent study using attending skills with one of your professors and see if there is any change in his/her behavior.
4 Select a topic of study such as electricity and list questions using the Bloom taxonomy. Be sure to use each level.
5 Create an experiment that could be used for an inquiry session. Remember to use dissonant events.
6 Select an object and brainstorm the various uses for that item for 5 minutes. Using the SCAMPER technique, brainstorm once again. Note any differences in your score.
7 Create a simulation game using a futuristic theme. Remember to use the format suggested in the section on simulation.

REFERENCES

American Psychological Association. *Publication manual: 2d edition*, 1984. Washington, DC: American Psychological Association.

Bloom, B. S. (1956). *Taxonomy of educational objectives. Handbook I: Cognitive domain*. New York: David McKay.

Bolton, R. (1982). *People skills*. Englewood Cliffs, NJ: Prentice-Hall.

Boyer, E. L. (1983). *High school: A report on secondary education in America*. Carnegie Foundation for the Advancement of Teaching. New York: Harper & Row.

The University of Chicago Press (1969). *A manual of style, 12th edition*. Chicago: The University of Chicago Press.

Clark, B. (1983). *Growing up gifted*. Columbus, OH: Charles E. Merrill.

Douglas, M. & Douglas, D. (1980). *Manage your time, manage your work, manage yourself*. New York: AMACOM Col, VIII.

Drew, J. (1984). *Governor's honors summer evaluation report*, Tampa: University of South Florida. Unpublished.

Dunn, R. & Price, G. (1980). The learning style characteristics of gifted students. *Gifted Child Quarterly*, 24, 33–36.

Durden, W. G. (1983). *Computers for the gifted at home and school.* Presentation at G/C/T Directors, Mobile, Alabama, February 4.

Gilbert, P. (1970). *Uphill controversy.* Simulation game developed in Charleston West Virginia Workshop on Gifted.

Goodlad, J. (1984). *A place called school.* New York: McGraw-Hill.

Horn, R. E. & Cleaves, A. (1980). *The guide to simulations/games for education and training.* Beverly Hills, CA: Sage.

Ivey, A. & Hinkle, J. (1970). *The transactional classroom.* Unpublished manuscript, University of Massachusetts.

Kaplan, S. N. (1979). *Inservice training manual: Activities for developing curriculum for the gifted and talented.* Ventura, CA: Office of the Ventura County Superintendent of Schools.

Kaplan, S. N. (1980). *Educating the pre-school/primary gifted and talented.* Ventura, CA: Office of the Ventura County Superintendent of Schools.

Kauffman, D. (1976). *Teaching the future: A guide to future-oriented education.* Palm Springs, CA: ETC Publications.

Krathwohl, D. R., Bloom, B. S. & Masia, B. B. (1964). *Taxonomy of educational objectives: The classification of educational goals. Handbook 2: Affective domain.* New York: David McKay.

Maker, C. J. (1982). *Teaching models in the education of the gifted.* Rockville, MD: Aspen.

Naisbitt, J. (1983). *Megatrends: New directions transforming our lives.* New York: Warner Books.

National Commission on Excellence in Education (1983). *A nation at risk: The imperative for educational reform.* Report to the nation and the Secretary of Education. United States Department of Education. Washington. DC: U.S. Government Printing Office.

Osborn, A. (1963). *Applied imagination, 3d edition.* New York: Scribners.

Parnes, S. (1975). *Aha: Insights into creative behavior.* Buffalo, NY: The Creative Education Foundation.

Parnes, S. (1972). *Creativity: Unlocking human potential.* Buffalo, NY: D.O.K. Publishers.

Reid, A. (1961). *Turn to page 84.* Unpublished paper. Glencoe, MN.

Renzulli, J. S. (1977). *The enrichment triad model: A guide for developing defensible programs for the gifted and talented.* Weltersford, CT: Creative Learning Press.

Renzulli, J. S. & Smith, L. H. (1980). An alternative approach to identifying and programming for gifted and talented students. *Gifted/Creative/Talented, 15,* 4–11.

Question construction wheel (1975). Garden Grove Unified School District, Garden Grove, CA.

Sanders, N. (1966). *Classroom questions: What kinds.* New York: Harper & Row.

Shallcross, D. (1981). *Teaching creative behavior.* Englewood Cliffs, NJ: Prentice-Hall.

Sisk, D. (1975, 1983). *Teaching gifted children.* Developed in conjunction with a Federal Grant from Title U, Section 505 (Florida).

Sisk, D. (1982, 1985). *Governor's honors summer evaluation report.* Report to the State of Florida, Tallahassee.

Sizer, T. R. (1984). *Horace's compromise: The dilemma of the American high school.* The first report from a study of high schools co-sponsored by the National Association of Secondary School Principals and the Commission on Educational Issues of the National Association of Independent Schools. Boston: Houghton Mifflin.

Stanford, B. & Stanford, G. (1969). *Learning Discussion Skills Through Games.* Citation Press, 1969.

Stanley, J. C. (1976). Use of tests to discover talent. In D. P. Keating (Ed.), *Intellectual Talent: Research and Development.* Baltimore, MD: Johns Hopkins University.

Stanley, J. (1984). The exceptionally talented. *The Roeper Review*, February, 160.

Strunk, W., Jr. & White, E. B. (1979). *The elements of style, 3d edition*. New York: Macmillan.

Suchman, J. R. (1961). Inquiry training: Building skills for autonomous discovery. *Merrill Palmer Quarterly, 7*, 147–69.

Taba, H. (1963). Learning by discovery: psychological and educational rationale. *Elementary School Journal, 63*, 308–316.

Taba, H. & Elzey, F. (1964). Teaching strategies and thought process. *Teachers College Record, 65*, 524–34.

Taba, H., Durkin, M. C., Fraenkel, J. R. & McNaughton, A. H. (1971). *A teacher's handbook for elementary social studies: An inductive approach*. Reading, MA: Addison-Wellsey.

Toffler, A. (1981). *Third wave*. New York: Bantam.

Twentieth Century Fund, Task Force on Federal Elementary and Secondary Policy (1983). *Making the grade: A report*. New York: The Fund.

Von Til, W. (1981). *Writing for professional publications*. Boston: Allyn and Bacon.

CHAPTER 6

SCIENCE AND MATHEMATICS FOR THE GIFTED

CHAPTER 6

SCIENCE AND MATHEMATICS FOR THE GIFTED

If I have been able to see farther than others, it was because I stood on the shoulders of giants.

Sir Isaac Newton

I believe in intuition and inspiration; at times I feel certain I am right while not knowing the reason.

Albert Einstein

Few people challenge the notion that highly technological cultures must be supported with educational systems in which science and mathematics are emphasized. However, it is unique for school districts to provide ongoing science and mathematics curriculum in which gifted students are being appropriately challenged. Such programs do exist in specific school districts, and there is a growing sense of urgency in American education to address the problem of meeting the needs of the gifted in specific academic areas. Yet, many forces hinder a systematic approach to addressing this problem. Part of the problem is confusion over the needs for such programs as well as the state of the art in science and mathematics education. This chapter addresses identifying gifted students in science and mathematics, those students' special characteristics, and the role of the teacher as facilitator. Organizing strands for science and mathematics programs for gifted students are discussed, and the unique problem of the mathematically gifted girl

Photograph on opposite page courtesy of Elizabeth Crews, Berkeley, California.

is explored. The last topic in the chapter is suggestions for instruction. The central theme of this chapter is that science and mathematics are crucial to the education of the gifted and that new programs are being developed but that continued efforts are needed.

Most intellectually gifted students enjoy science, as studying it challenges their insatiable curiosity. Elementary and middle school gifted students are fascinated by laboratory equipment, and science instruction can be exciting as students learn about the products of science. More importantly, gifted students need to learn to search for truth, and science can aid in this search. Exciting discussions take place in science education as students talk about the supersonic airplane, nuclear energy, DNA, biogenetic engineering, the use of artificial hearts, and implants of animal organs in humans. Through lively discussions, gifted students recognize and value how national policy and ordinary day-to-day life are affected by scientific decisions.

STATE OF THE ART IN SCIENCE EDUCATION

The scientific and engineering communities are exploring ways to maintain the vigor of research and technological innovation in the United States. In the course of discussions, several problems emerge, and one is the state of the art in science education. The facts about the "Quantity of Science and Mathematics in the Education of Pre-college Students" (Hurd, 1983), as shown in Exhibit 6-1, are useful background information on science education and the need for continued reform for all students, including the gifted. One of the essential problems is the identification of students with scientific aptitude.

EXHIBIT 6-1

FACTS

Quantity of science and mathematics in the education of pre-college students
- Science enrollments in high schools have been decreasing, and students are unmotivated to study science
- Students are taking more semesters of mathematics but show an overall decline in achievement
- Students receive 44 minutes per day of math and 20 minutes per day in science (grades 1 to 5)
- In grades 7 to 9 all students take general math and general science
- Two-thirds of ninth graders enroll in algebra and a specialized earth, physical, or life science
- Out of 3 million seniors in 1980, 93 percent took 1 year of math, 67 percent took 2 years of math, and 34 percent took 3 years of math
- Only 54 percent of the 21,000 high schools in the 1980 study taught trigonometry
- Asian-Americans take more science and math than whites
- Males take more science and math than girls, except for algebra 1

Identifying the Gifted in Science

Early identification of students with scientific aptitude is advocated, but it means different things to different educators. When Brandwein (1981) and Bloom (1955) suggest early identification of scientific talent, they are speaking about ninth and tenth grade level (ages 13 to 15) students. Other researchers advocate early identification, but they are speaking about interest and self-selection, rather than high scores on tests such as those used to identify gifted students in science at the secondary and middle school level.

One point that needs to be made early on in the discussion of specific academic aptitude in mathematics, science, or other content areas is that students of high general intellectual ability may not always demonstrate high specific academic aptitude in every area. Educators must select the appropriate educational program for the type of giftedness being served. Callahan (1985) states that the relationship between intellectual ability and science aptitude may best be considered a relationship of intersecting sets. An examination of admissions and selection criteria indicates a variety of standards. Most elementary schools use either general intellectual ability and interest or general intellectual ability, interest, and achievement. However, at the middle school and senior high levels, the admissions and selection criteria often depend on the objectives of the program. For example, the Bronx High School of Science (BHSS), one of the nation's best-known specialized high schools, has as its major objective the identification of highly motivated students who will conduct original, independent research. Consequently, the students are screened by both verbal and mathematics segments. This selection process identifies students with high achievement and aptitude in science and mathematics and with laboratory ability through examinations and direct observation.

Another specialized school is the North Carolina School for Science and Mathematics (NCSSM). This school was established in 1978 by Governor James B. Hunt and opened in the fall of 1980 with 150 gifted students in the eleventh grade. NCSSM is highly selective in its admissions policy. The school uses multiple criteria to screen students, including standardized tests, personal recommendations, writing samples, and out-of-class participation in science fairs and other projects. An idea of the caliber of the school's students can be surmised from Brown (1983) who reported that the 1983 class of freshman had median SAT scores of 520 (verbal) and 600 (quantitative).

Scientific aptitude, according to Stanley (1976), consists of reasoning about events in which the student generates inferences and then tests them for possible verification.

Some investigators are convinced that science talent is not a single trait but an aspect of high general intelligence which emerges through environmental stimulation and available opportunities for development (Gold, 1982). Others believe that such a trait or traits exist, but they disagree as to its components. These components may include the following: sensitivity to problems, ability to develop novel ideas, and the ability to evaluate (Guilford, 1950); specialized and persistent curiosity, alertness in detecting inconsistencies, and a high degree of mechanical-mindedness (Subarsky, 1948); industry, devotion to work, energy, and initiative (Cole, 1956); spatial visualization, manipulative ability, and ability to communicate (Super & Bacrach, 1957); and persistence and questioning (Brandwein, 1981).

Roe (1956, 1961) studied the personality and intellect of successful scientists and found the most striking characteristics to be high IQ, general need for independence, autonomy, and personal mastery of the environment; attraction to the facts that appear mutually contradictory; delight in finding a way to reconcile them; and precocious self-confidence about solving intellectual problems.

Renzulli (1979) also examined the literature and concluded that giftedness is characterized by interaction among three traits: above-average ability, creativity, and task commitment. Callahan (1985) states that these three clusters are crucial to a final definition of the scientifically gifted, in that a student with great commitment and interest in science but with little aptitude or creativity is unlikely to be a gifted scientist. The three traits must be brought to bear on some potentially valuable human endeavor in science for the talent to manifest itself.

Teacher as Facilitator in Science

A survey by Scobee and Nash (1983) polled eighty highly successful space scientists who stated that teachers who were willing to challenge students to think for themselves (i.e., to provide activities directed toward problem solving or scientific investigations) were very instrumental in their success. Other aspects of an effective program that were identified were opportunities to hear experts in the field; interaction with peers with the same or better mental ability; opportunity to have a mentor; hands-on experiences with scientific equipment; and opportunities to learn about interrelation among the disciplines of science and/or the humanities.

"Most important science is doing, not reading about, not looking at, not replicating someone else's discoveries," states Roufberg (1984). She describes the role of the teacher as a facilitator who helps the student work like a scientist: questioning, observing, analyzing, testing, and, finally, answering.

Sellin and Birch (1980) list four special roles of the teacher who instructs gifted students in science: model, values educator, interest booster, and functional assessor. As a model of scientific method, the teacher demonstrates his/her curiosity and skill. As a values educator, the teacher encourages gifted students to openly explore the vital issues in science. As an interest booster, the teacher of the gifted stimulates initial interest and expands it. In the functional assessor role, the teacher takes note of the speed and fullness of the gifted students' comprehension, their learning style and preference of mode of instruction (lecture, discussion, or learning center), and their overall comprehension. Lastly, it is most important for the teacher to give gifted students feedback on their functioning or performance levels to enable their growth as potential scientists.

One of the essential roles of the teacher as facilitator in science is to guide independent study. The following ten steps are modified from the Renzulli Triad (Renzulli, 1979) and should prove helpful:

1 Assess student interest
2 Expose students to numerous interest areas
3 Conduct personal interviews
4 Develop a written plan
5 Determine direction and timeline with the gifted student
6 Assist the student in locating multiple resources
7 Brainstorm final product
8 Provide necessary methodological assistance
9 Help the gifted student identify the audience for her/his findings
10 Evaluate the course of study with the gifted student and assess new areas for study.

RECOMMENDATIONS AND SUGGESTIONS FOR SCHOOLS

Organizing Strands for Science for the Gifted

In a summer workshop on gifted education, teachers identified skills or strands of activities that gifted students in science should pursue:

1 Building a background of scientific information through reading and interpreting scientific writing
2 Locating authoritative sources of scientific information
3 Carrying out experiments for testing ideas and hypotheses
4 Mastering and using the techniques and tools of science
5 Selecting pertinent and adequate data
6 Making valid inferences and predictions from data
7 Recognizing and evaluating assumptions underlying techniques and processes used in solving problems
8 Expressing ideas both quantitatively and qualitatively
9 Using and applying the scientific knowledge for social change
10 Forming new relationships and ideas from known facts and concepts (Sisk, 1984)

Callahan (1985) lists ten organizing concepts for science for the gifted which are complementary and translate well into goals. They are:

- The process of formulating scientific questions
- Methods of scientific inquiry
- The structure of the disciplines of science
- The interrelationship between the sciences and other disciplines
- The history of science
- The use of intuition in science
- The use of inductive and deductive reasoning in scientific problem solving
- The language of science

Scientifically Gifted Girls: A Special Challenge

The question of what can be done to encourage young gifted girls to work up to their level of ability was recently addressed in a program called *Action Science*. It had three unique features: (1) Only girls could attend the program; the groups of twenty-five girls were divided by grade, first through third or fourth through sixth; (2) the program was taught only by women who were working scientists committed to their fields of study; and (3) at least one parent or adult was to attend the program with his/her daughter.

In project *Action Science*, the girls were exposed to sophisticated scientific equipment; they were encouraged to use their own judgment and to develop independence in decision making. It was found that girls rely more than boys on the judgment of an adult or peer to answer questions or to validate whether or not something is correct.

Parents and teachers need to stress self-reliance, independence, and decision making in girls who demonstrate giftedness in science. Another possible option is to provide a conference for young girls gifted in science to motivate them to pursue advanced math and science courses. A handbook for planners of conferences like this is *Expanding Your Horizons in Science and Mathematics* (Reis & Rand, 1983).

Administrative Arrangements for the Scientifically Gifted

Several administrative plans accommodate the needs of gifted students in science. Extended experiences and an enriched science curriculum provide additional exposure, as well as special grouping in extra classes and special schools. Acceleration is another means of working with gifted students in science, and many middle and secondary programs move up subject offerings in science at least a year for the scientifically gifted. Some schools offer students a life science as well as a physical science in the seventh grade; an earth science in the eighth grade; biology in the ninth grade; chemistry in the tenth grade; physics at the eleventh-grade level; and advanced courses in astronomy, geology, human physiology, or advanced placement in physics, chemistry, or biology in the twelfth grade. However, one problem with acceleration is that instruction may become textbook oriented with little opportunity for in-depth or student-initiated learning. It takes time to develop complex, abstract, and higher level thinking skills. When teachers concentrate too determinedly on acceleration, topics can become teacher selected and teacher directed.

Two of the more famous special schools in science are the BHSS in New York City and the NCSSM in Durham. Both schools emphasize enrichment and acceleration. At the Bronx High School of Science, gifted students learn with the socratic method, locate problems, and set up independent research. In the eleventh grade, they conduct research under the direction of one teacher or a team of teachers. Every gifted student in the research honors program submits his/her research to the school's science congress, the New York Biology Teacher's Congress, the science fair, and the Westinghouse Science Talent Search. The best of the papers are featured in the student publication *The Journal of Biology*. These activities build pride in the school and in the individual gifted student.

The curriculum at the NCSSM is highly geared to the math and science areas. There are courses in microbiology, astrophysics, calculus, and organic chemistry, as well as many small seminars. NCSSM has a well-developed mentor program in which gifted students work with a variety of professionals in the research triangle (Raleigh, Durham, and Chapel Hill). The focal point of the curriculum is having the students write, analyze, compute, synthesize, and evaluate.

Both of these special schools offer challenging programs for the scientifically gifted. One of the benefits NCSSM offers to North Carolina is the annual summer teacher institute. North Carolina teachers attend the school to learn new and exciting teaching methods to use in their home school. The Bronx High School of Science also holds workshops and disseminates materials to interested educators in New York and other areas. These efforts represent sizeable investments on the part of the state of North Carolina and the city of New York, but the return is highly developed scientific talent in their gifted youth.

Suggestions for Instruction

One of the more frustrating aspects of being a teacher of the gifted is trying to work with one or two gifted students within a regular classroom. Blurton (1983) suggests teacher-made science packets to assist gifted students. A teacher-made science packet could contain the following:

1 An attractive cover with illustrations and a brief synopsis of the unit
2 A list of objectives which includes the content knowledge and process skills to be taught
3 A table of contents
4 A pretest
5 A series of lessons which includes: (1) clear, concise directions, (2) a list of necessary materials, and (3) a structure which incorporates a three-phase learning cycle (exploration, elaboration, and application)
6 A posttest

Teacher-made packets are used to accelerate and enrich gifted students at a particular grade level. Gifted students work on advanced materials and broadened applications in science in the regular classroom while the other students do the regular grade-level work.

Exhibit 6-2 is an example of a student activity model with a different format by King and DeRose (1980).

Suggestions for science instruction usually include a recommendation for special grouping and differentiated science activities. The following lessons (Exhibits 6-3 to 6-7, pp. 135–139) were developed using a format consisting of objectives, tasks, materials, and procedures including verbal, visual, and manipulative activities. The last section is evaluation. The brief lessons can be accomplished in a 55-minute classroom period. They are planned to encourage gifted students to observe closely, to remember, and most of all to become involved in the scientific process.

EXHIBIT 6-2

CHECK IT OUT!
Scientific Method/Stations

Objectives

The student will be able to:
- Describe the properties of an object and record data from these observations in the forms of pictures and measurements
- Demonstrate a method for sorting the objects by their properties
- Construct a simple classification system according to the variations in characteristics
- Construct hypotheses on relative age, use, and owners based on a set of observations and inferences
- Locate information, revise inferences, and draw conclusions based on this research

Directions

Students will investigate a set of objects at five different stations and record their observations and analyses.
Students will respond to the following questions:
- *Observing*—Describe the properties of each object. What is its shape, texture, special features? What material is it made from? Etc.
- *Measuring*—Record the length, width, weight, etc.
- *Other data*—Sketch the object.
- *Classifying*—Identify a property to classify the object (e.g., stone or not stone, tool or not, etc.)
- *Making a hypothesis*—Write a hypothesis, based on your observations, for each of these problems:
    1 What is the relative age of the objects? (number them)
    2 What is the use of each of the objects?
    3 What people or culture used the objects?
- *Testing a hypothesis*—Use books, periodicals, pamphlets, etc., to test the hypotheses. Record your conclusions.
Examples of artifacts in a station:
    Station 1: arrowhead
                  glazed pottery piece
                  1818 coin
                  piece of cannonball
                  Dragoon button
    Station 2: pictures of Ubraid
                  Sumerian, and
                  Babylonian pottery

Source: King and DeRose (1980).

Another example of instruction using enrichment and acceleration was developed in the Cambridge, Massachusetts, public school system. Teachers and school officials searched for suitable models for instruction and found none. They tried ability grouping, special classes, learning centers, and study groups and still didn't have the model for giftedness that suited them. They finally chose one

---

EXHIBIT 6-3

GRADES 4 TO 6
Great Balloon Race

Objectives

Students will:
1 plan and devise a balloon rocket
2 test their rockets and make changes
3 evaluate methods used in constructing a balloon rocket

Tasks

Students will take their existing information on friction, aerodynamics, and relative fields and develop what they believe is the best working model for a rocket balloon.

Materials

String, different sizes and shapes of balloons, straws, masking tape

Procedures

1 Verbal: Lecture on friction, aerodynamics, and rockets.
2 Visual: Demonstrate an actual example.
3 Manipulative: Have them work in small groups devising ideas for their balloon race.

Evaluation

1 Discuss strengths and weaknesses of the different types of rockets.
2 Propose a composite rocket model using all of the strong points brought up in discussion.

Source: B. Buda, J. Kinney, T. Nesman, and I. Nesvimal. Used by permission.

---

called Core-Explore-More. This plan develops the interest and abilities of gifted students in the fourth through sixth grades, by focusing on a number of topics. Each topic has a fifteen- to twenty-page workbook that includes task cards, specific ideas for activities, articles of interest, and a list of available resources. In this way, the gifted are in the "mainstream," and they are provided with a challenging program (Hannigan, 1983).

De Bruin and Schaff (1982) designed and implemented a scientific research program using community-based research laboratories and facilities in Toledo, Ohio. In addition to using laboratory equipment, materials, and supplies, students are advised by scientific personnel including research scientists and laboratory specialists with special research skills and abilities. As a result of this program, gifted students expand their background and understanding of research and work cooperatively with scientists who are actively engaged in research.

For example, a 12-year-old works with a university professor who is studying the effects of vitamin C on protein development in fruit flies. Another gifted student is developing computer programs under the guidance of an engineer at a local community-based research site. Through projects such as this, which foster com-

EXHIBIT 6-4

GRADE 10
Crystal-Growing Lab

Objectives

Students will:
1 apply the principle of crystal growth to discover variables which promote optimum growth
2 cooperate in planning, predicting, and decision making as they grow a crystal of $CuSO_4$

Tasks

1 Develop and test hypothesis for the best crystal growth.
2 Provide suggested procedures for best crystal growth.
3 Identify control and experimental groups.

Materials:

containers, chemicals, thermometer

Procedures:

1 Verbal: Introduction and prelab discussion
2 Visual: Illustrate characteristic shapes of crystals using charts.
3 Visual: Demonstrate the procedure for crystal growth.
4 Manipulative: Students in small groups devise a hypothesis for best crystal growth.
5 Manipulative: Students measure and make up solutions for crystal growth.
6 Manipulative: Students label the control and experimental groups appropriately.

Evaluation

1 Compare crystals with other groups and reach class consensus as to the best technique for crystal growth.

Source: B. Buda, J. Kinney, T. Nesman, and I. Nesvimal. Used by permission.

EXHIBIT 6-5

GRADE 6
It's a Gas

Objectives

Students will:
1 observe the effect of heat and cold on the size of balloon and form their observations, predicting the relationship between temperature and volume
2 observe the effects of pressure on the size of a balloon, a marshmallow, and some shaving cream and from their observations, predict the relationship between pressure and volume
3 apply these relationships to a given problem

Task

1 View demonstrations and derive the relationship between temperature and volume of a gas.
2 View demonstrations and derive relationship between pressure and volume.

EXHIBIT 6-5 *(Continued)*

3 When given a hard-boiled egg (shell removed) and a flask, devise a way to get the egg into and out of the flask without breaking it.

Verbal procedure

Students will:
1 hear a brief introduction to the nature of gasses and a description of temperature, pressure, and volume.
2 be asked to observe the change in volume of a balloon when it is placed in a large container of ice water for about 1 minute. They are then told to observe the change in volume which occurs when it is removed from the ice water.
3 be given a description of the working of the vacuum pump.
4 be asked to observe the effect of pressure change on the volume of a balloon, a marshmallow, and some shaving cream.
5 be asked to remove the shell from a hard-boiled egg they brought from home and place it on top of a flask. They will then be instructed to find a way to get the egg into and out of the flask, without its being broken.

Visual procedure

Observe drawings of gas diagram model on board or overhead projector.

Observe the balloon as it changes volume.

Observe the vacuum pump and its effect on the volume of objects.

Written procedure

Students will:

record their observations and explain why they occur

state the relationship between temperature and volume

state the relationship between pressure and volume

explain why their design worked, in terms of the gas laws

Manipulative procedure

Students will work with egg and flask to get egg in and then out again.

Evaluation procedure

Was their method of entry and exit successful?

Students will demonstrate their method to the class and explain why it worked.

Source: C. Tommello and A. Blosfield. Used by permission.

munication and cooperation, the future needs of gifted science students are being met in a dynamic way.

In Chapter 5, "Curriculum Strategies for the Gifted" the section on inquiry covers the use of discrepant events to teach principles of science. Most of the discrepant events developed by Suchman (1966) are on the elementary level. Wright (1982) lists fifteen simple discrepant events to use with secondary students. He states that they are a good device for stimulating interest in scientific concepts and principles, as well as simple enjoyment.

Several of the discrepant events follow.

EXHIBIT 6-6

GRADE 9

Some Basics of Bases (and Acids)

Objectives

Students will:

predict strong versus weak acid or base by observing their reactions with a conductivity apparatus (a 40-watt light bulb and electrodes)

predict strength of acids and bases based upon color changes of three indicators—purple cabbage juice, grape juice, and hot tea

Given an unknown solution, students will identify it as strong or weak acid or base

Tasks

Observe the intensity of a light bulb's glow when it is placed in several solutions: strong acid, strong base, weak acid, weak base.

Test a number of substances provided. Make a chart of the substances tested, and classify each as a weak or strong acid or base.

Observe the color changes of three indicators—purple cabbage juice, dilute grape juice, and hot tea—with SA, WA, SB, WB.

Given several unknown solutions, determine whether they are SA, WA, SB, WB, based upon previous observations.

Verbal procedure

Receive instructions on the handling of the conductivity apparatus. These include: observing safety techniques, cleaning electrodes between solutions, and ensuring that both electrodes are immersed in each of the solutions to be tested.

Receive preliminary information on the nature of acid/base indicators.

Visual procedure

Demonstrate the use of the conductivity apparatus.

Demonstrate several color changes of common laboratory acid/base indicators.

Written procedure

Study a chart for listing these indicators' conductivity data.

Study a chart for listing their colorimetric observations.

Study a chart for listing their observations and predictions concerning the unknown solutions.

Manipulative procedure

Set up conductivity apparatus and test solutions.

Measure equal amounts of solutions to be tested with the three indicators and test each with an equal amount of an indicator.

Evaluation procedure

Determine the nature of the unknown solutions by the use of conductivity and colorimetry.

Explain why the glow of the light bulb varies with the strength of the acid or base.

Suggest some other solutions found around the house that could be tested.

Source: C. Tommello and A. Blosfield. Used by permission.

EXHIBIT 6-7

GRADE 8
The Woolyboogers

Objectives
Students will make observations in lieu of conclusions in early problem-solving methods.

Materials
Dilute nitric acid (1/20), potassium dichromate crystals, liquid mercury, green food coloring, wood splint, petri dish

Tasks
To view a petri dish of the mercury and acid and make observations for 15 minutes

Verbal procedures
Participate in a discussion on what attributes constitute life. They have been given a home-work assignment to make a list of attributes.

Review proper observational methods to focus students on the idea that observations come before conclusion drawing.

List all observations made of the eggs as soon as they hit the life water and after food coloring is added for up to 15 minutes. Just observations are to be listed.

Visual procedures
Show a piece of chalk and indicate the observations that can be made of it as a quick review.

Written procedures
List observations in whatever format they desire for the 15-minute period.

A copy of the chalk demonstration is given to each student.

Manipulative procedures
Students are given the small dishes to which is added the green life water to about half full. The teacher adds one drop of the mercury ("eggs" they are called). Student may poke eggs with the wood splint; students may sprinkle the food crystals over the eggs and then continue their observations for the remaining 15 minutes.

Evaluation procedures
Class discussion and listing on board of the groups' observations and of any early conclusions that were drawn. Discussions of why some statements were conclusions and why they are out of place may be held. For example, the woolyboogers had babies. This statement indicates they are alive. What could have been said is that their numbers seemed to increase.

Source: C. Tommello and A. Blosfield. Used by permission.

Rising Rice This is an event in which a repetitious series of actions is con-tradicted in the last trial.

Materials: A glass jar full of raw rice and a table knife.
Procedures: Plunge the knife into the jar of rice several times. When the students begin questioning your sanity, jab the knife in once

more and slowly lift. The whole jar will be lifted up. The rice packs so tightly that it provides enough friction to lift the jar.

Light Lead   You cannot always trust your senses.

Materials: Piece of sponge (about 50 g, cut to size), piece of lead (about 45 g), and an equal arm balance.

Procedure: Prepare a chunk of lead and a piece of sponge where the sponge is slightly heavier than the lead. Give students the chance to compare weights by lifting them. Ask "Which is heavier?" or "How many times heavier is the lead than the sponge?" To most students, the lead will seem heavier. Place the two items on opposite ends of an equal arm balance and have students react.

Cooking by freezing

Materials: One dozen apples, freezing unit, blender, hot plate, and cooking utensils.

Procedure: Prepare for the demonstration by placing apples in a freezer. After the apples are thoroughly frozen, let them thaw. Freezing breaks down the cells in the apples just the same as cooking does. Prepare another batch of apples by cooking them in the normal manner. Process both batches in a blender. When both are served to the students, they will not be able to tell which was "cooked" by freezing.

Still another effective way of instructing gifted students is through the use of convocations. Convocations have been used in Union City, New Jersey, since that city's gifted education project was funded by the National Office of Gifted and Talented. Strobert and Alvarez (1982) report that seminar programs offer gifted students an opportunity to study scientific issues in depth and to do creative work by proposing solutions to real-life problems. Prior to the convocation, each gifted student receives a packet including information based on the issue under investigation, vocabulary lists, references, and resources. The convocations stress the scientific skills of observation, data collection, and interpretation. This model allows gifted students to work with community specialists; to use nonconventional settings beyond the classroom; to use community and regional resources; and to address societal issues. Convocation themes are science related and oriented toward the future, such as space, oceanography, energy, computers, health, and environment.

Anderson (1983) also advocates issue-related curriculum in science and suggests a number of issues similar to those used in New Jersey: the interdependence of today's world, stresses on biological systems, the energy issue, and the world's dependence upon science and technology.

Education of gifted students in the eighties is not complete without an understanding of the sciences, their relation to societal change, and their many applications. Gifted students must recognize that world problems cannot be understood without a grasp of scientific and technological matters. When teachers realize that science must be taught as a process as well as a product, and as gifted students are given opportunities to experience scientific inquiry, programs in science will be strengthened.

Most socialist and third world countries are also in the process of strengthening their precollege science and mathematics programs. Facts on science education from other countries (Exhibit 6-8) illustrate this interest and effort. Commonalities exist in the way science and mathematics are taught in the USSR, East Germany, the People's Republic of China, and Japan (Hurd, 1981; Klein, 1980; and Kumanyov, 1980).

These facts indicate there is widespread recognition of the importance of science and technology in fostering human well-being and in meeting the economic and political demands of living in the twentieth century in other countries. The facts also indicate that teaching the vast amount of scientific information available to students is useful in advancing human welfare and the welfare of nations.

To achieve a science education for gifted students that will meet their needs, enterprising teachers and administrators must continue to develop challenging science and mathematic program offerings for these students.

EXHIBIT 6-8

SCIENCE AND MATH EDUCATION IN OTHER COUNTRIES

- Socialist countries are strengthening their precollege science and math programs.
- School years average 240 days (U.S., 180 days).
- Six- to eight-hour school day
- National education policies emphasize importance of science and mathematics. In China, science education policies are written into the constitution.
- Specially trained science and math teachers take over instruction in grades 4 to 12.
- Specialized study in the sciences begins in the sixth grade with courses in mathematics, biology, chemistry, physics and earth science (one to three times a week).
- Three or four sciences are taken each term.
- In secondary school, students take seven to nine courses.
- English is the language of science. There are more people learning English in China than there are English-speaking people in the U.S.
- Gifted students in math and science have national contests, research projects after school, mentors (teachers, scientists), and early admission.
- Key schools for gifted in math and science have been identified.
- Comprehensive exams follow primary, middle, and secondary school to assess progress. Objective is to avoid failures.
- At age 14 to 15, a student decides to pursue vocational or college preparatory programs.
- Science and math teachers are specially trained. The Soviet Union uses research projects similar to dissertations. In-service education is required.
- In China a national symbol is the Bohr atom model with the slogan "Science is the eternal spring."
- Parents show concern, involvement, and responsibility.

STATE OF THE ART IN MATHEMATICS EDUCATION

Few subjects have been taught in a more rigid textbook fashion with so little imagination, particularly at the elementary level, as mathematics; yet mathematics is vital to the education of gifted students in this age of automation and technology. Mathematics for the gifted must provide for the diverse needs of the individual gifted student, as well as respond to a changing society.

Wheatley (1983) states that today's curriculum was based on an industrial society and requires major restructuring to prepare students for a future where computers will be the major tool. He sees the curriculum of today's mathematics as being representative of a society that is very different from the present and calls for change.

Stanley (1976, 1984) has been instrumental in helping educators see the capabilities of gifted students in the area of mathematical achievement. He has found sixth graders capable of performing at the university level in his Talent Search at John Hopkins University (1976–1986). Yet these same gifted students are often blocked from rapid advances in conceptual thought by an almost exclusive emphasis on skill learning in the regular school program. Too often, the gifted may become overwhelmed by skill acquisition and never experience the excitement of thinking "like a mathematician." Stanley suggests that the mathematics curriculum be reoriented toward principles and concepts for the gifted. Skill acquisition can be efficiently achieved when viewed from this perspective of problem solving and application.

Identifying the Gifted in Mathematics

Stanley (1976) suggests that if one set of tests, such as the Iowa Test of Basic Skills, has been used for a gifted student, the ceiling may be too low to show the limits of the student's knowledge; therefore, teachers can use tests designed for older students to test achievement. Fox (1976) also has done in-depth work in identifying gifted mathematics students. Fox suggests:

> The whole picture of the cognitive strengths and weaknesses of the student should be carefully assessed by using batteries of difficult tests. One might first begin by screening students on in-grade achievement tests, such as the Iowa Tests of Basic Skills. Students who score above the ninety-fifth percentile on mathematics or verbal tests and the ninety-fifth percentile overall on the in-grade norms could be further tested on special tests of ability at a higher level, such as the Scholastic Aptitude Test (SAT), Preliminary Scholastic Aptitude Test (PSAT), Differential Aptitude Test (DAT), or School and College Ability Test (SCAT). These tests should then be followed by other tests of special abilities, such as Raven's Progressive Matrices, Bennett's Mechanical Comprehension Tests of Educational Progress, Science (STEP), and College Entrance Examination Board (CEEB) achievement tests. (p. 30)

Other tests that might be useful are the Ross Test of Higher Cognitive Processes (Ross & Ross, 1976) or the Watson-Glaser Test of Critical Thinking (Watson & Glaser, 1964).

Characteristics of the Mathematically Gifted   Greenes (1981) lists six characteristics of the mathematically gifted. They are:

1 Flexibility in handling data
2 Outstanding ability to organize data
3 Mental agility
4 Original interpretations
5 Outstanding ability to transfer ideas
6 Outstanding ability to generalize

Greenes also states that the mathematically gifted prefer oral rather than written communication because it is faster. Many of the gifted students interviewed had difficulty explaining their thought processes, because they tended to combine several mental processes or operations in one step and to make intuitive leaps. This kind of mental agility is a real problem for gifted students in responding to classroom questions. For example, one gifted fifth grader, according to Greenes, did not immediately answer the question of how many kilometers Mrs. Johnson traveled each hour if she went 360 kilometers. The youngster told the teacher that the problem was not clear because it did not state that the same number of kilometers was traveled for each hour. The solution, according to the student, could be any set of six numbers that add up to 360, and there is an infinite set of such sets.

Teacher as Facilitator in Mathematics

Teachers faced with comments from gifted students such as the one just described can become frustrated. To overcome this frustration, Borenson (1983) suggests that teachers become mathematics facilitators who group students so they can share ideas; accept all student responses, encourage boardwork; and promote a climate for all to be heard. He further states that the teacher should promote mathematical creativity in the classroom by providing a nonstructured class with emphasis on independent judgment and thinking; but most of all, the teacher should be a risk taker and facilitator.

RECOMMENDATIONS AND SUGGESTIONS FOR SCHOOLS

Organizing Strands in Mathematics

Rather than wait for textbooks to be rewritten for gifted students, Wheatley (1983) suggests ten elementary school mathematics strands for the gifted with suggested percentages of time. The relatively small amount of time relegated to facts and computation is consistent with the emphasis that has been placed on problem solving and principles (Stanley, 1976; Fox, 1976; Greenes, 1981). The ten strands appear in Table 6-1.

TABLE 6-1
ELEMENTARY SCHOOL MATHEMATICS STRANDS

Strands	Time (%)
Problem solving	20
Estimation and mental arithmetic	6
Numeration	6
Geometry	15
Spatial visualization	5
Probability and statistics	6
Arithmetic and algebra concepts	12
Facts and computations	15
Applications	5
Computer programming	10

Mathematically Gifted Girls: A Special Challenge

Research on highly able mathematical reasoners in grade 7 provides insight into the needs of highly gifted girls. Over the past several years, almost 20,000 students, primarily seventh graders, participated in the talent search at the Johns Hopkins University (Stanley et al., 1974; Keating, 1976; Stanley et al., 1977). Even though the mean score for boys in the talent search is only about 35 points higher than the mean for girls, all boys did score higher than all girls on individual tests. Yet many girls are extremely gifted, as evidenced by the fact that each year about a fourth of the girls in the talent search score higher than the average for college-bound senior girls on the mathematics portion of the Scholastic Aptitude Test (SAT).

Fox (1981) suggests teachers play an important role in encouraging girls at school and suggests six strategies:

Identify gifted girls early.
Counsel parents.
Encourage girls directly.
Individualize instructions.
Reduce sexism in the classroom.
Provide career education and role models.

The challenge for teachers is to identify mathematically gifted girls and to help them discover their talent and potential. Both highly able boys and girls need moral and intellectual role models to show them what they can achieve. However, for gifted girls the exposure to women who use the full range of their abilities, particularly in mathematics, is essential. Outstanding women in the field of mathematics are still rare. A 2-year study on the achievement and participation patterns of women in mathematics by Armstrong (1980) indicated that women in engineering represented just $\frac{1}{10}$ of 1 percent of the total number of engineers in the United States. Only 2 percent of all physicists are women. A study by the Carnegie Commission on Higher Educational Opportunities for Women reported by Fennema & Sherman (1977) concluded that a major barrier to the advancement of women in scientific and technological fields was due to their mathematical training.

Mathematics is a critical filter. Sells (1980) reports alarming statistics at the University of California at Berkeley in which 57 percent of entering males compared to 8 percent of entering females—a difference of more than 7 to 1—had 4 years of high school math. At the time of the study, all but five of the twenty majors offered at Berkeley required calculus or statistics; thus, 92 percent of the women entering Berkeley were not qualified at entry for 75 percent of the available majors.

Armstrong (1980) identified three variables which affect achievement of women in mathematics:

A positive attitude toward mathematics.

A perception that math is necessary and useful to the individual.

A positive influence of parents, teachers, counselors, and peers on the individual advocating mathematics.

Rekdal (1984) adds math avoidance as another variable in females as a result of stereotypical thinking that mathematics is a field for males.

Administrative Arrangements for Mathematics Instructions for Gifted Students

There are several methods of providing for gifted students in mathematics. Extended experiences or enriched mathematics curricula provides additional experience, but this extension may mean little more than extra problems. Extra classes, special classes, and special schools, such as Fairfax High School for Technology with its emphasis on mathematics and science, are provided. The BHSS offers gifted students an enriched mathematics sequence throughout their 4 years. This sequence includes courses in algebra, geometry, intermediate algebra, and calculus. These offerings provide greater coverage in mathematics and include all mathematics necessary for college entrance.

Acceleration is another means of working with the gifted, although most special classes and special schools combine acceleration with enrichment. In some schools, gifted students complete seventh- and eighth-grade arithmetic and ninth-grade general mathematics in the first 2 years. In the ninth grade, they take algebra and receive high school credit for an extra math course.

In Santa Barbara, California, gifted students spend 3 days each week on materials studied by the regular class and they spend the other 2 days in a seminar-type program with emphasis on varied experience and independence.

Suggestions for Instruction

Mathematics is a "natural high" for the mathematically gifted. The young gifted student uses a leap-and-check method similar to a technique used by many mathematicians called "hypothesis-test." They begin with answers and check them out. An example of this type of thinking is demonstrated by a 5-year-old gifted girl who picked up a candy bar and announced "A fourth of a fourth of this piece of candy is sure small." The teacher stopped short and gasped "What?" The child said "A fourth of a fourth—that's a sixteenth." When the teacher asked the child where she had learned all that, she said "I just figured it out." The leap-and-test approach is very useful as mathematics moves from simple rituals of calculations to quantitative thought. Alfred North Whitehead (1929) stated that the goal of mathematics is thought. He recommended that mathematics be the development of relations in space. Several general ideas for teaching mathematics to gifted students are:

1 Discourage compartmentalization of mathematics instruction in the various mathematics courses.
2 Integrate and focus mathematical thinking through the study of the history of mathematics.
3 Encourage the use of different methods to solve the same problem.
4 Encourage checking or computational devices.
5 Encourage the gifted student to perform unusual mathematical operations.
6 Assign challenging and unusual problems.

One of the biggest problems in providing for the needs of the mathematically gifted student is individualizing his/her instruction. A model depicting this process calls for the selection of a particular object or concept, followed by preassessment and diagnosis of need (see Figure 6-1). If enough students need instruction, the teacher can organize a large group, or, if only a few students need instruction, small groups can be used; if only one or two students need help, individual instruction can be used.

Following the instructional phase, the teacher once again diagnoses students' needs, through test or observation, and either assigns enrichment activities, practice, or reteaches if necessary, before moving on to the objectives for Concept II.

FIGURE 6-1
A model for individualized instruction.

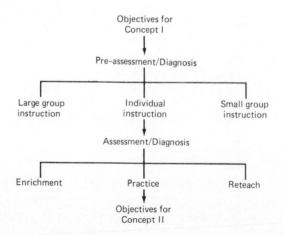

This individualized learning model is a form of mastery learning and follows several sequential steps: specification of objectives, designation of mastery score for summative evaluation, unit teaching, formative tests, immediate feedback, diagnosis of errors, alternative procedures, retest, and summative evaluation.

Kersch and Reismann (1985) report mastery learning units usually concentrate on lower-level cognitive objectives; but for the gifted student the mathematics objectives focus on application, analysis, synthesis, and evaluation.

To assist the secondary teacher of mathematics in developing curriculum for the gifted, a format that encourages a number of modalities is helpful. In this format, the teacher identifies the objectives, materials needed, tasks, and procedures. The procedures include verbal, visual, manipulative, and written tasks. Several examples are given in Exhibits 6-9 to 6-12, below and on pp. 148–152: (1) a statistics survey project for grade 8, (2) high school mathematics for grades 9 to 11, and (3) geometry for grade 10.

EXHIBIT 6-9

GRADE 8
Statistics Survey Project

The gifted students will study the applications and interpretations of statistics and surveys. This activity will allow the gifted students to explain their understanding of statistics and surveys through visual and graphing processes.

Objectives

Explain the use of statistics and its importance in everyday life.

Develop, conduct, implement, and compile an original survey on a subject in which they are interested.

Demonstrate the interpretation of their surveys through the use of graphs.

Write a concise summary explaining the outcome of their survey and how they reached their outcome.

Materials:

Determined by students according to individual needs.

Tasks

Choose a subject they are interested in.

Write a question pertaining to that subject.

Choose a sample of people (30) who will answer their questions.

Keep a written log of the sample population by name, age, and sex.

Compile a summary of the project and what they learned.

Share individual projects and interpretations with the class.

Verbal procedure

Students will:

receive instruction on statistics and basic requirements to be included in their survey, e.g., questions to ask, population survey, and use of graphs to interpret outcomes of survey.

EXHIBIT 6-9 *(Continued)*

include sample populations interviewed by name, age, and sex.

receive verbal feedback on their surveys.

Manipulative procedure

Students will:

cut out and show examples of the use of statistics from newspapers, magazines, etc.

interview thirty different people and keep a log of their responses.

Visual procedure

Display of different graphs used for compiling data from survey.

Study a copy of a sample survey to establish a better understanding of how to compile a survey.

Evaluation procedure

Did students explain the use and importance of statistics?

Did students compile an original survey on the subject of their interest?

Were students able to demonstrate with two different graphs the interpretation of their survey?

Were students able to compile a written summary explaining the outcomes of their survey?

Were the students able to explain how they arrived at a particular outcome?

Many programs for the gifted develop special courses for students with mathematical aptitude. These courses are being designed and designated titles such as "Gifted Geometry" (see Exhibit 6-13, p. 153). Petri (1983) reports one such course. The format Petri uses includes major objectives and subobjectives (numbered 1.0 to 6.7). The subobjectives (2.1 to 6.7) address the needs of the gifted student. It can be noted that the activities become more complex as the gifted student progresses in his/her mastery of geometry.

Integrating Mathematics for Upper Elementary and Middle School Gifted Students   Pereira-Mendoz and May (1983) suggest that the upper elementary and junior high grades are a difficult period for students, not particularly in terms of the mathematics curriculum but in terms of their maturity. They suggest integrating mathematics into categories such as home, community, sports, travel, and nature. These enriching activities bring the environment into the mathematics classroom and provide concrete ways for gifted students to see the relevancy of mathematics.

Another example of upper elementary and middle school integration is the activity for gifted students called "Plan a Business" in Exhibit 6-14, p. 155.

Van de Walle and Thompson (1981) list a number of problem-solving activities to be integrated into the daily classroom scheme:

1 *Full class quickies.* Problem-solving skills that can be developed in verbal teacher-directed sessions of 3 to 5 minutes. These are quite effective with estimation skill problems. Place the problem on a transparency, show it for 5 to 15 seconds, and ask the gifted students to estimate the answer.

EXHIBIT 6-10

GRADE 9
High School Mathematics

In this activity, the gifted student will learn characteristics and requirements of polygonal tesselations.

Objectives
Given a regular polygon, the gifted students will determine whether it will tesselate the plane.
They will use the formula for determining the angle measure of a regular n-gon.
Students will suggest possible combinations of polygons that will compose a semiregular tesselation.

Task
Formulate a definition of a regular and semiregular tesselation.
Name various tesselations found in the real world.

Verbal
Attend a teacher-oriented lecture on tesselations, incorporating the formula for tesselations.
Teachers will point out possible uses of tesselations.

Visual
Use mirrors to make illustrations of infinite tesselations; create sample tiles shown, patterns on transparencies, and geometric shapes to demonstrate what will tesselate and what will not; and demonstrate complete charts on regular and possible combinations for semiregular combinations.

Written
Explain why a regular pentagon cannot be used to tesselate a plane.

Manipulative
Construct and cut out a pattern that will tesselate using a protractor.

Evaluate
Discuss the geometric theorems used in this activity.

Source: P. Allison, S. Gibson, and David Nash (1984). Used by permission.

---

2 *Shoebox problems.* Packaged manipulative problems in a shoebox. An example would be pictures of six or more shapes that can be made with tangrams. Gifted students use the tangrams to find out which is the largest and smallest shape.

3 *Folder problems.* Nonroutine problems are written, including drawings, on the inside of a file folder and covered with transparent plastic. Other ideas suggested by Van de Walle and Thompson are the use of tape recorders, playground problems, and a think-game center with games such as Mastermind and the Tower of Hanoi.

EXHIBIT 6-11

GRADE 10
High School Mathematics—Geometry

In this activity, the gifted students will learn the differences and similarities between the altitudes, medians, angle bisectors, and the perpendicular bisectors of the sides of a triangle.

Objectives

To observe the relationships between the orthocenter, incenter, centroid, and circumcenter of any triangle.

Materials:

Paper, compasses, straight edges

Tasks:

To construct the altitudes, medians, angle bisectors of a triangle, and the perpendicular bisectors of the sides of the triangle

To identify the points of concurrency of these segments or lines

To predict conclusions concerning various kinds of triangles

Verbal Procedure

The students will:

attend a lecture defining the terms altitude, median, angles bisector, perpendicular bisector, and concurrency.

be instructed on (or reminded of) the procedure for construction of altitudes, medians, angle bisectors, and perpendicular bisectors of segments.

Visual procedure

Observe the currency of the perpendicular bisectors of the sides of the triangle, the altitudes, the medians, and the angle bisectors of the triangle.

Observe that the points of concurrency will move as the triangle is changed from scalene to isosceles to equilateral.

Manipulative procedure

Construct a scalene triangle with its altitudes, medians, angle bisectors, and perpendicular bisectors.

Repeat the process with an isosceles triangle and an equilateral triangle.

Written procedure

Record the findings from the isosceles and equilateral triangles.

The natural curiosity of gifted students can be further stimulated through activities such as "Create a Puzzle" (Exhibit 6-15, p. 156) for grades 6 to 9.

The development of gifted students' problem-solving abilities can be presented on a regular basis with only minor alterations to the teacher's existing time schedule. These activities are excellent items for the practice selection on the mastery model, as well as enrichment. Since present textbooks do not stress higher-level

EXHIBIT 6-12

GRADE 11
High School Mathematics

In this activity the gifted students will study the wrapping function as a simple model for periodic functions.

Objectives:
To define periodic functions by means of a unit circle
To define the periodic functions cosine and sine

Tasks:
To construct a unit circle centered at the origin of a coordinate plane
To construct a real number line which is completely flexible and with the same scale as the coordinate plane
To secure the line to the circle so that it is tangent to the circle at the point (1,0)
To wrap the line about the circle, the positive ray winding counterclockwise, so that each real number on the line wraps into one and only one point on the circle.

Verbal procedure
Students will:
be instructed on the density of the real number line, with specific reference to irrational values and rational multiples of π
recall and share the following information: the equation for a circle, the formula for the circumference of a circle, the relationship between the lengths of the sides of the special right triangles, the notation of an ordered pair.

Visual procedure
Observe that each time the line is wrapped about the circle another real number is paired with each point on the circle.
Identify values of cosine x and sine x for the points on the real number line having coordinates 0, $\pi/2$, π, and 3 $\pi/2$.
Observe the symmetry of the unit circle with respect to both the origin and the axes, and then identify the coordinates of all points shown in the figure.

Written procedure
Record the definitions of the two periodic functions cos and sin.
Use the equation $u^2 + v^2 = 1$ to compute special values of the new functions.
Compute and record the values for sin x and cos x shown in the table.
Attempt to write a definition of periodic function.

Manipulative procedure
Construct the circle using straight-edge and compass.
Label, secure, and wrap the string.
Project points of the circle into the u axis in order to see the special right triangles.
Investigate the winding process to determine the period of each of the function cos and sin.
Determine the changes (increases and decreases) of each of the functions as x ranges from 0 to 1 to 0 to -1 to 0.

EXHIBIT 6-12 *(Continued)*

Evaluation

Were the students' definitions valid (good)?
Did the wrapping produce correct function values?

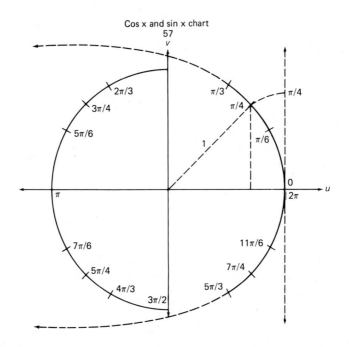

Cos x and sin x chart
57

x	cos x	sin x	x	cos x	sin x
0			π		
$\pi/6$			$7\pi/6$		
$\pi/4$			$5\pi/4$		
$\pi/3$			$4\pi/3$		
$\pi/2$			$3\pi/2$		
$2\pi/3$			$5\pi/3$		
$3\pi/4$			$7\pi/4$		
$5\pi/6$			$11\pi/6$		
π			2π		

Source: P. Allison, S. Gibson, and David Nash. Used by permission.

EXHIBIT 6-13

GIFTED GEOMETRY
Grade 9

Brief course description
The focus of this course is on the fundamental of plane Euclidean, coordinate, and solid geometries and trignometry. Creative thinking is used with both formal and informal methods of deductive proofs and indirect proofs. Group and individual research skills are incorporated into the program using topics such as the history of geometry, geometers, geometry and nature, and geometry and its influence on the world's art, music, and view of the universe.

Objectives and subobjectives

Major objective 1.0
The learner will accomplish all the objectives of the regular geometry curriculum using an accelerated approach.

Major objective 2.0
The learner will pursue and internalize the facts that a theorem begins as a conjecture about an observed pattern and that, without proof, there is no guarantee that the pattern will continue infinitely.

The learner will:

2.1 Examine two patterns, not knowing in advance that one fails after a certain point:
   a Patterns in figurate numbers, such as triangular, square, and pentagonal numbers
   b Pattern of the maximum number of regions in which a circle is divided by connecting points on the circle; first use two points, then three, four, and five points
2.2 Compose a table with the findings for both patterns
2.3 In suggested patterns, sense the relationships for both patterns
   a The figure numbers and their differences
   b The number of points connected and the number of regions formed
2.4 Invent a hypothesis about the relationships discovered
2.5 Anticipate the outcome of continuing the pattern using the hypothesis; In suggested patterns:
   a Guess the difference between the hexagonal numbers.
   b Guess the maximum number of regions into which six points divide a circle
2.6 Validate the hypothesis by physical calculations
2.7 Describe feelings when the second hypothesis did not agree with the findings
2.8 Discuss how famous people might have felt whose hypotheses or conjectures either were initially accepted by their peers and later failed or did not fail but were not accepted by their peers
2.9 Discuss the topic "If I were to invent a hypothesis which was destined to fail after a period of time, I would rather it should fail during/after my lifetime."
2.10 Discuss the topic "If I could choose, I would rather invent a hypothesis that was accepted by my peers, but later failed/was not accepted by my peers, but did not fail."

Major objective 3.0
The learner will use formal methods to prove a theorem.

Subobjectives. The learner will:
3.1 Write deductive proofs in two-column form
3.2 Write indirect proofs

Major objective 4.0
The learner will use informal methods to prove or validate a theorem.

EXHIBIT 6-13 *(Continued)*

Subobjective. The learner will:
  5.1 Read selections from *The Divine Proportion: A Study in Mathematical Beauty* by H. E. Huntley
  5.2 Construct a bulletin board display portraying his observations of occurrences of mathematics in the real world

Major Objective 6.0
The learner will examine the concept of the trigonometric ratio and its applications.

Subobjectives. The learner will:
  6.1 Derive the basic trignometric ratios using similar right triangles
  6.2 Use tables to evaluate trigonometric ratios
  6.3 Relate the trigonometric ratios to the winding functions
  6.4 Develop identities concerning trigonometric ratios
  6.5 Research the principle of the clinometer and hypsometer
  6.6 Construct a clinometer and a hypsometer
  6.7 Use the clinometer and hypsometer to compute the height of objects

Source: M. Petri, West Palm Beach Public Schools. Used by permission.

reasoning but overemphasize computational rules, it is essential that teachers of the gifted encourage the gifted to reason and relate ideas. This section on mathematics in gifted education has given suggestions to assist teachers in stepping back for a broad view of the teaching of mathematics for gifted students, with emphasis on preparing them for the future.

SUMMARY

The central ideas of this chapter are that science and mathematics are crucial to the education of today's students and that new program developments are being made but that continued development is needed. Science enrollments in high schools have been decreasing as students become less motivated to study science. Even though more students are taking more semesters of mathematics, there is still an overall decline in achievement.

The importance of identifying both mathematically and scientifically gifted students at an early age was discussed, as well as the need to consider the fact that intellectual giftedness does not always equate with a specific academic aptitude in science or mathematics. Characteristics of the scientifically gifted were identified as sensitivity to problems, ability to develop novel ideas, ability to evaluate, persistent curiosity, alertness in detecting inconsistencies, high degree of mechanical mindedness, spatial visualization, planning ability, and ability to communicate.

In mathematics, the characteristics of the mathematically gifted were flexibility in handling data, outstanding ability to organize data, mental agility, original interpretations, and outstanding ability to transfer ideas and to generalize. The role of the teacher as a facilitator in both science and mathematics was stressed and the importance of process versus product was discussed.

EXHIBIT 6-14

PLAN A BUSINESS
Grades 6–9

In this activity the gifted students will develop word problems that would be associated with running a business of their choice. These problems are translated into equations using variables in order to find solutions.

Objectives
The student will:
Create original advertisements to promote sales of the product.
Write word problems concerning situations that would arise from that business.
Translate problems into equations using variables.
Solve equations using equation-solving skills.

Tasks
To find information about costs and products related to the business
To find mathematical problems that result from operating the business.

Procedures:
The student will:
View filmstrips on net profit and sales tax
Work with computer programs (i.e., Lemonade Stand) dealing with operating a business
Work in small groups to write problems and equations
Explain projects to the class and receive feedback

Evaluation
Did the verbal explanation and problems demonstrate a practical application for the use of equations and variables in the real world?

Used by permission of Genevieve Gambrell.

Organizing concepts and strands were identified for mathematics and science with the notion that gifted students in both areas function as practitioners.

Administrative arrangements for the gifted in both mathematics and science consist of acceleration, enrichment, and special grouping. Examples of each were discussed along with suggested strategies.

The importance of identifying and meeting the needs of gifted students in mathematics and science for the welfare of the nation and the individual was emphasized for an increasingly technological society.

EXTENDING ACTIVITIES

1 Conduct a survey of school and teacher policies concerning education of students gifted in mathematics and science. List examples of how your survey participants suggest implementing their ideas or how they have implemented their suggestions. What con-

EXHIBIT 6-15

CREATE A PUZZLE
Grades 6 to 9

In this activity gifted students develop puzzle problems that involve three intersecting sets.

Objectives
The student will:
Plan a situation using three categories
Draw a Venn diagram with three intersecting sets
Write numbers in each part of the diagram
Translate this information to write a puzzle
Solve the puzzle

Example
Ninety gifted students went to Burger King.
a Three had a Whopper, a coke, and fries.
b Twenty-four had a Whopper.
c Five had a Whopper and a coke.
d Thirty-three had a coke.
e Ten had fries and a coke.
f Thirty-eight had fries.
g Eight had fries and a Whopper.
* How many had nothing?

Procedures
The student will:
View Venn diagrams
Work with sample problems
Work in small groups to create puzzle problems
Explain projects to the class and receive feedback

Evaluation
Did the verbal explanation and problems demonstrate practical application for the use of Venn diagrams in solving puzzles?

Used by permission of Genevieve Gambrell.

clusions can you draw about these practices in helping these students develop their abilities?
2 If you were going to place an advertisement of 75 to 100 words to obtain a mentor for a gifted student in science, what key features would you emphasize?
3 Review a biographical sketch of a person considered gifted in science and/or mathematics and describe the three most important factors in your opinion that account for her/his achievement. Be prepared to share this with your classmates.
4 Devise a checklist that could be used to select educational materials for the gifted in science and/or mathematics. Share your ideas with the class.

REFERENCES

Anderson, R. (1983). Are yesterday's goals adequate for tomorrow? *Science Education,* 67(2), 171–176.

Armstrong, J. M. (1980). Achievement and participation of women in mathematics. *Educational Commission of the States,* Denver, CO.

Bloom, S. (1955). The early identification of potential. *School Science and Mathematics,* 55, 287–295.

Blurton, C. (1983). Individualized science packet for gifted students. *School Science and Mathematics,* 83(4), 326–332.

Borenson, H. (1981). Promoting mathematical creativity in the classroom. *The Education Forum,* May, 471–476.

Brandwein, F. (1981). *The gifted as future scientists.* Ventura, CA: Ventura County Superintendent of Schools Office.

Brown, R. (1983). Unique science school offers hope. *State Educational Leader,* Winter, 14–15.

Callahan, C. (1985). Science. *Teaching Gifted Children and Adolescents.* Columbus, OH: Charles E. Merrill.

Cole, C. (1956). *Encouraging scientific talent.* New York: College Entrance Examination Board.

De Briun, J. & Schaff, J. (1982). Community-based science research program for gifted and talented high schools. *Roeper Review,* 5(2), 12–14.

Fennema, E. & Sherman, J. A. (1977). Sex-related differences in mathematics achievement, spatial visualization and affective factors. *American Educational Research Journal, 14,* 51–71.

Fox, L. (1976). Sex differences in mathematical precocity: Bridging the gap. In Keating, D. (Ed.), *Intellectual Talent Research and Development,* Baltimore: Johns Hopkins University Press.

Fox, L. (1981). Mathematically able girls: A special challenge. *Arithmetic Teacher,* February, 22–23.

Gold, M. (1982). *Education of the gifted/talented.* Ventura, CA: Ventura County Superintendent of Schools Office, September.

Greenes, C. (1981). Identifying the gifted student in mathematics. *Arithmetic Teacher,* February.

Guilford, J. P. (1950). Creativity. *American Psychologist, 5,* 444–454.

Hannigan, I. (1983). Enrichment through core-explore-more. *Gifted Children Newsletter,* 4(5), May, 14–17.

Hurd, P. (1981). *Science education in the People's Republic of China.* Washington, DC: National Science Foundation, Science Education Directorate.

Hurd, P. (1983). State of precollege education in mathematics and science. *Science Education, 67(1),* 57–67.

Keating, D. P. (1976). A Piagetion approach to intellectual precocity. In D. Keating (Ed.), *Intellectual Talent,* Baltimore: The Johns Hopkins University Press.

Kersch, M. & Reismann, F. K. (1985). Mathematics for gifted students. In R. H. Swassing (Ed.), *Teaching gifted children and adolescents.* Columbus, OH: Charles E. Merrill.

King, L. & DeRose, K. (1980). *Archaeology—We dig it.* Paper presented at NSTA Cleveland Convention, Cleveland, OH.

Klein, M. S. (1980). *The challenge of communist education: A look at the German Democratic Republic.* Boulder, CO: East European Monographs.

Kumanyov, V. A. (1980). *Problems of public education in the USSR.* Halifax: Atlantic Institute.

Pereira-Mendoz, L. & May, S. (1983). The environment—A teaching aid. *School Science and Mathematics, 83*(1), January, 54–60.

Petri, M. (1983). *Geometry/gifted project.* Paper presented to West Palm Beach Board of Public Instruction, West Palm Beach, FL: Department of Exceptional Child Education.

Reis, S. & Rand, D. (1983). Encourage girls in science and math. *Gifted Children Newsletter, 4*(8), 1–7.

Rekdal, C. K. (1984). Guiding the gifted female through being aware: The math connection. *GCT, 35,* November/December, 10–12.

Renzulli, J. S. (1979). *What makes giftedness? A re-examination of the definition of the gifted and talented.* Ventura, CA: Ventura County Superintendent of School Office.

Roe, A. A. (1956). *The psychology of occupation.* New York, Wiley.

Roe, A. A. (1961). The psychology of the scientist. *Science, 134,* 456–459.

Ross, J. D. & Ross, C. M. (1976). *The Ross test for higher cognitive processes.* Novato, CA: Academic Therapy Publications.

Roufberg, R. (1984). A world of science for expanding the mind. *Gifted Children Newsletter, 5*(1), 15–16.

Scobee, J. & Nash, W. (1983). A survey of highly successful space scientists concerning education for gifted and talented students. *Gifted Child Quarterly, 27*(4), 147–151.

Sellin, D. & Birch, J. (1980). *Educating gifted and talented learners.* Rochelle, MD: Aspen Publications.

Sells, L. W. (1980). The mathematics filter and the education of women and minorities. In L. H. Fox, L. Brody & D. Tobin (Eds.), *Women and the Mathematical Mystique.* Baltimore: Johns Hopkins University Press.

Sisk, D. (1984). *Organizing strands for science of the gifted.* Paper presented at National Association for Gifted Children, St. Louis, MO.

Stanley, J. C. (1976). Use of tests to discover talent. In D. Keating (Ed.), *Intellectual Talent: Research and Development.* Baltimore: Johns Hopkins University Press.

Stanley, J., Keating, D. & Fox, L. (Eds.) (1974). *Mathematical talent: Discovery, description and development.* Baltimore: Johns Hopkins University Press.

Stanley, J., George, W. C. & Solano, C. H. (1977). *The gifted and the creative: A fifty year perspective.* Baltimore: Johns Hopkins University Press.

Stanley, J. (1984). The exceptionally talented. *Roeper Review, 6*(3), 160.

Strobert, B. & Alvarez, F. (1982). The convocation model project: A creative approach to the study of science for gifted disadvantaged students. *The Elementary School Journal, 82*(3), 230–235.

Subarsky, Z. (1948). What is science talent? *Scientific Monthly, 66,* May, 377–382.

Suchman, J. R. (1966). *Developing inquiry.* Chicago: Inquiry Development Program, Science Research Associates, Inc.

Super, D. C. & Bacrach, P. B. (1957). *Scientific careers and vocational development theory.* New York: Teachers College, Columbia University.

Van de Walle, J. & Thompson, C. (1981). Fitting problem solving into every classroom. *School Science and Mathematics, 81*(4), 289–302.

Watson, G. & Glaser, E. M. (1964). *Watson-Glaser critical thinking appraisal manual for forms Ym and 2m.* New York: Harcourt Press.

Wheatley, G. (1983). A mathematics curriculum for the gifted talented. *Gifted Child Quarterly, 27*(2), 77–80.

Whitehead, A. N. (1929). *The aims of education.* New York: Macmillan.

Wright, E. (1982). Fifteen simple discrepant events that teach science principles and concepts. *School Science and Mathematics, 81*(7), 575–580.

CHAPTER 7

LANGUAGE ARTS AND SOCIAL STUDIES FOR THE GIFTED

ESEA Title I

CHAPTER 7

LANGUAGE ARTS AND SOCIAL STUDIES FOR THE GIFTED

Language arts and social studies are grouped together because their aims complement one another. The skills of language arts are the means of self-expression and the means of sharing thoughts and emotions; the skills of social studies are those of developing leadership to affect political and ethical decision making. Together, language arts and social studies prepare responsive and responsible citizens.

In many school districts, programs for the gifted have developed units of study that integrate language arts and social studies, particularly at the secondary level. At the elementary and middle school levels, through cooperative planning and communication, the two subject areas can also share the common goal of developing young people's ethical sensitivity, critical skills, and creative productivity.

This chapter examines the definition of language arts and social studies, the identification procedures and identifying characteristics of gifted students in both areas of study, and the role of the teacher as a facilitator. Recommendations and suggestions for language arts are discussed and suggested topics in social studies are offered. Administrative arrangements for both areas are examined with emphasis on enrichment, acceleration, and special grouping. The sections in this chapter under headings relating to recommendations and suggestions for language arts and social studies contain suggestions for instruction with emphasis on practical classroom applications.

The first subject area covered is language arts. According to Barbe and Milone (1985), language arts (reading and writing) are the foundation for both personal and academic success, for through reading students gather vast storehouses of

Photograph on facing page courtesy of Elizabeth Crews, Berkeley, California.

knowledge, as well as experiencing one of life's most enjoyable pastimes; and through writing students convey their ideas and thoughts.

STATE OF THE ART IN LANGUAGE ARTS FOR THE GIFTED

Language arts for the purpose of this chapter are defined as reading, writing, listening, and speaking. Language is considered the tool of socialization and is basic to the development of intelligence. Language usage often stimulates parents and teachers to identify the intellectually gifted child. The intellectually gifted child's rapid growth in language, early reading, quick retention of words, and a vocabulary far beyond his/her age group cause her/him to be easily identified.

A 1983 survey found that among boys tested, gifted boys scored highest in reading, with language usage in second place, using the Stanford Achievement tests. For girls, the order was reversed, but language and reading held the two highest places. Intellectually gifted young people are likely to be more distinctly different from their age peers in general information and in language than in other readily observed characteristics. Teachers report that by the middle of the first grade many gifted students are reading and comprehending books at the fourth-grade level.

The obviousness of these language abilities may cause teachers and administrators to adapt curriculum for the language arts to the abilities of gifted students; for whatever reasons, there are many more curricula for gifted students in language than in other subject areas. Programs for gifted students provide opportunities for them to read, write, and talk with emphasis on developing their creativity.

Parents of 1000 gifted children were surveyed and 87 percent reported having suspected their children were gifted before they entered kindergarten. Twenty-two percent guessed their child as being gifted during the child's first 12 months of life; 48 percent between the ages of 1 and 3; 17 percent between 4 and 5 years of age, and 13 percent when their child was older. Johnson (1984) lists characteristics of gifted preschoolers which can be useful in identifying giftedness in language arts:

- has an unusual memory
- teaches himself/herself to read
- will offer several solutions to the same problem
- recites from memory
- has a large vocabulary
- can solve problems and process ideas in a complex way
- has a long attention span
- has an almost adult sense of humor
- gives his/her opinions about things, whether asked or not
- is a nonstop talker
- asks questions constantly
- seems to understand books, films, and discussions at high level
- can perceive and articulate the unstated feelings of others

Identifying the Gifted in Language Arts

Educators, psychologists, and parents agree that gifted students should not be identified by a single test or score (Clark, 1983; Gallagher, 1985), yet this practice still persists. The test most often used to identify the gifted in language arts is the group intelligence test. Many times decisions are also made using group achievement tests, particularly if the program emphasizes acceleration.

Barbe and Milone (1985) report that exceptional ability in the language arts is usually accompanied by superiority in other areas. Consequently, the linguistically gifted child is sometimes discovered by means of standardized tests. However, Barbe and Milone suggest that school performance and parent and teacher recommendations be added to the identification procedure.

It is important to note that not all gifted students are superior in the language arts, and programs for gifted children should be geared to the individual student's ability. In addition, exceptional ability in one area of language arts, such as reading, does not necessarily mean that the student is gifted in other areas of the language arts.

A viable identification procedure should include multiple indices such as: teacher recommendation of demonstrated interest; superior ability in language arts such as reading, writing, and speaking; superior test scores, with emphasis on the verbal score; and indices of creative performance.

Characteristics of the Gifted in Language Arts

The student who is gifted in the language arts often begins the first grade being able to read. Parents of 6-year-olds report that their gifted children recognize words at ages 3 and 4 and read simple books at ages 4 and 5. Many more have the capacity to read, but because the environment does not give them either the opportunity to read or the encouragement, they do not.

A characteristic of the child gifted in the language arts is early ability to write capitals and sometimes small letters in manuscript. Along with this interest and skill in writing goes an interest in spelling. Many young gifted children spontaneously spell their favorite words and show a keen interest in word recognition. However, the most notable characteristics of the gifted in language arts are sentence structure and speech patterns which are related to their mental advancement. As a result of this advancement, they often verbalize and sound much older than they are. General characteristics of the gifted in language arts are: (1) early speech development, (2) unusual vocabulary, (3) intelligent conversation, (4) wide range of general information, (5) retentiveness, (6) keen powers of observation, and (7) sensitivity.

Teachers and parents can refer to the above list of characteristics in order to recommend children who demonstrate a majority of these characteristics for the gifted language arts programs.

Teacher as Facilitator

The role of the teacher in language arts is defined by Sellin and Birch (1980) as (1) maximizing the key features of language arts, (2) helping students understand language as communication, and (3) assisting students in integrating literary skills in the content dimensions to school and life experiences.

To facilitate the development of language arts ability, the teacher of gifted children needs to reflect many of the characteristics identified by Davis (1954), such as cooperative democratic attitude, kindliness and consideration for the individual, patience, wide interests, flexibility, and use of recognition and praise. Teachers who demonstrate these characteristics provide a psychologically safe and free atmosphere which encourages gifted students to flourish in language arts.

Kaplan (1979) discusses the role of the teacher of the gifted in language arts and identifies three elements that are essential: exposure, analysis, and expression. The teacher should be capable of identifying what is expected (exposure) and arranging activities that afford gifted students time to experience the "doing" (analysis) and "producing" of language arts (expression).

RECOMMENDATIONS AND SUGGESTIONS FOR LANGUAGE ARTS

The National Education Association (NEA) committee of the English Council made a number of recommendations for the gifted in the 1960s that are still relevant (NEA, 1960):

1 Set advanced goals and more rigorous standards of expression for the gifted.

2 Limit drill on routine correctness as determined by early administration of diagnostic tests.

3 Provide a literature program that is characterized by reading of original works in their entirety, attention to cultural goals, and integration of objectives in reading and literature.

4 Provide seminars for gifted students.

5 Set a goal of effective expression with appropriate emphasis on both creative and expository writing and speech.

This list is in *English for the Academically Talented Students in the Secondary School*, and reflects the emphases of many current programs for the gifted in language arts.

Gold (1982) outlines eight suggestions for middle and upper grade language arts programs for gifted. They are:

1 Determining the purpose of reading a particular item and adapting one's ideas, ordering ideas in sequence, relating details to ideas they elaborate

2 Increasing ability to comprehend difficult material: finding the main ideas, ordering ideas in sequence, relating details to ideas they elaborate

3 Responding actively to reading materials: drawing inferences, seeing relationships, arriving at conclusions

4 Reacting critically to material: discriminating among sources, weighing the validity of information presented, selecting what is important and relevant, distinguishing fact from opinion, turning to other sources to check accuracy and significance of material read

5 Locating information: using table of contents and index in book; employment of dictionary, glossary, encyclopedia, atlas, and other reference books; reading maps, charts, graphs, and tables; use of library tools such as the card catalogue and periodicals guides

6 Note taking in reading reference material; selecting facts worth remembering, practicing recall, reorganizing material in different ways, using mnemonic devices

7 Organizing material read or heard; outlining and writing summaries

8 Learning ways to remember important material; selecting facts worth remembering, practicing recall, reorganizing material in different ways, utilizing mnemonic devices (pp. 210–211).

These skills have relevance for all students, but they are particularly relevant for gifted students in language arts since they relate to superior verbal ability, which is a characteristic of the gifted in language arts. Suggestions for the elementary program would include:

1 Integrate reading and writing.

2 Provide a variety of reading material in every subject.

3 Help the young gifted student to become an effective reader and enjoy the process.

4 Determine the exact instructional needs of individuals and group instruction.

5 Encourage critical reading as well as creative reading.

6 Provide opportunities for listening and speaking.

7 Engage gifted students in problem solving.

Gifted students at the elementary and secondary levels need to experience a balanced curriculum in language arts with opportunity to express thoughts and feelings in writing and speaking. Barbe and Milone (1985) stress that the gifted should also learn to use writing to support positions they adopt, since these skills will be most important for them as adults.

One last important aspect of language arts for the gifted is the mastery of a foreign language. The more languages an individual learns, the easier it is to acquire new ones. Goodman and Scott (1981) state that with rare exception, the child's first language is actually enhanced by early exposure to a second. They state that a person who is at home with two languages has an educational advantage by being aware of the customs, habits, and thought patterns of two languages. Exposure to other cultures has a positive effect on the gifted student's sensitivity and tolerance. International awareness is essential in today's world. The President's Commission on Foreign Language and International Studies reflected this value and recommended that an international point of view be developed (*Strength Through Wisdom*, 1979).

Administrative Arrangements for Language Arts

The three major ways of programming for the gifted are used in language arts: acceleration; special grouping, including special classes and special schools; and enrichment.

Although acceleration is an option in language arts, it is infrequently used at the elementary level. However, many schools report the use of acceleration in telescoping material at the middle school level, and the use of advanced placement and cooperative efforts with colleges and universities at the secondary level. Enrichment is much more frequently used at the elementary level and involves gifted students in in-depth study of new areas. Enrichment in language arts includes a certain amount of acceleration, in that concepts and skills normally taught at later years can be introduced.

There are no special schools specifically designated as schools for gifted in the language arts; however, there are several schools which offer programs for the gifted in language arts. The Denver International School is an example of a special school that focuses on the language arts. Young children learn a second language using the immersion concept (studying and learning in French, except for 1 hour per day). The students are screened for both ability and motivation. From ages 4 to 7, they study and learn in French. This is accomplished using songs, dramatization, art, and games. In the second grade, students learn to write, first in French, then in English. Even though the school has grade levels, children frequently cross grades. Students move ahead as they achieve mastery; for example, an advanced, highly motivated second grader can go into fourth grade. Another strength of the Denver International School is its small classes and individual attention. The school is an example of acceleration, enrichment, and special grouping in the language arts (Cox, 1985).

A similar type of program at the secondary level is the Bellaire High School in Houston (Cox, 1985). This school offers the International Baccalaureate (IB) program which is administered by its home office in Geneva, Switzerland, and is designed to facilitate student admission to colleges and universities worldwide. When students satisfy the requirements of the IB diploma, they can be admitted to college with sophomore standing. The Geneva office was founded in 1965. Currently, there are IB programs in the United States in over half of the states. The IB curriculum requires two languages and emphasizes a multicultural perspective. It is a 2-year program for eleventh- and twelfth-grade students. Each IB student takes nine academic requirements over the 2-year period. Six are traditional courses, three of which meet five times a week while the other three meet for about half that time. Courses can be selected from the following:

1 Language A (first language, usually English in North America), including a study of world literature
2 Language B (second language, distinguished from language A in not requiring the same depth and breadth of understanding of cultural and historical context of language)

3 Study of Man*—one of the options: history, geography, economics philosophy, psychology, social anthropology, business studies
4 Experimental sciences—one of the following options: biology, chemistry, physics, physical science, scientific studies
5 Mathematics
6 One of the following: art, music, a classical language, a second language B, computer studies

Students are selected for Bellaire by a committee of teachers, counselors, and administrators. They consider a number of factors: attendance, conduct, extracurricular activities, motivation, academic performance, and written statements by the students. Most of the students at Bellaire score at the ninetieth percentile or above in achievement and ability.

The IB program can be offered within the walls of an existing school, as the core curriculum, or it can be offered as a school-within-a-school. Its major strength is the rigorous emphasis on language development and the international focus.

Suggestions for Instruction

Barr (1984) reports on a curriculum development effort in which a group of secondary language arts teachers, selected for their skills and interest in teaching gifted students, were specifically trained in the writing of curriculum units. These teachers were instructed on the principles of differentiating curricula for gifted students. Each unit outlined the philosophy, goal, and objectives for curriculum emphasis, staffing, and the means by which the program was to be delivered. The units also included an organizing element and a series of objectives with the following components: content, process, and product. The components were based on selected principles of a differentiated curriculum for the gifted developed by the LTI (Kaplan, 1979). These principles were grouped according to whether they addressed content, process, or product. They are:

- Present content that is related to broad-based issues, themes, questions, problems (content)
- Integrate multiple disciplines into the area of study where possible (content)
- Allow for in-depth learning of a self-selected area within the area of study (process)
- Develop independent, self-directed study skills (process)
- Integrate basic skills (process)
- Develop complex productive, abstract, and higher level thinking skills (process)
- Develop research skills and methods (process)
- Focus on open-ended tasks (process)

* Study of Man, as it is listed by the International Baccalaureate Program Handbook.

• Encourage the development of products that challenge existing ideas or produce "new ideas" (product)
• Encourage the development of products that use new techniques, materials, forms (product)

Units were based on broad themes such as individuality and survival. The curriculum design sheets illustrate the planning and developing process, and sample instructional plans indicate the activities and resources a teacher of the gifted in language arts can use. Terms on the curriculum sheet that may need definition are: *introduction*, which refers to learning activities which motivate gifted students or develop prerequisite skills necessary for the learning experience; *practice*, which refers to learning activities that provide continuous practice or reinforcement to help students acquire the needed skills or develop conceptualizations of the content; and *extend*, which refers to an outline of independent opportunities for gifted students who want or need further learning.

The units reported by Barr (1984) are used in special classes for gifted secondary students in language arts. The emphasis in the special classes is on acceleration and enrichment.

An example of enrichment activities in language arts using the Enrichment Triad Model is reported by Renzulli and Stoddard (1983). The training activities used were the "Sentence Craft" materials (O'Hare, 1973) and the *New Directions in Creativity* program (Renzulli & Callahan, 1976). The materials were selected for their relative simplicity in format. *Sentence Craft* is a workbook of sequenced lessons offering examples and exercises in sentence-combining techniques. For example, in one lesson students learn how a series of "base" sentences can be combined into a single longer sentence:

> Battaglia glanced at first base.
> He went into his wind-up.
> Then he threw a hanging curve.
> Ryan knocked it out of the stadium. (O'Hare, 1973)

When the clues are provided in the textbook, a student might rewrite these sentences by combining them in the following manner: Battaglia glanced at first base, went into his wind-up, and threw a hanging curve that Ryan knocked out of the stadium.

New Directions in Creativity is a five-book series of reproducible worksheets which present open-ended challenges for students. With gifted fifth and sixth graders using these activities in two 40-minute sessions per week for 6 weeks, Renzulli and Stoddard (1983) found that the syntactic maturity and overall quality of the writing samples were positively affected. As the gifted students were involved in both pull-out sessions and regular classes, it was significant that there were no differences in the outcomes of the two approaches. Both were successful in achieving increased writing skills.

Fearn (1983) suggests several enrichment strategies which are applicable for elementary and middle school gifted students. One example of an effective activity is the instruction "Write directions for finding the difference between 40 and 26

(40 − 26). Be as exact as you can, because someone else will have to follow your written directions."

After perhaps 5 minutes, Fearn suggests that the gifted students give their paper to someone else and announces two rules. First, no one may explain his/her directions orally to whomever has his/her paper; and second, everyone is to follow the directions before them precisely as written. Since every set of directions is an exact reproduction of a mental construction of subtracting with borrowing, there are two quality variables in the writing. The first is the writing. These quality variables quickly surface during feedback and discussion of the exercises as the gifted students experience success or meet with confusion.

The implications, according to Fearn, are numerous. He reports that the activity forces gifted students to think through the topic, either making their mental constructions conscious or, if the situation requires, to form them. It also helps them learn to specify their constructions, receive real feedback, and, by implication, make revisions based on feedback. Directions and cues can request a list of directions or an essay. Some examples are:

- Write a fifty-word essay that tells exactly how raisins are made from grapes.
- Explain in not more than twenty-five words exactly what inertia means.

Activities such as these suggested by Fearn provide challenging enrichment for gifted students in language arts and can be used in the regular classroom or in special classes. Other examples of enrichment activities in language arts are suggested by Embry (1983). These activities involve logic and drawing conclusions. They challenge analytical thinking and call for deductive thinking in which a conclusion is drawn from two statements or premises. An example is: An artist is a talented person. Jeff is an artist. Therefore, Jeff is a talented person. Note that the conclusion is not necessarily a true statement. It is only true when the premises of the problem are true. Other examples are:

- Whoever wrote the poem is a perceptive writer.
- Anthony is quite perceptive.

Conclusion:

1 The poem was written by Anthony.
2 The poem was not written by Anthony.
3 The poem may have been written by Anthony.

Or (example),

- If the vase is not broken, it can be used.
- If the vase can be used, it is either the copper one or the brass one.

1 If the vase is broken, it is made of glass.
2 If the vase is broken, it is not the copper one or the brass one.
3 Copper and brass will not break.

The answers to the first and second examples are 2 and 3, respectively. Gifted students in language arts enjoy creating problems and stumping one another.

CHALLENGING THE YOUNG GIFTED CHILD WHO CAN READ

One unique problem in language arts is dealing with the kindergarten child who can read. Lowe (1983) addresses this problem with some very practical suggestions. She recommends that specific tests be given to the young gifted child, such as reading subtests of the more commonly used standardized achievement tests, the Metropolitan, California, or Stanford, to gain baseline information. Areas of special interest to the child should be determined through written inventories or informal discussions. Some possible approaches for teachers to use after ascertaining the reading level and specific skills and interests are:

1 Try library-learning contracts in which the teacher and the gifted kindergarten student decide on a topic to be explored. Use a simple "What-I-want-to-know" and "How-I'll-find-out-about-it." During class reading-readiness time, the gifted student can use the library to work on his/her special topic.

2 Utilize kits (Science Research Associates, etc.), games, and programmed learning devices such as Systems 80 for young gifted readers.

3 Use the experience-based "young author" approach. If the child is unable to print or write, he/she can use a primary school typewriter or dictate the story on tape. These activities allow the gifted child to compose, drawing on his/her own experiences. He/she can write stories, poems, and plays for the rest of the class.

Gold (1982) suggests that gifted students learn mnemonic devices and create some of their own. Gardner (1983) suggests several mnemonic devices such as remembering letters in the name of "Roy G. Biv" to recall the colors of the rainbow in order: red, orange, yellow, green, blue, indigo, and violet. Another is to remember the names of the Great Lakes, by thinking of "homes": Huron, Ontario, Michigan, Erie, and Superior. Or, what does the first letter of each word in this sentence spell? A rat in the house might eat the ice cream. (Answer: arithmetic.) Gardner stresses memory by writing stories in which a mystery is solved by someone remembering an important detail or simply playing memory games in which a student leaves the room and one person changes one thing about her/his appearance. The student who leaves the room is to come back and tell what changed. This activity evokes increased perception skills and positive social interaction.

Other enrichment activities are suggested by Hoomes (1983) and called "A Mishmash of Misbehaving Monsters." This unit develops gifted students' abilities in observing, recalling, understanding, concluding, applying, assuming, evaluating, and divergent and convergent thinking. The unit is divided into five activities. Activity 1, "Monster IQ Test," is a matching activity exercise designed as an introduction to a variety of monsters such as minotaur, centaur, cyclops, and hydra. Activity 2 leads students to design their own monsters. Activity 3 helps students create an adversary for their monsters, and Activity 4 directs students in writing short adventure stories featuring their monsters. Activity 5 is a series of suggestions of continuing the use of monsters in creative exercises. Monsters can be a springboard to the study of other subjects such as folklore, mythology, sociology, history, and biology, and meets the principle of a differentiated curriculum—integrating subject matter.

Examples of enrichment for gifted students, especially those that deal with higher-level thinking, are seemingly endless. One interesting example from Eiss (1984) uses conundrums with gifted students. The goal is to provide teachers with techniques to:

1 Open students' eyes to the sense of wonder in language
2 Reveal the conceptualization processes involved in poetry
3 Discuss the connections between poetry and other forms of expression
4 Indicate important types and techniques of poetry

Eiss defines conundrums as riddles solved with a pun. Some of the conundrums he suggests are:

What happened to the duck who flew upside down? (He quacked up)
Where did the first corn come from? (The stalk brought it)
Why did the farmer scold the chickens? (They used fowl language)
What animal never plays fair? (The cheetah)
What animal is always short of breath? (The panther)

Enrichment activities such as these motivate gifted students to further develop their skills in language arts and, more important, to love language and its usage.

The next subject area to be discussed is that of social studies, which integrates the social sciences. Many of the activities described for the gifted in language arts can become companion experiences in the area of social studies.

SOCIAL STUDIES FOR THE GIFTED

Social studies lends itself to enrichment for the gifted. In terms of methods, the unit, project, and activity approach which is popular and effective with the intellectually gifted student are especially effective in social studies. However, the teaching of social studies to gifted students is not without its problems. Gold (1982) identifies one major problem in social studies as the difficulty of matching social studies content to the immaturity and inexperience of the elementary and middle school gifted student. Another problem in social studies is that the content changes quickly and includes large amounts of new knowledge to be learned, almost simultaneously, by the gifted student and the teacher of the gifted. Many teachers have difficulty with the feeling that they are not totally knowledgeable about social studies. Yet, social studies, more than other subjects, offers the gifted student a chance to deal with real problems in the world, problems that have their roots in the past, direct application to the present, and implications for the future. Social studies also provides for deliberate education about values. Stewart (1985) states that, since teaching social studies to the gifted takes place in a broad and ever-shifting context, these changes bring a new sense of urgency to the role of social studies.

STATE OF THE ART IN SOCIAL STUDIES FOR THE GIFTED

Social studies is usually defined as an integration of subjects (Ponder & Hirsh, 1981; Superka et al., 1980) with a contemporary problems-issues-and-principles approach. Subject areas included in social studies are history, geography, economics, anthropology, sociology, psychology, and political science (Mitsakos, 1981; Smith, 1979). According to Mitsakos, social studies can be viewed as citizenship transmission, as social science, or as reflective inquiry. In practice, most programs in social studies for the gifted use all three descriptions, with emphasis on inquiry and discovery.

Identifying the Gifted in Social Studies

Identifying students with outstanding ability in social studies can be accomplished in a number of ways. One way is to search for students who demonstrate certain characteristics that seem to identify giftedness in social studies, such as those proposed by Plowman (1980).

Characteristics of the Gifted in Social Studies

Plowman (1980) suggests social studies teachers look for the following characteristics to identify the gifted student:

1 Conceptually advanced for her/his age
2 Possesses a storehouse of advanced, technical, or very specific knowledge
3 Enjoys difficult or complex tasks
4 Sets high standards for independent projects
5 Viewed by classmates as a source of new ideas and knowledge
6 Viewed by classmates as a group strategist or organizer
7 Sees humor in human relationships and is able to laugh at his/herself
8 Tells or writes imaginative stories
9 Has wide-ranging and/or highly focused interests
10 Sees relationships that other people do not
11 Absorbs knowledge easily and quickly
12 Is an advanced, intensive, extensive reader (two grade levels above grade placement)
13 Uses self-survival mechanisms (fantasy when bored) (p. 14)

Other criteria suggested for selecting gifted students for advanced study in social studies were compiled by the NEA in 1960 and are still useful (NEA, 1960):

1 A searching and open mind toward social problems and data
2 Social sensitivity, a genuine interest in people and in the consequences of social interaction, and appreciation of other people's ideas and ethical values
3 Capacity for critical judgment, with particular reference to the assessment of human behavior
4 Emotional balance and a sense of perspective in evaluating the evidence of social science

5 Imagination, the ability to project oneself into social situations that differ in time and place from one's own

6 A sense of time and the ability to see events in their relationship to other events that precede and follow

7 The ability to carry on research in social problems, to perceive the limits of a problem, to secure data, to weigh evidence, to formulate hypotheses, to reach meaningful conclusions, and to organize the results effectively for written or oral presentations

If the program emphasizes inquiry and a problems approach, the Revolving Door Identification Model (RDIM) (Renzulli et al., 1981) may be feasible. This model focuses on the interaction of above-average ability, creativity, and task commitment. It assumes that giftedness is relative or situational and, consequently, a student can function as "gifted" and display the creative, productive behavior necessary to explore in-depth topics in social studies. The Renzulli model works well in the regular classroom served by a pull-out or an enrichment program. As the gifted student completes a given project, he/she returns to the regular classroom. It is also conceivable that the regular classroom teacher could monitor the independent inquiry.

Teacher as Facilitator in Social Studies

Kaplan (1979) conceptualizes the teaching of social studies for gifted as a set of accommodations. One accommodation is adjusting the nature and structure of the social studies curriculum. Another accommodation must be made for the unique attributes and status of the gifted learner. These accommodations are accomplished through replacing the standard curriculum with new material, applying process activities and modifying the learning modes. She suggests three modifications that teachers may make to the curriculum: vertical modification, in which the gifted student receives more advanced content; horizontal modification, in which the content and information in social studies is expanded (commonly viewed as enrichment); and modification with supplemental learning, in which the gifted student may work on studies or investigation of real problems of personal interest.

Pearson (1979) suggests that the teacher's role in teaching social studies is that of a consultant who is involved in teacher–pupil planning. Pearson also advocates small group work in which students are responsible for a given segment of a topic. For example, students can study a given country or state in small groups of five, with each student responsible for a topic such as government, topography and climate, history, industry, and people. The teacher's role is to evaluate through criterion-referenced procedures and to serve as a facilitator.

Gold (1982) identified another important attribute for the teacher of the gifted in social studies, the ability to handle controversial and sensitive material. This is important in that the teacher of the gifted must avoid dominating or indoctrinating behavior and must encourage gifted students to engage in critical thinking. In addition, Gold suggests teachers of the gifted in social studies continue to be involved in their own studies, since the field is constantly changing. Lastly, it is helpful for the teacher, as model, to display a keen interest and involvement in civic activities through personal participation.

RECOMMENDATIONS AND SUGGESTIONS FOR SOCIAL STUDIES

The social studies curriculum, according to Kaplan (1979) should consist of broad-based topics such as the needs of people to survive and should involve searching, assimilating, and reporting. These three dimensions allow the gifted student to be actively involved, to broaden her/his interests, and to practice techniques for learning.

Gold (1982) lists fourteen basic themes suggested by the National Council for the Social Studies:

1 The intelligent uses of the forces of nature
2 Recognition and understanding of world interdependence
3 Recognition of the dignity and worth of the individual
4 The use of intelligence to improve human living
5 The vitalization of our democracy through an intelligent use of our public educational facilities
6 The intelligent acceptance, by individuals and groups, of responsibility for achieving democracy
7 Increasing the effectiveness of the family as a basic social institution
8 The effective development of moral and spiritual values
9 The intelligent and responsible sharing of power in order to attain justice
10 The intelligent utilization of scarce resources to attain the widest general well-being
11 Achievement of adequate horizons of loyalty
12 Cooperation in the interest of peace and welfare
13 Achieving a balance between social stability and social change
14 Widening and deepening the ability to live more richly

The focus in social studies for the gifted should be on concept formation and generalization, rather than on information and facts. Gifted students can easily organize facts into meaningful relationships and make generalizations. Key ideas, such as the reasons why individual cultures have developed as they have in particular geographic settings, are much more meaningful for the gifted than memorizing cities, products, and other facts about countries.

Administrative Arrangements

In the elementary school, provisions for the gifted in social studies range from enrichment in the regular classroom, to enrichment in special classes or learning centers, to acceleration and enrichment combinations in special classes. At the middle school level, the administrative arrangement that is becoming increasingly more popular is the special class for the gifted in social studies with emphasis on both acceleration and enrichment.

The segregation of gifted students in the social studies class is controversial to classroom teachers who believe personal integrity, human sympathy, social responsibility, and realistic self-evaluation must be developed in the context of the full range of abilities. However, many educators of the gifted contend the gifted should study in segregated classes to allow for full educational development. At the high school level, ninth- and tenth-grade students usually take world history and geography emphasizing the Western world or world history with emphasis on Asia. In some larger schools there may be an introduction to the social sciences in which the students learn the techniques, processes, and perspectives of anthropology, sociology, economics, and political science. In grades 11 and 12, American history and government are usually required. Options might be an advanced introduction to social sciences, similar to one given in grades 9 and 10, or electives in modern European history, Far Eastern history, the Middle East, history of Great Britain and the Commonwealth, Latin American history, Africa, international relations, economics, sociology, psychology, and seminars in contemporary issues.

In spite of the continuing controversy over special class versus regular class instruction for the gifted in social studies, there is agreement on basic practices for the gifted in social studies. These are:

1 Programs are organized around units or broad-based themes.
2 Personal interest and understanding of self and others are encouraged.
3 Emphasis is placed on self-directed study.
4 Opportunities to develop leadership.
5 Emphasis is placed on skill building such as creative thinking, investigative inquiry, and verbal and nonverbal communication skills.
6 The complexity, tentativeness, and debatable nature of most solutions and conclusions is emphasized.

Classroom procedures for the social studies include problem solving; group processes with emphasis on debate, role playing and panel discussions; critical use of modern mass media; independent study or investigations, simulations, critical and creative thinking; futuristics; and inquiry. These basic practices will be illustrated with a variety of administrative arrangements (special classes, enrichment or acceleration) and grade levels.

Suggestions for Instruction

Subotnik (1984) reports on a social studies curriculum which is modified for gifted intermediate and secondary students by incorporating strategies designed to foster creative thinking. The strategies, an outgrowth of futures and creativity research, include brainstorming, attribute listing, morphological synthesis, reverse historical chronology, webbing, consequence charts, and guided fantasy. One of the activities, "Reverse Historical Chronology," traces a current news item back in time in a step-by-step plan of action. Students begin by identifying a goal and imaging the goal as actualized. Working backwards, they invent the cause-and-effect highlights which mark the path from the goal to the present. Subotnik states that with practice, gifted students realize that action taken today may have a significant impact on the future. Another activity, webbing, is similar to the futures wheel technique discussed on curriculum strategies for gifted in the Chapter 4. In webbing, the concept is placed in the middle and free association of concepts are branched and looped from the concept, like a flow chart.

Emphasizing inquiry, McCauley (1984) writes about her experiences using a Renzulli Type III Activity involving the history of a neighborhood vacant lot. She used the activity with her fifth-grade gifted students in Rockford, Illinois. They learned investigative skills: collecting raw data, categorizing data, and reaching conclusions based on the information. Procedures included observing, listing, looking, sketching, notetaking, mapmaking, and interviewing. The history of the neighborhood evolved through the reconstruction of the family stories of the residents of the houses on the property until 1975. The findings were published in a book distributed to the community members.

Both of these suggestions for instruction concentrate on skill building in creative thinking and inquiry. Another example of adapting curriculum for the gifted is reported by Shaver (1984) who uses a jurisprudential approach to social studies. He states that this is appropriate for gifted because of their concern with moral issues and interest in leadership. His approach focuses on the analysis of public issues, both political and ethical. The students discuss the proper aims and actions for society. Shaver's approach is based on the assumptions that controversy is inevitable and that learning to recognize and handle disputes is essential to making decisions about public issues. The rationale underlying the jurisprudential approach can be summarized, according to Shaver:

1 Social studies education is basically citizenship education.

2 Citizenship education ought to reflect the nature of the society and the policy decisions made by the society.

3 Our society is pluralistic, with a variety of frames of reference resulting in continuous disagreement over the political–ethical issues which are at the heart of policy disputes.

4 Because political–ethical decisions must rest at least in part on one's views of what is morally desirable, values are crucial to their justification.

5 Values are defined differently and, when in conflict, weighted differently by people with different frames of reference.

The jurisprudential approach provides a viable answer to the problems versus content question that bothers social studies teachers. The approach offers gifted students many opportunities for cognitive moral development and helps prepare them to deal with public issues.

The work of Subotnik and Shaver are examples of adapting curriculum to be used in special classes for gifted, and they represent enrichment and acceleration strategies. The activity described by McCauley can be used either with a small group of gifted or with individual gifted students.

Haggart (1983) reports on the use of the art and science of heraldry as an enrichment activity. This self-directed study encourages students to conduct research. Haggart defines heraldry as the use and study of coats-of-arms, and provides each gifted student with an outline and list of suggested resources. The outline is as follows:

Skeleton for Heraldry—Basic Ideas in Outline

I   History
   A Ancient world
   B Middle Ages
   C Modern
II Uses of heraldry
III Symbols used in heraldry
   A Tincture
   B The field
   C Blazon
   D Charge
   E Device
   F Cadency

IV Building a Coat of Arms
   A Designing the shield
   B Designing other parts
     1 Supporters
     2 Helm, mantle, ground
   C Choosing a motto
V   Finding your family's coat of arms
VI People who work with heraldry
   A Herald
   B Pursuivant

The excitement of doing research with real sources makes social studies come alive for gifted students. This heraldry lesson is appropriate for gifted students in upper elementary, and stimulates their personal interest as well as helps them develop understanding of self and others.

An effective way for teachers to work with the gifted in the regular classroom or in a special class is to provide centers for self-directed study. Slovenske (1983) uses a center for current events called "Hail to the Chief." The activities in the center are for gifted fourth graders, incorporating current events with creativity in language and social studies. Interest is generated by displaying newspaper articles, current magazines, caricatures of top political figures, and a tape of "Hail to the Chief." Selected activities are:

Presidential Business   It has been reported that President Reagan reads six newspapers each day beginning at about 5 a.m. For the next 5 days, keep track of what you read between 9 a.m. and 12 a.m. each day.

Presidential Problem Solving   Suddenly a crystal ball has appeared on your desk. You are now able to look into the future, and read the fortunes of special people. Describe what you see in the future for President Reagan.

Reagan Commemorative   Although the Soviet Union issues more commemorative stamps (stamps made to honor people or special occasions) than any other country, the United States prints the largest quantities of stamps. Design a stamp to commemorate President Reagan and something important that has happened in his administration. Remember to identify the value of your stamp.

Hollywood   It's been said that a picture is worth a thousand words. When President Reagan was an actor, his facial expressions had to express various feelings without using words.

Illustrate the feelings listed below. Then using a mirror, try to show thinking skills.

If the entire class is studying a given topic such as Africa, the independent projects of the gifted student can enrich the other students' studies. An example of an independent study contract is shown in Exhibit 7-1. It is appropriate for elementary gifted students, grades 2 to 5. (Berger and Bernstein, 1986).

EXHIBIT 7-1

AFRICA
Independent Study Contract

1 Create a map of the continent of Africa. Choose one of these types:
  A Relief map
  B Political map
  C Collage map (cut out scenes of African life, pictures of people, foods, etc., and paste on an outline map of Africa)
2 Take an urban Africa safari to the largest city in your chosen country. Draw pictures of the scenery and events you see on your trip. Cut these out and paste them on black paper. Write captions in white ink. Viola! An urban African safari photograph album!
3 Choose one country in Africa to visit. List five interview questions that you would like to ask someone who lives in that country or who has visited that place.
4 List five ways that your African country is like the United States and five ways that it is different from the United States.
5 Think of objects that could be placed on a mobile to illustrate the wide variety of life in various African countries. Create and display your mobile.
6 Do research on African art in encyclopedias, library books, or magazines. After examining the art and sculpture of Africa, design an art piece that might be representative of Africa.
7 Read these African proverbs. Can you think of similar American proverbs? Choose one African proverb and write a fable with this proverb as the moral of your story.

  When the ape cannot reach the ripe banana with his hand, he says it is sour.
  He was born with a full set of teeth.
  Don't despise the gift because it is small.
  A roaring lion kills no game.
  The stick which is at your friend's house will not drive away the leopard.

I will complete the contract by _____

Signature _____
Data starting _____

Other techniques to use with groups of gifted students to build self-concept and understanding of others include role playing, problem-solving situations, values clarification, encounter lessons, and simulation. All of these techniques provide the gifted students opportunity to communicate and better understand themselves.

Leadership development is suggested as an important component of programs for the gifted in social studies. Roets (1983) states that all students in special gifted classes or enrichment classes should complete leadership training programs at least every 3 or 4 years. She uses groups of 8 to 20 gifted students in her leadership training programs and emphasizes debate and discussion. The gifted are identified by teachers, parents, and self-nomination. Roets also suggests the use of checklists on leadership such as the Scales for Rating Behavioral Characteristics of Superior Students (Renzulli et al., 1976) and the Roets Rating Scale for Leadership (Roets, 1983). The time requirement for the leadership training is 10 to 12 hours. Objectives of the program are:

1 To understand the process of leadership of self and others
2 To practice and master the skills of selecting role models, the language of leadership, project planning, and group discussion
3 To apply all these leadership skills to planning and implementing projects
4 To encourage positive self-image that says "I can do it"

Items from Roets Leadership Scale include:

- I feel at ease asking people for help or information
- I can speak to persons in authority (Roets, 1983)

The Roets program of leadership has four components: people of achievement, the language of leadership, project planning, and debate and discussion. Gifted students at the elementary level enjoy studying people of achievement such as Martin Luther King, Clara Barton, and Carry Nation. The language of leadership helps students understand the verbal and nonverbal communication skills required by leaders: reading facial expressions, using body language, using symbols, practicing social phrases of courtesy and inquiry, public speaking, making impromptu speeches of persuasion, using tone of voice, encouraging and discouraging a speaker, listening, and responding in different ways. Project planning enables students to learn how to put an idea into reality, and debate and discussion helps students deal with issues of leadership such as peer pressure and qualities of young leaders.

The last two examples of social studies instruction discussed in this chapter include an enrichment program for young gifted children (Maker, 1984) and a ninth-grade special class for social studies (Rouse, 1985). Both of these programs can serve as models for developing appropriate differential curriculum. The problem of developing challenging materials for the young gifted student is complex, in that such a program must also develop abstract concepts.

Maker accomplished this in a special program for young gifted children. The content areas are anthropology, physical science, and sculpture. For discussion in the area of social studies, the emphasis is on anthropology. Experts in each content area developed a framework in the format of generalizations, concepts, and data, including a few sample activities. Classroom teachers used this information, with Maker's assistance, to develop teaching activities appropriate for gifted children.

1 All people, past and present, have shaped their beliefs and behavior in the face of universal human problems and needs.

2 Concrete remnants of a culture do not accurately reflect the abstract beliefs of a culture.

The concepts studied were culture, cultural universal, human needs, artifact, excavation, and archaeology. The basic method or data used was the simulation game *Dig*, discussed in Chapter 5 on curriculum strategies. *Dig* was developed for older students (grades 7 to 12), and it was modified for the young gifted students. The major purpose of the game is to develop a culture and to function as an anthropologist. Throughout the session, speakers, films, and discussions of the various aspects of anthropology and archaeology were used.

The discussions were based on the Taba Teaching Strategies. Below are examples of the type of discussions with the Taba headings.

Concept Development   What do you think were the uses of these objects or artifacts?

Interpretation of Data   What are some techniques used by the archaeologist?

Application of Generalizations   What do you think people will believe when they find your artifacts?

Resolution of Conflict   How can a child resolve the conflict with her/his parents or parent over old ways versus new ways?

The secondary program in social studies was developed using a methodology similar to that used in Maker's program for young gifted children. University professors from the disciplines of history, geography, economics, anthropology, sociology, psychology, and political science identified key concepts, generalizations, data, and techniques essential to their disciplines. In addition, a specialist on gifted students worked with the teachers of social studies emphasizing the unique learning, emotional, and social needs of gifted students. Successful strategies to be used with gifted students were demonstrated, such as role playing, simulation, inquiry, independent study, creative problem solving, futuristics, and group processes.

Following exposure to the discipline, key concepts, strategies appropriate for gifted teaching, and the nature and needs of gifted students, the teachers developed lessons for ninth-grade social studies. These lessons were shared with the content specialists and the specialist in gifted education. After the sample lessons were evaluated and revised, they were incorporated into the curriculum and field tested (Rouse, 1985).

A key concept from economics which was part of the gifted student's basic understanding was "Wants are always greater than the ability to satisfy them and economic choices must be made." Making choices was translated to a need to develop skills in decision making. Exhibit 7-2 shows a sample lesson from the unit on economics; it lists the economic principles that guide the project.

EXHIBIT 7-2

SOCIAL STUDIES UNIT
Decision Making

Purpose

Introduce students to a sample decision-making process useful in making personal and social/economic decisions.

Objectives

After completing this lesson, the student will apply the decision-making process to a real or hypothetical economic problem.

Teacher instructions

Introduce students to charts of the decision-making process. (Ideas for the charts came from the "Give and Take" series, twelve 15-minute color film programs in personal economics for students in grades 8 to 10 (Programs 1 and 2). Have students brainstorm a list of common economic problems faced by ninth graders. Choose one or more problems to use as illustrations.

The decision-making process

Sally wants to go on the school band trip. She has $30 in her savings account. Her parents recently paid for tuition for summer band camp and are unwilling to finance this trip. The cost of the band trip is $85. Sally can make a lot of money babysitting on weekends and after school. But Sally also has homework and soccer. What should Sally do?

    Step 1—Define the problem. Sally has a scarcity of time and money. She wants to go on the trip.

    Step 2—Identify the alternatives for dealing with the problem. The grid shows four alternatives. Students may be able to think of others.

    Step 3—Specify criteria to be used in evaluating alternatives. The grid shows four criteria. Students may be able to think of others.

    Step 4—Evaluate the alternatives. Place a plus or minus in boxes on the grid to show whether each criterion is being met by the alternatives. In some cases, more than one plus or minus can be used to show the strength of the alternative or the preference of one criterion over another. The grid illustrates possible evaluations. Individual students may evaluate differently.

    Step 5—Make a decision. Students may not see a single "right" decision; rather they should see the implications (underlying values) of the decision.

Following the decision-making, the students produced the following alternatives and criteria:

	Criteria			
Alternatives	Pleasure	Time for homework	Time for sport	Avoid debt
1 Work 37 hours @ $1.50 per hour to earn $55.00 needed for trip.	+ −	−	−	+
2 Work 18 hours @ $1.50 per hour to earn $27.00. Get a loan for remainder.	+	+	+	−
3 Get a loan for total amount needed.	+	+	+	−
4 Do not go on trip.	− −	+	+	+

Source: J. G. Rouse, Project Triology Pinellas County B.P.I., Clearwater, Florida, 1985. Used by permission.

The key concepts for the unit in Exhibit 7-2 are listed below:

1 Economics is the study of how people use their resources to satisfy their competing wants.
2 Each economy must answer these basic questions:
   a what goods and services will be produced;
   b how much will be produced;
   c who obtains these goods and services.
3 The factors of production include land, labor, capital, and human managers. Business uses these to produce goods and services for which they pay rent, salaries, interest, and profits.
4 A market economy relies heavily on the profit motive. Investing in a business implies a risk. If successful, the business makes a profit; if unsuccessful, a loss.
5 Increases and improvements in technology, education, and capital make production more efficient.
6 All economies have a circular flow of goods and services and an opposite flow of money.
7 All economies fall into one of three categories:
   • market (free enterprise)
   • traditional
   • controlled (command)
8 The gross national product of a nation is the dollar value of all goods and services produced in the economy in 1 year.

These two projects represent efforts to build curricula using ideas similar to Bruner's (1971), which emphasize the structure of a discipline and define relevant learning as "What do you know that permits you to move toward goals you care about?" (Bruner, 1971, p. 114).

Social studies for the gifted, as illustrated in these two models, focuses on developing creative producers in the social sciences who are capable of adding new information and concepts to the disciplines. In these projects, the gifted students experience an integration of the various social sciences. In addition, they experience the process of learning the structure of the various disciplines and how to function as social scientists.

SUMMARY

This chapter examined language arts and social studies for the gifted. The two subject areas were grouped together because they complement each other. Language arts were defined as including reading, writing, listening, and speaking. Language was considered not only as the tool of socialization but as basic to the development of intelligence. The identification of the gifted in language arts was approached with a multiplicity of tools, including standardized intelligence and achievement tests and creative performance.

The characteristics of the gifted in language arts included early speech development, unusual vocabulary, intelligent conversation, wide range of general information, retentiveness, keen powers of observation, and sensitivity. The role of the teacher as facilitator was discussed, along with Kaplan's recommendation that teachers blend three elements in language arts development for gifted students: exposure, analysis, and expression.

Suggestions for language arts instruction in elementary and middle schools and secondary programs were given. Emphasis was placed on developing skills for self-direction; productive, abstract, and higher level thinking skills (process), and on presenting material using broad-based issues and themes.

It was noted that many efforts have been made for gifted students in language arts, due to their obvious superior language abilities.

The goals and methods of social studies were examined and it was noted that the methods used in social studies are similar to those used in programs for the intellectually gifted, such as the unit approach and emphasis on inquiry. Social studies was defined as an integration of subjects including history, geography, economics, anthropology, sociology, psychology, and political science. Social studies also includes citizenship transmission and social science as reflective inquiry. Identification procedures for the gifted in social studies were discussed and a multiple-source approach was recommended, as well as the approach of Renzulli's revolving door. It was noted that the multiple source approach is more viable for special classes and accelerated programs, whereas the revolving door approach appears to work better in the regular classroom or in enrichment pull-out programs.

The role of the teacher of the gifted in social studies was discussed, as well as the need for the teacher to avoid dominating students' attitudes, ideas, and opinions. And the teacher should encourage open discussion of controversial and sensitive material. The broad-based themes suggested by the National Council for the Social Studies were covered, including themes such as the recognition and understanding of world interdependence.

Administrative arrangements were covered, including acceleration, special grouping, and enrichment. Classroom procedures and instructional strategies for the gifted in social studies include problem solving; group processes with emphasis on debate, role playing, and panel discussion; critics' use of modern mass media; independent study or investigations; simulation; critical and creative thinking; futuristics; and inquiry.

The emphasis in social studies was providing the gifted with tools for making original contributions to society and for being responsible and responsive citizens.

EXTENDING ACTIVITIES

1 Review the curriculum content in language arts and social studies in your school district. Are there any provisions being made to alter the pace, content, or procedure for instruction?
2 Prepare a short (15-minute) presentation on the importance of encouraging gifted students to become creative producers in language arts and social studies. Identify your major points.
3 Conduct a survey to identify teacher perceptions on segregating the gifted for social studies. Share your feelings with the class.
4 Consider this proposition: Teachers of the gifted should be involved in civic activities to serve as role models for their students.
5 Interview professionals who operate day care centers, nursery schools, and/or kindergartens. Identify their key ideas on language development with which parents and teachers should be familiar. Be sure to note if any potential gifted preschool children have been identified. How were they identified?

REFERENCES

Barbe, W. & Milone, M. (1985). Reading and writing. In R. Swassing (Ed.), *Teaching gifted children and adolescents*. Columbus, OH: Charles E. Merrill.
Barr, C. (1984). *Language arts for the gifted*. A challenge grant submitted to the Florida Department of Education, Tallahassee.
Berger, L. & Bernstein, J. (1983a). Discovering myself. *Challenge, 1*(4), 44–45.
Berger, L. & Bernstein, J. (1983b). Africa. *Challenge, 2*(2), 26–29.
Bruner, J. (1971). *The relevance of education*. New York: W. W. Norton.
Clark, B. (1983). *Growing up gifted*. Columbus, OH: Charles E. Merrill.
Combs, W. E. (1975). *Some further effects and implications of sentence combining exercises for the secondary*. Language arts curriculum doctoral dissertation. Minneapolis: University of Minnesota.
Cox (1985). *The Richardson study, a national investigation, educational opportunities for able learners*. Fort Worth: Texas Christian University Press.
Davis, N. (1954). Teachers of the gifted. *Journal of Teacher Education, 5*(3), 221–224.
Eiss, H. (1984). Reflections of the crystal. *Challenge, 3*(1), 28–35.
Embry (1983). How logical are you? *Challenge, 1*(4), 12–14.
Fearn, L. (1983). Beyond basic writing skills: Using writing constructively. *Challenge, 1*(4), 15–16.

Gallagher, J. (1985). *Teaching the gifted child*. Newton, MA: Allyn and Bacon.

Gardner, J. (1983). Based on books. *Challenge, 1*(4), 29–31.

Gold, M. (1982). *Education of the gifted/talented*. Ventura, CA: Ventura County Superintendent of Schools.

Goodman, D. B. & Scott, G. (1981). International high school: A challenge for scholars. In *Action for the 80s: A political, professional, and public program for foreign language education*. Skokie, IL: National Textbook Company.

Guilford, J. P. (1967). *The nature of human intelligence*. New York: McGraw-Hill.

Haggart, J. (1983). Of unicorns and kings. *Challenge, 1*(4), 24–28.

Hoomes, E. A. (1983). Mishmash of misbehaving monsters. *Challenge, 1* (4), 24–29.

Johnson, N. (1984). Gifted pre-schoolers: Children of promise. *Challenge, 3*(1), 6–9.

Kaplan, S. (1979). Language arts and social studies curriculum in the elementary school. In A. H. Passow (Ed.), *The gifted and the talented: Their education and development*. 78th Yearbook of the National Society for the Study of Education. Chicago: The University of Chicago Press.

Lowe, S. (1983). What to do with the kindergarten child who can read. *Challenge, 1*(4), 2–4.

Maker, C. J. (1984). An experimental program for young gifted children. *Challenge, 3*(1), 44–48.

McCauley, E. M. (1984). The story of a vacant lot. *Roeper Review: A Journal on Gifted Education, 7*(1), 11–12.

McCumsey, J. (1983). Meeting the affective need of gifted children. *Challenge, 2*(7), 17–20.

Mellon, J. T. (1969). *Transformation sentence-combining*. Report No. 10, Urbana, IL: Council of Teachers of English.

Mitsakos, C. L. (1981). The nature and purposes of social studies. In J. Allen (Ed.), *Education in the 1980s: Social studies*. Washington, DC: National Education Association.

National Education Association (1960). *Project on the academically talented student*. Washington, DC: English for the Academically Talented Student.

O'Hare, F. (1973). *Sentence-combining*. Report No. 15, Urbana, IL: National Council of Teachers.

Pearson, C. (1979). Cooperative learning. *Learning, 7*, 34–37.

Plowman, P. (1980). *Teaching the gifted and talented in the social classroom*. Washington, DC: National Education Association.

Ponder, G. & Hirsh (1981). Social studies education for the gifted: Lessons from other pests. *Roeper Review: A Journal on Gifted Education*, November, 17–19.

Renzulli, J. (1979). *What makes giftedness? A re-examination of the definition of the gifted/talented*. Los Angeles: National State Leadership Training Institutes for Gifted.

Renzulli, J. & Callahan, C. (1973). *New Directions in Creativity*. New York: Harper & Row.

Renzulli, J., Smith, L., White, A., Callahan, C. & Hartman, R. (1976). *Scales for rating the behavioral characteristics of superior students*. Wetherfield, CT: Creative Learning Press.

Renzulli, J. & Stoddard, E. P. (1983). Improving the writing skills of talent pool students. *Gifted Child Quarterly, 27*(1), 21–27.

Renzulli, J. S., Rees, S. M. & Smith, L. H. (1981). *The Revolving Door Identification Model*. Mansfield Center, CT: Creative Learning Press.

Roets, L. (1983). Leadership: An instructional program for ages 8–12. *Challenge, 2*(2), 12–16.

Rouse, J. (1985). *Social studies for the gifted: Project triology.* A challenge grant submitted to the Florida Department of Education, Tallahassee.

Sellin, D. & Birch, J. (1980). *Educating gifted and talented learners.* Rockville, MD: Aspen.

Shaver, J. (1984). Helping gifted students to analyze public issues: The jurisprudential approach. *Roeper Review: A Journal on Gifted Education, 7*(1), 4–7.

Slovenske, J. (1983). Hail to the Chief. *Challenge, 1*(4), 32–34.

Smith, J. (1979). *Creative teaching of the social studies in the elementary school.* Boston: Allyn and Bacon.

Stewart, E. (1985). Social studies. In R. Swassing (Ed.), *Teaching Gifted Children and Adolescents.* Columbus, OH: Charles E. Merrill.

Strength through wisdom: A critique of U.S. capabilities (1979). A report to the President from the President's Commission on Foreign Lawyers and International Students. Washington, DC: U.S. Government Printing Office.

Subotnik, R. (1984). Emphasis on the creative dimensions: Social studies curriculum modification for gifted in intermediate and secondary students. *Roeper Review: A Journal on Gifted Education, 7*(1), 7–11.

Superka, D., Hawke, S. & Morrisett, I. (1980). The current and future status of the social studies. *Social Education, 44,* 362–369.

Terman, L. (1954) The discovery and encouragement of exceptional talent. *American Psychologist, 9*(6), 221–230.

CHAPTER 8

TEACHERS OF THE GIFTED

CHAPTER 8

TEACHERS OF THE GIFTED

Treat people as if they were what they ought to be and you help them to become what they are capable of being.

Goethe

Little specific documentation exists to prove that good regular classroom teachers do not also make good teachers for the gifted, but considerable data does support the notion that nothing matters in the school more than the teacher (Dunkin & Bidler, 1974; Callahan & Renzulli, 1977; Gaze & Berliner, 1979). Teachers set goals, assist in establishing values, select learning experiences, choose methods or teaching strategies, and, most importantly, serve as models for gifted students. However, Mandell and Fiscus (1981) state that not every teacher should teach gifted students, and they report studies in which gifted students may react with hostility or resentment if the teachers try to oppress them (Merman, 1971; Maker, 1975; Impelizzeri et al., 1976). This chapter examines research suggestions concerning qualifications for teachers to teach gifted and criteria for teacher selection. Particular attention is given to competencies for certification of teachers of the gifted and to teacher preparation. A distinction is made between degree-seeking programs with training at the university and college level and training for teachers provided by local educational systems and state departments of education. Specific examples of in-service training based on unique problems are addressed.

Photograph on opposite page courtesy of Elizabeth Crews, Berkeley, California.

The section on in-service training indicates how these programs can develop appropriate characteristics for teachers of gifted students.

QUALIFICATIONS FOR TEACHING THE GIFTED

Early researchers, such as Carroll (1940) in *Genius in the Making* and Bentley (1937) in *Superior Children*, suggest that the teacher of the gifted should be enthusiastic about learning, thoroughly competent in educational methods, free of jealousy and selfishness, and modestly brilliant. Bentley (1937) also added specific training in gifted education and previous teaching experience to his list of qualifications.

Many of the characteristics suggested in the thirties and forties are still valid today, as witnessed by the number of states requiring special training or certification in education of the gifted. The variety of lists of characteristics or qualifications for teachers of the gifted have been gathered through questionnaire responses in which gifted individuals or graduates of gifted programs have identified qualities of excellent teachers. One such list compiled by Davis (1954) lists the following qualifications: cooperative democratic attitude, kindliness and consideration for the individual, patience, wide interests, pleasing personal appearance and manner, fairness and impartiality, sense of humor, good disposition and consistent behavior, interest in people's problems, flexibility, use of recognition and praise, and unusual proficiency in teaching a particular subject.

As a follow-up procedure of a summer residential secondary gifted program, sixty students ranked the Davis (1954) list of characteristics by order of preference and added characteristics or qualifications they thought important in teaching the gifted (Sisk, 1984). The gifted students' preferences were quite clear. They added competency and an interest in learning and ranked it as 1. Their preferences are displayed in Table 8-1.

TABLE 8-1
IMPORTANT TEACHER CHARACTERISTICS IN EDUCATION OF THE GIFTED

Order of preference	Percentage (%)
1 Competency and an interest in learning	98
2 Unusual proficiency in teaching a particular subject	95
3 Cooperative democratic attitude	92
4 Wide interests	85
5 Use of recognition and praise	88
6 Flexibility	90
7 Fairness and impartiality	93
8 Sense of humor	90
9 Interest in people's problems	83
10 Pleasing personal appearance and manner	79

It is evident from the preferences listed that professional characteristics such as an interest in learning and proficiency in teaching a subject were more important than personal characteristics or pleasing appearance and manner.

Another way to examine teacher characteristics in gifted education is suggested by Maker (1982) who divides the characteristics into three groups: philosophical, personal, and professional.

Philosophical characteristics are important because the way teachers view education has an impact on their approach to teaching. For example, a teacher who believes education for gifted students in itinerant pull-out programs, special classes, or special schools creates an elitist group will approach the program with negative feelings and a lack of enthusiasm for the gifted students or the program. When teachers view giftedness as including high intellectual potential, task commitment, high achievement, and creativity, they will approach the gifted students from a strength approach, tending to focus on subject matter. In contrast, teachers who view giftedness as composed of individual strengths and weaknesses will approach the teaching situation with a focus on individual gifted students.

Philosophical characteristics need to be considered in the selection of gifted teachers. For example, an elementary school principal outlined a proposed school-based gifted program with special classes for gifted in mathematics and language arts including both acceleration and enrichment. After an explicit faculty meeting where the goals of the program were outlined, the principal then invited the teachers who could support the proposed philosophical approach to participate in the gifted program and those who opposed the ideas to request a transfer. This situation is an example of a principal matching the philosophy of teachers with the programs. However, it is rare that school administrators can be that unequivocal in their beliefs and action. However, in that particular case, as a result of the total commitment on the part of the entire staff, the program thrived.

Other philosophical conflicts that teachers may have with gifted students are explored by Strom (1983). He states that teachers often think gifted students can make it on their own, and so they ignore them. Strom reports that teachers sometimes have a tendency to think that as long as gifted students earn high grades and stay out of trouble, it is unnecessary to consider their dissatisfactions. As a result of such reasoning, gifted students may become alienated and underachieve. To substantiate this danger, Strom points to the Iowa studies in which 45 percent of the students with IQs over 130 were receiving grades averaging lower than "C."

Wellborn (1980) reports that teachers may have philosophical difficulty with creativity in the classroom and that creative and talented students report incidents in which they were scorned, ridiculed, and deprived of suitable challenge.

Moreover, the attitudes of teachers do not necessarily need to be negative to be detrimental. For example, teachers may believe that gifted students can and will do better and consequently form favorable opinions concerning them as students. Strom (1983) states that once that favorable attitude is formed, it is sustained in spite of conflicting information. He relates a study in which teachers were asked to teach a card trick to one person of moderate ability and to another who was gifted. In fact, the students were of equal ability, yet the teachers expressed the belief that the gifted students performed better than the nongifted students, even when the reverse was true.

The importance of teachers' and administrators' recognition of philosophical stances and their consequences in the classroom is essential, since overly optimistic and unrealistic expectations are as detrimental to the education of gifted students as negative attitudes.

Professional characteristics of teachers, such as the ability to use group dynamic skills, advanced techniques, and strategies in a given subject area; to conduct inquiry training; and to possess knowledge of computer sciences, can be developed through in-service training.

One comprehensive list of professional criteria has been compiled by the state of California. The list includes using teaching methods, developing experiences, and employing methods of evaluation consistent with the needs and interests of individual gifted students.

In addition, several states are currently studying the feasibility of testing professional competency of teachers of the gifted through paper and pencil tests with items based on competency clusters consisting of (1) strategies to maximize the learning of gifted students, (2) guidance and counseling skills, and (3) knowledge and awareness of the psychology of the gifted student (Lavely, 1986).

The professional characteristics just mentioned have been delineated into specific competencies for teachers of the gifted. One example of this delineation is the San Diego Unified School District list (Appendix A). Selected items are:

Candidate will demonstrate familiarity with programming characteristics to include, but are not limited to, segregation, enrichment, acceleration, and early school entrance.

Candidate will be able to utilize systematic observation, academic assessment, clinical teaching, or information assessment procedures for individualizing instruction.

These competencies serve as an example of how professional characteristics can be identified and opportunities provided for teachers to build these professional competencies.

Plowman (1983), in a meeting of the Richardson Foundation in Fort Worth, Texas, reported that the California state criteria are divided into ten clusters of professional characteristics or competency groups such as (1) assessment of gifted, (2) knowledge of the nature and needs of gifted, (3) utilization of assessment data in planning individual programs for gifted, (4) knowledge of curriculum models relevant to gifted education, (5) knowledge and ability to utilize group dynamics, (6) knowledge of different programmatic efforts for gifted, (7) interest and commitment to teacher growth and effectiveness, (8) knowledge of rules and laws relative to gifted education, (9) knowledge and ability to counsel gifted students and their parents; and (10) knowledge of current trends and issues in gifted education. A portion of the California criteria is listed in Table 8-2, showing the breakdown of attributes.

TABLE 8-2
CALIFORNIA CRITERIA FOR TEACHERS OF THE
GIFTED

1.5   Knowledgeable—possessing broad knowledge, includ-
       ing superior knowledge in one field, an understanding
       of related fields, and insight into how knowledge from
       various fields may be applied in analyzing and in arriving
       at solutions to problems

1.6   Flexible

1.61   In recreating and restructuring the physical environment

1.62   In using materials and equipment

1.63   In structuring and restructuring interest-learning-person-
       ality-developing groups and classroom experiences

1.64   In planning lessons and in modifying lessons to capi-
       talize on a "moment of" or opportunity for learning

Source: California State Department of Public Instruction. Used by
permission.

Teachers who possess the competencies listed will be highly professional individuals. The teacher profile it suggests is similar to the profile suggested by
Whitmore (1980), who describes teachers of the gifted as teachers who model
the traits and lifestyle of a scholar, who challenge the students to think at higher
levels, who stimulate interest and independent pursuits, who are responsive to
the need for flexibility, and who enjoy the energetic and inquiring minds of gifted
children.

Personal characteristics are probably the least amenable to change. Personal
characteristics are inherent traits including motivation, self-confidence, sense of
humor, patience, wide interests, and flexibility. Consequently, in many situations
teachers are unable to adjust to the personality characteristics needed for gifted
programs.

Lindsey (1980) has synthesized the personal characteristics of teachers who
are successful in working with gifted students. They include understanding and
accepting one's self, having outstanding ego strength, being sensitive to others,
having above-average intellectual interests, and being responsible for one's own
behavior and its consequences.

Still another example of desirable personal characteristics for teachers of the
gifted is documented by Kathnelson and Colley (1982). They asked gifted students,
ages 6 to 16 years, to record descriptions of what they would like the ideal teacher
to do as a teacher and as a person. The personal characteristics included someone
who understands them; who has a sense of humor; who is cheerful, supportive,
and respectful; and who is patient and flexible.

Other personal characteristics have been documented by numerous researchers
such as Bishop (1968); Drews (1972); Freehill (1975); Gallagher et al. (1967);
and Baldwin (1977). They are empathy, tolerance, authenticity and congruency,
self-actualization, and enthusiasm.

Maker (1982) suggests that school districts and school officials should decide on the curriculum approach or administrative model for the program and choose teachers who possess the necessary skills, personal traits, and philosophy to complement the program, or they should choose teachers who possess a given set of personal and professional characteristics and encourage them to develop their own curricular approach. The more open-ended the school district's approach to gifted programming, the more likely the school administrators are to select the latter approach. However, in well-defined and well-established programs, it is imperative that teachers have skills, personal traits, and philosophies compatible with the gifted program to enable the program to be successful. Teachers who possess the competencies discussed in this chapter will be vital, growing, caring, knowledgeable individuals.

The teachers' role in gifted education is effectively clarified by Drews (1976):

> The teacher's task is to inspire and release . . . the teachers who have the greatest appeal to the gifted are those who combine two characteristics. First of all, they must know a great deal, and their knowledge should extend to the far reaches of their subjects. (Those who are themselves excited learners can communicate this feeling to their students). Second, they must have a superlative ability to relate to others. For the gifted, as well as for all students, the creative teacher is one who has faith in young people and loves students, who is cooperative and kind, who is democratic and considerate. Such teachers act on the belief that all human beings are naturally good and have transcendent potentiality. With such values and guidance, the student can make the most fundamental decisions—choices of lifestyles and world-views—as well as the minute-to-minute choices of which most people actually remain unaware . . . (p. 28).

TEACHER PREPARATION

There are many ways teachers can become more effective in working with gifted children and youth. Teacher educators in university and college settings may offer courses, and state and local education agencies may offer in-service training workshops. Yet, in spite of outstanding degree and nondegree seeking teacher training programs, there is no absolute assurance of success in working with gifted students, unless the teachers bring knowledge, awareness, and experience to teaching of the gifted. To maximize the opportunity for successful teaching of gifted students, several models for training are examined and discussed.

College and University Programs

During the last decade college and university programs have grown from a little over ten reported programs in the Marland report (1972) to over 140 college and university program offerings in more than forty states (Hultgren, 1982). Karnes and Parker (1984) report 101 programs leading to M.A., Ed.S., and Ph.D. degrees. The programs vary from college to college and university to university, with some offering one or two courses and others offering full degree programs with emphasis on gifted education. However, most of the surveys indicate that courses are geared toward the graduate level with teaching experience required (Lindsey, 1980).

In 1981, The Association for Gifted (TAG) and a committee on professional training from the National Association for Gifted Children (NAGC) identified three areas for the establishment of a set of professional standards in gifted education (Seeley, 1981).

1 *In gifted/talented education*—Establishing standards encourages the continued growth of the field. Standards provide a basis for communication and reciprocity among programs, and for continued dialogue relative to the nature of training in an evolving field.

2 *For institutions*—Adopting standards for approved programs performs a crucial function on this level: ensuring a minimum university commitment to professional training. By "institutionalization" of programs, we are eliminating much of the "patched on" quality which is unfortunately beginning to characterize many higher education programs.

3 *In training programs*—It is not the purpose of standards to guarantee that graduates have mastered particular skills. However, professional standards would ensure that trainees at various levels have been exposed to essential information in theoretical and applied contexts. (pp.165–166)

The six standards that were proposed are:

1 *Admission and selection criteria.* The institution should publish specific criteria for admission to programs at each degree level. These criteria should include cognitive and affective evidence obtained from multiple sources and should be congruent with stated program philosophy and goals.

2 *Curriculum and competence areas.* Training programs should establish a coherent, comprehensive, and discernible curriculum that addresses the major areas of gifted education as well as related studies. The curriculum should address theory, practice, and research in each of these areas.

3 *Degree programs.* Degree programs with a major emphasis in gifted education should be offered only at the graduate level and should be differentiated from one another appropriate to level (i.e., masters, specialist, doctoral).

4 *Faculty for graduate programs.* Faculty members with major teaching responsibilities in graduate programs should hold the doctorate with advanced study in gifted child education, or have competence in the field as demonstrated by significant research, writing, or leadership in gifted education. Faculty members who conduct the advanced programs should be engaged in scholarly activity which supports their specialization in the field and have experiences which relate directly to gifted education.

5 *Administrative structure—staffing.* The faculty for advanced programs should include at least one full-time doctoral-level person who holds an appropriate degree or has demonstrated competence, and at least three persons who hold the doctorate in fields which directly support the program.

6 *Administrative structure—evaluation.* The program's mission and course offerings should be reviewed regularly. The results of this evaluation should be used in program modification and improvement efforts. Systematic opportunities should be provided for student and faculty input into program administration, review, and planning.

7 *Resources and facilities.* Institutions that offer graduate programs in gifted education should assure adequate human and material resources and facilities to implement their prescribed course of study. (pp. 166–168)

With greater interest in building training programs at the university and college levels, such standards as the above developed by TAG and NAGC are most helpful. In a survey conducted by Hultgren (1982), several areas were identified as needing continued study. These were listed as a need for programs to include knowledge of leadership skills and career options for the gifted, programming for culturally diverse gifted, use of educational technology, programming for under-achieving gifted, better community relations and resource development, and the need for practical experience for teachers of the gifted.

Zettel (1979), Hultgren (1982), and others have surveyed the number and types of courses offered to the gifted and in spite of reported variance, the courses do cluster around several topics or areas: (a) Psychology or nature and needs of the gifted; (b) methods and strategies of teaching the gifted; (c) creative behavior or creativity development; (d) counseling and guidance of gifted; and (e) research on the gifted.

Programs for Degree-Seeking Graduate Students

Programs for training teachers of the gifted at the Master of Education level (M.A.) are usually competency based. Many programs use the competencies compiled for the Office of Gifted and Talented and disseminated by the LTI:

- Knowledge of nature and needs of gifted
- Skill in developing higher cognitive thinking abilities
- Knowledge of affective/cognitive needs of gifted
- Ability to develop creative problem solving
- Ability to develop materials for the gifted
- Ability to utilize individual teaching strategies
- Ability to demonstrate appropriate teaching techniques and materials for the gifted
- Ability to guide and counsel gifted students and their parents
- Ability to carry out action research in the classroom

The above competencies are achieved in a number of courses, including *Nature and Needs of the Gifted, Educational Procedures for the Gifted, Creative Problem Solving, Guidance and Counseling for Gifted and Their Parents, Research Programs in Gifted* and *Supervised Practicum With Gifted.* In addition to these professional courses, some M.A. programs include courses in liberal arts, with graduate students enrolling in liberal arts as well as professional education courses.

Many training programs are based on teacher competencies as well as on the perceived needs of gifted students and the teacher's ability to work with gifted in direct experiences. These training programs can be figuratively depicted (Figure 8-1) with the professional education courses in the center, complemented by the

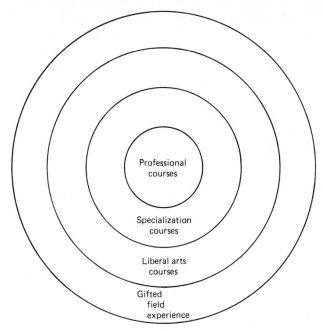

FIGURE 8-1
Visualization of MA programs.

specialization courses in gifted education, strengthened by increased competency in the liberal arts, and reinforced by field experiences with gifted students.

The M.A. programs can be visualized with the aid of Figure 8-1.

These types of program offerings in teacher education for the gifted are made at universities such as the University of Connecticut, Purdue University, the University of Georgia at Athens, and the University of South Florida at Tampa. For descriptions of other programs see Renzulli (1973), Gear (1974), Maker (1975), and Sisk (1975).

In-service Training for Teachers of the Gifted

Training for teachers of the gifted which is provided by school districts, state education departments, and colleges and universities is different from the basic graduate programs in gifted education, in that the training sessions offer experiences with specific goals. These goals include topics such as developing higher level thinking skills, communication, and creative thinking skills; leadership skill development; learning techniques to work with underachieving students; developing strategies for reducing stress; and planning advanced placement courses. In-service education for teachers of the gifted includes summer institutes, demonstration projects, the use of in-service centers, technical assistance, and other related support activities.

One of the better summer institutes is the one run by the LTI, originally funded by the federal Office of Gifted and Talented. The LTI conducts annual 2-week intensive institutes designed for teachers and leaders of the gifted. These institutes include the latest teaching strategies and timely topics pertaining to the gifted. In addition, the LTI provides individually contracted workshops for local and state education agencies.

In-service training can be ineffective if it is conducted in a traditional manner, with outside experts involved in short-term workshops, institutes, or projects and with no opportunity or time for follow-up. To counterbalance these problems, Gallagher (1983) proposes a three-point plan: (1) a needs assessment, (2) a formal contract of agreement that relates to personnel time and the manner of delivery of the services, and (3) a talent bank to store all kinds of information about available personnel and resources.

Still another suggestion for building and achieving relevance in in-service is suggested by Renzulli (1977). He suggests an instructional management system (IMS) with three major objectives: (1) to compress much highly relevant information into a relatively short training period; (2) to provide a structure of knowledge about the topic or teaching strategy presented; and (3) to provide a series of packaged workshops that can be used by other trainers. Renzulli identifies several general types of informational content including rationale; packaged workshop activities, including theoretical information; demonstration activities, samples of exemplary teaching, lists of exemplary programs, catalogs and descriptions of available materials, and material evaluation forms; student materials, including no-fail introductory activities, student information about the IMS; and program evaluation. The advantage of the Gallagher and Renzulli training proposals is that workshops and institutes can go beyond being entertaining or even informative to providing concepts and tools for continuous learning by teachers and gifted students.

A Specific In-service Example Organized Around a Unique Problem

Many schools might offer advanced placement (AP) programs if they had secondary teachers who felt confident to teach what are often viewed as college-level courses. This problem is complicated by the realization that few teacher education institutions have courses for the training of individuals who are interested in teaching advanced placement of gifted students. Only rarely do departments consider this part of their mission.

Spear (1983) reports this omission was addressed through the cooperation of the College Board and a consortium of southwestern colleges and universities, who agreed to provide special summer courses for AP and prospective AP teachers. The teachers were given graduate credit and financial assistance to attend. The biology course used multiple approaches for the advanced placement teachers including up-to-date knowledge of the field, knowledge of frontier research areas in biology, new ideas for laboratory exercises, information on how to begin an advanced placement course, information on how to construct tests for AP students, and information on the College Board's AP exams. Emphasis was also placed on providing teachers with the needed confidence to offer AP courses. The topics were selected by giving the teachers copies of the biology AP syllabus, prepared by the National College Board's committee on AP biology, and adding to the list ten topics they wanted reviewed and ten topics they would like to discuss. After the teacher responses were compiled, the topics receiving the most votes were the ones covered. This example of in-service training addresses specific needs, and exemplifies the suggestions of Gallagher (1983) and Renzulli (1973).

Lowenstein (1981) reports on the effectiveness of in-service training on guidance and education of gifted students. The "experimental teachers" were compared with teachers in twenty schools with no in-service program (control). The former used more classroom activities for enrichment and were more successful than the latter. Lowenstein states that one of the greatest jobs psychologists have, in addition to assessing students who might be gifted, is helping teachers help students who have been diagnosed as gifted. He further states that teachers working with gifted students should be special people themselves to be effective in understanding teaching the gifted. He states it is vital for teachers to have continuous training to learn to develop an individual or small group teaching approach, to consider the speed with which tracking takes place, and to base tracking on the needs and capacities of the individual gifted student rather than on a highly organized and inflexible approach determined by chronological age or limited by the course curriculum.

OTHER TEACHERS OF THE GIFTED

In comprehensive gifted programs, many different people are considered teachers of the gifted and these people play significant roles in the gifted program. For example, leaders in the community can serve as mentors, parents can be considered teachers in the home, and ancillary personnel, psychologists, counselors, and psychometrists can provide services for the gifted.

Use of Mentors as Teachers

A classic model of mentorship was initiated by Hirsch under a grant by the Office of Gifted and Talented in 1976–1979 (Hirsch 1979). Hirsch used her mentorship model primarily with high school students. Gifted students received one semester of credit and were assigned to mentors or community leaders in decision-making positions. In addition, they attended weekly seminars using the Harvard case study method to share experiences, insights, and problems.

Such mentor relationships can be enhanced through the use of teacher-led questions suggested by Maker (1982). Selected questions are:

- Are you a calculated risk taker? What are some specific situations in which you tried something without full assurance of success?
- What are the different ways you have used to get information and insight from your career exploration experiences?

- What is your role as a mentee? How do you feel about that role? How well do you play that role?
- What experiences have you had as a mentee that require you to be flexible? How do you feel about those experiences?
- What is self-direction? What have you done that you consider demonstrates initiative? Why?
- What are the different ways you can show someone what you have learned?

In spite of the fact that most mentor programs are planned for secondary gifted students, there is no reason that mentor programs cannot be made available to elementary and middle school gifted students. Using the classical definition of mentor, i.e., an individual with expertise sharing with a gifted student, a mentor can be an older gifted student sharing experience with a younger one, or it may be an adult in the community and/or business sector. Still another neglected source of mentors is older people. Many retirees have considerable experience and knowledge that can be tapped by gifted students. In addition, the retired have unlimited time to devote to gifted students in comparison to mentors engaged in daily work. A valuable resource for school districts contemplating beginning a mentorship program is the mentor academy model, described by Runions (1980).

One potential problem with mentor programs is that the expert or leader may not be able to relate effectively to gifted students. However, in spite of this problem, gifted students receive great benefit from shadowing their mentors. Gifted students assigned to sites such as congressional offices, business firms, banks, scientific laboratories, schools, hospitals, and other sites observe the dynamics in a given field and experience the leadership characteristics of their mentors in action.

A useful source for understanding the role of the mentor is the *Sorcerer's Apprentice: A Case Study in the Role of the Mentor* (Boston, 1976). Boston analyzes the relationship between the mentor and the mentee and concludes: (1) mentor programs in gifted education should be rooted in experimental learning; (2) both mentor and mentee to some degree should select each other in the context of a dual commitment; (3) mentoring programs for the gifted should be open-ended; and (4) instruction and evaluation should be competency based.

An example of a successful mentor program for gifted was initiated under a federally funded Title IV stimulation grant in cooperation with a local university. The project concentrated on building school/community relationships and identifying mentors to work with gifted students. Adults were located in a wide variety of fields including the arts and the sciences and an agreement was made between the school and the individual mentors to work on a one-to-one basis with the gifted and talented students (Ting, 1967). The mentor project was successful in serving gifted students and in building community commitment to gifted education.

Sellin (1980) suggests a useful technique for bringing more precision to the mentoring process. The technique, developed by Charkhuff, consists of a four-part model: (1) attending, (2) responding, (3) personalizing, and (4) initiating. A mentor's attending and responding helps convince mentees of their personal worth, and through responding and personalizing, the mentor serves to convince the mentee that he or she is being understood. In addition, through initiating or devising a plan of action for the mentee, there is a natural growth in trust and empathy.

Parents as Teachers

Parents and teachers of the gifted want what is best for gifted students, yet parents may need to better understand the characteristics of their gifted children. Clark (1983) lists topics for five parent sessions which she offers in a university setting:

1 *Understanding giftedness*—Who are the gifted? How do you nurture giftedness?

2 *Emotional and social development of the gifted*—Developing self-esteem, values, and creativity. ·

3 *Meeting the needs of the gifted*—Program alternatives, differential curriculum, learning and challenges, integrating all four areas of learning, and evaluation.

4 *Effective teachers at home and at school*—The nurturing home, growth, families, communication, the teacher in the classroom as a part of the learning community.

5 *What can you do now?*—Planning with the school, student–parent–teacher interaction, legislative possibilities and provisions, and becoming active for gifted education in your community.

In-service training experiences encourage parents to work toward quality education for gifted children. After in-service training experiences, many parents can function as teachers or teacher assistants, creating learning or interests units and supplying materials. In many universities' Saturday seminars for gifted students, parents serve as teacher/helpers with small groups and in some cases teach classes in which they hold expertise, such as computers, art, chemistry, akaido, and other topics. The following points offer some guidelines for parents as teachers.

1 Try to listen and interact nonjudgmentally when communicating with your gifted child or other gifted children. Share your own ideas, and remember you are talking with a younger person. Be sensitive to the amount of information they are willing and able to absorb.

2 Volunteer to help in areas where you have expertise and in areas where your enjoyment and enthusiasm can be shared. An essential part of your teaching role is to be a vital model for learning.

3 Encourage the individuality of each child. Provide opportunities for the gifted to form their own ideas, values, and ways of doing things. Respect their separateness.

4 Allow the gifted child to observe his or her own personal doubts and shortcomings. Sometimes, gifted students are very uncomfortable with failure and seek perfection. By learning that adults learn from their mistakes, gifted children learn the value of setting realistic personal standards and learn to be comfortable in the process of "becoming" or learning.

5 Help your gifted child set time and energy priorities. Gifted children perceive the world as exciting and stimulating and, as a result, they may try to be a part of everything. By modeling the good use of time and the planning of activities, you can help your child become a better user of time, personal interests, and energy.

6 Share your excitement and love of life. Gifted children need to feel understood and they need to feel they are part of the growing family of humanity. They can experience this phenomenon through loving, caring relationships with adults.

Other suggestions which are geared to fostering achievement and creativity are reported by Telford and Sawrey (1981):

- Perpetuate curiosity
- Free people from fear of error
- Encourage fantasy- as well as reality-oriented cognition
- Encourage contacts with creative people
- Encourage diversity and individuality
- Encourage individual initiative
- Avoid stereotyping the potentially creative

These suggestions apply to parents and individuals who willingly come into contact with gifted students to help stimulate their growth and development. The overall interaction profile conducive to achievement and creativity in gifted students calls for people willing to reward curiosity. Gifted students need to be encouraged to be spontaneous and use critical evaluation with an emphasis on accepting and appreciating differences. Three action components for parents, teachers, and others are: (1) emphasize curiosity, (2) build self-esteem, and (3) stimulate creativity. According to Maw and Maw (1980) these components develop and grow together.

ROLE OF ANCILLARY PERSONNEL WITH GIFTED

The role of ancillary personnel, such as psychologists, counselors, psychometrists, and others must be continuous if the education of the gifted is to be dynamic.

Role of the Psychologist

Psychologists can be helpful in developing intensive training opportunities for classroom teachers of the gifted, by helping teachers build a better understanding of these students' nature and needs and developing methods to encourage creativity, self-esteem, and curiosity. Other ways for the psychologist to lend support to the gifted program are by helping parents work with their gifted child's unique needs and interests and by assisting in the identification of and programming for special populations of gifted such as the disadvantaged, the handicapped, and the creatively gifted. With the psychologist's guidance in developing profiles of individual gifted pupil needs, teachers can develop more appropriate educational plans.

Role of the Counselor

Counselors can help gifted students learn to better understand themselves and to make wise decisions, particularly in the area of career choices. One successful method is the use of joint parent and teacher sessions, in which the participants experience a group helping process, which can be very positive. A helping process, called the "child study technique" is explained in considerable detail in Chapter 11 on guidance and counseling. Through the use of this technique the counselor can help the participants experience powerful problem solving.

Role of the Psychometrist

Psychometrists can assist classroom teachers, administrators, parents, counselors and psychologists by sharing specific information concerning the test behavior of the gifted student during the individual testing session. Individual student behavior during testing reflects a microcosm of his/her overall behavior. The gifted student's degree of perseverance, cooperation, and initiative, as well as test behavior in skill areas such as creating, valuing, choosing, communicating, and discovering can be very useful in grasping an overall view of the functioning level of gifted students.

Implicit in comprehensive planning for gifted students is the notion that schools involve ancillary personnel for advice, support, and help in identifying a variety of possibilities for their growth and development. It is important for teachers to realize that there is no one curriculum for gifted students' diversity. Also, it is essential that there be dialogue and cooperation among all school personnel, the parents, and the community members. To achieve this, Kovner (1979) suggests a program development effort utilizing community members, museums, colleges and universities, and other students as an organizational framework. Such total approaches offer greater opportunity for all students, as well as for the gifted, to achieve excellence.

SUMMARY

Qualifications for teachers of the gifted were discussed, and these characteristics were divided into philosophical, professional, and personal characteristics, as suggested by Maker (1982).

Philosophical characteristics were deemed important, because the ways in which teachers view education affects their approach to students and the classroom. Teachers of the gifted need to reflect a cooperative, democratic attitude and have a competency and/or interest in learning. Professional characteristics are strategies to maximize the learning of gifted students, guidance and counseling skills, and knowledge and awareness of the psychology of the gifted student. Personal characteristics include empathy, tolerance of ambiguity, authenticity, congruency, self-actualization, and enthusiasm. Plowman's specific state criteria for teacher selection in California were examined (Plowman 1983).

Teacher preparation was covered, and the purposes and standards developed and reported through the joint efforts of (TAG) and (NAGC) were noted. (Seeley, 1981). Programs at the M.A. level were discussed. These programs consist of four parts: (1) professional education, (2) specialization courses, (3) liberal arts, and (4) practicum or field experiences.

In-service training was defined as short-term training, and the suggestions offered by Gallagher (1983) and Renzulli (1977) for planning effective experiences for teachers were outlined. A unique consortium effort to meet a specific in-service need of planning advanced placement courses in biology was covered.

Mentors as teachers was discussed and the role of the mentor and mentee was defined. Specific suggestions were given for seminar questions such as "What experiences have you had as a mentee that require you to be flexible?" Techniques for bringing more precision to the mentoring process were listed: (1) attending, (2) responding, (3) personalizing, and (4) initiating (Sellin, 1980).

The topic of parents as teachers was examined. Parent session topics and guidelines for parents as teachers were suggested. The role of ancillary personnel in gifted programs was covered, with emphasis on the need for continuous interaction and dialogue for advice, support, and help to provide for full growth and development of gifted students.

EXTENDING ACTIVITIES

1 Using the Davis list of characteristics (Davis, 1954), interview a sample of gifted students (a cohort of ten) and rank order their preferences. Then rank order the list, using your own perceptions of teachers. Compare your perceptions of teachers with those of your sample group of gifted students.
2 Research your state's criteria for teacher selection and/or teacher competencies for gifted. Be prepared to discuss one or both.
3 Arrange to attend an AP class. Note the teacher's efforts in varying the process, product, or content. Also, notice the learning environment in the classroom.
4 Take Telford and Sawrey's (1981) specific suggestions to foster achievement and creativity, and modify them to use as an informal assessment instrument, such as "Do you encourage contacts with creative people?" Interview a parent of a gifted student. Encourage the parent to give examples of his/her parenting behavior and share your findings in class.

REFERENCES

Baldwin, A. (1977). Seven keys in program planning for gifted and talented. *Roeper City and County School Parent Communicator, 2*, 3–6.
Bentley, J. E. (1937). *Superior children: Their physiological, psychological and social development.* New York: W. W. Norton.
Bishop, W. (1968). Successful teachers of the gifted. *Exceptional Children, 34*, 317–325.

Boston, B. (1976). *The sorcerer's apprentice—A case study in the role of the mentor.* Reston, VA: EMC Clearing House on Handicapped and Gifted Children, The Council for Exceptional Children.

Callahan, C. M. & Renzulli, J. S. (1977). The effectiveness of a creativity training program in the language arts. *Gifted Child Quarterly*, April, 538–545.

Carroll, H. (1940). *Genius in the making.* New York: McGraw-Hill.

Clark, B. (1983). *Growing up gifted.* Columbus, OH: Charles E. Merrill.

Davis, N. (1954). Teachers of the gifted. *Journal of Teacher Education, 5,* 221–224.

Drews, E. M. (1972). *Learning together: How to foster creativity, self-fulfillment, and social awareness in today's students and teachers.* Englewood Cliffs, NJ: Prentice-Hall.

Drews, E. M. (1976). Leading out and letting be. *Today's Education,* 26–28.

Dunkin, M. S. & Bidler, B. J. (1974). *The study of teaching.* New York: Holt, Rinehart and Winston.

Freehill, M. (1975). Teachers for the gifted. In B. Boston (Ed.), *A Resource Manual of Information for Educating the Gifted and Talented.* Reston, VA: Council for Exceptional Children.

Gallagher, J. (1983). A plan for catalytic support for gifted education in the 1980's. *The Elementary School Journal, 82*(3), 180–185.

Gallagher, J., Aschner, M. & Jenne, W. (1967). Productive thinking in the classroom. *Interaction.* Reston, VA: The Council for Exceptional Children.

Gaze, N. L. & Berliner, D. C. (1979). *Educational psychology.* Chicago: Rand McNally.

Gear, G. (1974). *Teaching the talented program: A progress report.* Storrs: University of Connecticut.

Hirsch, S. (1979). *Executive intenprogram.* Report to the office of gifted and talented, Washington, DC.

Hultgren, H. (1982). Competencies for teachers of the gifted. *Dissertation Abstracts.* Doctoral dissertation, University of Denver.

Impelizzeri, A. E., Farrell, M. S. & Melville, G. G. (1976). Psychology and emotional needs of gifted youngsters. *NASSP Bulletin*, March, 43–52.

Karnes, F. & Parker, J. (1984). Graduate degree programs in the education of the gifted. *Journal of the Gifted, 7,* 205–216.

Kathnelson, A. & Colley, L. (1982). *Personal and professional characteristics valued in teachers of the gifted.* Unpublished paper presented at California State University, Los Angeles, CA.

Kovner, A. (1979). Improving the quality of programs for gifted and talented students. *Kappa Delta Pi*, April, 114–115.

Lavely, C. (1986). *Competency test for teachers of the gifted.* Report to the state of Florida, Tampa.

Lindsey, M. (1980). *Training teachers of the gifted and talented.* New York: Teachers College Press.

Lowenstein, L. F. (1981). *The psychological problems for gifted children.* Coxtons Publishers.

Maker, J. (1975). *Training teachers for the gifted and talented: A comparison of models.* Reston, VA: The Council for Exceptional Children.

Maker, J. (1982). *Curriculum development for the gifted.* Rockville, MD: Aspen Systems Corporation.

Mandell, C. & Fiscus, E. (1981). *Understanding exceptional people.* New York: West Publishing Company.

Marland, S., Jr. (1972). *Education of the gifted and talented.* Report to the Congress of the U.S. by the U.S. Commission of Education. Washington, DC: U.S. Government Printing Office.

Maw, W. H., & Maw, E. W. (1970). Self concepts of high and low curiosity boys. *Child Development*, 41, 123–129.

McCumsey, J. (1985). Conducting: A longitudinal study. *Challenge*, 3 (4), 42–48.

Merman, J. J. (1971). Education of the gifted in the '70s. *Gifted Child Quarterly*, Autumn, 217–224.

Newland, T. E. (1976). *The gifted in socioeducational perspective*. Englewood Cliffs, NJ: Prentice-Hall.

Plowman, P. (1983). *Competencies for California teachers*. Unpublished paper presented at the Richardson Foundation, Fort Worth, TX.

Renzulli, J. (1973). *Graduate study in special education of the gifted and talented*. Storrs: University of Connecticut, Department of Educational Psychology.

Renzulli, J. (1977). *The enrichment triad model—A guide for developing programs for the gifted and talented*. Oransfield, CT: Creative Learning Press.

Runions, T. (1980). The mentor academy program: Educating the gifted/talented for the 80's. *Gifted Child Quarterly*, 24(4), 152–157.

Seeley, K. (1981). Professional standards for training programs in gifted education. *Journal of the Education of the Gifted*, 4(3), 165–168.

Sellin, D. & Birch, J. (1983). *Psychoeducational development of gifted and talented learners*. Rockville, MD: Aspen Systems Publishers.

Sisk, D. (1984). *Evaluation report of governors honors program*. State of Florida.

Sisk, D. (1975). Teaching the gifted and talented teacher: A training model. *The Gifted Child Quarterly*, 19, 81–88.

Spear, I. (1983). *Texas cooperative project in advanced placement*. Unpublished paper presented at the Richardson Foundation, Fort Worth, TX.

Strom, R. (1983). Expectations for educating the gifted teacher. *The Education Forum*, Spring, 279–303.

Telford, C. & Sawrey, J. (1981). The gifted and highly creative. *The Exceptional Index*. Englewood Cliffs, NJ: Prentice-Hall.

Ting, M. (1967). *Evaluation report of project matchmaker*. Florida Department of Education.

Wellborn, B. (1980). The gifted child: Big challenge for college. *U.S. News and World Report, 89*.

Whitmore, J. (1980). *Conflict and underachievement*. Boston: Allyn and Bacon.

Zettel, J. (1979). Gifted and talented education over a half decade of change. *Journal for the Education of the Gifted, 3*, 14–31.

CHAPTER 9

EVALUATION OF PROGRAMS FOR THE GIFTED

CHAPTER 9

EVALUATION OF PROGRAMS FOR THE GIFTED

Were it offered to my choice, I should have no objection to a repetition of the same life from its beginning, only asking the advantage authors have in a second edition to correct some faults of the first.

Benjamin Franklin

The evaluation of programs for the gifted has become increasingly important, as local and state educational agencies and private and federal funding sources examine budgets and decide on funding priorities. Questions pertaining to effectiveness and efficiency are commonplace. To continue their vital growth and development, programs for the gifted must include ways and means to answer these questions.

This chapter examines the definition of evaluation and focuses on the key features of evaluation: (1) establishing the purpose of evaluation; (2) examining and determining measurable program goals and student performance objectives; (3) choosing valid and reliable measures; and (4) communicating data to all audiences. Unique problems of evaluation with gifted students, such as the use of inappropriate levels of tests; the use of a single test score for both selecting and pretesting participants in a gifted program; incorrectly interpreting data; and teacher alienation are discussed. Evaluation models of Stufflebeam (1971) and Provus (1971) are examined, and suggestions for choosing evaluators are made. The last section offers selected sample instruments for the evaluation of gifted programs.

Photograph on facing page courtesy of Elizabeth Crews, Berkeley, California.

DEFINITION OF EVALUATION

The term "evaluation" has many connotations to educators, administrators, and parents. "Evaluate," as defined, means "to find the value or amount of; to determine the worth of; appraise." Consequently, to many individuals including those mentioned above, evaluation means "to test." In the context of this chapter, evaluation is defined as determining the value of or gathering information about the gifted program. This concept of evaluation broadens the process beyond the realm of testing to include the gathering of a number of types of data or information in order to help decision makers improve programs for gifted students. This point of view has been supported by a number of researchers, such as Hedges (1979) and Cammeron (1978), who state that the purpose of evaluation is to provide data to educators. They define evaluation as a means to improve instruction or the quality of services. This definition is similar to that of Brinkerhoff (1979), in which evaluation is defined as the extent to which the program's standards have become reality and these standards are compared to actual performance. Cammeron further insists that accountability and evaluation procedures *guide* educators rather than dominate or intimidate them. Raybin (1971) clarifies the concept of evaluation by stating that evaluation is a means towards an end—a tool.

In discussing program evaluation, it is essential to examine the key features of evaluation in gifted programs and to examine the purpose of evaluation as one of the most essential elements in a comprehensive program evaluation.

KEY FEATURES OF EVALUATION

Establishing the Purpose of Evaluation

The purpose of evaluation must be agreed upon by all of the individuals involved in the gifted program. Sometimes the process of evaluation is seen as pure experimental research carried on by external evaluators or the "central administration." When the purpose of evaluation is viewed as experimental research, the emphasis is on establishing experimental and control groups and on gathering data, including both pretest and posttest data. Also, an attitude may prevail that the data will suggest whether the program should be continued or discontinued.

Evaluation as discussed in this chapter is a process used to determine outcome effects, as suggested by Callahan (1983). In order to gather program information to make the programs better for gifted students, outcome evaluations are needed. Outcome evaluations are referred to as "summative" evaluations (Howell et al., 1979). In utilizing such an attitudinal approach, educators direct their efforts toward identifying the elements of the gifted program which contribute to positive growth in gifted students and those which do not. Evaluations should give information about which aspects to revise and change. Evaluations that can point to areas that need change in the program are continuous and called "formative" (Howell et al., 1979). The use of continuous evaluation allows program planners and developers to revise faulty elements in gifted programs rather than continue them to the end.

Once the purpose of evaluation has been decided upon, then program planners, teachers, parents, and evaluators must reach consensus on information needed. Clark (1983) lists six points that are helpful in planning the focus of data gathering and clarifying the purpose of evaluation:

1 Know clearly what each person or group involved in your program needs to know.

2 Choose instruments and tools to give you the information.

3 Set up collection points throughout the year in addition to your assessment procedures.

4 Collect only useful data.

5 Communicate your information to all concerned persons and groups.

6 Use your evaluation data to produce growth in the program.

The above suggestions require expansion with emphasis on the evaluators proceeding from the overall program goals and objectives to the student performance objectives to make sure they are measurable. Once this is accomplished, then the correct tools can be selected and Clark's procedures carried out.

Examining and Determining Measurable Program Goals and Student Performance Objectives

Renzulli and Smith (1979) state that one of the major problems in program evaluation is that the perspective of the evaluator and the program staff often differ. To the evaluators, the goals of the program may seem vague and unmeasurable, such as "The students will become more motivated" or "The students will become more creative." Yet the program staff may view the evaluators as using jargon such as the following statement contains, introduced primarily by Mager (1962): Eighty-five percent of the students will achieve 90 percent of the items on the Creativity Matrix as measured by the Williams Inventory.

Somewhere between "The students will become more creative" and "eighty-five percent of the students will achieve at 90 percent of the items on the Creativity Matrix as measured by the Williams Inventory" are simply stated and measurable objectives. It is important that the objectives be capable of communicating the direction and goal of the gifted program to a wide audience. For example, a gifted program in Alberquerque, as reported by Maker (1982), entitled SPACE (or the Special Program for Advanced Career Exploration) has three major student performance objectives stated as follows. The student will demonstrate:

1 *Self-knowledge:* evaluation of their abilities, interests, and aptitudes that will enable students to consider the compatibility of their strengths and interests in relation to the requirements of their career goals.

2 *Interpersonal skills:* interviewing techniques, responsible, assertive behavior, self-confidence, adequate assessment of skills and abilities, and ability to establish a one-to-one working relationship with a professional.

3 *Work competencies:* seriousness of purpose, willingness to undertake assignments, dependability in meeting commitments, discretion in handling confidential situations, sensitivity in interpersonal relations, independence, accuracy, creative problem solving, promptness, appropriate dress and appearance, and a generally responsive and positive attitude.

These student performance objectives are very explicit and involved. In evaluating the student performance objectives, evaluation should be based on a variety of types of information such as objective measures, interviews, written reports from the students, and parent information. Assessment of students include standardized testing using the Wide Range Achievement Test (WRAT), the Woodcock-Johnson Psychoeducational Battery, and the Watson-Glaser Test of Critical Thinking. This information is supplemented by student self-evaluation and teacher appraisal of growth.

Overall program evaluation is accomplished using the Class Activities Questionnaire (CAQ), developed by Steele (1969), and with forms compiled by students, parents, and mentors. The CAQ has been used extensively in evaluating programs for the gifted in the state of Illinois and other selected areas. It is designed to assess the classroom climate and has five dimensions: (1) lower thought processes, (2) higher thought processes, (3) classroom focus, (4) classroom climate, and (5) student questions.

The CAQ is based on the lower and higher thought processes of Bloom's taxonomy and examines the classroom focus or the role the teacher plays, with particular emphasis on whether he or she is active or passive. The classroom climate section yields information on students' attitudes and feelings, and the student opinions section reflects students' thoughts about their class and particularly what items they would like to influence or change. Sample items are in Exhibit 9-1.

The overall SPACE objective, to increase the articulation between the school and community, is assessed using questionnaires to measure the effectiveness and quality of the mentorship. One questionnaire is completed by the mentor from the community, another by the parents, and another by the students. Each questionnaire assesses the student entry and exit characteristics, the overall operation of the program, and the value of the experience for the mentor.

The SPACE evaluation also attempts to gather information about the overall value of the gifted program. Tests are used as part of the data gathering and supplemented by discussion, observation, questionnaires, and daily input. The gathered data is used to help gain a better understanding of the gifted students in the program and to improve program planning and implementation.

Choosing Valid and Reliable Measures

One of the major questions to be dealt with in evaluation is "Does the program for the gifted have an educational effect?" Still another major concern and question for evaluation is "Can the existence of an educational effect be established with valid and reliable measures?" A simple definition of a valid measure is that it is one that has a logical relationship to what is being measured, whether it is creative reading, self-concept, program planning, or decision making.

EXHIBIT 9-1

SAMPLE OF ITEMS FROM CLASS ACTIVITIES QUESTIONNAIRE

For each sentence below, circle the letters which show the extent to which you *agree* or *disagree.*

Base your answer on how well each sentence describes what is stressed in your class . . . what your teacher has you do.

Circle SA   If you *strongly agree* with the sentence.
Circle A   If you *agree* moderately with the sentence.
Circle D   If you *disagree* moderately with the sentence.
Circle SD   If you *strongly disagree* with the sentence.

1 Remembering or recognizing information is the student's main job.	SA	A	D	SD
2 A central activity is to make judgments of good/bad and right/wrong, and to explain why.	SA	A	D	SD
3 Students actively put methods and ideas to use in new situations.	SA	A	D	SD
4 Most class time is spent doing things other than listening.	SA	A	D	SD

For example, if a gifted project is designed to enhance creative thinking skills of low achieving gifted students, the students could be pretested to measure their creative thinking status before the project begins and posttested at the end. When the test instruments are relevant to the content of the instruction, i.e., creative thinking, a valid assessment of progress can be made. However, if the students were tested on the California Achievement Test, reading subtest, it would not be likely that the obtained scores could reflect the outcomes of the gifted program. Consequently, a test such as the Torrance Test of Creative Thinking would more likely be a valid instrument.

Another example to help clarify the need for valid and reliable measures in gifted programs is that of a program's attempt to increase parent involvement. Such a program could, on the one hand, validly report increased parent visits, greater attendance at parent/teacher meetings, and greater knowledge of and participation in local school board elections. On the other hand, reporting on how well the parents liked the gifted program would not be as compelling evidence of the gifted program's effectiveness. Such "I like it" responses by parents have frequently been used to justify program effectiveness. However, in the current climate of more sophisticated accountability, teachers and administrators need to use more valid measures.

When the measures being used are directly related to the purpose and intention of the gifted program intervention, the measures can be said to be valid. Educators must be confident that they are not only measuring the right things but that the measures are reliable. Reliability can be defined as measures that consistently rank the same things in the same order, time after time (Tallmadge, 1977). Tallmadge lists measures considered reliable by the Joint Dissemination Review Panel, for the United States Department of Education: achievement test scores, scores on attitude or self-concept scales (tests); measures of absenteeism, classroom observations of teaching behavior, measures of service delivered, and indicators of parent involvement (direct observational measures).

Other unobtrusive measures which indirectly assess the achievement of objectives are measures of vandalism, the number of books checked out of the library, and the use by women of facilities formerly restricted to men.

Another concern in evaluation is the question of whether or not intervention is the reason for change in the students. That is, would the conditions being reported have happened without the intervention? This question implies a comparison or a weighing of the results of the gifted program against regular education programs. Such comparisons are critical in educational situations, because the growth or change may have occurred with no intervention. For example, in a gifted program, attempting to foster independence and the commitment to tasks are goals which might be attained simply as a result of maturation.

There are two ways to handle the above-mentioned problem. One is to get an estimate of the development of these qualities in "no gifted program students" (gifted students having no gifted program) to compare with students enrolled in the gifted program; the other is to get an estimate from the performance of the gifted students prior to the intervention. The latter is usually more feasible in school districts in which it would be somewhat difficult to explain to both community members and parents why one group of gifted students is receiving service and another is not. However, when school districts are performing pilot projects for the gifted, the use of a comparison group is both desirable and practical. It is important to find the most believable comparison, the one that represents the most confidence that the innovation in the gifted program was and is an improvement over regular school offerings for the gifted.

The ongoing problem in any type of educational intervention for the gifted is similar to that in any other type of innovation or experiment. The school program may hypothesize that the gifted students will improve in any number of specific ways, and yet the results may suggest other possible causes for these effects. In a laboratory setting, many of these variables can be controlled, but in the educational setting this is not possible. However, when evaluation procedures are well designed, they provide appropriate comparisons and controls for other possible causes of observed effects, and yield the needed data to ensure continued program development in gifted education.

Communicating Data to All Audiences

Much evaluative data is communicated in terms of percentages, raw scores, standard deviations, and other measurement terms, but there is need for more human data to reflect the personal side of the gifted program. Case studies on individual children are helpful in reporting student growth, and anecdotal information such as the following is very useful to members of boards of education, community members, regular classroom teachers, and administrators. The information is taken from a middle school gifted program in leadership.

Stephanie: As long as I can remember I've always wanted to be a lawyer, so that's why I enjoy my mentorship with a court reporter. My observations of the day-to-day involvement with Ms. Paul are exciting, and there isn't a day that goes by that I don't thoroughly enjoy seeing the human action of life. I know I will be a much better lawyer as a result of this experience. I am certainly learning a lot about efficient use of time and the importance of scheduling.

An important factor to be considered concerning Stephanie is that she is an underachieving, gifted black middle school girl from a low socioeconomic background. Through the mentor intervention, she is demonstrating better study skills, her absenteeism has been drastically reduced, and her school achievement has improved.

Still another example, in the same program, is that of Robert.

Robert: I've always been a ham and interested in acting, but I just didn't think I could make it. But since I've been at the Inner City Theatre with Mr. Jones I feel it is not only a possibility for me, but I am going to do it. I can act. I have had several parts and Mr. Jones has helped me believe in myself. I know when I am reaching the audience and when I am not. There is a feeling of realness that goes through me when I am on the stage, and it is wonderful . . . so wonderful I can hardly explain it to anyone but Mr. Jones. He listens and he never becomes angry with me when I forget a line. If my other teachers were like he is, I wouldn't have wasted so much time in school.

Robert and Stephanie are students in a program for low socioeconomic level gifted students. The program was in danger of losing its funding until these anecdotes were shared and program visits were made by local city council members. After brief deliberation, the members decided to extend the program to the elementary grades, to focus on locating minority gifted children at an early age, and to refund the program at a higher level. The power of personal anecdotes substantiated by measurable data is profound. All data and information should be continuously gathered over the full period of the program, to substantiate its total growth and development.

UNIQUE PROBLEMS OF EVALUATION WITH GIFTED STUDENTS

The Use of Inappropriate Levels of Tests

One unique problem in evaluating programs for gifted students is that they achieve very high or very low test scores. For many gifted students, tests are inappropriate for assessing their performance. Ideally, students should score in the middle of the range of possible raw scores. Average performance for groups of students should generally fall between 30 and 75 percent correct answers out of the total number of items. Consequently, test levels for gifted students should be selected on the basis of their achievement levels, not on the basis of their grades in school. For gifted students, one or two test levels above their grade level is recommended. Most major test publishers have interlocked their test levels and have provided expanded standard scores which allow educators to determine score equivalencies between adjacent test levels. These scores make it possible to predict, from a given gifted pupil's score on one test level, how he or she would have scored on the next higher or lower level. Still another possibility is that the manual may provide normative data for students who are tested out of their level.

Stanley (1976) suggests that tests should be chosen which have enough "ceiling" for each gifted student to be tested. "Ceiling" refers to how difficult the test items must be before the student misses all the items. Difficulty is associated with age or grade level; older ages and higher grades are asked more difficult items. Stanley also recommends the use of advanced achievement tests for gifted students with specific academic aptitudes, since this approach would be appropriate to their abilities. Recognizing that this practice is not consistent with school and/or testing practices, he suggests that teachers act boldly and test the gifted student's limits through advanced instrumentation.

The Use of a Single Set of Test Scores for Both Selecting and Pretesting Participants

Another problem in evaluation of gifted education programs is the means by which gifted students are selected for participation in a program; for example, creative thinking may be reflected in relatively high test scores on creativity tests, and the use of these test scores as a pretest measure invalidates any kind of norm-referenced evaluation. If students are selected from a group because of their high test scores and are retested on the same or on a comparable test to establish a baseline value for evaluation, the retest may not reflect the actual level. To avoid this problem, gifted students should be selected for participation in a gifted program based on one set of test scores and pretested using an alternate form of the same test or a different test.

The Use of Grade Equivalent Scores

Still another problem in evaluating gifted programs is the use of grade equivalent scores. Grade equivalent scores provide an insensitive and, in some cases, a systematically distorted assessment of cognitive growth. For the layperson, particularly parents, and for statistically naive educators, the concept of a grade equivalent score can be misleading. For example, a grade equivalent score of eighth grade on the WRAT in mathematics achieved by a third-grade student does not mean that he or she knows eighth-grade math. In some cases, the gifted third grader can do math as well as the average eighth grader, but it is likely that no average eighth-grade student has ever taken the third-grade level of the test. The use of grade equivalents for evaluation purposes can also create another problem, in that the scores do not form an equal interval scale and should never be averaged. Even more importantly, grade equivalents are construct-based, on the assumption that individual student growth takes place at an even pace throughout a school year. Tallmadge (1977) reports that learning typically does not follow this regular pattern, and gains for gifted students measured in grade equivalents can be artificially inflated.

One way to avoid the problems of the use of grade equivalent scores in the evaluation of gifted programs is to use normalized standard scores. These scores are provided by test publishers and can be used for computations. In this way, gains can be interpreted through reference to pretest and posttest percentile standings with respect to a group norm.

Incorrect Interpretation of Data

Sometimes directors of gifted programs claim that their programs lead to observed progress in the gifted students, when there may be alternative explanations for these changes in performance or behavior. For example, in one gifted program, students learned substantially more than expected in social studies, but the gifted project, per se, was not responsible. In this case, the school district had instituted multiple changes including smaller class size, new facilities, and additional personnel in the library, as well as a curriculum specialist who worked with the teachers on using new strategies for teaching. The gains for students in the gifted project could be attributed to the Hawthorne effect, which is that they did well simply because they were in a special program, and the situation was compounded by the unrecognized effects of the multiple changes. Under conditions such as those described above, evaluators are wise to suggest alternative explanations for the perceived growth or change and to be conservative in their claims.

Teacher Alienation

An important concern to address in examining evaluation as a concept is that of increased teacher alienation. Teachers in the regular classroom may perceive the addition of a gifted program and its offerings as a judgment about them, that they are not doing their jobs adequately. Consequently, when the evaluation process is initiated, regular classroom teachers and teachers in the gifted program may become pitted against one another. For this reason, it is imperative that evaluation be viewed as the evaluation of alternative means to achieve specific expectations with specific children. For example, one district reports being engaged in the evaluation of the use of creative problem solving with third-grade gifted students in a small-group setting. This type of specific delineation of parameters for evaluation is less apt to threaten teachers in the regular third-grade classes, who may or may not be using a type of problem solving in the regular classroom with their full classes. Raybin (1971) calls this notion "minimum essentials"; thus, in an evaluation, individual pupil performance is examined in relation to the unique circumstances associated with the performance.

EVALUATION MODELS

Costanzo-Sorg (1970) found that specialists in gifted were using a number of specific models to evaluate gifted and talented programs, notably that of Stufflebeam (1971) and Provus (1971). The Stufflebeam model consists of interactions between four types of decisions and four types of program operations. Decisions relate to: (1) planning, (2) structure, (3) implementation, and (4) recycling. Operations include: (1) context, (2) input, (3) process, and (4) product.

In the Stufflebeam model, decisions and operations can be defined as:

Planning—The establishment of goals and objectives

Structure—Procedures and resources to be implemented

Implementation—Introduction and maintenance of program

Recycling—Reacting to attainments and results and impact

Context—Needs assessment, results, mission statement, assumptions, constraints, facilitators

Input—Pupil needs and characteristics, staff resources, material and physical resources, costs and receptivity

Process—Activities, instruction, experiences, reactions, and tactics

Product—Outcomes matched against context and input

To use the Stufflebeam model, planners and developers in a school district or in a state educational agency examine the decisions: planning, structure, implementation, and recycling, as they relate to the operations: context, input, process, and product. For example, if a school district is considering a gifted program, the planners and developers need to ensure that there is a policy statement concerning criteria for selection and evaluation in order to maintain a consistent policy toward gifted students. Within this policy, there needs to be a commitment to evaluation of the program itself. Relating the planning phase to the context, program assumptions need to be clarified. From this data, decisions are made as to the selection of appropriate measurement instruments to assess the sources of input and mode, and the procedures are selected to introduce and employ the evaluation tactics (process). In the planning phase's interface with the product, the emphasis is on availability of data sources and whether outcomes match against context and input. Questions concern the use of the objective data and the qualitative data.

In decisions concerning structure and its relationship to context, the program planners will want to secure the endorsement of all participants and be sure that all have been given ample opportunity to share their points of view and insights. This is very important, for many programs fail because of negative perceptions held by various individuals in the educational system or wider community. To ensure input, the planners can schedule various training sessions for parents, students, and other participants. Taking this process into consideration, there should be opportunity for any participant's insights to be incorporated. The product is the assessment of the credibility of intentions among all the participants.

The implementation phase is the initiation of the program and evaluation procedures with efforts at maintaining a schedule. The input at this stage involves the assurance that all resources are available as needed. Process is the assurance that the schedule and commitments are met. The product of the implementation phase is the assembling and assessing of the data and the preparation of progress reports as well as final reports.

The recycling phase involves reaction to attainment of goals and objectives, and the context phase includes any revision necessary to achieve consistency. The input phase includes the examination of the comprehensiveness of the input. Process is the reviewing of the adequacy of the activities associated with the gathering and use of the data. Lastly, the product is making decisions regarding continuation and improvement.

Sellin and Birch (1981) list five evaluation tactics which summarize the evaluation process and clarify the use of the Stufflebeam model.

1 Establishing the context of quality in which the program will operate, typically labeled "mission statement"

2 Identifying the existing resources and attributes of participants that are starting points, typically labeled "input"

3 Monitoring the actions of participants toward the goals of the mission, usually labeled "process"

4 Analyzing results, usually labeled "outcomes," expressed in performance of products

5 Making recommendations inferred from the interactions of the preceding four elements, usually described as "impact statements"

Provus (1971) uses similar terms, such as design, installation, process, product, and comparison. He defines design as the plan selected for evaluation. Installation is concerned with the circumstances and actual operation of the program, and process is the characteristics or attributes of the gifted students and their performance, as well as the means by which the students are studied and observed during the evaluation process. Product is defined as the reports and recommendations growing out of the evaluation. The Provus model is a discrepancy model and places emphasis on comparing the intentions or objectives and the results or outcomes. These discrepancies suggest possible action or the need for action by the program's decision makers.

Several guiding questions evaluators can use in working with gifted programs are listed by Costanzo-Sorg (1979): (1) Did I seek improvement in services to children and youth? (2) Did I insist on advance planning to secure the necessary consensus? (3) Did I use sufficient and varied sources of data? (4) Did I relate procedures to goals and maintain consistency? (5) Did I provide in-service training or orientation for participants? (6) Did I insist on sufficient time for program operations? Securing responses to these types of questions ensures credibility in carrying out evaluation.

CHOOSING EVALUATORS

When a school district is choosing an outside evaluator and there is no full-time evaluation director in the school system, it is important for the employed evaluators to be competent at evaluating gifted programs either through training or experience, as there are unique problems in evaluating these programs.

In addition, the evaluator must be able to work comfortably with school officials in reaching decisions or agreements as to what is needed in the evaluation. If these agreements are not worked out with sufficient clarity in the initial discussions, the information gathered may not be meaningful or have any use in future decision making for the gifted program.

Evaluators and educators may have difficulty coming to an agreement. One reason may be that school officials are not objective concerning the gifted program. However, it is important for school officials to remember that the job of the evaluator is to be objective and to deal with the facts. The evaluator is not being hired to conclude in advance of information or data his or her favorable assessment of or support for the program for the gifted.

According to Cooley and Lohnes (1976), evaluators may have training in a wide variety of disciplines such as behavioral sciences, in the fields of philosophy, psychology, sociology, research, and statistical inference. Yet the most important skills for evaluators are the ability to organize, manage, and adhere to a comprehensive evaluation plan using models such as those of Stufflebeam (1971) and Provus (1971). Finally, essential to this discussion on evaluation is that the eventual beneficiary of the evaluation process is the gifted student and the improvement of the educational program for the gifted. Hall (1980) states that even though the evaluation process may seem complex, the time spent on evaluation is well spent if it results in programming continuation and funding within school climates commonly bent on program cuts and cost-cutting procedures.

SAMPLE INSTRUMENTS FOR THE EVALUATION OF PROGRAMS FOR THE GIFTED STUDENT PRODUCT EVALUATION

One way to measure objectives for gifted programs is to judge student products in relation to the stated objectives. Hall (1980) shares the procedures used by the Michigan State Department of Education in developing a set of scales to measure the objectives of the state pilot projects. Each instrument was especially designed for each objective. The most useful scales as reported by districts were the ratings of student products for creativity and excellence. Exhibit 9-2 lists two project objectives.

The evaluation of instructional programs for gifted and talented can be accomplished through formative and summative evaluation. In formative evaluation, the essential ingredient is a representation of the strengths and weaknesses in an assessment of what is going on day to day. Several examples of formative evaluation are reported in the document *Sample Instruments for the Evaluation of Programs for the Gifted and Talented* compiled by the evaluation committee TAG (The Association for Gifted). Exhibit 9-3 is a modified form from this document and contains two questions from each of the major program evaluation components: description, identification, evaluation, administration, and service.

Summative evaluation reflects an annual overview of the program. Summative evaluation assures that the needs assessment was conducted, the identification procedures were utilized, and specific program techniques were selected and

---

EXHIBIT 9-2

SAMPLE ITEMS FROM INSTRUMENTS FOR RATING THE PROJECTS SUBMITTED
BY STUDENTS IN MICHIGAN'S SECTION 47 PROGRAM

Project objective 3

Eighty percent of a random sampling of the students involved in the pilot programs will attain
a satisfactory score on an "excellence scale" when the student products are individually
rated by a group of three judges.

- To what extent does the product represent an in-depth, superior handling of the subject?

5	4	3	2	1
To a great extent		Somewhat		To a very limited extent

- To what extent is this product of a quality level beyond what one might expect of a
student of this age?

5	4	3	2	1
To a great extent		Somewhat		To a very limited extent

Project objective 5

Eighty percent of a random sampling of the students involved in the pilot programs will attain
a satisfactory score on a "process/product creativity scale" when the student projects are
individually rated by a group of three judges and when the process that went into the projects
is rated by a classroom observer.

- Considering the project as a whole, to what extent would you say that it indicates a high
degree of originality and freshness for a student of this age?

5	4	3	2	1
To a great extent		Somewhat		To a very limited extent

---

implemented. The questions suggested in Exhibit 9-3 are interchangeable for both
formative and summative assessment. Through the use of model questionnaires
supplemented by objective data, evaluation becomes a process or means of determining outcomes (summative evaluation); it also becomes a means of gathering
information about programs in order to continue developing quality programs for
gifted students.

Longitudinal information on gifted programs can insure better recommendations in programming and can also help administrators, the board of education,
and the community to continue to endorse and support the program. A useful
resource in planning a longitudinal study is McCumsey (1985).

SUMMARY

In this chapter, evaluating was defined as determining the value of or gathering
information about the gifted program. Key features of evaluation were discussed,
such as establishing the purpose of evaluation and examining and determining

EXHIBIT 9-3

Model A

Evaluation Team: Chicago   Staff Form-REV.

_____ Team Reported   Date of Visitation _____

GIFTED PROGRAM–FIELD EVALUATION

Program description	**OK**	**PROBLEM**	**DID NOT OBSERVE**

1 Are the depth and focus of activities in the program generally such that they meet the special needs of gifted children?

2 Are the program's activities compatible with the program objectives?

Program identification

1 Do the identification procedures correspond to those stated in the original proposal?

2 Is student identification based primarily on objective data?

Program mechanics

1 Are the students involved in the program at least 150 minutes per week?

2 Are special counseling and/or guidance provisions made available to all students in the gifted program?

Program evaluation

1 Is a systematic plan of evaluation being used to assess the program?

2 Does the evaluation provide necessary information to assess the effectiveness of the program?

Program administration

1 Were the teachers in the program involved in developing the current program?

2 Are materials and services being purchased necessary to the activities which comprise the program?

Program services

1 Are materials and services ordered for the programs received within a reasonable length of time?

2 Are you receiving the services and consultative help necessary to assist you in implementing your program?

measurable program goals and student objectives. The use of a gifted mentor was offered as an example of program evaluation.

The importance of choosing valid and reliable measures was discussed, as well as the need to communicate data to a variety of audiences. Several unique evaluation problems with gifted programs were listed, such as the use of inappropriate tests, the use of a single set of test scores for both selection and pretesting participants, the use of grade equivalent scores, and the incorrect interpretation of data.

Two evaluation models, Stufflebeam's (1971) and Provus's (1971), were highlighted and their application to gifted programs was illustrated. The problem of choosing evaluators was briefly examined, and several sample instruments were discussed to demonstrate concrete ways of gathering both formative and summative data.

EXTENDING ACTIVITIES

1 Locate and review a federally or state funded project in gifted education. If available, read the final report. Is there a match between the stated goals and objectives and the outcomes?
2 Select a recent article on evaluation. Relate the article to this chapter on evaluation. Share your insights on evaluation, as a result of this chapter and the article.
3 Choose one objective measure and read the Buros' general description of the test or instrument (*Book of Mental Measurement*). Note the discussion on reliability and validity.
4 If you were hiring an evaluator for your school district and writing a job description, what type of individual would you want? Write a job description and be specific as to qualifications.

REFERENCES

Brinkerhoff, R. O. (1979). Evaluating full-service special education progress. In E. L. Meyer, G. A. Vergason & R. J. Shelan (Eds.), *Instructional Planning for Exceptional Children*. Denver: Love.

Callahan, C. (1983). Issues in evaluating programs for the gifted. *Gifted Child Quarterly*, 27 (1), 3–7.

Cammeron, W. A. (1978). Project evaluation. In H. Berger (Ed.), *Science Career Education for the Physically Handicapped*. Thomasville, GA: Thomas County Public Schools.

Clark, B. (1983). *Growing up gifted*. Columbus, OH: Charles E. Merrill.

Cooley, H. & Lohnes, W. (1976). *Evaluation research in education*. New York: Irvington Publishers, Halsted Press Division of John Wiley and Sons.

Constanzo-Sorg, N. J. (1970). *An implementation evaluation of a school system wide program for gifted students*. Unpublished doctoral dissertation, University of Pittsburg, Pennsylvania.

Hall, E. (1980). Comprehensive evaluation of gifted programs: A matrix model. *GCT, 11*, 12–16.

Hedges, W. D. (1979). How to raise your school's ranking. *Phi Delta Kappan, 60*, 377–378.

Howell, K. W., Kaplan, J. S. & O'Connell, C. Y. (1979). *Evaluating exceptional children: A task analysis approach*. Columbus, OH: Charles E. Merrill.

Mager, R. F. (1962). *Preparing instructional objectives*. Palo Alto, CA: Fearon Publishers.

Maker, J. (1982). *Curriculum development for the gifted*. Rockville, MD: Aspen System Publishers.

McCumsey, J. (1985). Conducting: A Longitudinal Study. *Challenge. 3* (4), 42–48.

New York Times Dictionary. (1982) New York: New York Times Company.

Provus, M. (1971). *Discrepancy evaluation*. Berkeley, CA: McCutchen Publishers.

Raybin, R. (1971). Minimum essentials and accountability. *Phi Delta Kappan, 60,* 374–375.

Renzulli, J. S. & Smith, L. H. (1979). Issues and procedures in evaluating programs. In A. H. Passow (Ed.), *The Gifted and Talented: Their Education and Development*. Chicago: University of Chicago Press.

Sellin, D. & Birch, J. (1981). *Psychoeducational development of gifted and talented learners*. Rockville, MD: Aspen Systems Publishers.

Stanley, J. C. (1976). Use of tests to discover talent. In D. P. Keating (Ed.), *Intellectual Talent: Research and Development*. Baltimore, MD: Johns Hopkins University Press.

Steele, J. M. (1969). *Dimensions of the class activities questionnaire*. Urbana: University of Illinois, Illinois Center for Institutional Research and Curriculum Evaluation.

Stufflebeam, O. (1971). Evaluation and decision making. In O. Stufflebeam, W. J. Gephart, E. Gerbs, R. Hammond, H. Merrion & N. Provers (Eds.), *Educational Evaluation in Decision-Making*. Itasca, IL: Peacock.

Tallmadge, G. K. (1977). *Idea book*. Washington, DC: Health, Education and Welfare.

SECTION THREE

UNIQUE PROBLEMS, TRENDS, AND ISSUES IN GIFTED EDUCATION

Much of what is good practice in gifted education, such as identifying students with special needs and characteristics using a multidimensional definition of gifted and programming for these unique characteristics, is of equal importance for subpopulations of gifted students: for the culturally diverse—blacks, Hispanics, Native Americans; for the disadvantaged, the highly creative, the handicapped gifted; for gifted female students, and for the highly gifted. Gifted students in the these subpopulations represent a unique problem and challenge in the field of gifted education. Chapter 10 addresses their needs and suggests programming implications. Case studies are given for each subpopulation. Chapter 11 covers the counseling and guidance needs of the gifted, a neglected area in the field of gifted education, including the importance of understanding the inner self and emotions, communicating with others, and of students' career aspirations. Chapter 12 focuses on the expanded dimensions of learning and provides information on brain/mind research, visualization, suggestopedia, biofeedback, and technology in education. Lastly, Chapter 13 deals with the trends and issues in gifted education, such as the gap between research and practice, and the equity issue in identification. In addition, the ongoing confusion over the definition of giftedness is discussed. Sustaining beliefs in gifted education are outlined.

CHAPTER 10

SPECIAL POPULATIONS
OF THE GIFTED

"If a man does not keep pace with his companions, perhaps it is because he hears a different drummer. Let him step to the music which he hears, however measured or far away.

Henry David Thoreau

A general area of concern in gifted education is the special populations who demonstrate superior ability or potential in spite of, or in addition to, special needs and characteristics which cause motivational, learning, or behavior problems. Included in this category of special populations are culturally diverse children, including the black, Hispanic, and Native American; disadvantaged or poor; creatively gifted; highly gifted; handicapped gifted; and gifted female students.

It is essential that the unique needs and characteristics of these subgroups not be considered deficits or weaknesses. If they have a deficit perception, teachers approach these students from subgroups as lacking the full qualifications of gifted students. This chapter addresses these special populations in a diagnostic–prescriptive approach. The emphasis is on identifying their unique characteristics, including intellectual, social, and emotional needs for educational program development. It is important to remember when we discuss strengths and weaknesses of test behavior that it may appear these are deficits in the child. However, the deficits are in the system's adaptations to the child. In addition, some of the results can be interpreted as behaviors manifested in the testing situation rather than as a general learning deficit.

The importance of recognizing indicators of giftedness in special populations stems from the recognition that traditional identification and selection methods overlook many gifted, including a disproportionate percentage of minority gifted, and that no single culture or group can adequately reinforce or develop all the diverse cognitive processes possible (Bernal, 1975).

The need for early identification is stressed. Exemplary case studies illustrate particular issues within the different subgroups. The first subgroup to be discussed is the culturally different or culturally diverse population. Before we proceed with this discussion, these terms must be clarified, since they are often used interchangeably in the literature on gifted education. In some cases, students who are culturally diverse may be disadvantaged, and in other cases they may not be. In this chapter, disadvantaged means being poor or being a member of the lower socioeconomic classes. In this case, difference is characterized by poverty rather than by culture. In contrast, culturally diverse means that students are members of a culture significantly different in values, attitudes, and practices from the majority culture.

CULTURALLY DIVERSE

Black Students

The first group of students to be discussed are black students. The difficulty in discussing black students as an example of cultural difference is that much of the literature on this subpopulation does not control for socioeconomic status, and consequently, it is difficult to identify specific differences between blacks and whites if they are not of the same socioeconomic level. However, Bacon (1982) reports a study in which 121 black students in grades 3, 4, 8, and 9 were studied. Differences were found in intellectual and language patterns. Using the Structure of Intellect (SOI) and observations of student behavior, Bacon found that black students showed difficulties in areas essential to the acquisition of academic skills. Yet as younger students became academically successful, they suffered creativity loss. Meeker (1978) controlled for socioeconomic status, and the differences she observed on the SOI between whites, blacks, and Mexican Americans can be viewed as cultural differences. She found black students tested lower in cognition, evaluation, and convergent products, and higher in memory. Meeker (1978) reports that blacks tested lower on figural content than did whites and Mexican Americans. If the above findings are viewed in terms of learning characteristics, black students show strengths in mastering material and in recall or memory. Weaknesses of black students tested were in evaluation and convergent production or in areas in which productive thinking called for a logical response. They also had difficulty working on abstract principles dealing with semantic concepts.

Halpern (1973) found black students had strengths in the symbolic areas and in logical reasoning that were independent of semantic material. The subtests that were the most successful for black students, using the Weschler Intelligence Scale for Children (WISC-R), were the arithmetic and digit span subtests. Other subtests successfully completed by black students were the comprehension and similarities subtests, measuring abstract reasoning and comprehension. Halpern's findings are similar to those of Bruch (1971), who attempted to identify strengths and weaknesses of black students using the Stanford-Binet. Similarly, Torrance (1977) found strengths in the figural area, using the Torrance Tests of Creative Thinking (TTCT).

Bacon (1982) further reports, in her study of black students, that student failure among black students is not as much related to deficits in ability or academic capability as it is to student behaviors and preferred learning styles. She states that schools emphasize conformity at the expense of independent and creative behavior of black students. The students in her study had trouble consuming and organizing large amounts of information; adjusting to long-term assignments requiring independent study and planning; adjusting to a depersonalized environment; extending their academic life into the home; and going beyond satisfaction with minimum standards and peer recognition.

Programming Implications   In examining the research on black students, Bruch (1971), Halpern (1973), Torrance (1977), Meeker (1978), and Bacon (1982) point to areas in which black students demonstrate evident strengths: memory, creativity, and symbolic skills. It would be feasible to concentrate on activities in the figural and spatial areas as introductory lessons. These lessons could be supplemented by activities in memory and divergent production. Drawing on black students' strengths in creativity, academic lessons could reinforce such activities in figural and spatial areas, using divergent production as a mediator.

An example of this type of modification is the experience of black gifted middle school youngsters who were introduced to creative writing through encounter lessons. Encounter lessons involve a combination of strategies: role playing, visual imagery, and intuitive thinking exercises. The students were placed in small groups and asked to become an imaginary object, person, place, or thing and to answer a series of questions calling for responses in these categories categorized as (1) perception (seeing, feeling, hearing); (2) relating to others; (3) creative responses; (4) fear responses; and (5) abstract thoughts. After completing the questions, the students were asked to do creative writing. Many chose to write poems, plays, and short stories; others chose to write editorials, one- or two-line "fine sayings," or short paragraphs (Sisk, 1982).

Bacon (1982) suggests educators deal with the black students' low school motivation through "survival skills." She outlines a survival skills program to assist them in assessing requirements for success in new situations: (1) set goals to determine personal direction; (2) identify positive alternative behaviors; and (3) develop peer relations for collaboration on academic tasks. She also suggests parents and teachers provide a stimulating environment, free from ridicule, and one which legitimizes interdependence and caring. Bacon advocates an educational setting consisting of appropriate routine, creative ritual, personal relevance, academic rigor, and group responsibility.

Maker (1982) recommends opportunities for choice of topic areas, capitalizing on interest and emphasizing self-evaluation for black students with low motivation. She also suggests that an emphasis be placed on success, particularly as the black students begin to work independently. She views teacher reinforcement and guidance as essential because of black students' difficulty with lack of knowledge, lack of familiarity with references, and low self-confidence.

It is important for educators to understand the dynamics behind the behaviors of this population. One way to encourage understanding is to examine case studies of youngsters from this subgroup. The case study of Regina in Exhibit 10-1 reflects much of the research reported in this section.

EXHIBIT 10-1

REGINA

Case Study

Regina, age 8, is a tall, attractive black student. Her eyes sparkle with a sense of humor that is apparent as she teases and plays pranks on her friends in her predominantly black neighborhood. Each day she is bussed across town to a predominantly white neighborhood, where she attends third grade. She is in a gifted enrichment class, held on Tuesday and Thursday at her home school. However, recently the enrichment teacher has been notified that Regina has not been finishing her regular classroom work, and it is being recommended that she be removed from the gifted program.

Regina is one of four children; three are older, married, and living away from home. Regina's mother is a staff assistant for a Headstart program, and her father is a reporter for the county courthouse. Regina's parents noticed her giftedness at an early age, and they report she knew TV commercials by heart and delighted in "parroting" these to her parents and neighbors. She showed interest in numbers and did simple addition and substraction before her first year at school. Regina loves going to church with her parents and demonstrated her quick memory by telling bible stories to other Sunday school children.

Regina's first year of school was in an all-black school, where she appeared happy and cheerful. At age 7, her parents moved to the city, and Regina was assigned to a predominantly white school, with a white teacher. There were four other black children in the class. Here, she began to complain of stomachaches and refused to do assigned homework. The teacher reported Regina would not go beyond minimum performance, and was happy with "C" work. However, Regina scored 8 and 9 stanines on various achievement subtests and consequently, she was given an individual Stanford-Binet. She achieved an IQ of 136, and was enrolled in the gifted program.

In the second grade, she attended a cluster group class of ten gifted students, including two black students; ten above-average students, including three black students; and ten average students, including one black student. The teacher noted in Regina's cumulative folder that she responded well to the stimulating environment of the cluster group. She stated that Regina was developing a good self-image.

The class was structured using the Taylor Totem Pole (Taylor, 1963), with planned activities on the six levels: academic, planning, communication, predicting and forecasting, creative, and decision making. Each gifted student completed one activity at each level, and they could do as many as they wanted upon completion of the other six. Regina was eager to do extra creative work.

In third grade, Regina transferred to her present school. Here there are two other gifted students in the classroom, both white. Regina's teacher describes the other two gifted

EXHIBIT 10-1 *(Continued)*

students as task-committed. The teacher wants Regina to be retested and states that the original test (given in first grade) was inaccurate.

Regina's parents are high school graduates and they want Regina to do well in school, but they are baffled by her lack of interest. They have no career plans for her, but say they want her to be happy.

Regina reports she has few friends in her new school, and that the teacher forces her to do work she already knows. Her favorite subject is mathematics. She is receiving a "B" in mathematics on her next report card, her only "B," as the other grades are "C"s. When observed in the regular classroom, Regina appeared listless, disinterested, and bored. Regina's parents have attended a parent conference, and they state that the teacher does not like their daughter. The papers they were shown of Regina's were incomplete and inaccurate. At home, Regina has a quick wit and memory, but her parents fear she will not complete school. At the last parent conference, it was recommended she be removed from the gifted program until she achieves in the regular classroom.

Regina is typical of many black gifted students; she has difficulty in completing assignments and working independently. Without the stimulating environment and support of her enrichment teacher in the cluster group setting, it is highly possible Regina will not develop her potential ability. Culturally different gifted students have the added difficulty of having to simultaneously function in two cultures. Too often black students do not know how to react to the highly competitive performance-based educational climate of predominantly white elementary and middle schools, and this problem is intensified in high school.

Bacon (1982) reminds educators not to apply universal cultural standards to any group—no matter what cultural background. To win the interest and attention of black students like Regina, educators need to focus on the individual, approach the students from their strengths, and develop the individual's sense of responsibility to work on his/her weaker areas.

Hispanic Students

The second group to be discussed as members of the culturally diverse sub-population is the Hispanic student. This group includes Mexican Americans and Cubans. Hispanics also include the Spanish-speaking people of Latin America (Central and South America) and the Caribbean, and Puerto Ricans. Clark (1983) lists the positive characteristics and unique needs of Mexican American students:

- Attitudes of cooperation
- Attitudes fostering education through high school
- Supportive family, community
- Affectionate, demonstrative parental relationship
- Unusual maturity and responsibility for their age
- Experience with giving advice and judgments in disputes
- Planning strategies
- Eagerness to try out new ideas
- Ability to initiate and maintain meaningful transactions with adults
- Facility for learning second language

These needs and characteristics are considered positives for the Mexican American student and were drawn from the research of Bernal (1978) and Aragon and Marquez (1975). A profile of the Mexican American gifted student was described by Bernal (1983) at a Sid W. Richardson Foundation meeting in Fort Worth. He stressed that the Mexican American gifted student is streetwise and is viewed by other Mexican American students as one who can make it in the white-dominated society. This streetwiseness involves leadership and interpersonal skills and a sense of risk taking. Bernal also stated that the gifted Mexican American has the ability to learn English rapidly, particularly if she/he is given opportunities in expressive activities, games, and simulations that include a sense of drama. The social responsibility of these students is noted by their willingness to accept the role of surrogate parent for younger brothers and sisters.

Bernal also reported that the Mexican American gifted student often prefers older friends and enjoys lively conversations with older boys and girls, sometimes using imaginative games and creative applications with simple toys and objects. Much of what Bernal reports can be summarized as strengths in the areas of leadership and creativity, and many of the positive characteristics of Mexican American gifted students can be readily identified. Yet, because early success in school is language dependent, these students who speak only Spanish or are bilingual, with Spanish being the dominant language, often fall behind in their first few years of school. With this experience of being behind, they develop poor self-concepts in relation to school and attitudes of underachievement.

Culturally limiting attitudes and abilities of the Mexican American as listed by Clark (1983) are:

- Language of dominant culture often unfamiliar
- Attitudes depreciating education after high school; education seen as unrealistic, especially for women
- Attitudes that differ in basic time, space, and reality may cause misunderstandings
- Attitudes against competition make it difficult to succeed in a traditional classroom
- Sex role stereotyping
- Lack of experience with values of other cultures
- Emphasis on family over achievement and life goals of children

The most glaring weakness in the above limitations involves career and educational aspirations. Clearly, if career goals of Mexican American youth conflict with family wishes or welfare, the youth put their needs and goals aside.

Programming Implications Mexican American gifted students' strengths are in the areas of creativity and leadership. Providing educational experiences in these areas can be highly motivating and can function as a bridge to academic skills and language acquisition. With an early deficit in language being a serious problem by grade 3, the first few years should emphasize a variety of language activities. The Mexican American student's interest in interpersonal skills makes him/her a natural candidate for simulation activities requiring creativity, leadership, and interpersonal involvement.

Another technique to be used with Mexican American gifted students was demonstrated by Dwyer (1983) in a curriculum developed for migrant children, many of whom were Mexican Americans deficient in language skills. The children were introduced to basic language and number skills in highly motivating activities using small toys and manipulative objects. The findings of Dwyer and his associates substantiate conclusions by Bernal (1975), Gerken (1978), Meeker (1978), and Maker (1982) that these youngsters can rapidly acquire English language skills once they are exposed.

Heavy emphasis should be placed on counseling Mexican American youth and their parents on career opportunities. Care should be taken to respect the home and family values (Lafrenz & Colangelo, 1981). Of particular concern is the need to assist Mexican American youth to cope with (1) keeping their identity as Mexican Americans and (2) being a part of the majority culture to realize their potential. Lafrenz and Colangelo (1981) also recommend helping these students learn to deal with peer pressure "not to succeed" in the majority white culture. Other teacher and counselor options for working with Mexican American gifted are suggested by Clark (1983):

- Help them to deal with excessive pressure to succeed
- Help them to learn to value all persons regardless of cultural and/or sexual identity
- Give them opportunities to share their ideas, attitudes, and values
- Help them to explore the strengths of various cultures and the unity of all people

These four recommendations are being put into operation in a special high school program for minority and disadvantaged in the city of San Diego public schools where the majority of the students are Mexican American and Asian. Their program goal is to send the students to college, and over 98 percent of the 156 students involved enroll in college.

An example of an activity to involve the Mexican American youth in exploring ideas, attitudes, and values in relation to basic cultural paradigms is a simulation game entitled "Parle" (Sisk, 1983). In this activity, the students are divided into teams of seven to ten, and they are asked to create their country's educational system, political system, religion, and history. The natural resources and military strength of the countries are given as starting points. The students then select leaders and negotiators and react to a variety of crises which are announced by the teacher or student leader. Through these activities, the students experience many attitudes and values, as well as the key concept of interdependence of people and nations. "Parle" provides positive experiences based on interpersonal activities and creativity, and there is opportunity for the Mexican American youngster to use imagination and risk taking. Through successful school experiences, such as this highly motivating activity, the strengths and weaknesses of Mexican American students can be identified and remedied. The case study of Jessie in Exhibit 10-2 reflects much of the research reported in this section.

EXHIBIT 10-2

JESSIE

Case Study

Jessie at age 7 was a small, wiry youngster with sullen black eyes, who rarely caught the eye of adults or children. He attended a second-grade classroom with a cluster group arrangement for gifted students because the teacher was supportive and had an ability to work with difficult students. The psychologist considered Jessie at age 7 as untestable, with little or no English, and feared that he was borderline retarded.

Jessie, one of six children, ages 2 through 10, lived in a two-room storefront in southern California. Both of his parents were workers in a cannery and immigrated from Mexico.

In his second-grade class, the teacher encouraged him to pass out books, sharpen pencils, prepare materials for art, and do similar chores to feel responsible. He prepared the art or science activities using the teacher's prescribed directions. He eagerly participated in science and art activities, and every attempt was made to allow him to progress at his own pace.

Jessie displayed language understanding, but he had little verbal interaction with other children. His black eyes would sweep around the room, taking in details, only returning to a downward gaze when he was directly looked upon by the teacher or other students.

The second-grade class was composed of ten gifted students, ten average students, and ten above-average students. Jessie's teacher stated that while he was planning independent study projects for the gifted students, Jessie asked if he could do a study. He said "yes," and Jessie asked to do a study on music using the following independent study plan:

What I want to know more about	Where will I find my information?	What will I do with it?
1 Music	1 My brother Paco	1 Write a song
2 My accordion	2 Books and records	2 Play my accordion for the class
3 Mexican songs	3 My head	

Jessie's second-grade class was lively, and the teacher often pushed chairs and tables aside for the children to square dance. When they appeared tired and listless, he led them in renditions of show tunes. Laughter and involvement were mixed with academics, and under these conditions, Jessie thrived.

On a home visit, the teacher enjoyed a bowl of chicken soup served in a tin cup. While sitting on their one chair, surrounded by five children, the mother, the father, and the grandmother, the teacher shared how well Jessie was doing. Jessie's family was supportive and demonstratively affectionate, and encouraged Jessie to play his accordion. He played several Mexican tunes and several of his own songs that he had "made up from his head." After the home visit, the teacher recommended Jessie be tested for the gifted program, in spite of depressed language skills.

Prior to the testing, Jessie developed a severe cold, as there was little or no heat in the home. He developed otitis sereous media which affected his hearing. The psychologist administered the Stanford-Binet and Jessie achieved an IQ of 88, reflecting dull normal ability.

Refusing to accept this classification, the teacher encouraged him to listen to simple plays which were taped. Gifted readers read poems and stories to him, and these were also taped, and a tape recorder was loaned to the family. Jessie was given a speaking part in a class play. At the end of the year, the psychologist gave Jessie the WISC-R and he scored 105. Again, the teacher was cautioned not to make much of the child's ability.

In third grade, his teacher was not willing to give him extra individual time. The principal

EXHIBIT 10-2 *(Continued)*

placed him in a regular classroom on the recommendation of the psychologist, who stated that Jessie should not be pressured or encouraged to go beyond his ability. Jessie became noncommunicative, and his third-grade teacher described him as dirty, sullen, and uncooperative. He developed severe colds, and missed over 120 days of school in the third grade. On a home visit, the social worker found Jessie supervising three younger children and preparing the evening meal. When questioned about school attendance, his parents, who had elementary school education (grade 6) in Pueblo, Mexico, said Jessie did not like school, and he was sick a lot.

He was detained in third grade, and assigned to his former second-grade teacher, who was teaching third-grade gifted and had asked that he be assigned to him. During the school year, he worked on Jessie's self-concept, emphasizing his natural interest in science and art, encouraging his music, and introducing mathematics to him using Cuisennaire rods. Jessie responded to the psychological safety and freedom and gained enough self-confidence to misbehave.

At the middle of the term, the teacher requested retesting. Jessie was given the Stanford-Binet and achieved a score of 120, and with that score and his teacher's recommendation, Jessie was enrolled in the gifted program. Jessie's family was counseled concerning his potential and need to attend school. He did not miss one day of school in the third grade.

At the end of the third grade, Jessie's father was fired from the cannery, and the family returned to Mexico. Whether or not Jessie continued to develop his ability is unknown since the family did not return to California, nor did they keep in contact with the school.

This case study of Jessie reminds educators that children who enter school as monolingual and are not challenged in school may feel unworthy. As a result, they may be lost to society as gifted students. Yet through emphasis on language-related skills, they can thrive, and begin to develop creativity. Jessie won first prize in an art contest with a chalk drawing of a harbor. The judge's comment was most telling, ". . . the energy of this painting bespeaks an ability far exceeding a 9-year-old boy."

Native American Students

The third group to be discussed as culturally diverse is the Native American which includes American Indians. Locke (1982) reports that only twenty-six American Indians in a school-age population of 400,000 were identified by the U.S. Department of Interior—Bureau of Indian Affairs as gifted students. Locke, vice president for education at the Sequoya American Indian Institute in Albuquerque, New Mexico views the problem of identifying American Indian gifted as complex, in that there are 490 tribes and 291 languages. Consequently, the identification process differs from tribe to tribe.

One tribe which has shown interest in identifying gifted is the Red Lake Chippewa, in northern Minnesota. The tribe participated in a cooperative institute sponsored by the National Office of Gifted and Talented and the Office of Indian Education. Brown (1976) reported that the elders of the Chippewa tribe view giftedness as divine and believe giftedness should be used to benefit the tribe.

Indian leaders and Indian schoolteachers compiled the following list of characteristics of American Indian gifted students (Locke, 1982):

- Curiosity
- Problem-solving ability
- Interested in many areas
- Like older children for playmates/companions

- Persistent
- Seen as leaders by others
- Trustworthy
- Independent thinking
- Well-developed memory
- Keen understanding and perceptive

Many of the characteristics of the American Indian gifted are similar to those generated by educators for the typical gifted student; however, several characteristics do not appear on the list, such as desire to excel, dominating peers or others, being individualistic or competitive. Locke and others were quick to identify these characteristics as having a negative value among American Indian tribes and, therefore, as traits that would be discouraged.

McShane and Plass (1982) worked with Chippewa Indian students in studying Wechsler scale performance patterns. They found that the Indian pattern consisted of spatial abilities higher than sequencing skills, followed by conceptual and acquired knowledge. In earlier studies, McShane (1980) found that the typical Indian child possessed relatively superior visual perception abilities and depressed language skills. McShane's study supports the findings that Indian students have superior or relatively high visual–spatial functioning (Berry, 1969; Kleinfeld, 1970, 1971; Lombardi, 1970). Berry (1971), working with Canadian Indian students, interpreted his findings as a functional adaptation of the demands of the North, where perceptual motor skills were highly useful. Still another reason for the well-developed perceptual motor skills may be the emphasis on concrete reality and the individuality of objects. This phenomenon makes it difficult for Indian students to classify or generalize.

Schuberg and Cropley (1972) studied differences between Indian and urban white children and found Indian children do not analyze experiences habitually or spontaneously in verbal terms. This finding expands the conceptual picture of the Native Americans as concrete learners. Shuberg and Cropley's findings were substantiated by Meeker (1978), who examined the SOI abilities of Navajo children in Arizona and New Mexico. She found high auditory memory and figural ability scores, with low semantic and low classification abilities.

The profile of the American Indian gifted student is one of strong visual spatial skills, strengths in observation, problem solving, and memory. Difficulties are noted in the semantic and classification areas. The gifted American Indian will not be dominant but will display independence and curiosity in influencing others for the benefit of the group.

Programming Implications   Weinberg (1977), in the National Institute of Education (NIE) study on minority groups, stated that schools begin with the American Indian student's inadequate mastery of English and fashion the curriculum to match that declared deficiency. This type of thinking must be changed if educators are to identify the American Indian gifted and to meet their educational needs. A curriculum emphasizing memory and figural areas will be successful. The subject areas of mathematics, music, and visual arts can be vehicles for concrete experiences and prove motivating and useful. To work on weaknesses such as semantic and classification skills, teachers can help by giving directions orally and providing opportunities for group work. Social studies, science, and logic exercises can also be good beginning points.

American Indian gifted students enjoy group work and do not want to be singled out from the group; consequently, cooperation should be emphasized. Locke (1982) suggests that mentorships be used in such fields as agriculture, aquaculture, building, and architecture, the arts, and physical and mental therapy. She cautions white teachers not to transmit their values to the American Indian student. She states that teachers must understand that it is dangerous to the mental health of the American Indian student to be taught values that are antithetical to his/her culture. Locke suggests that the curriculum be taught as skills, not as values to be internalized.

This fine line between nurturing the gifts of the Native American, developing her/his special sensitivities to the self and environment, and introducing the skills of the majority culture is a challenge to educators. An examination of the case study of Mary Anne in Exhibit 10-3 is relevant to this challenge.

EXHIBIT 10-3

MARY ANNE

Case Study

Mary Anne, who likes to be called Mae, lives with her mother on a reservation. They live alone, since this past year both Mae's grandmother and father died of lingering illnesses. Mae, who is 7, and her mother were emotionally drained by the experience. Mae came to the attention of her teachers in the reservation preschool by asking many questions and appearing interested in everything. She listened to the stories told in the classroom and then told her grandmother the same stories with detail and accuracy. Ina Blackbear, the mother, has a high school education and works in the preschool cafeteria. Ina noticed Mae's ability at an early age. Mae is her only child, as her husband was considerably older than she; however, he had grown children who live on the reservation. These older brothers and sisters have little interaction with Mae and her mother, as they do not approve of the second marriage of their father.

Mae's mother is a bright woman and displays an understanding of her ability. She reports that Mae walked early, talked early, and was a restless, alert baby. Mae's early companions were two older girls who lived near her family, ages 9 and 10. They enjoyed playing school, and Mae was often the teacher. In school, Mae is viewed as a leader and is often asked to intercede in classroom disagreements.

Mae's teacher states that she is trustworthy and responsible. Recently, Mae was referred to the gifted program. She was given the WISC-R and achieved two standard deviations above the mean, and qualified for the gifted program. However, her teacher says she is not interested in reading. On the Wide Range Achievement Test (WRAT), her reading grade was 1.6. On the Woodcock Reading Mastery test, she achieved a reading grade level of 1.8 with deficits in the area of decoding meaningless trigrams.

The teacher of the gifted meets Mae weekly for an hour and a half and works with her on reading skills. She uses an experience approach. Mae dictates stories, and the teacher types these for her to read. In addition, Mae's mother has been taking books and records home.

> **EXHIBIT 10-3** *(Continued)*
>
> The family does not have television, so there is free evening time.
>
> Mae's tribe has submitted a project to the state for funding a reservation resource center for the gifted. If funded, the center will provide opportunities for Mae to work daily with a resource teacher. Mae does well in math, achieving a 3.3 grade level equivalent on the WRAT, and she likes puzzles.
>
> Mae reflects membership in a culture which is less fluent with English, yet her mother's education and her tribe's interest in providing gifted education may help develop her talent. In conflict with this, Mae's mother, her teachers, and the director of the school state that they are not interested in having any Indian child appear different from the group. However, they do recognize the need to develop leadership among their people and Mae is viewed as a potential leader.

THE DISADVANTAGED

The term "disadvantaged" as used here refers to poor or lower socioeconomic class students. In examining the research on disadvantaged gifted, Baldwin (1973), Farrell (1973), McMillin (1975), and Frasier (1979) identify a number of traits of disadvantaged gifted:

- Alertness, curiosity
- Independence
- Nonverbal fluency
- Experiential learners
- Creative
- Risk takers
- Sense of humor
- Language rich in imagery
- Enjoys music and art
- Leadership
- Responsible
- Adaptable
- Externally motivated
- Low in knowledge/vocabulary
- Well-developed memory and observational skills
- Responsiveness to the concrete

The learning profile of the disadvantaged gifted is one of a student with weakness in knowledge and reading, requiring external motivation. Yet, when the characteristics of leadership and creativity are examined, the disadvantaged student demonstrates curiosity, an ability to generate ideas, and an ability to excel in problem solving (Torrance, 1968, 1971, 1977). In problem-solving experiences, Torrance found that the disadvantaged gifted exhibited leadership, risk taking, and a willingness to try new ideas.

The portrait of the disadvantaged gifted is amplified by Arnold (1974), who described disadvantaged learners in the Los Angeles project for gifted as students more dependent on the teacher, able to reason step by step, and comfortable with instructions and procedures that are sequentially organized. Yet, the students persevered with tasks and saw them to completion if they were supported by the classroom teacher.

The above classroom behaviors describe students who need classroom direction and support. When they do not receive this support and direction, these students can become negative toward school, teachers, and achievement. Baldwin (1973, 1982) states that disadvantaged gifted students are seldom exposed to books and are starved for verbal encounters with other gifted students and significant adults.

Interest in the disadvantaged gifted had its peak in the sixties with the work of Sexton (1961), Coleman et al. (1966), Passow et al. (1967), and Pressman (1969). These researchers reported that disadvantaged students do poorly in school and that as they proceed through the grades, they continue to do less and less well. The school problem was highlighted at a national conference on disadvantaged gifted in Washington, D.C. Representative Shirley Chisholm (1978) asserted that the term "disadvantaged gifted" is a misunderstood term and noted the plight of the disadvantaged gifted student when standard English tests were used. She said schools fail to identify and nurture the talents of the disadvantaged and react with hostility to skills they cannot measure and potential they cannot understand.

Programming Implications   There are two stages of development when programs for disadvantaged gifted are essential, the early preschool years and the period of adolescence. Smilansky (1984) states that there is no period in human development where 3 or 4 years produces the transformation of a person and his or her capacities to the extent that adolescence does, unless it is early childhood. With the young child, early experiences enhance her/his creativity and leadership, and the provision of intensive language experiences helps remedy deficiencies in knowledge and vocabulary. Most of the strengths listed, such as sense of humor, enjoyment of music and art, alertness, curiosity, nonverbal fluency, and experiential learning can be utilized in an early childhood sensory bombardment program. In a sensory bombardment program, there is the opportunity to see, hear, and feel with emphasis on stories and active participation.

For the adolescent, Smilansky (1984), the director of Exceptional Child Education in Israel and an outspoken supporter of gifted education, suggests that educators work on values and commitment to the political process. In Smilansky's program, the gifted students meet twice a week in the afternoon and during the entire summer for 3 consecutive years (sixth, seventh, and eighth grades). They attend an enrichment center where there is an emphasis on intellectual development on the development of an esprit de corps, and on the idea that their group can create a different culture. This new culture emphasizes intellectual development and gives priority to learning as a "counterculture" in relation to the dominant culture in the disadvantaged area.

Another administrative model that is useful with the disadvantaged gifted in Israel is the boarding school. It is believed that these students need additional help in developing their potential because they are growing up in areas where quality education is unavailable. The boarding centers have been in operation since 1960 and have worked with over 4000 youngsters. The program costs twice as much as the regular high school, but Smilansky states that the results indicate that boarding centers double the rate at which disadvantaged high school students attend college and increases the proportion of those who graduate from universities by twofold. Boarding schools may cost twice as much as regular schools, but they are twice as effective at realizing the students' potential.

Smilansky suggests that a program for the disadvantaged gifted should focus on self-development and coping capacities to understand the self and the environment and, more important, to prepare the students to take part in their environment. To accomplish these goals, the Israelis developed units of curriculum on topics such as sexual identity and leadership. Sexual identity is defined to include sex roles, sex-role stereotyping, sex education, career education, and relations between the adolescent and the family. Another unit is leadership, to help understand the community. In a peer counseling unit, the students learn to give orders and to receive them. Responsibility goes hand-in-hand with receiving privileges. Students take responsibility in order to upgrade the total level of learning and living in the classroom, and they assume the responsibility of counseling younger students or adults.

Another exciting program for disadvantaged gifted students is the San Diego program called Achievement Via Individual Determination (AVID). This program works with Mexican American, Asian, and black students to encourage them to go to high school. AVID has graduated 158 students over its 5-year history, 156 of whom have gone on to college (89 percent to 4-year institutions, 11 percent to 2-year institutions).

EXHIBIT 10-4

MALCOLM

Case Study

Malcolm at age 14 is almost six feet tall, lacking one inch. His long, lean form is usually draped over a chair while watching television, or he may rough-house with his younger brother and sister, ages 9 and 10. Malcolm is one of nine children. His older brother Tyrone, 16, is in a state training school for burglarizing a neighborhood gas station. Yvonne, 17, and Mary Lee, 18, live at home and work part time in a nursery. Both Yvonne and Mary Lee are school dropouts, as is Tyrone. The older three brothers are married and live in New Iberia, Louisiana, the original home of the family.

Their home is rented and it is their sixth home in the last 4 years. Malcolm's father is a day worker and his mother does domestic work when it is available. Each morning Malcolm's father goes downtown to the work station at 6:00 a.m. By 7:00 a.m., the various employers who need help come to select workers. Sometimes, he works in the box plant, or on the dock, or at any number of unskilled jobs. Malcolm's parents quit school at the eighth grade, and none of the family graduated from high school. Malcolm, a ninth grader at Riverview High School, has attended more school than anyone in the family.

He is in the gifted math and science sections, and his teacher states that he does average work but shows interest in computers. Malcolm has been meeting with the teacher at 7:30 a.m. to help program the computer and has developed several computer games.

EXHIBIT 10-4 *(Continued)*

He seldom studies at home or reads books. His reading scores, according to his achievement test records, are stanine 6. He says reading bores him, and he would rather watch television. His estimate of the number of hours spent watching television is over 40 hours per week.

Malcolm has located other students who are interested in computers and science, and his current attitude is positive about school. Prior to this year, he was talking about dropping out of school. His math teacher has arranged for him to use a computer program to develop vocabulary skills, and he has shown interest in improving this weakness. Although he openly states there is no reason to go to college, for after all what can he do about it, . . . he does attend school regularly.

Malcolm is upset about his brother being in the state training school, and he feels his brother is innocent. Yet the mother reports Tyrone was always in some kind of trouble. She is interested in her boys being successful, but she admits little enthusiasm about her girls and wishes they would get married. She and Malcolm's father married at age 15. There is open affection between them.

Malcolm's father becomes very depressed when he isn't working and on those days he is in the neighborhood bar; he has been known to come home "roaring drunk" in the words of Malcolm. "He can be abusive," and "I usually split," are Malcolm's comments.

Malcolm supervises his younger brother and sister and prepares meals when his mother and father are working. He doesn't seem to mind this, and he helps them with their homework, particularly if it is music or art. He sang in the church choir but has dropped out because, as he says, "Church is for sissies."

Malcolm was identified as gifted when he was 10 and scored 135 on the WISC-R. He has attended a learning center for gifted since he was in the fifth grade. In the middle school years, the program became school based with special classes for the gifted in science, math, and language arts. Malcolm's achievement in language arts has been consistently low, notably in knowledge and vocabulary. As a result, he has not been included in the gifted classes in language arts. In the science and mathematics class, he has done average work and learns best when the work is experiential. He loves the computer.

His teachers indicate he has a rich sense of humor and at times likes to be the class clown. He does a "Funky Joe" routine to the amusement of everyone. Funky Joe is a thinly disguised caricature of the language arts teacher.

Currently, Malcolm is studying fruit flies in a science project with two other boys. His teacher indicates that the project has potential to win a state prize.

The counselor is working with Malcolm and his parents on a proposed career in science or mathematics, but he says that it is "uphill" as neither the parents nor Malcolm are interested in "bettering themselves."

Maker (1982) suggests the strengths of creativity in disadvantaged gifted be further strengthened through the use of open-ended activities such as those that emphasize idea production; divergent thinking; and creative production in language arts, music, science, and the visual arts. For the disadvantaged student it is essential to combine the development of strong areas with weaker ones and to begin with strengths and gradually work on the weaker areas (Exhibit 10-4).

Malcolm is typical of disadvantaged students and possesses many of the characteristics listed: creativity, a sense of humor, language rich in imagery, enjoyment of music and art; he is externally motivated (the science prize he wants to win), low in knowledge/vocabulary; he has a well-developed memory and observation skills (mimicking the language teacher) and is responsive to the concrete. Whether or not he uses his potential will depend in part on the success or failure of the school's efforts to counteract his environment's negative pull toward dropping out of school and antieducation attitudes. By giving Malcolm and other disadvantaged gifted students an appropriate education and guidance, educators can help them help themselves as well as society. Too many of our institutions are filled with people who have potential, who were not able to use their ability in a positive way. Early identification and talent development for the disadvantaged must become a priority in education of the gifted.

THE HIGHLY CREATIVE

Creativity can be conceptualized in a number of ways, and various researchers have offered definitions. For example, Torrance (1962) defines creativity as the process of sensing gaps or discerning missing elements; forming new hypotheses and communicating the results; and possibly modifying and retesting the hypotheses. Parnes (1967) defines creativity as a function of knowledge, imagination, and evaluation. Williams (1968) defines creativity as a conscious act of human intelligence. He further defines the act as including knowledge; mental processes based on cognition; divergent–productive and associative thinking; evaluative behaviors; and communication skills. Guilford (1959) states that creativity includes aptitude traits such as fluency, flexibility, and originality in thinking; along with being sensitive to problems and the ability to redefine and elaborate. He calls this group of traits divergent thinking abilities.

Not only are there many and varied definitions of what creativity is, but there are many educators who equate giftedness with creativity. Clark (1983) states that it seems incorrect to use creativity synonymously with giftedness or to limit its definition to the expression of feelings and affective development. She conceptualizes creativity as the highest expression of giftedness.

Gowan (1981), in an attempt to further explain the relationship between giftedness and creativity, made a distinction between personal and cultural creativity. He stated that anyone can be taught personal creativity, but that giftedness is necessary for cultural creativity, the form that produces major discoveries and ideas which change society's future and direction.

Highly creative children and adults are composed of paradoxes. Williams (1982) lists a number of these: open yet closed; zany but serious; well adjusted but still maladjusted; thriving on disorder but seeking order. To teachers and parents of highly crative children, these paradoxical qualities pose a great challenge; but if it were not for their existence, creativity would not flourish. Below are listed some of the characteristics of the highly creative:

1 Needs comfort and security to fit the mold; compulsive need to be different

2 Will not accept as true one single answer or solution; rigidly closed at whatever level they have arrived at

3 Highly independent and self-sufficient, loving to discover and to make inquiries on their own; strong need for sharing and for group acceptance and approval following creative ideas, productions, or accomplishments

4 Strong preference for complexity and difficult tasks; must simplify most things to bring temporary closure

5 Very serious about consequences and implications; good sense of humor, with playful attitude and behavior

6 Very aware of criticism and lack of acceptance; not bothered by failure or unresolved situations

The above paradoxes are selected from Williams's (1982) list of paradoxical traits of highly creative students, and it can be noted that highly creative students need support from parents and teachers to deal with these paradoxes in order to develop and use their ability.

In examining characteristics of highly creative individuals, Clark (1983) lists the following attributes:

- Self-disciplined, independent, often anti-authoritarian
- Zany sense of humor
- Able to resist group pressure
- Adaptable
- Adventurous
- Tolerance for ambiguity and discomfort
- Little tolerance for boredom
- Preference for complexity, asymmetry, open-endedness
- Divergent thinkers
- High in memory, good attention to detail
- Broad knowledge background
- Need supportive climate and recognition
- Need think periods
- High aesthetic values
- Free in developing sex-role integration

As a result of the above list of characteristics, the highly creative student poses a challenge to education. Yet, by taking note of the unique characteristics of the highly creative, educators can adapt and modify schooling to meet their needs.

Programming Implications   Before discussing programming implications, it is important to point out that the growth of creativity, as defined by test performance, increases from age 3 to 4 and then begins to drop, rising again to drop at the fourth grade. Torrance (1962) reports that some fifth graders do worse on creativity tests than they did in first grade. Any number of factors have been identified that cause this creativity development to be discontinued, such as the environment and teaching strategies used in the regular classroom; parental discouragement of exploration, imagination, and inquiry; sex-role stereotyping; authoritarianism; ridicule of fantasy and imagination; and an emphasis on conformity.

In nurturing and developing the highly creative child, Williams (1982) makes the following suggestions:

- Establish a responsive and expressive climate
- Provide encouragement for self-resourcefulness
- Recognize, respect, and give emotional support

- Expect and allow for comfortable regression in growth patterns
- Allow and provide some balance between interpersonal and intrapersonal experiences
- Establish well-defined standards of discipline and conduct
- Establish an achievement-oriented climate
- Establish an attitude of basic trust

Specific strategies that are helpful in meeting the needs of the highly creative student are simulation, with a focus on open-ended production of ideas and divergent thinking; and independent work followed by group processing and verification. In addition, the conditions of psychological freedom and safety are necessary along with teaching specific skills for developing creativity within subject matter. For example, in science, creative thinking may call for inquiry and the five-step problem-solving process of Parnes (1963). To maximize the classroom climate for creativity, there should be an emphasis on higher levels of creative thinking, defined by Guilford (1959) as being sensitive to problems, and defining and redefining problems in order to discourage the limiting of creative performance. The case study of Stephan in Exhibit 10-5 depicts the unique challenge to education posed by the creative student.

EXHIBIT 10-5

STEPHAN

Case Study

Stephan is a 7-year-old, dark-haired, dark-eyed boy with a look that could be described as baleful. He has appeared in several television commercials and community theater productions.

At the recommendation of his second-grade teacher, Stephan was brought to the local university for an intellectual evaluation. He was given the Stanford-Binet and achieved an IQ of 165. During the testing situation, Stephan indicated he was tired and his imaginary friend Jeff, a clown doll draped on his arm, would take the test. The psychologist directed questions to the boy's arm, with little or no eye contact with Stephan. About half-way through the test, Stephan said that Jeff was tired and that he would respond. He placed the doll on the chair, face down, and proceeded to accomplish several of the items at the average adult and superior adult levels. The psychologist noted that the boy needed time to ponder his responses, particularly the abstract reasoning items. Stephan's answers to these items reflected broad knowledge and background. On the psychological report, the psychologist stated that Stephan responded well in a supportive climate.

He also stated that the more complex the item, the more Stephan seemed to enjoy it. When questions were easy, he openly indicated his boredom. The psychologist recommended that Stephan enter the gifted program in his hometown.

Stephan's parents are college educated; the father is an engineer and the mother teaches high school English. The mother is active in theater work and has had several supporting roles in New York in off-Broadway productions. The parents are affectionate with Stephan, who is their only child.

Stephan is an achieving student, as reflected by achievement test stanines of 8 and 9 in most subjects. He receives "A's" on report cards, but receives "N's" for "needs to improve"

EXHIBIT 10-5 *(Continued)*

in self-discipline and work habits. His teachers report sloppy and disorganized work. They also indicate he is silly and demands a lot of class time.

When Stephen was interviewed at a specialized school for the gifted, he met with the principal and three classroom teachers. On his entry to the room, he announced he was tired, and his imaginary friend Jeff, again draped on his arm, would be interviewed. The interviewers interpreted this behavior as immature and denied entrance to the gifted program, stating he would be unable to adapt to their routine and demand for independence.

Stephan and his parents were shocked and disappointed by the decision. His parents enrolled him in a nearby private school. A psychologist is working with the private school in establishing a responsive and expressive climate for Stephan. He has recommended continued theater work. In addition, the school is establishing an achievement-oriented climate using Stephan's interests as a guide.

The ways in which society and, most particularly, the schools value and deal with the highly creative not only affect the development of the creative individual but also affect the society itself. For every individual creative potential lost, there is a loss to society.

THE HANDICAPPED GIFTED

An essential point in discussing the handicapped gifted student is to refrain from making generalizations. Every handicap affects an attribute such as intelligence, ability, creativity, divergent thinking, or self-concept in a unique way. There is agreement among educators who work with handicapped gifted students that there must be an emphasis on cultivating strengths rather than remedying deficits. A bright blind adult stated it well when he said, "It was years before I stopped bludgeoning the world with my handicap and began caressing it with my gift." If parents and educators view handicaps as the main attributes of individuals, so will handicapped children, if they are not helped to recognize, develop, and prize their gifts.

Mullins (1979) uses the term "handicapism" to describe the stereotyping of handicapped persons. Some examples are: "lame brain," "turning a deaf ear," "crippled by a strike," "short-sighted," "blind as a bat," "twisted logic," and "myopic point of view." Mullins suggests increased sensitivity on the part of the media in presenting the handicapped in a positive way.

The single most definitive work in the area of the handicapped gifted is that of Maker (1977). She analyzes the available studies regarding visually impaired, hearing impaired, physically disabled, learning disabled, and emotionally impaired gifted. One important finding was that handicapped gifted have many similarities to the nonhandicapped gifted population relating to characteristics of giftedness in general.

The visually impaired gifted whom Maker (1977, 1982) studied were similar to nonhandicapped individuals according to overall ability, with memory and general information being strengths. In some cases, there was an indication of superiority in auditory perception. They were verbally fluent and the curiosity they manifested bore a direct relation to how mobile they were. Examining the self-concept of the visually impaired, Maker (1982) found a wide gap between ideal self and actual self, as well as concern with identity as a person.

The hearing-impaired gifted student's intelligence was comparable to the normal gifted, with similar creativity to the nonhandicapped gifted child's. Yet there was slower emergence of specific abilities as the individual matured. The hearing-impaired gifted student's self-concept was a concern, but it dealt mostly with the ability to succeed socially.

The emotionally impaired gifted student showed comparable intelligence and ability structure with the nonhandicapped gifted student, except for evaluative skills, in which there was evidence to suggest that divergent thinking was different (Meeker, 1969). The emotionally impaired gifted displayed concerns about relationships with parents and peers, as well as about their ability to do well in school (Whitmore, 1980, 1986).

The learning disabled gifted had higher-level abilities in reasoning and problem solving in comparison to their scores in perception and short-term memory. Their inability to achieve in school masked their creativity, and there were overall problems with self-esteem. Bruninks (1978) found that the learning disabled also had difficulty in peer relationships.

Diagnostic teaching can help close the gap between what the handicapped gifted individual is capable of doing and his/her current performance. However, it is important, in discussing a child's underachievement, that parents and educators be realistic in their expectations, especially when the assessment of potential for performance is based on standards for nonhandicapped children such as test scores, teacher judgment, or classroom performance. The performance of the handicapped student or the measurement of his/her potential is often impeded by environmental factors. Consequently, in working with handicapped gifted students, the teachers' approach should be an all-around effort toward academic performance, affective development, and as with most gifted students, an emphasis on the higher level cognitive skills in whatever modality is available.

With students who have a sensory handicap, on the one hand, the emphasis is on the development of abstract thinking through intuition; on the other hand, with learning-disabled students, the teacher focuses on their reasoning, rather than on memory, for discussion or problem solving.

With most of the handicapped gifted, group dynamics and discussion activities based on understanding self and others are helpful. Creative problem solving and discussions using simulation activities also afford opportunities for them to use evaluation.

Lastly, emphasis should be placed on career counseling to enable the handicapped gifted student to raise his/her sights beyond the more traditional careers for handicapped people. Handicapped scientists are found in mathematics, physics, engineering, medical sciences, agriculture, industrial technology, education, dentistry, pharmaceutical science, computer science, statistics, and atmospheric and hydrospheric sciences. Limitations for the handicapped gifted are found in their own attitudes and aspirations as well as the opportunities provided by parents and educators.

Early efforts to locate handicapped gifted and to demonstrate effective means of working with them were accomplished in several projects in 1978. These federally projects were Retrieval and Acceleration of Promising Youth Handicapped Talent (RAPYHT) located at the Institute for Child Behavior and Development at the University of Illinois and the Chapel Hill Gifted–Handicapped Project for children between the ages of 2½ and 6. Each project was funded by the federal government for 3 years, and they each developed appropriate identification procedures and curricula to challenge the gifted handicapped students' special abilities (Greene et al., 1978).

The projects stressed the need for early identification and for assessment to be done in a nondiscriminatory manner. An example is reported by Greene et al. (1978):

> Paige is a cerebral palsy child who cannot walk, control her arm and hand movements, or talk. Yet with her head stylus, she can flip puzzle pieces in their appropriate place. When Paige was first evaluated at age 3, her IQ was reported as 21. At age 4, it was measured as 80. Yet, in the special project, her abilities are assessed differently. She is observed as being keenly alert and interested in a whole range of topics, all of which are characteristics of being gifted. Upon the recommendation of her current teacher, they used only the tests that did not require verbal answers or the manipulation of objects and allowed Paige to point to answers with her head. Now she is recognized as gifted.

Service in both projects includes the gifted child and the parents. The parents are taught extending activities to use at home. In addition, weekly experiential workshops are held to help the parents recognize their role in their child's growth and development. Parents are taught to use spontaneous daily experiences to expand their child's abilities. See Exhibit 10-6.

EXHIBIT 10-6

MICHEL

Case Study

Michel is a 4-year-old spina bifida child whose condition is complicated by a brittle bone syndrome, making it necessary for him to be strapped into a special device to simulate standing. A desk top can be extended to allow him to write, eat, play games, and do puzzles.

Recently during a visit to Michel's special school for handicapped, the school psychologist was greeted by a cheery "Hi," and asked a quick series of questions: Why are you here? What is in your briefcase? Are you a medical doctor?

After completing his rounds, the psychologist found the boy, who quickly invited him to dinner. Somewhat nonplussed, the psychologist took his home telephone number and promised to call. When he questioned the school about Michel's educational program, he found that he received occupational therapy for part of the day and free play with other handicapped preschool youngsters for the remainder of the day.

What the psychologist noted was an alert, curious, outgoing, eager mind. He called the mother and asked if he could test the youngster at his office. She began weeping, saying

EXHIBIT 10-6 *(Continued)*

he was the first person who believed Michel had a mind. Bitterly, she recounted doctors, a divorced husband, and school officials who wanted to talk about his handicap but not about his gifts.

Michel was given the WISC-R and achieved an IQ of 151. He demonstrated rudimentary reading skills and the creative ability to tell favorite stories with his own variations, with changes of characters and settings.

As a result of the psychologists' intervention, Michel attended the first and second grade classes for reading and social studies and the kindergarten class for the remainder of the day. His disposition brightened considerably, and he and his mother related that they were doing science experiments at home. They are deeply grateful for the school's new perception of Michel as gifted. His medical prognosis is less than 2 years of life; however, the quality of his mental and emotional life is easing the struggle and pain of his physical life.

When handicapped children are given appropriate opportunities, they can demonstrate their giftedness. This is particularly true when a broadened definition of giftedness is used and when educators creatively search for signs of outstanding ability or potential for high performance in one or more areas of development.

GIFTED FEMALE STUDENTS

Concern about gifted female students is not new; it can be traced to the early work of Terman who made comparisons of the scores of boys and girls. He found there were smaller numbers of girls with higher scores. Callahan (1980) states that this trend still exists and increases in adolescence. The general assumption prevailing among psychologists and educators is that differences in achievement, motivation, and academics are all culturally influenced. Fox (1981) states that as people grow from infants to adults, their self-perceptions and values are shaped by their experiences in the home, the school, the playground, and the world at large.

Some of the reasons for these perceptions and values can be noted in the work of Rodenstein et al. (1977), who report on the contrasting social expectations for gifted students and for adult women. Gifted students are expected to (1) develop their talents and be "selfish" in energy use; (2) be active, exploring, and assertive; (3) pursue a challenging career; (4) develop their talents; and (5) succeed in traditional male-dominated careers. Women, in contrast, are expected to (1) be selfless, nurturing, and giving; (2) be passive and dependent; (3) run a household; (4) put career second to "the man's career"; and (5) be feminine.

When young gifted women accept the "feminine virtues," as defined by Rodenstein, the results are often noted in their comments as adult women. For example, in the follow-up studies of Terman's original gifted group, Sears and Barbee (1977) interviewed these gifted women at age 76. Looking backward, many said they should have chosen a career, and few said they would still have chosen homemaking as their primary occupation.

Another barrier to women's achieving success is their poor mathematics background. Fox (1981) stresses the importance of women's perception of mathematics as being useful to one's future and career interests. She defines the willingness to take intellectual risks as a learned attitude and behavior, and she states that many gifted adolescent females fear success and "looking" intellectual.

Ernest (1976) studied 1324 children in grades 2 through 12 and found no significant differences between boys and girls in reported enjoyment of mathematics. However, when Ernest (1980) studied the number of girls enrolled in mathematics when it was not required, dismally few were reported.

The Association for Women in Mathematics has been concerned about women's performance in mathematics. Luchins and Luchins (1980) worked with 350 female members of the Association for Women in Mathematics, as well as with a group of male mathematicians. In comparing the differences between career counseling and encouragement or discouragement about viewing mathematics as a potential career, they found that the women mathematicians had been told boys did not like girls who were smart, were advised to go into traditional careers, and were given little support. In their jobs, they reported encountering fewer job offerings, lower salaries, and less advancement potential than equally or less qualified males.

Callahan (1982) reports women are often perceived by themselves and others as standing at the periphery of a profession. She states that while underachievement is usually a male problem, the reverse is true of lifetime achievement—here it is a female problem. This may be a result of feeling insignificant and a concomitant lack of motivation to make significant contributions in a profession they feel has no real, vested interest in them.

Still another factor relevant to the productivity of women is marriage. Callahan (1980), reporting on a Radcliffe Committee on Graduate Education for Women study, found married women professionals did not expect full equality in the profession nor were they expecting to accept the same responsibility as men for achieving career success. In a sample of families where wives were physicians, college professors, and attorneys, Callahan reported that these women regarded their career as a hobby and their primary role as wife and mother. Interestingly, there were no age-linked differences in these perceptions among women in the sample, ages 23 to 50.

The most comprehensive review of sex differences was done by Maccoby and Jaclin (1974). They were concerned with how the sexes differ in general learning ability, achievement, cognitive style, and specific aptitudes. They found no real differences in the way boys and girls learn and, most notable up to age 10 or 11, there were no differences on verbal measures. Yet at age 11, girls begin to outscore boys on tests of verbal performance. At ages 9 to 13, boys begin to do better in mathematics. These quantitative differences were also noted in science achievement. At the beginning of adolescence, there is a difference in spatial ability, with boys having an advantage. No differences were found on problem solving or on concept mastery, reasoning, and nonverbal creativity. However, girls were superior on measures of verbal creativity after age 7. In summary, after adolescence boys appear to be clearly and consistently superior to girls in visual–spatial ability and achievement in mathematics and science.

Programming Implications The women in the study for the Association for Women in Mathematics made specific suggestions for educators and parents. They suggested that bright young girls should be given female role models; teachers and educators should treat girls and boys as being equally capable in mathematics, and they should consistently encourage girls' interest in mathematics. Lastly, they suggested that mathematics be approached as both intuitive and recreational to help dispel any inherent fear boys or girls might have of the subject.

In addition, Wolleat (1979) suggests a counseling program to help gifted females deal with their academic and personal resources. Connelly (1977) points out that gifted girls often experience loneliness, and when they show their ability, they are accused of being bossy, unfeminine, and show-offs. Similarly, Solano (1977) reports that average-ability classmates and teachers who had no background in gifted education perceived gifted girls more negatively than they did gifted boys.

Some specific counseling areas, according to Connelly (1977), would be teaching women: (1) How to establish their credentials; (2) how to cope with anger; (3) how to use power effectively; (4) how to use networks; and (5) how to self-actualize, go beyond the "feminine role," and still survive.

The curriculum for the gifted female must provide opportunities to work on visual–spatial problem solving, and it must include female role models. Gifted females need to critically read nonstereotyping literature, asking questions such as (1) How are girls and women portrayed in this book? (2) How are men and boys portrayed? (3) How realistic is the portrayal for the time and place in which it was written or for today? (4) How might I have changed the book if I had been the author?

These questions help provide opportunities for gifted females to establish their own personal goals and to develop an internal locus of control, as suggested by Callahan (1980). This development is essential before women can enter the ranks of leadership.

Even today, women are conspicuously absent from the ranks of leadership and underrepresented in most high-prestige, high-salary occupations. The majority of the high-salary, high-prestige occupations require mathematical and technical training as a prerequisite, and gifted females are moving away from these subjects and these careers. In Exhibit 10-7, a young male and female of similar ability at age 12 differ significantly at age 17. Research suggests that the future for these two may also be very different.

EXHIBIT 10-7

RYAN

Case Study

Ryan is a 17-year-old, attractive blonde girl with large blue eyes. Her parents state that she has taken to brooding in her room and to watching television. School bores Ryan and she is undecided about going to college or career plans. Ryan has not taken advanced physics or calculus, even though it was offered in her high school.

EXHIBIT 10-7 *(Continued)*

In the seventh grade, Ryan was involved in the Johns Hopkins University Mathematics Talent Search. She scored in the top 1 percent of her age group on the mathematics portion of the Iowa Tests of Basic Skills in the fifth grade and was recommended by her teacher to take the Scholastic Aptitude Test–Mathematics (SAT-M). Ryan scored over 500 on the SAT-M and was invited to attend special accelerated summer classes and to take college courses for credit.

Her best friend, Nelson, also achieved an SAT-M test score of over 500 and took advantage of the Johns Hopkins offerings. At age 17, Nelson left the high school where he and Ryan attended, and entered a nearby university with sophomore status. He acquired 1 year of college credit through AP examination (the Advanced Placement Program, APP), from college courses taken in the summers and on released time during his last year of high school. Nelson plans to major in electrical engineering.

Ryan talks about getting married and having children, but she is not dating anyone exclusively. Her current teachers question her giftedness and are not recommending her for any outstanding senior awards.

If educators are committed to gifted female students as a special population, it is essential that they foster the gifted female's development of positive values and attitudes toward mathematics, career interest in the sciences and, above all, the willingness to take intellectual risks.

THE HIGHLY GIFTED

The problem of discussing the extremely high IQ or highly gifted student has been stated simply, but accurately by Tannenbaum (1983). "Defining precisely what is meant by extremely high IQ is somewhat like judging precisely how high is up." A comprehensive study of extremely high IQ children was conducted by Hollingworth (1942), who established an IQ of 180 as a cut-off point. She found that the higher the ability level, the earlier the need to provide educational programs. Hollingworth noted that twelve children in her sample lacked the ability to make close, congenial friendships and evidenced play interests dissimilar to their age mates. As a result, these highly gifted young people were often isolates and had negative attitudes toward authority. For them, ordinary schooling was a waste of time, and school was described as drudgery.

Feldmen (1979) stated that extremely high levels of intellectual giftedness have seldom been studied. Outside of Cox's (1926) research effort to study 300 geniuses from the years 1450–1850 by estimating their childhood IQ, and the work of Hollingworth (1942), there is little or no material available. Feldman studied three young people who had early prodigious musical achievement and performed at an adult professional level before the age of 10. He reported that the most striking quality they displayed was the passion with which they pursued their excellence. Commitment, tenacity, and joy in achievement were noted.

Newland (1976) reports on similar outstanding performance at an early age for highly gifted and gives examples such as Karl Witte, who was proficient in several languages at the age of 9; Joseph Haydn, who was playing and composing at the age of 6; William Cullen Bryant, who was writing poetry at the age of 8;

and Albert Einstein who was playing the violin at age 7. Newland states that since the antecedents to early manifestation of interest and sustained involvement are essentially unknown, it may be that such behaviors can be attributed to an inner drive or motivation to "press into one's environment" rather than wait to be stimulated.

In Terman's original study, Terman and Oden (1947) found that there were forty-one males and thirty-four females with IQs of 170 and above. In examining family backgrounds of the gifted, they found that the parents were more often college graduates engaged in professional and higher-status work than the remainder of the Terman sample. Also, the highly gifted children learned to read earlier and earned somewhat better marks in school than the rest of the sample. They finished high school earlier and tended to earn "A" averages in college. The most interesting piece of data on the highly gifted from Terman's study was the fact that they were poorly adjusted socially. This was explained by Terman and Oden as due, in part, to their not having children of their own age who could provide intellectual stimulation.

Being highly gifted and highly visible is not easy. One group of highly gifted children who were visible to most individuals in the forties were the *Quiz Kids*. When several of them were assembled on a national television show, one of them described his experience as a "quiz kid" as ambivalent—the attention was initially welcomed but soon became overwhelming (Alvino, 1983). The further the highly gifted student is from his/her referent ability group, that is, from the other students who are intellectual peers, the more apt she/he is to feel different and to have poor adjustment. This finding was reported by Gallagher and Crowder (1957), who compared fifteen students with IQs of 65 and fifteen students with IQs of 150 to 165.

As a result of this type of finding, many educators (Gallagher & Crowder, 1957; Newland, 1976; Stanley, 1979; Maker, 1982) and others are advocating that the highly gifted be grouped with their intellectual peers as much as possible, particularly in areas such as mathematics and reading.

Programming Implications Programs need to be based on the highly gifteds' individual strengths and interests. Emphasis must be placed on helping them understand their giftedness and develop tolerance for people with lesser ability and for authority. Since highly gifted individuals deal with people of lesser ability and authority all their lives, it is important to teach them coping skills for expressing their feelings in socially acceptable ways. At the same time, the highly gifted should be permitted to acknowledge their real feelings. Grouping highly gifted students with their intellectual peers lessens adjustment problems.

An interesting educational program was developed for an 11-year-old college freshman, Susie Susedik, with an IQ of 160 (Bell, 1982). Susie has three sisters; Stacey, age 9 (eighth grade); Stephanie, age 7, (seventh grade); and Johanna, age 5 (not in school, but who reads at a junior high school level and likes long division and chess.) Susie talked in sentences at age 3 months; at 9 months she knew the alphabet; at age 1 year she read first-grade material. She recently took the SAT-M and scored 690, higher than 99 percent of high school seniors. The teaching techniques developed by the Susediks included using colorful flashcards with letters, numbers, and simple words and selected books with clear pictures and large type. They describe their materials as academic games which they began using when Susie was 3 days old. The Susediks taught firmly but used soft and gentle tones. Daily learning sessions were rarely longer than 15 minutes, and a different-color ribbon was tied around each finger to stimulate counting. These special techniques were stopped when the children knew enough math and read well enough to build on their own knowledge (age 2).

The Susedik children were born with high IQs, but the special home-teaching methods contributed to their outstanding performance. The important factors behind the Susedik home teaching were consistency, the use of short periods of time, and the gamelike atmosphere established by the parents.

The pacing of instruction for the highly gifted needs to be quick, as they become impatient, and abstract ideas and higher levels of thinking need to be emphasized. The highly gifted can profit from learning as many tools as possible that will allow them to become independent learners, such as critical reading, writing, time management, note taking, research skills, and computer skills.

Rapid pacing, however, may emphasize the discrepancy between the highly gifted students' academic and chronological age. This natural discrepancy can be a problem. See Exhibit 10-8. In Kate's case, locating the correct educational setting to develop her educational potential and to provide the nurturing and safe atmosphere she needs is difficult. She can be grouped with either her intellectual peers or with older, gifted peers. However, one important need for Kate and other highly gifted students is a kind, supportive, flexible teacher to help them learn topics of interest and develop coping skills to deal with their potential.

When gifted programs provide opportunities for all gifted students from subpopulations to explore wider interests, develop broad abilities, and learn firsthand the respect and understanding of differences necessary for intelligent and creative participation in society, we will be one step closer to achieving the ideals of the American way of life.

EXHIBIT 10-8

KATE

Case Study

Kate is a 5-year-old gifted girl, with intense black eyes and black straight hair. She is tall, taller than her brother, who is 7, and they are thought to be twins. She reads at a junior high school level, and can do mathematics at the sixth-grade level. Kate is quiet, serious, and sensitive.

Recently, she has been having temper tantrums in her kindergarten class and refuses to return. She says the games and activities are stupid, and she doesn't like reading by herself or helping other children.

Her mother and father, professional physicians, are seeking a private school. They are considering an Episcopalian day school that provides independent studies. Kate would attend reading and mathematics classes with sixth graders, and work on independent activities with

---

EXHIBIT 10-8 *(Continued)*

her age group. The school reports two other first-grade students with IQs of 150. Kate achieved an IQ of 170 on the Stanford-Binet. The parents hope these other two children at school will provide peer stimulation for her. The school is highly disciplined and the children are caned by the headmaster when they disobey rules. Kate's father has little problem with this type of discipline, but her mother is dubious. The children in the school are learning calligraphy and express delight with the skill. Kate has poor fine motor coordination and is unsure about trying calligraphy.

Kate has begun bed-wetting, sleeping fitfully, and slipping into her parents' bed during the night. Her parents are distressed by her behavior and are seeking counseling.

SUMMARY

An area of concern in gifted education, the special populations or special subgroups who have learning, motivational, or behavior differences was examined. Included in this category were culturally diverse, black, Mexican American, Native American, creatively gifted, highly gifted, handicapped gifted, and gifted female students.

The unique needs and characteristics of these subgroups were viewed as beginning points for instruction based on the individual student's strengths and weaknesses. Early identification was stressed, and exemplary case studies illustrated the different subgroups.

Several areas of strength were identified in black students: memory, creativity, and symbolic areas. It was suggested that academic lessons be built upon divergent production activities for black students. It was also recommended that black gifted students who demonstrate low motivation be provided choices based on their interests, with an emphasis on self-evaluation.

The suggestion was made to approach Mexican American potential gifted students through their identified strengths in creativity and leadership. The Mexican American student's interest in interpersonal skills was noted and the use of simulation was recommended to develop her/his strengths in creativity, leadership, and interpersonal involvement.

The problem of identifying Native American gifted, with 490 tribes and 291 languages, was reported. The desire to excel, to be competitive, to dominate peers or others, and to be individualistic are not characteristics of Native American gifted. These characteristics hold a negative value in Native American cultures and are discouraged. The Native American gifted student is comfortable with groups and dislikes being singled out from the group. The curriculum suggested by Native American leaders emphasizes skills rather than values. This emphasis would minimize cultural conflict for the young, Native American gifted student.

Disadvantaged gifted students were discussed, and a profile of the disadvantaged gifted was compiled: weakness in knowledge, reading, and responses to external motivation. Learning centers and boarding schools were suggested as ways of meeting the needs of the disadvantaged. It was recommended that their creativity and responsiveness be encouraged through open-ended activities.

The highly creative gifted student was described as responsive and expressive. These students need encouragement to be resourceful, with well-defined standards of discipline and conduct. Highly creative students and adults demonstrate paradoxes such as "needs comfort and security to fit the mold" and "compulsive need to be different." The way in which society and the schools value and deal with the highly creative affects their development and society's progress.

The importance of stressing the strengths of the handicapped gifted was discussed to encourage full development of their abilities. Career counseling for the handicapped gifted was also stressed, so as not to limit their horizons to more traditional careers. When handicapped students are given appropriate opportunities, they demonstrate their giftedness. This is particularly true when a broadened definition of giftedness is used and when teachers creatively search for outstanding ability or potential in one or more areas of development.

Gifted female students, as a group, grossly underachieve and are underserved. Mathematics is a real barrier to girls' later achieving success, as women in professional lives. Specific counseling areas were suggested: (1) how to establish credentials; (2) how to cope with anger; (3) how to use power effectively, (4) how to use networks; and (5) how to self-actualize and go against the feminine role to survive. The curriculum for the gifted female needs to provide opportunities to work on visual–spatial problem solving, with female role models.

The difficulties in studying the highly gifted because of the small numbers and emphasis on the less-gifted range of abilities was discussed. Ordinary schooling is viewed as a waste of time and drudgery for the highly gifted. A unique educational program for four highly gifted girls was reported. It emphasized daily lessons; consistency; firmness; and gentle, soft tones, beginning the third day of life and ending at age 2 with the child independently reading and counting.

All of the subgroups have characteristics which cause them to learn in different ways. To become independent and self-directed learners, they need flexibility in programs based on their strengths, interests, and weaknesses. When their special needs are viewed as deficencies, these subgroups of gifted students are not identified or, if they are identified, they do not demonstrate achievement or motivation.

EXTENDING ACTIVITIES

1 Select a "special population" gifted adult and research his or her life. Did she/he have a mentor? What were the contributing factors to her/his development? Be prepared to share your ideas with the class.
2 Girls need opportunities to manipulate, try things, and explore just as boys do. What specific activities can be suggested for parents and teachers of girls?
3 Monitor the kinds of advice guidance counselors give at a given school, particularly as it relates to special populations. Are special populations dissuaded from pursuing certain fields or areas of study?
4 Review *Einstein: The Life and Times* (Clark, 1972). Einstein had a deep antagonism to educational authority, which he later generalized in a challenge to accepted beliefs. He regarded his educational experience as a negation of the human being. Note similarities between the young highly gifted Einstein and today's youth. Do you agree that Hollingworth was correct in observing that gifted children in the IQ range of 130 to 150 have better possibilities of relating to the group than the highly gifted? Why?
5 Research the availability of federal aid or programs to assist the special population of

Native Americans. Are these programs part of the Department of Interior? What is its jurisdiction over the welfare of the Native American?

REFERENCES

Alvino, J. (1983). Quiz kids reflect on their glory and gloom. *Gifted Child Newsletter*, 4(4), 3.

Aragon, J. & Marquez, L. (1975). Spanish speaking component. *Promising Practices: Teaching the Disadvantaged Gifted.* Ventura, CA: Ventura County Superintendent of Schools.

Arnold, A. (Ed.) (1974). *Programs for gifted: Research abstracts (1973–1974).* Los Angeles: Los Angeles City Unified School District.

Bacon, M. (1982). A matter of black and white. *Gifted Child Newsletter*, 3(11), 4.

Baldwin, A. (1973). *Identify the disadvantaged.* Paper presented at the First National Conference on the Disadvantaged Gifted, Ventura, CA. March.

Baldwin, A. (1982). Identify gifted minority children. *Gifted Child Newsletter*, 3(3), 7–8.

Bell, S. (1982). The super Susedik kids. *Families*, June, 95–100.

Bernal, E. M. (1975). Gifted Mexican American children: An ethno-scientific perspective. *California Journal of Educational Research*, 25, 261–273.

Bernal, E. M. (1978). The identification of gifted chicano children. In A. Y. Baldwin, G. H. Gear & L. L. Lucito (Eds.), *Educational planning for the gifted: Overcoming cultural, geographic and socio-economic barriers.* Reston, VA: Council for Exceptional Children.

Bernal, E. M. (1981). *Identifying minority gifted students: Special problems and procedures.* Paper presented in New Orleans, Council for Exceptional Children's Conference on Bilingual Child, February.

Bernal, E. M. (1983). *The characteristics of the Mexican in gifted.* Report to the Richardson Foundation, Fort Worth, TX.

Berry, J. W. (1969). Ecology and socialization as factors in figural assimilation and the resolution of binocular rivalry. *International Journal of Psychology*, 4, 270–280.

Berry, J. W. (1971). Psychological research in the north. *Anthropologist*, 13, 142–157.

Brown, C. (1976). *Gifted native American.* Presentation at the Gifted Conference, Chippewa Reservation, Red Lake, MN.

Bruch, C. B. (1971). Modification of procedures for identification of the disadvantaged gifted. *The Gifted Child Quarterly*, 15, 267–272.

Bruninks, V. (1978). Peer status and personality characteristics of learning disabled and non-disabled students. *Journal of Learning Disabilities*, 12, 484–489.

Callahan, C. (1980). The gifted girl: An anomaly? *Roeper Review*, 2(3), 16–20.

Callahan, C. (1982). Gifted girls: A neglected minority. *Gifted Child Newsletter*, 3(3), 5.

Chisholm, S. (1978). *The plight of the disadvantaged.* A Presentation at the National Conference on Disadvantaged Gifted, Washington, DC.

Clark, B. (1983). *Growing up gifted.* Columbus, OH: Charles E. Merrill.

Clark, R. W. (1972). *Einstein: The life and times.* New York: Avon Books.

Coleman, J., Campbell, E., Hobson, C., McPartland, J., Mood, A., Weinfeld, F. & York, R. (1966). Equality of educational opportunity. Washington, DC: U.S. Government Printing Office.

Connelly, M. (1977). Gifted girls and gifted women. *Roeper Review*, 12, 12–13.

Cox, C. (1926). The early mental traits of three hundred geniuses. In L. Terman (Ed.), *Genetic Studies of Genius, Volume 2.* Stanford, CA: Stanford University Press.

Dwyer, R. (1983). *Strategies for working with minority gifted.* A paper presented at an Advanced Institute for Gifted, Tampa, FL, January.

Ernest, J. (1976). Mathematics and sex. *American Mathematical Monthly*, *83*(8), 595–614.

Ernest, J. (1980). Is mathematics a sexist discipline? In L. Fox, L. Brady & D. Tobin (Eds.), *Women and the Mathematical Mystique*. Baltimore, MD: Johns Hopkins University Press.

Farrell, P. (1973). *Teacher involvement in identification*. Paper presented at the First National Conference on Disadvantaged Gifted, Ventura, CA, March.

Feldman, D. (1979). The mysterious case of extreme giftedness. H. Passow (ed.), *The Gifted and the Talented: Their Education and Development*, NSSE, 78th Yearbook.

Fox, L. (1981). Preparing gifted girls for future leadership. *Gifted Child Quarterly*, March/April, 7–11.

Frasier, M. (1979). Rethinking the issues regarding the culturally disadvantaged gifted. *Exceptional Children*, *45*, 538–542.

Gallagher, J. (1985). *Teaching the gifted child* (2d ed.). Boston: Allyn and Bacon.

Gallagher, J. & Crowder, T. (1957). The adjustment of gifted children in the regular classroom. *Exceptional Children*, *23*, 306–312.

Gerken, K. C. (1978). Performance of Mexican American children in intelligence tests. *Exceptional Children*, *44*, 438–443.

Gowan, J. (1981). Introduction. In J. Gowan, J. Khatena & E. P. Torrance (Eds.), *Creativity: Its Educational Implications* (2d ed.). Dubuque, IA: Kendall/Hunt.

Greene, J., Malley-Crist, J. & Cansler, D. (1978). Chapel Hill's services to the gifted handicapped. *GCT*, *4*, 29–33.

Guilford, J. P. (1959). Three faces of intellect. *American Psychology*, *14*, 469–479.

Halpern, F. (1973). *Survival: Black/white*. Elmsford, NY: Pergamon Press.

Hollingworth, R. S. (1942). *Children above 180 IQ*. Yonkers, NY: World Book.

Kleinfeld, J. O. (1970). *Cognitive strengths of eskimos and implications for education*. Fairbanks: University of Alaska.

Kleinfeld, J. O. (1971). *Instructional style and the intellectual performance of Indian and eskimo students*. Anchorage: University of Alaska.

Lafrenz, N. & Colangelo, N. (1981). Counseling the culturally diverse gifted. *Gifted Child Quarterly*, *25*(1), 27–30.

Locke, P. (1982). The American Indian: Too few identified. *Gifted Children Newsletter*, *3*(9), 4.

Lombardi, T. P. (1970). *Psycholinguistic ability of Sioux Indian children*. Unpublished doctoral dissertation, University of South Dakota.

Luchins, E. & Luchins, A. (1980). Female mathematicians: A contemporary approval. In L. Fox, L. Brady & D. Tobin (Eds.), *Women and the mathematical mystique*. Baltimore, MD: Johns Hopkins University Press.

Maccoby, E. & Jaclin, C. (1974). *The psychology of sex differences*. Stanford, CA: Stanford University Press.

Maker, J. (1977). *Providing programs for the gifted handicapped*. Reston, VA: The Council for Exceptional Children.

Maker, J. (1982). *Curriculum development for the gifted*. Rockville, MD: Aspen Publications.

McMillin, D. (1975). *Separate criteria: An alternative for the identification of disadvantaged gifted*. Paper presented at the National Teacher Institute on Disadvantaged Gifted, Los Angeles, May.

McShane, D. A. (1980). A view of scores of American Indian children on the Wescheler Intelligence Scales. *White Cloud Journal*, *1*(41), 3–10.

McShane, D. & Plass, J. (1982). Wechsler performance patterns of American Indian children. *Psychology in the schools, 19*(1), 8–17.

Meeker, M. (1969). *The structure of intellect: Its interpretation and uses*. Columbus, OH: Merrill Publishing Co.

Meeker, M. (1978). Nondiscriminatory procedures to assess giftedness in black, chicano, Navajo and Anglo children. In A. Baldwin, G. Gear & L. Lucito (Eds.), *Educational planning for the gifted: Overcoming cultural, geographical, and socio-economic barriers*. Reston, VA: The Council for Exceptional Children.

Mullins, J. (1979). *Making language work better for handicapped people and everyone else*. Paper presented at the annual convention of the Council for Exceptional Children, Dallas, TX, April.

Newland, T. E. (1976). *The gifted in socio-educational perspective*. Englewood Cliffs, NJ: Prentice-Hall.

Parnes, S. (1963). Education and creativity. *Teachers College Record, 64*, 331–339.

Parnes, S. (1967). *Creative behavior guidebook*. New York: Charles Scribner and Sons.

Passow, A., Goldberg, M. & Tannenbaum, A. (1967). *Education of the disadvantaged: A book of readings*. New York: Holt, Rinehart and Winston.

Pressman, H. (1969). Schools to beat the system: Can we open the gates of the gifted and let the children out? *Psychology Today, 2*, 58–63.

Rodenstein, J., Pfleger, L. & Colangelo, N. (1977). Career development of the gifted woman. *The Gifted Child Quarterly, 21*, 340–358.

Schuberg, J. & Cropley, A. (1972). Verbal regulation of behavior and IQ in Canadian Indian and white children. *Developmental Psychology, 7*, 259–301.

Sears, P. & Barbee, A. (1977). Career and life satisfaction among Terman's gifted women. In J. Stanley, W. George & C. Solano (Eds.), *The gifted and creative: A fifty year perspective*. Baltimore, MD: Johns Hopkins University Press.

Sexton, P. (1961). *Education and income*. New York: Viking Press.

Sisk, D. (1982). Strategies for working with black gifted students. *Florida Association for the Gifted Newsletter*, July.

Sisk, D. (1983). *Parlé: Simulation game*. Unpublished simulation game.

Smilansky, M. (1984). *The gifted disadvantaged in Israel*. Paper presented to the Ingenium Conference in South Africa, August.

Solano, C. (1977). Teacher and pupil stereotypes of gifted boys and girls. *Talents and Gifts, 19*, 4–8.

Stanley, J. C. (1979). The case for extreme educational acceleration of intellectually brilliant youths. In J. Gowan, J. Khatena & R. P. Torrance (Eds.), *Educating the ablest: A book of readings* (2d ed.). Ithaca, IL: F. E. Peacock Publications.

Tannenbaum, A. (1983). *Gifted children: Psychological and educational perspectives*. New York: Macmillan.

Taylor, C. W. (1963). Clues to creative teaching: The creative process and education. *Instructor, 73*, 4–5.

Terman, L. & Oden, M. (1947). The gifted child grows up. In L. Terman (Ed.), *Genetic studies of genius, Volume IV*. Stanford: Stanford University Press.

Torrance, E. P. (1962). *Guiding creative talent*. Englewood Cliffs, NJ: Prentice-Hall.

Torrance, E. P. (1968). Finding hidden talents among gifted disadvantaged. *The Gifted Child Quarterly, 12*, 131–137.

Torrance, E. P. (1971). Are the Torrance tests of creative thinking biased against or in favor of disadvantaged groups? *The Gifted Child Quarterly, 16*, 75–88.

Torrance, E. P. (1977). *Discovery and nurturance of giftedness in the culturally deficient*. Reston, VA: The Council for Exceptional Children.

Weinberg, M. (1977). Minority students: A research appraisal. *The national institute of education (NIE) study on minority groups*, Washington, DC.

Whitmore, J. (1980). *Giftedness, conflict and underachievement*. Boston: Allyn and Bacon.

Whitmore, J. (1986). Understanding a lack of motivation to excel. *Gifted Child Quarterly*, *30*(2), Spring, 66–69.

Williams, F. (1968). *Creativity at home and in school*. St. Paul, MN: Macalester Creativity Project.

Williams, F. (1982). Developing childrens' creativity at home and in school. *GCT*, *24*, 2–6.

Wolleat, P. (1979). Guiding the career development of gifted females. In N. Colangelo & R. Zaffromm (Eds.), *New voices in counseling the gifted*. Dubuque, IA: Kendall-Hunt.

CHAPTER 11

COUNSELING AND GUIDING
THE GIFTED

*So many things fail to interest us, simply because they don't find in us enough surfaces
on which to live, and what we have to do is to increase the number of planes in our mind,
so that a much larger number of themes can find a place in it at the same time.*

Ortega Gasset

Special counseling should be an essential part of the school program for all gifted
students from kindergarten to the twelfth grade, yet the gifted students who most
often receive help are the special populations of gifted: the culturally diverse, the
disadvantaged, and the handicapped. Although gifted students possess differential
affective needs and characteristics that demand nurturance, they receive minimal
counseling and guidance services. This chapter examines the notion of counseling
as the concept of integration of self and the foundation for gifted students' total
development. Van Tassel-Baska (1983) gives two reasons that the gifted receive
so few guidance services: (1) many educators see counseling as being primarily
for problem students, and (2) there are few trained personnel who feel adequately
prepared to deal with the counseling needs of gifted students.

The responsibility for counseling and guiding the gifted students lies with the
parents, teachers, and other personnel concerned with their welfare. This chapter
offers help to individuals who are interested in building and improving their
counseling and guidance skills to work with the gifted. The topics to be considered
are understanding the emotional self, awareness of self, and expressing emotions.

Photograph on facing page courtesy of Elizabeth Crews, Berkeley, California.

Through knowing and learning more about oneself one can reach out to others. Reaching out becomes the stimulus for several other topics, namely, communicating with others, integrating oneself, and becoming more self-directed.

Specific facilitating strategies discussed are awareness activities, relaxation, imagery, group dynamics, and bibliotherapy. The topic of career counseling is examined as a necessary component to a total guidance and counseling program for the gifted.

THE IMPORTANCE OF UNDERSTANDING THE EMOTIONAL SELF

The consciousness of self is not purely an intellectual idea. Shallcross and Sisk (1985) state that individuals experience the self as a thinking–intuiting–feeling–acting unit. Consequently, the self is more than the various roles assumed; it is the capacity by which a human being knows that he or she can play these roles. The thinking self exercises the power of judgment, conception, or inference, and employs logic and reason. The intuiting self perceives immediate cognition, knowledge, or conviction. The feeling or emotional self is the affective part of consciousness. Furthermore, the acting self responds to inputs of knowledge and impressions. People constantly strive to understand and to be aware of themselves. Self-awareness develops through involvement with others and through various activities. Awareness of self is continually expanding.

Awareness of the need for gifted students to cope with their giftedness is not new. It has been discussed by many researchers: Terman (1925), Hollingworth (1942), Schetky (1981), Maker (1982), Clark (1983), and Van Tassel-Baska (1983). Issues involved in coping with giftedness are:

- Understanding one's differentness, yet recognizing one's similarities to others
- Understanding how to accept and give criticism
- Being tolerant of oneself and others
- Developing an understanding of one's strengths and weaknesses
- Developing skills in areas that will nurture both cognitive and affective development (Van Tassel-Baska, 1983)

These issues represent essential components in a total guidance approach for the gifted, with the goal or objective being integration of self.

A MODEL FOR AWARENESS OF SELF

Shallcross and Sisk (1985) suggest a model to conceptualize the ways in which a sense of self develops and the integration of self is accomplished. The model is depicted in Figure 11-1.

Sensing, as depicted in the model, consists of basic sensory experiences: seeing, hearing, tasting, touching, feeling, and smelling. The highly curious and alert gifted student gathers sensory information. He/she then interprets and uses this information to build linkages and connections with past information or experiences. This interpretative thinking process is related to the emotions surrounding

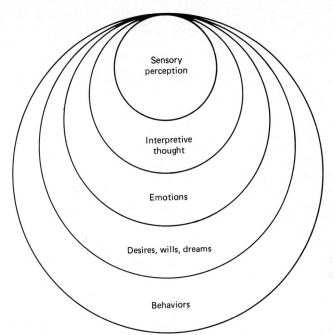

FIGURE 11-1
A model for self-awareness. (*D. Shallcross and D. Sisk*, The Growing Person, *Bearly Limited, Buffalo, New York, 1985. Reprinted by permission.*)

the information or the experience being perceived. These emotions are further refined to become wishes, desires, and dreams, resulting in action or behavior.

The information contained within awareness is not always readily available. One way to stimulate greater self-awareness is to consciously examine the various components in the model; the sensing, interpreting, emoting, desiring, and behaving, and to consciously try to experience the components.

Sensing

Most young gifted students are comfortable with the sensing level of self. As they walk near a building, they trail their hands lightly over the surface, experiencing the building completely. However, not all gifted students experience this sense of wonder. An effective tool to stimulate wonder is an activity called "Guided Fantasy." Exhibit 11-1 is an example to help gifted students experience their senses.

When this exercise is carried out in a group, the teacher uses a modulated but natural level of voice. It is important that the exercise take place in a quiet, relaxed atmosphere to permit the sensory experiences to be heightened. After the guided fantasy, the gifted students can share their various physiological experiences. For example, some students may have a particularly strong sensory or auditory experience such as "I could hear the laughter, it was very real" or, "I could see the fish swimming in the surf, they were all colors."

EXHIBIT 11-1

GUIDED FANTASY

Close your eyes and become conscious of your breathing. Relax and become very comfortable. See yourself at the seashore. . .

- See the waves splash against the seashore (pause)
- Hear the wild cry of the seagulls (pause)
- Smell the tang of the sea air (pause)
- See the sun's diamondlike sparkle on the water (pause)
- Hear the excited laughter of children chasing one another (pause)
- See the tiny fish swimming in the surf at your feet (pause)
- Reach out and experience the beauty (pause)
- Sit quietly, enjoy the feeling; feel calm and satisfied
- Slowly see yourself in the classroom

EXHIBIT 11-2

UNFINISHED SENSORY THOUGHTS

I see _____.

I hear _____.

I touch _____.

I feel _____.

Still another way to approach the development or refinement of the gifted student's senses is to use unfinished sensory thoughts. Exhibit 11-2 shows several that work well.

The facilitating parent, teacher, or friend can choose a topic and encourage the gifted students to take turns sharing finished thoughts. A topic might be A Walk in the Woods. A gifted 8 year-old's response was the following:

> A Walk in the Woods
> *I see* the sun shining in the trees.
> *I hear* the call of the birds.
> *I touch* the shaggy bark of the old oak.
> *I feel* good inside.

Another response, by a 5-year-old gifted student, using a different topic was:

> A Walk in Space
> *I see* the Moon Man approaching.
> *I hear* his words and I do not understand.
> *I touch* my invisible ray button.
> *I feel* safe, as he cannot see me.

I see him looking surprised.
I hear him call out.
I touch my home ray button.
I feel safe in my home.

When gifted students complete these phrases, they concentrate on sensory experiences. The finished product is similar to simple poetry, replete with sensory data. Gifted students enjoy seeing and hearing one another's finished products.

Interpretation

The senses supply raw information, purely sensory data, what was seen, heard, or observed. How it is interpreted or what is done with the data is called interpretation.

For example, a cat is walking toward the house. The cat is meowing loudly and carrying a limp kitten in its mouth.

The sensory data is interpreted as: The mother cat is very sad as she walks slowly back to the house, carrying her seriously injured kitten. She is bringing it home to be helped.

Then again, another interpretation: A mother cat found her kitten exploring the outdoors. The kitten had wandered from the cat box and the mother cat is upset and bringing her home.

Both of the interpretations are based on the raw or basic data, and were written by fourth-grade gifted girls. Interpretation is defined as a function of reality as individuals see it, and for the majority of the time, most interpretations individuals make are correct and provide useful data for action. However, when interpretations are incorrect, the sensory information needs to be separated from the interpretation. This is an important idea for teachers to share with young gifted students and to assist them in distinguishing one from the other.

Role playing builds interpretative skills for individual gifted students and for groups of gifted. Gifted students enjoy using data cards labeled What, Where, and When. These cards can be distributed and, after 60 seconds of preparation, the students can be asked to act out the prescribed action. Some favorite data cards are:

- You are a robot lost in the rain at night.
- You are a princess in New York City at dawn.
- You are a mosquito surrounded by cans of Raid in a modern kitchen.

As the leader or facilitator, the teacher or parent will note: (1) Did everyone participate? (2) Were the groups able to interpret the actions of one another? and (3) Did the groups correctly demonstrate their interpretations from the sensory data?

Interpretations are a necessary part of daily life. From sensory data, interpretations are made about simple acts like frowning. The interpretation may be that the individual is perturbed, has a headache, or is bothered by the glare from the sun. Interpreting is an essential skill that gifted students need help in using accurately to better communicate with others.

Feelings and Emotions

Feelings and emotions are experienced inside and, as they are experienced, individuals respond. These outward feeling responses can be traced to the sensory information being interpreted. An activity designed to help gifted students determine how accurately they are perceiving responses is to have them express emotions such as pleased, comfortable, calm, satisfied, angry, nervous, and eager.

In today's complex and changing world, many people have learned to hide their feelings. Gifted students mirror their significant adults, parents, or teachers, and they too may be reluctant to share emotions and feelings. The price that gifted students pay for withholding emotions is that others may never truly understand them as individuals. One way to encourage gifted students to share emotions and feelings is through the use of journals or daily logs. One teacher of the gifted has her students tape a large manila envelope to the side of their desks to hold their logs. The students have red tags or flags which they display if a feeling, emotion, or event needs to be shared.

A gifted student noted in his log:

> I was really upset in class today when I didn't get to be the team leader. I thought I was going to cry, but then I remembered how much Sarah wanted the job and I decided to volunteer as her assistant. She said yes, and now I feel much better. I guess I don't have to be first all the time. Was that what you said about not always tooting your own horn? I'm getting there. . . . Thanks.

This gifted student wanted to communicate not only his feelings but his insight. Informal communications such as these help teachers better understand gifted students' concerns and represent concrete reflections of their personal growth.

Still another problem is when feelings become so important that it is difficult to use one's intellect. Gifted students, with their keen sensitivity and strong sense of ego often experience this problem. Yet feelings can aid intuitive reactions, and intuition can bring new and different ways of looking at things, particularly in problem-solving situations. The challenge for education is to help gifted students use their emotions in a positive manner and not be used by their emotions. To accomplish this, gifted students must understand their emotions and feelings.

Bibliotherapy, the use of books to solve problems, can be very helpful in understanding emotions and feelings. Frasier and McCannon (1981) state that bibliotherapy is a vicarious experience. Through imagination, gifted students experience various approaches to problems without the real-life consequences that go with decision making. Frasier (1982) lists a number of needs of the gifted that bibliotherapy addresses:

To learn to clarify the feelings and expectations of others

To be exposed to alternatives, abstractions, consequences of choices, and opportunities for drawing generalizations and testing them

To transcend negative reactions by finding values to which he or she is or can be committed

To learn to set realistic goals and to accept setbacks as part of the learning process

To be allowed to pursue ideas and integrate new ideas without forced closure or products demanded

To explore the highest levels of human thought and apply this knowledge to today's problems

To find purpose and direction from a personal value system

To learn how behaviors affect the feelings and behaviors of others

Through bibliotherapy, gifted students identify with characters in books who are having similar problems. As emotional and social issues are raised in the stories, gifted students experience catharsis, or a release of emotional or psychological tension, as well as gaining insight into their own or similar problems. Gifted students quickly perceive problems and their solutions as universal happenings.

Bibliotherapy supplemented by discussions led by a sympathetic person is helpful for even the youngest gifted reader. The major problem in using bibliotherapy with gifted students is getting the right book to the right student at the right time.

An excellent source for locating books is the *Book-Finder's Guide*, which lists books according to topics. For example, gifted students who are coping with divorce in their family may well choose Judy Blume's book, *It's Not the End of the World*, illustrating a child's experience with divorce in the family. As divorce becomes more common, many gifted students need emotional support to cope with this problem, and many may need to give emotional support to their friends.

A common fear of gifted students is not doing well in school. This fear stems from their sense of perfection. Judy Blume deals with this problem in a sensitive, caring manner in *Otherwise Known As Sheila The Great*. Nine-year-old Sheila's frustration, fear of dogs, and being unable to swim are similar to fears of many young gifted students. As gifted students discuss their fears in bibliotherapy sessions, they gain insight into their own behavior and the behavior of others.

Another example of an appropriate book for bibliotherapy is *The Cat Ate My Gymsuit* by Paula Danziger. In this book, Danziger explores the problems of being bright, 13, and growing up. Specific problems dealt with are boredom with school and coping with one's parents. Both of these problems are shared by many gifted adolescents.

In discussing the use of bibliotherapy, one problem that surfaces is how can teachers and parents find the time to read the books. One solution is to locate groups of parents or teachers who are willing to prepare bibliotherapy sessions or sheets and share these with one another. One group of parents and teachers prepared fifty bibliotherapy sheets. They used Taylor's (1963) creativity model for the questioning or discussion process. Taylor, a psychologist and educator at the University of Utah, states that creativity can be developed by using different levels or kinds of thinking. He calls these academic, creative, planning, predicting, forecasting, communicating, evaluation and decisionmaking.* Definitions of the Taylor terms are:

Academic: the ability to understand, remember well, and get good grades

Communication: the ability to clearly express oneself so that others understand

Planning: the ability to organize something; time, work, or play

Predicting: the ability to determine the outcome of things and to know what to expect

Creating: the ability to have new ideas, or to invent, compose, or design something

Evaluating: the ability to make productive decisions and choices

Mechanics of Bibliotherapy

A bibliotherapy session usually lasts 20 to 30 minutes and involves a group of seven to fifteen students. The ideal group size for open discussion is seven to ten, allowing time for full participation and exchange of ideas.

When gifted students have read a given story or book, they make an appointment with their teacher, guidance counselor, librarian, or parent volunteer to participate in a bibliotherapy session. One teacher of the gifted in a self-contained classroom uses an appointment sheet that looks like Figure 11-2.

	Monday	Tuesday	Wednesday	Thursday	Friday
Time	9–9:30	10–10:30	1–1:30	2–2:30	9–9:30
Student leader		Sue L. +5		Paula H. +6	
Book title		*Ramona and Her Father*		*Blackbird Singing*	

FIGURE 11-2
Bibliotherapy appointments.

This teacher plans weekly 30-minute periods for bibliotherapy sessions for her gifted students. This schedule reflects two sessions, one using *Ramona and Her Father* (Cleary, 1972) and the other using *Blackbird Singing* (Bunting, 1980). *Ramona and Her Father* deals with how family routine can be upset when a father loses a job. *Blackbird Singing* deals with 10-year-old Marcus's struggle to come to terms with himself, his parents, and a complex ecological dilemma when their crops are threatened by huge numbers of migrating birds. The gifted students in this teacher's class live in a poor socioeconomic region and many of them are concerned about their parents' lack of work. Thirteen of the teacher's gifted

*Discerning opportunities, social behavior, and implementing action have been added by Taylor in 1985.

students are involved in the two sessions, leaving twelve who have not indicated an interest in the sessions as yet. While the teacher works with the two small groups in bibliotherapy sessions, the other gifted students can work on independent activities.

In bibliotherapy sessions, the leader uses questions to explore a variety of types of thinking. Exhibit 11-3 shows a sample bibliotherapy session using *The Cat Ate My Gymsuit* (Danziger, 1973). The format includes a brief summary and three questions at each level of thinking.

Exhibit 11-3

THE CAT ATE MY GYMSUIT
Paula Danziger

Summary

Marcy is a 13-year-old girl with problems and a tendency to hide them. She is bored with school and hates her father's behavior. She is also worried about being fat and thinks she may get a bad case of acne any minute. Ms. Finney, a new English teacher, brings life and purpose to school using new teaching methods. The teacher is suspended for refusing to pledge allegiance to the flag. The school goes into an uproar, and Marcy and her family are deeply involved and changed by the whole episode.

Questions

Academic

1 What are some of the excuses Marcy uses for not going to gym?
2 What were some of Ms. Finney's teaching methods?
3 What happened on Marcy's first date?

Planning

1 What could the students do to plan for Ms. Finney's rehiring?
2 How could Marcy's mother plan to help Marcy lose weight?
3 What would have been your plan for convincing the school board that new teaching methods are needed?

Predicting and forecasting

1 If the school board had voted against Ms. Finney returning to school, what do you think Marcy and her friends would have done next?
2 Put yourself in Ms. Finney's shoes. What do you think she was saying to herself during her suspension?
3 If Marcy and her friends had not organized a protest, do you think the school board would have made a different decision?

Creative

1 Ms. Finney's class wrote a children's book for a class assignment. What would be the title of your book? What would it be about?
2 What do you think Marcy would have said if she had been interviewed by the evening news?
3 If you were to draw a picture of your favorite excuse that Marcy used for not wearing her gymsuit, what would it look like?

EXHIBIT 11-3 *(Continued)*

Decision making/evaluation

1 Do you think Marcy's feelings about herself changed? In what ways?
2 Why do you think Ms. Finney resigned? Do you agree with her?
3 Did you like the Smedley activity? Why?

Groups of parents and teachers can work together, preparing sheets on books. These sheets can be combined into a resource for teachers and parents to use when conducting bibliotherapy sessions. Using these bibliotherapy sheets, parents, teachers, and volunteers can easily lead bibliotherapy sessions. Emphasis is on giving emotional support, and leaders note how individual characters in books give and receive emotional support.

Frasier (1982) suggests a number of follow-up activities to bibliotherapy, such as posted notices on story-related radio and television programs, role playing, dramatization, opportunities to illustrate stories that have been read, and watching films or filmstrips on similar topics. Bibliotherapy can help gifted students solve many of their problems and challenges in a caring atmosphere. Insightful discussion offers opportunities for solving existing problems and may also prevent future problems for gifted students.

Role playing can be useful in exploring emotions. A helpful strategy is "Double Technique." This is accomplished by asking gifted students to portray a conflict situation and asking another gifted student to interact with the original actor, as a type of other self. The idea is to explore as many different moods and psychological perspectives as possible. Gifted students enjoy opportunities for role playing, particularly if those opportunities are followed by discussion.

Desire/Intention/Will

Desire is what an individual wants to accomplish; an *intention* is the moving toward or away from something; and *will* is what is decided. Intentions can be desires or wills of which gifted students are aware, but they may be hidden. Desires, intentions, or wills can be defined as objectives. Objectives become directives to accomplish specific tasks or activities.

In some cases, intentions, desires, and wills may be in conflict with one another. Gifted students want to be liked by others, but they also want to win and to be the best. Trying to decide which intention is the more important is difficult. One way for gifted students to test intentions is to note the behavior and the resultant feelings. A given response or behavior may bring warm, satisfying feelings, while another response or behavior may bring irritation and unhappiness.

Some conflicts gifted students deal with are questions such as, Shall I get good grades? or, Shall I try to be popular? By observing action in role playing or viewing videotapes of group interaction, gifted students learn to read facial expressions, posture, voice characteristics, and actions to better understand desires, wills, and intentions, as they relate to behavior. They also note how they listen, build on one another's ideas, express emotions, or socially interact. As gifted students become more aware of themselves, they also gain tools in understanding others.

Action Behavior

The actions or behavior of gifted students is the part of them which is often reported and noticed by others. Alvino (1981) relates the frustrations of a first-grade girl named Susie who was consistently shut out of cliques and play groups. The child blamed herself for her fellow students' behavior and their rejection of her intellectual ability, outspokenness, and nonconforming attitude. Susie's ideas were reinforced by her teacher, who said she would get along better with the others if she tempered her advanced vocabulary. The teacher stated, "Why don't you try talking like a first grader?"

To better understand their actions and how they are perceived, gifted students can view themselves on videotape. However, viewing tapes can be devastating, particularly if the intention of the gifted student is to be friendly and supportive and the action appears hostile or unproductive. Teachers need to provide a positive atmosphere for these experiences, using many questions directed toward introspection, such as, How could you go about this action in a more positive way? What are some of the ways you could approach this problem?

A recognition of what they are doing at any given time is a valuable tool for gifted students and it will help them become aware of their developing selves. Yet, these activities can produce stress, and teachers need to help the gifted students learn to cope.

Williams (1979) suggests dealing with stress by using the four stages of the creative process. She calls her techniques a stress coping model, and lists six problem-solving steps which gifted students can master to help analyze stess-causing behaviors:

1 Gathering concepts
2 Recognizing the problems
3 Developing a hypothesis
4 Designing the investigation
5 Coming up with possible solutions
6 Confirming or disputing

Suggested activities to be used in the Williams coping model include concentration exercises, creative dramatics, discussions, emotion–memory exercises, fantasy journeys, observation activities, relaxation, and role playing. Williams tested her model over a period of 3 years and found many behavioral changes in gifted students. There was a reduction in fear and failure and the students were more willing to display risk-taking action. As they became more aware of themselves and more aware of their actions, their actions become more congruent with their desires, intents, and wills.

Expressing Emotions

Gifted students need to learn to express their emotions as well as to express cognitive ideas. All students need socially acceptable mechanisms to share their feelings and, in a verbally oriented society, gifted students, with their high verbal ability, need the "right words" to convey their emotions. By owning their statements or by using "I," gifted students learn to see the connection between expressing feelings and owning those feelings. Gifted students possess a dramatic flair and enjoy role playing, particularly charades, in which a variety of emotions or situations are placed on slips of paper to act out. Sample words might be *eager, confused, afraid, worried, excited, joyous, lonely,* and *anxious.*

Following improvisational activities, the teacher can lead the gifted students in processing the activity. Some questions that might be explored are: Did you say and do what you had planned? Did the other players say and do what you expected them to do? How did you decide on which emotion to portray? Did you feel yourself in the part? What was the exact thing that happened to cause you to react that way? What major emotion did each character portray? Have you experienced something similar to the scene you saw?

A natural follow-up to role playing and group improvisational work is an activity known as "Boundary Breaking." Boundary Breaking, as explained in Shallcross and Sisk (1985), follows simple ground rules:

1 One person speaks at a time.
2 Everyone has the right to say "Pass" if they need more time to think or choose not to take part.
3 No one is allowed to criticize, interrupt, or laugh at another person's response.
4 All responses are accepted; there are no right or wrong responses.
5 Everyone gets a turn, following a pattern to the left or right of the circle.
6 The leader takes a turn with the group members.
7 The group should be limited to no more than ten members.
8 The questions are asked in a nonthreatening atmosphere.

Examples of questions which have been successfully used in Boundary Breaking sessions with gifted students are:

1 If you could change one thing about yourself, what would it be?
2 If you could be any famous person in history, who would you be?
3 What is one trait that you feel most people admire about you?
4 What is one trait that you feel most people dislike about you?
5 If you could visit anywhere in the world, where would you visit?
6 If you could change one thing about your best friend, what would it be?
7 If you could change one thing about the world, what would you change?
8 If you could be any kind of animal, what would you like to be?

At first, gifted students may need to be reminded of the ground rules, but they quickly internalize the underlying structure and protect the mutual acceptance, understanding, and trust experienced in Boundary Breaking. In Boundary Breaking, gifted students are provided opportunities to freely express feelings without judgment or comment. This activity helps gifted students experience a sense of dignity and worth, which counterbalances negative experiences.

Many gifted students make little or no effort to hide their difference, and, consequently, they have difficulty establishing relationships. Their divergent thinking and action is not always appreciated, and in the words of Alvino (1981) they seem "off the wall." In addition, they are very sensitive to concerns and issues that other students may not be concerned about and may appear self-righteous or self-serving. When gifted students display their high standards of truth and morality and are quick to point out how others don't measure up, they are often rejected.

In Boundary Breaking, gifted students experience total acceptance of their personalities, but they also hear other points of view which provide new material for further refinement and development of their own standards of behavior and action.

COMMUNICATING WITH OTHERS

Through communication, individuals learn to understand others and to help others to understand them. Communication is defined as sending a message to a person or persons that will, in turn, evoke a response. Communication is verbal, non-verbal, and a combination of both. Through effective communication, gifted students learn to build trusting, cooperative, growing relationships; when necessary, they learn to terminate relationships or to shift them to a different level.

Tomer (1981) suggests using Bloom and Krathwohl's affective taxonomy of educational objectives as a means to develop interpersonal communication for gifted students. On the first level, awareness, Tomer (1981) suggests that gifted students can improve their communication with others by becoming more realistic about their own expectations and about those imposed on them by parents and teachers. This can be accomplished through bibliotherapy and discussion. The second level, responding, can be accomplished by reaching out to others and receiving knowledge verbally and nonverbally through art, music, mime, and symbols. In the third level, valuing, the gifted students accept, choose, and become committed to values which exemplify acceptance and responsibility for oneself and others. At this level, gifted students can do problem solving and role playing. On the fourth level, organization of a value system, gifted students become more deeply committed as they learn to establish an integrated sense of values through activities such as values clarification and boundary breaking. On the fifth level of the taxonomy, characterization of a value, through their actions gifted students display the congruence between their values and actions using simulation activities and role playing.

Communication is an involving process, affecting the sender and the receiver. Communication can move forward in a positive, growing manner and cause the sender and receiver to experience positive feelings toward one another, or it can stagnate and produce negative feelings between the sender and the receiver.

Two exercises to build better communication for gifted students are "one-way communication exercise" and "two-way communication exercise" (Shallcross & Sisk, 1985). The "one-way exercise" is usually done first. In this exercise, a sender is chosen and given a simple design to describe to a group of receivers. The directions are given with no feedback, and the sender faces away from the receivers. One design to use with young gifted students is three intersecting circles with two squares, one on each end. Other more simple designs can be used if necessary. As gifted students experience this activity, they suggest designs of their own, and, as their skills in communicating with one another develop, their designs become more and more complex.

The simple design of circles and squares is illustrated in Figure 11-3.

In "one-way communication," the sender initiates the beginning of the exercise. The sender gives the one-way directions and does not see the receiver's confusion, hesitation, progress, or success.

In the "two-way exercise," the sender may answer questions from the receivers and may engage in helping, interested behavior. In the "two-way exercise," the same design is used or a similar one can be developed.

One-way communication is quicker, and many gifted students, because of their impatience, prefer one-way communication, particularly when they are the sender. However, as receivers, gifted students prefer two-way communication, and the level of confidence of the receiver is lower. The two-way communication exercise takes longer, but it is usually more accurate and the receiver is less perturbed.

Gifted students recognize that the commanding "Do it!" approach in one-way communication helps get the job done quickly but less effectively. They also experience the dimension of hurt and disturbed feelings of their fellow classmates.

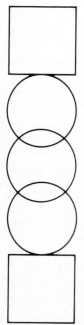

FIGURE 11-3
One-way communication.

Still another important communication skill is listening. Both the sender and the receiver engage in listening. One way to demonstrate that a response has been understood is paraphrasing. Carl Rogers (1980) found that listening intently to what a person says, trying to understand how it seems to the speaker, and grasping the personal significance of the message is crucial to total communication. Rogers (1980) states in *A Way of Being* that empathic understanding, as reflected by paraphrasing, helps to build close relationships, which in turn bring about positive personality growth.

Another activity that works well with gifted students is *I Speak, You Speak*. In this activity, one gifted student is designated as the sender, and this student works with one other gifted student, a receiver. The sender is asked to talk for 1 minute on a selected topic. Following this 1 minute, the receiver cannot talk until he or she has first restated the ideas and feelings of the sender. This activity encourages laughter and frustration in gifted students, as they learn to listen more closely and accurately. To help gifted students learn to communicate totally, parents and teachers can use three specific communication skills: (1) clarifying strengths, (2) making personal statements, and (3) making relationship statements.

By modeling these communication skills with gifted students, teachers and parents can help the gifted become more effective in communicating. Teachers can clarify strengths in informal ways by stating how well a gifted student is doing. Powell (1983) states that as a gifted child growing up, his parents valued caring for others and being a person of worth. In addition, they were able to reflect those values to him and to convey that he had strengths. He also said that he had teachers who expected positive things from him and clarified his strengths. Through their support, he was able to use his strengths.

Contrived classroom situations can be arranged to clarify strengths, using activities such as the "1-minute brag." Gifted students are given 1 minute to brag about all the things they think they do well. Following that 1-minute brag, the gifted students and their teachers reinforce those strengths by naming other specific strengths. After one particularly productive session, a gifted fourth grader shouted, "I feel so good, if I were a dog, my tail would be wagging!" The rest of the class agreed that his phrase was "happiness personified."

Still another way to clarify strengths is to construct a badge of distinction. A badge of distinction is a collage of torn pictures from magazines portraying interests, strengths, or wishes. These badges can be displayed and time can be provided for the gifted student to stand up and talk about herself/himself. This activity can introduce the concept of personal statements, as the gifted student tells about herself or himself. For example, "I put a sail boat here, because I like to sail," or, "I put a loving mother and child on my collage because my family is like that. I feel loved."

Through the use of the collage, gifted students make many personal statements; by making these statements they experience a safe and secure environment, safe enough to express feelings. Personal statements help gifted students reveal to others who they are, and by saying "I," gifted students own the statements and are responsible for them.

Relationship statements are the messages which are communicated to other people concerning our thoughts and feelings about them. Making relationship statements clarifies where two persons stand in relationship to each other and helps to facilitate greater openness in expressing feelings. An example of a relationship statement is, "When you smile at me in the morning when I come into the classroom, I feel appreciated," or, "When you tell me my poems are sensitive, I feel as if I want to write more," or, "When you don't call on me, I feel hurt and rejected." By making relationship statements, gifted students make their own feelings known through clearer communication.

Many of the difficulties encountered by gifted students are a result of poor communication, and the quality of their personal relationships can be improved through the use of better communication skills. The use of the skills may seem awkward at first, because they are new. But as they are used, the skills become a natural part of the gifted student's way of communicating.

INTEGRATING ONESELF

Gestalt is a German word meaning "the whole," but in the everyday use of gestalt, the term can mean "getting it all together." When we get it all together, it can also be said that we are integrated. Each of us has many selves. An exercise that is interesting and entertaining for gifted students is having them tear a sheet of 8½- by 11-inch paper into nine pieces and write their different selves or roles on each piece of paper, such as (1) girl scout, (2) daddy's little girl, (3) Marge's sister, (4) mother's helper, (5) Tom's girlfriend, (6) Sue's best friend, (7) the good student, (8) grandma's angel, and (9) tomboy. A 12-year-old gifted girl prioritized her different selves. She was given a chance to discard one of her selves and to discuss why, or to keep all of the selves. She chose to discard "daddy's little girl," as she was able to do many things on her own and perceived herself as being capable. Gifted students enjoy moving around the room, discussing their different roles and how they view them. This activity offers a positive reason and opportunity for interaction.

The concept of a psychological self is apparent in an individual's action. When students feel that they are not doing well, that attitude may keep them from trying. The same is true in the physical area. A lack of confidence shows in the way students look, walk, or stand. Many times gifted students will deny awareness of a specific attitude that they have, but teachers and parents often note the attitude in their personal demeanor. The next exercise demonstrates that feelings do show in behavior. It is called "Walk Like" (Shallcross & Sisk, 1985). The teacher or parent can say "walk like" and give each student an opportunity to demonstrate how they think each person would walk. "Walk Like" gives the following instructions or directives:

1 Walk like a brave person.
2 Walk like an angry person.
3 Walk like an embarrassed person.
4 Walk like a guilty person.

The activity can also be personalized by saying:

1 Show us how you walk when you are scared.
2 Show us how you walk when you feel happy.
3 Show us how you walk when you feel playful.
4 Show us how you walk when you are hurt.

Other ways of having students explore their total realm of being, or their integration of self, are by portraying an inanimate object and by exploring a series of questions concerning the object. Perls (1969) stated that any time we are talking, no matter what we are talking about, we are talking about ourselves. Therefore, when the gifted speak about inanimate or make-believe objects, they are revealing to themselves and to others a pattern of values, interests, and ideas that are a part of them. Awareness activities, such as encounter lessons, follow a pattern of questions that deal with perception (seeing, feeling, hearing, smelling, tasting); fear; relating to a group; creativity and change; and lastly, an abstract question that provides an opportunity for expression as a whole (Sisk, 1979). Exhibit 11-4 gives an encounter lesson with the questions and responses of a 10-year-old gifted boy. (The teacher's statements are designated as *T* and the student's as *S*.)

Much of what the young gifted student is saying about himself as a leaf is probably true of him as a young man, especially the part about needing friends since he just recently moved to a new school. He does not want to be taken for

---

EXHIBIT 11-4

AUTUMN FANTASY

T: I want you to become a leaf on a tree. It is autumn.
T: Perception: As a leaf on a tree, what are you seeing, feeling, or hearing?
S: I am high on a tree, and I see tiny little people below. No one notices me, since I am up so high. The wind is blowing and I feel slightly dizzy.
T: Fear: There is smoke in the air; what are you feeling?
S: I'm afraid. Smoke means fire, and we are so dry. It would be very easy for a fire to start.
T: Relating to a group: There are many leaves being blown around. Some are being blown into our tree; how do you feel about them?
S: It is alright if they come here. I need some new friends, maybe we can have some good times. They look friendly.
T: Creativity: If you could change yourself, as a leaf, in what way would you change yourself?
S: I would not be an autumn leaf that's about to die. I would be a pine tree and live forever. They don't lose their leaves in the fall. They also smell good, and people decorate them for Christmas trees.
T: Abstract thought: If you could talk, what would you say to the world, from the point of view of a tree?
S: I would tell them never to take trees for granted. Trees are alive and worth a great deal. We are all part of this world and give beauty to one another.

granted but rather to be a part of the world and to give and receive value. Powell (1983) expresses the same view in another way, when he states "we need someone, someone to love us before we can learn how to make it and learn to love ourselves."

Through positive interactions with teachers, parents, and other significant others gifted students begin to integrate themselves. Van Tassel-Baska (1983) lists several activities to promote integration of self. One is called "the eminence game," and the objective is to highlight role models for gifted students. The students read biographies of Frank Lloyd Wright, Pablo Casals, Marie Curie, and Albert Einstein and in small groups discuss questions such as the following:

1 Did each of these eminent individuals become famous because of innate abilities, a nurturing environment, or just plain luck?

2 What similarities and differences do you perceive among the four?

3 What personal qualities enhanced their work?

4 How did they cope with being different, being loners, being laughed at or scorned?

5 In your opinion, what made these individuals able to create at high levels?

These activities help gifted students begin to perceive their lives as holistic. As they discuss common interests and problems with other students and supportive teachers, they sense the reinforcement and encouragement being offered and begin to cope with their differentness and build a more integrated self.

Becoming More Self-Directed

As gifted students develop a sense of self and a sense of self in relationship to others, they experience personal power and worth. Each time gifted students test themselves, this sense of personal power is stretched. This power can be used to change parts of the self that are not to one's liking. By letting go of parts of the self, gifted students become more competent, creative, and self-directed. The gifted child's natural desire is to become knowledgeable, skilled, competent, and ultimately successful in achieving valued goals (Whitmore, 1986).

One way teachers can help gifted students become more self-directed is by having them experience planning, working on tasks and completing the tasks. Creative problem solving, as defined by Parnes et al. (1977), is useful in completing tasks. First, gifted students identify a problem and then follow a problem-solving process. The following is an example of how a group of gifted students used the process, becoming more self-directed: A fifth-grade gifted class has shown an interest in going to Epcot Center in Disney World. Their teacher said they could go if they financed the trip. They defined their problem with a statement which asked, "In what ways could we earn money to go to Disney World?" Then they chose a class leader and brainstormed as many ideas as possible without making judgments. The class leader listed their ideas on the blackboard:

1 Write creative stories and tape record them to be sold to parents, or read them to small children for a fee.

2 Put on a class play and charge 25 cents for admission.

3 Bring old things, like toys and knick-knacks, for a flea market.

4 Bake cookies and sell them at recess.

5 Read poetry or do a play for a Rotary or other groups.

6 Organize an after-school program for first and second grade and charge 50 cents admission.

7 Have a school fair.

8 Ask a store to donate toys or bicycles to raffle.

9 Have the parents each donate $20.

10 Ask Disney World for a discount.

11 Have a contest for the most special pet and charge 50 cents to enter.

As the gifted students listed their ideas, one idea triggered another (hitchhiking), but the brainstorming process took less than 8 minutes. The criteria they used for decision making were (1) the idea should be enjoyable, (2) the idea should be something we can do ourselves, and (3) the idea should make money. The students chose options 2 and 5. They decided to give a class play and charge a quarter for admission. They decided to offer the play to public groups for $50 per performance. They reasoned that most groups would have 100 members and that it would cost the individual members approximately 50 cents.

Once the decision was made as to what ideas they were going to use, the teacher then divided the class into groups and the students began to plan their work. One group was in charge of publicity, another was in charge of selling tickets, and still another was in charge of rewriting and editing the play. The play was a huge success and the class performed to various groups such as the Rotary, Eastern Star, and a garden club. They were able to go to Epcot Center, and, in addition, they became more self-directed and experienced the pleasure of achieving a task.

Still another way for gifted students to learn to be more self-directed is through group dynamic activities which create an invitational climate (invites participation—see Purkey, 1984) such as "Taking Charge," shown in Exhibit 11-5.

EXHIBIT 11-5

TAKING CHARGE

If you were king for a day and were in charge, what three things would you change?

_____

_____

_____

After answering that question, what three things would you leave the same?

_____

_____

_____

The following are selected responses from elementary school gifted students who worked in small groups to answer the question, "What three things would you change?"

- Governments would be more peaceful
- Parents would have to be nice
- School would start later
- School would be all year around
- No more homework
- No more pollution
- Things would be fair
- Disease would be gone forever
- No more war
- People would live forever
- No more pain in the world
- Everybody would have a pet
- There would be love in the world
- Teachers would all be nice

The gifted students had a lively discussion using the question, "What would you change?" As can be noted by their responses, some gifted students were more serious than others, but they all stated that they felt a sense of power when they took charge and gave their responses. One gifted boy said, "I wish mine would come true. If people lived forever, they would have time to solve all their problems." This comment opened a new line of discussion, by living longer, more problems could be produced.

To the question, "What would you leave the same?" the gifted students had the following responses:

- Living and dying
- Church
- School
- My family
- Our gifted class
- The government in the USA
- Our city
- Our language

This last group of responses was difficult for the gifted students, and they needed more time to generate the list. It is interesting to note that many of their responses were not wanting social institutions or social paradigms to change. As gifted students discuss their choices, they become aware of their own values and of others. Knowing one's values in relation to others and experiencing new ideas in a safe atmosphere stimulates self-directedness.

Encouraging gifted students to list the roles they play is helpful in building awareness of the many roles they have assumed. Through evaluating these roles, gifted students can experience more self-direction, and take charge of discarding unwanted or unnecessary roles. This activity was discussed in the subsection "Integrating Oneself." It is interesting to note the differences in the responses of a 10 year old, as discussed earlier, with those of a 15 year old.

The directions for this activity are simple. Ask the gifted students to list all the roles they play. If they have difficulty in deciding which roles to list, ask them to think of the various tasks they complete each day. After they have listed the roles, ask them to prioritize the list, with the most important item as being 1, and so on.

The list of roles completed by a gifted 15-year-old girl are:

daughter
sister
granddaughter
MYF secretary
drum majorette
tennis team member
student
babysitter
choir member
girl friend
swim team member
Muffin's owner

Her roles indicate that she is a busy young woman. Given an opportunity to discard any of the roles, she chose to give up either the swim team or the tennis team but indicated she needed more time to decide. The decision as to which role was number 1 was also difficult, and she related that being a daughter was number 1 in her life and that she and her family were very close. However, recently she had been spending a great deal of time with her grandmother, who was a widow; her grandmother was becoming more and more important to her. She related how they spent many quiet evenings sitting and reading together or discussing old movies which they both enjoyed.

Thinking about who they are and what they value is meaningful to all gifted students, but it is especially important to adolescents. To be able to have such discussions in psychologically safe atmospheres with supportive teachers and parents is essential if gifted students are to realize their ability to become self-directed. Educators need to help gifted students develop their authority within, which is based on a healthy knowledge of who they are and a belief in their ability to cope and to function in a positive way.

RAISING CAREER ASPIRATIONS

All gifted students need guidance and support from their teachers. This is expressed by Powell (1983):

Three impressive teachers supported and encouraged me. One was my homeroom teacher who always felt that I was superior college material and said so. Another was the black electric shop teacher I had during my junior year who was rough, tough, loving and very intelligent. . . . the third was my principal who called me into the office one day to inform me of my potential.

A specific attempt to raise career aspirations for the gifted was reported by Kerr (1982), in which twenty-three gifted girls and twenty-five gifted boys, all of whom were eleventh graders from four different urban high schools, attended a guidance laboratory. The participants took the Self-Directed Search prior to the workshop and the Myers-Briggs Type Indicator. Following this assessment, the participants were allowed to select any part of the university to visit and to attend a self-selected university class related to their career interest area. After the class visitation, the gifted students had lunch with the guidance laboratory counselors and university faculty members, who discussed with them their morning's experiences, school activities, and future plans in pairs and triads. In the afternoon, the gifted students participated in individual and group counseling sessions in which the counselors interpreted test results and discussed the gifted students' career interests and values. The counselors helped the gifted students set tentative career goals and attempted to raise their aspirations if they named a career goal that met the following conditions: (1) was clearly below their ability, (2) was a sex-role stereotyped choice, or (3) was a low-paying or low-status job or career.

After the individual counseling, the gifted students were led on a guided fantasy into their "perfect future day." They shared their fantasies with one another and then discussed barriers to their achievement of their perfect future day.

Lastly, the counselors distributed fact sheets for gifted women and men which briefly described the results of research on gifted men and women emphasizing the importance of high aspirations and the possibilities for combining family and career.

Between 20 and 28 weeks later, the researchers found that the gifted girls did raise their career aspirations from pretest to posttest. The gifted boys did not change their career aspirations, but they began with very high aspirations and had little room to change. This study is a fine example of how counselors and teachers can raise the career aspirations of gifted young men and women.

Conversely, Casserly (1980) reports that counselors sometimes admit they explicitly discourage gifted girls from studying science and mathematics and from pursuing careers in fields such as engineering. This type of behavior should be noted and corrected if girls are to reach their potential. When teachers are conscious of promoting the achievement of girls, it does make a difference. Casserly reports, in a study of high schools that enrolled relatively large number of young women in advanced placement science and calculus courses, that the teachers in these schools had actively recruited females for these classes and tried to nurture their self-confidence and interest in mathematics achievement.

In addition to the importance of counseling, Fox (1981) found few available female models who were scientists and mathematicians. She suggests role models be sought for gifted girls and opportunities provided for the young women and the role models to interact.

Variables Affecting Career Choices

Willings (1983) collected 2000 work histories from respondents in England, Scotland, Europe, the United States, and Canada and isolated a number of discrete variables in career choice. Almost all of the research indicated parental influence was the strongest single influence, followed by school influence, inadequate or faulty information, and overcompensation.

Overcompensation was illustrated by a shy student who tried to overcome her problem by becoming a door-to-door salesperson and consequently had a nervous breakdown.

Willings (1983) discusses the unique pressures on gifted students such as fear of failure and parents using the gifted child as a status symbol or, as reported by Ainsley (1984), seeing the gifted child as a second chance for themselves.

Job study is suggested as one way to combat the problem of career selection for gifted (Willings, 1983). Job study is divided into four stages. The first three involve an in-depth study of mental requirements, physical requirements, and job factors. In the fourth stage, elements such as the image of the job, hidden factors, special skills and difficulties, and distastes are explored.

Still another way to help gifted students make career choices was tried by Digenakis and Miller (1979). They used simulation of real-life situations to enhance the learning process and to form part of the enriched career search. They suggest that gifted students plan and run their own simulation exercises as part of their career search.

Career aspirations for gifted students, both male and female, need to be addressed in a comprehensive manner by counselors, teachers, and parents. The specific role for parents in guiding and counseling the gifted is covered in the last section of this chapter. For teachers and guidance counselors, one useful way to identify the career counseling needs of the gifted is to examine their characteristics and to note the counseling implications. For example, gifted students have an exceptional ability to quickly comprehend material, and, as a result, many of them are placed in advanced and honors classes. Yet in many cases, the gifted student becomes discouraged with these classes, particularly if he/she perceives that the class involves more preparation, more assignments, and more outside readings than the average class. In this instance, it is helpful for counselors and teachers to provide support for the gifted student to continue to pursue advanced material. The benefits of advanced classes should be pointed out, such as being able to select an academic major in a college or university, especially in the case of advanced mathematics, which is a requirement for most science majors.

Another characteristic of gifted students which becomes a problem is their need to make demands on themselves and to be achievement oriented. In this area, teachers and counselors need to help gifted students to set realistic goals and to realize they can and will meet failure at times. It is especially important that they recognize their perfectionism and deal with it in a realistic manner. Quality work is needed in most careers, but a sense of perfectionism gets in the way of interpersonal relationships, such as those with fellow workers, as noted by Willings (1983).

Still another group of characteristics of giftedness clusters around learning style. Gifted students tend to be critical thinkers; solve problems and solutions quickly, often intuitively; demonstrate a high energy level; and display a so-called intellectual mode of learning and interacting with others. This cluster of characteristics calls for the school system to place gifted students with others of similar ability, in order that they may work at their own pace; and to provide a flexible arrangement for the gifted to attend college classes while still enrolled in high school or middle school; as well as to gain early entrance to college. Teachers and counselors should help gifted students to function at a more mature intellectual level, if they are attending college classes while still in high school, and to develop social skills. Too often, the gifted student may become socially inept. Yet through group dynamics and awareness activities followed by discussion, gifted students can see the need for achieving a balance between intellectual and social activities. These social skills are essential for effective work skills in the gifted student's chosen career.

Lastly, the gifted student is keen on trying new approaches to activities and wants to ask many questions, often displaying a high degree of sensitivity and emotional involvement in the topic or issue being discussed. The counseling implication for teachers and counselors is to provide a personal relationship for gifted students to help them function at their optimum level and to help them understand their own sensitivity.

Further examination of the characteristics of the gifted and the career counseling implications indicates a need for emotional support, an emphasis on problem solving, and the development of sensitive human relationships. The gifted are capable of flexibility and yet require self-initiated programs of learning. A difficult point for them to understand is the balance between required work and self-initiated work. The efforts of the teachers and the counselors must be cooperative with the parents' efforts on behalf of gifted students, if they are to be successful.

ROLE OF THE PARENTS IN GUIDING AND COUNSELING THE GIFTED

Coleman (1982) determined by administering a questionnaire that parenting a gifted child demanded about 150 percent of one's time. Parental concerns determined by Coleman were:

1 Recognizing giftedness in the very young child
2 Ways of stimulating and fostering emerging talent
3 Problems related to discipline—social interaction—allowing the gifted child to live his/her own life

A growing number of articles are available for parents, such as an article by Schatz (1983), a parent of two gifted boys and a teacher and counselor for gifted, who lists guidelines for nurturing and identifying the very young gifted. Schatz notes early signs of giftedness such as exceptional creativity, curiosity, and intellectual ability and then goes on to identify four determinants of guidance within the home: (1) materials, (2) modeling, (3) space, and (4) time. She suggests that young children be provided with books, papers, pencils, and crayons to nurture their interests and potential ability. She also states that the opportunity for gifted to write, doodle, and freely draw using their imagination can mean high premiums for low investment in simple materials. Schatz emphasizes the parents' role in modeling, reading, and inquiry, and she suggests that parents and gifted children read together in order to think, feel, laugh, cry, listen, talk, fear, wonder, hate, and love together. She sees gifted children needing physical space to explore and to store their projects. She also talks about psychological space and the gifted student's ability to manipulate others. Schatz suggests that parents should tolerate acceptable manipulation but put a gentle and firm stop to potentially harmful manipulations. Lastly, she recommends that time management skills be taught to gifted students.

Another source of information for recognizing giftedness and for stimulating and fostering the gifted child's talent is provided by Coffey et al. (1976) and is called *Parentspeak*. Selected suggestions for parents are:

1 Gifted children are children first and gifted second. A 5-year-old boy may be able to solve mathematical problems worth bragging about to the grandparents, but he has only lived 5 years, and only behavior reasonable for a 5-year-old should be expected of him.

2 Let them specialize if they want to. You may not enjoy living with dinosaurs by the year, but there are fringe benefits. They could be learning to do research, keeping notes, knowing the Dewey Decimal System, and keeping some kind of order in that disaster area that passes for a room, after you learn that there are things more important than neatness.

3 Discipline is necessary and comes in the same shape for all brothers and sisters, whether gifted, curly headed, or slowpokes. Giftedness is no excuse for unacceptable behavior.

4 Let your home be a place where knowledge is valued and the quest for learning respected.

5 Remember that the fine line between encouragement and pushing may make the difference between a happy and productive youngster and an unfulfilled, underachieving child.

6 Praise your gifted child because he or she needs all the encouragement available; praise him or her for the wonderful things accomplished. If the great experiment does not work and the shaky tower of blocks comes tumbling down, praise the child for trying. Inquiring minds must take intellectual risk, and risk taking needs to be supported and praised. Constructive criticism and recognizing good effort is a form of praise too.

Still another source of help for parents in supporting gifted students is provided by the American Association for Gifted Children in a series of bulletins. One bulletin called "Guideposts for Gifted Young People" discusses such topics as Why Do Some Bright Students Fail in School Subjects? Resisting Group Tyranny, and Looking Ahead. The section on bright students failing is particularly well done. The bulletin states that some bright students fail in school when the morale is low and there is an anti-intellectual attitude. In these cases, gifted students who enjoy reading and studying may be looked down upon and ridiculed, and they may begin to fail in order to survive. Then again, gifted students may fail because of poor relationships with specific teachers or because they lack study skills. The association's bulletin entitled "Guideposts for Administrators" discusses the issues of providing special programs and provisions for the gifted and gives a list of types of programs. For parents who are approaching schools on behalf of their gifted children, such bulletins are helpful in ensuring that they are knowledgeable about the needs of gifted and what can be provided for them by the educational system.

Yet another source of information for parents of gifted is the *Gifted Children Monthly*. Fisher (1981), in an article in the *Monthly* entitled "Being a Good Model for Your Gifted Child," relates how fourteen parents developed a child reading endeavor to develop a home environment that would encourage "do as I do" rather than "do as I say, not as I do." Some of the behaviors parents identified as needing attention were (1) fear of taking risks, (2) misuse of leisure time, (3) poor social skills, and (4) overdependency on others. In all cases, the parents attempted to model the appropriate behavior, such as being risk takers themselves; trying new things; experimenting and developing a tolerance for their own possible failures; demonstrating healthful, constructive, enjoyable ways of using spare time; being aware of not setting up a hierarchy of valued persons; modeling independence; and finding solutions by alternative means.

In a meeting of over 300 parents of gifted in New York, the parents indicated a growing sense of stress in their gifted children, which manifested itself in symptoms such as headaches; mood changes; poor sleeping habits or inability to fall asleep; bedwetting and nail biting; and general anxiety displayed in fears, worry, and oversensitivity. Stress is an ongoing problem for gifted students, and much of it stems from their characteristics of being perfectionists and their desire to achieve, together with their sensitivity, as mentioned in the earlier section on career counseling. Hayes and Levitt (1982) suggest a number of ways parents can help gifted students deal with stress, such as the following:

1 Concentrate on positive spiritual as well as physical development.
2 Adopt an attitude that no problem is too monumental to be solved.
3 Establish a sense of purpose and direction.
4 Establish and maintain a strong support network.
5 Develop effective behavioral skills (time management).
6 Learn to come to terms with your feelings.
7 Take a systematic approach to all problem solving.

The National Association for Gifted Children (NAGC) has published a book entitled *Mountains to Climb*. Haensly and Nash (1983) cover topics such as the options for acceleration into and through college, special institutes and summer programs available for gifted, as well as information on talent and scholarship searches.

This chapter has stressed the need for a holistic approach in educating the gifted student. To nurture intellect is important, but to nurture emotions is equally important. More and more educators and counselors realize that it is not enough to have a good mind and that gifted students must be guided in knowing how to use their minds.

SUMMARY

This chapter examined understanding the emotional self and awareness of self. A model of self-awareness consisting of (1) sensory perception; (2) interpretive thought; (3) emotions; (4) desires, wills, and dreams; and (5) behaviors was discussed. Examples were given for parents and educators to use in developing and nurturing each of the five areas.

Through knowing ourselves we reach out to others. This notion was explored along with topics such as communicating with others, integrating oneself, and becoming more self-directed. Facilitating strategies were discussed, including awareness activities, imagery or guided fantasy, group dynamics, and bibliotherapy.

The topic of career counseling emphasized raising the career aspirations of gifted students, and the role of parents in guiding and counseling the gifted was discussed. In the parent section, specific problems identified by parents of gifted students were listed, and suggestions and resources were noted. A cooperative effort between school and home was stressed throughout the chapter to ensure an holistic approach to the gifted student.

EXTENDING ACTIVITIES

1 Select a gifted student to observe, and note behaviors of stress that may be demonstrated. Chart the examples according to whether they are behavioral changes or cognitive changes.
2 Select two activities suggested for building awareness of self and share them with a small group of gifted students.
3 Interview several gifted high school students and ask them to indicate career preferences. Note whether the career choices are clearly below the gifted student's ability, are sex-role stereotyped, low-paying, or low-status jobs or careers.
4 Conduct an intensive literature review for the years 1980–1985 to find outstanding female mathematicians or scientists. Compile a list of the female leaders and a bibliography of their works.
5 You have been asked to conduct a brief seminar for parents of gifted students on counseling and guidance needs. Outline your topics. Include a listing of selected characteristics of gifted students and their counseling implications.

REFERENCES

Ainsley, W. (1984). *Counseling gifted students*. A presentation to the Hillsborough Council for Gifted Education, Tampa, FL.
Alvino, J. (1981). Guidance for the gifted. *Instructor*, November/December, 64–66. New York: Macmillan.
Blume, J. (1972). *It's not the end of the world*. New York: Dalton Publications.
Blume, J. (1972). *Otherwise known as Sheila the great*. New York: Dalton Publications.
Bunting, A. E. (1980). *Blackbird singing*. New York: Macmillan.

Casserly, P. L. (1980). Factors affecting female participation in advanced placement programs in mathematics, chemistry and physics. In L. H. Fox, L. Brody, & D. Tobin (Eds.), *Women and the mathematical mystique*. Baltimore: Johns Hopkins University Press.

Clark, B. (1983). *Growing up gifted*. Columbus, OH: Charles E. Merrill.

Cleary, B. (1972). *Ramona and her father*. New York: William Morrow.

Coffey, F., Ginsberg, G., Lockhart, C. & McCartney, D. (1976). Nathan and wood. *Parentspeak*. St. Paul, MN: National Association for Gifted.

Coleman, D. (1982). Parenting the gifted: Is this a job for superparents? *GCT, 22*, 47–50.

Danziger, P. (1973). *The cat ate my gymsuit*. New York: Delacorte Press.

Digenakis, P. & Miller, J. (1979). What's my line? An in-depth experience with professional occupations, *GCT, 8*, 14–16, 18–19.

Dreyer, S. (1981). *The bookfinder: A guide to children's literature about the needs and problems of youth, aged 2–15*. Circle Pines, MN: American Guidance Services.

Eberle, B. (1974). *Classroom cue cards for cultivating multiple talents*. Buffalo, NY: DOK Publications.

Fisher, E. (1981). Being a good model for your gifted child. *Gifted Child Monthly, 2*(6), 1–2.

Fox, L. (1981). Preparing gifted girls for future leadership roles. *GCT*, March/April, 7–11.

Frasier, M. (1982). Bibliotherapy: Educational and counseling implications for the gifted/disadvantaged. In D. Smith (Ed.), *Identifying and Educating the Disadvantaged Gifted*. Ventura, CA: Office of the Superintendent.

Frasier, M. & McCannon, C. (1981). Using bibliotherapy with gifted children. *Gifted Child Quarterly, 25*(2), 81–85.

Haensly, P. & Nash, W. (1984). *Mountains to climb*. St. Paul, MN: National Association for Gifted.

Hayes, D. & Levitt, M. (1982). An inventory for parents. *GCT, 24*, 8–12.

Hoffer, E. (1973). *Reflections on the human condition*. New York: Harper & Row.

Hollingworth, L. S. (1942). *Children above 180 IQ*. Yonkers, NY: World Book.

Kerr, B. (1982). Career education strategies for the gifted. *Chronicle Guidance Publications*, 1–4.

Maker, J. (1982). *Curriculum development for gifted*. Rockville, MD: Aspen Systems Corporation.

Myers, I. B. (1975). *Manual: The Myers-Briggs typal indicator*. Palo Alto, CA: Consulting Psychologists Press.

Parnes, S. J., Noller, R. B. & Biondi, A. (1977). *A guide to creative action*. New York: Charles Scribner and Sons.

Perls, F. (1969). *Gestalt therapy verbatim*. Lafayette, CA: Real People Press.

Powell, P. (1983). *Identification of gifted minorities and poor socio-economic groups*. Unpublished communication submitted to the Richardson Foundation, May.

Purkey, W. W. (1984). *Inviting School Success*. Belmont, CA: Wadsworth.

Rogers, C. (1980). *A way of being*. Boston: Houghton-Mifflin.

Schetky, D. (1981). The emotional and social development of the gifted child. *GCT*, 2–4.

Schatz, E. (1983). Determinants of guidance within the home. *GCT*, March/April, 59–60.

Shallcross, D. & Sisk, D. (1985). *The growing person*. Buffalo, NY: Bearly Limited.

Sisk, D. (1979). Encounter lessons: Tapping the fantasy of gifted. *Gifted Child Quarterly, 23*(1), 213–216.

Taylor, C. (1963). Clues to creative teaching: The creative process and education. *Instructor, 73*, 4–5.

Terman, L. M. (Ed.) (1925). *Genetic studies of genius. Volume 1: Mental and physical traits of a thousand gifted children*. Palo Alto, CA: Stanford University Press.

Tomer, M. (1981). Human relations in education: A rational for a curriculum in interpersonal skills for gifted students—Grades k–12. *Gifted Child Quarterly, 25*(2), 94–97.

Van Tassel-Baska, J. (1983). The teacher as counselor for the gifted. *Teaching Exceptional Children*, Spring, 145–150.

Whitmore, J. (1986). Understanding a lack of motivation to excel. *Gifted Child Quarterly, 30*(2), 66–99.

Williams, A. (1979). Teaching gifted students how to deal with stress. *Gifted Child Quarterly, 23*(1), 136–141.

Willings, D. (1983). Training for leadership. *Roeper Review, 20*, 18–23.

CHAPTER 12

EXPANDING DIMENSIONS OF LEARNING

We are made wise not by the recollections of our past, but by the responsibility for our future.

George Bernard Shaw

Education is in need of healing; as positive expectations produce positive effects in the body, the removal of psychological barriers—the cynicism, mistrust, and fear which prevent exploring new concepts of learning and new ideas—produces transformations for educators (Ferguson, 1981).

This chapter examines mind/brain research and the implications for gifted education, such as the use of visualization to develop intuitive and imaginative skills. Suggestology, or superlearning (these terms are used interchangeably), is discussed as an innovative way to learn, incorporating attention, relaxation, imagery, and breathing. Biofeedback is covered as a means of promoting holistic health and functioning. Lastly, the role of technology, notably the computer, is examined as it affects the human mind and learning, and general recommendations for computer education for gifted students are listed.

Within the last generation, a new empirical discipline, cognitive science (a hybrid of psychology, computer science, psycholinguistics, and several other fields) has developed. Cognitive science explores the interior universe—the mind and the processing of thought. This exploration bears examination by educators interested in building quality education.

Photograph on facing page courtesy of Elizabeth Crews, Berkeley, California.

BRAIN/MIND RESEARCH

Interest in brain/mind research has increased in the last decade, and, as this research is interpreted and disseminated, several implications for gifted education are emerging. One area of implication involves the definition of giftedness. Clark (1983) suggests, in the light of human brain/mind research, that giftedness can be defined as advanced or accelerated development of brain function. Inherent in this proposed definition is the concept of whole brain functioning. High levels of giftedness or intelligence can be viewed as being an interaction process between advanced brain growth and environment. This concept of whole brain functioning is being proposed and used in the training of leaders in business by Herrmann (1986).

Acceptance of and willingness to study brain/mind research and its implications for education of the gifted can lead to teaching methods using both sides of the brain and can foster recognition of individual differences in learning styles. As skills in brain research increase, the endless possibilities for understanding more about learning and brain/mind research become more challenging and exciting.

Two areas of brain research with potential impact on education of the gifted are the studies of brain growth laterality (left-brain and right-brain research) and brain growth. A brief review and discussion of implications for education of the gifted student is offered.

Brain Laterality

Brain laterality studies began with the early writings of Nigan (1844), followed by the work of Broca, a French surgeon who performed autopsies on patients with no power of speech. The brains of these patients showed damaged left hemispheres, and this damaged area became known as Broca's area (Springer & Deutsch, 1981).

Wernicke, a German neurologist identified the part of the brain that helps us understand speech, which is known as Wernicke's area. His early work contributed to the idea that speech and understanding of speech are located in the left hemisphere. In the sixties, Sperry and his associates at the California Institute of Technology conducted brain research on split-brain patients. Sperry reported that the left hemisphere was adept at sequential processing analysis. Yet when the corpus callosum, or thick bundle of transverse fibers connecting the two cerebral hemispheres, was severed in severe epileptic patients, Sperry found the right hemisphere to be capable of understanding concrete language (nouns) but not of dealing with the complex grammatical structure of verbs (Sperry, 1974).

Levy (1977, 1983), in studies on hemispheric skills, concluded that the left brain is analytic, finding patterns in words, recognizing attributes in groups, putting parts into wholes, and using language to express what is understood. She describes the right brain as holistic in reasoning, but reports that both parts of the brain are capable of reasoning, using different strategies. A list of left/right mode behavior is offered by Herrmann (1986) in Table 12-1.

TABLE 12-1
LEFT/RIGHT MODE BEHAVIOR

Left Mode	Right Mode
Logical, analytical, linear sequential— drawing conclusions based on logical order of thinking	Intuitive, nonlinear utilizing intuitive feeling of how things fit, making leaps on insight
Utilizing precise, exact connotations— right/wrong, yes/no, etc.	Multiple processing of information
Convergent thinking	Divergent thinking
Rational—basing on facts and reason	Nonrational—does not require basis of reason
Conscious reasoning	Subconscious or preconscious reasoning
Verbal—semantic language	Nonverbal—use of imagery
Abstract	Concrete
Controlled	Emotive
Realistic	Fantasy
Intellectual	Sensuous
Active	Receptive
Linear time	Timelessness
Propositional	Imaginative
Mathematical, scientific	Artistic, musical symbolic
Objective	Subjective
Judgmental	Nonjudgmental, noncritical

Implications for brain laterality research are discussed by Ornstein and Brand-wein (1977); they report that each hemisphere possesses a method of thought processing. The left brain controls the function of language and sequencing, while the right brain controls intuitive and holistic thinking.

From this brief review and discussion, it appears that the two hemispheres complement one another and that total whole brain functioning provides different types of processing or thinking. Researchers in education and industry have established that people have hemispheric preferences, and they report that many opportunities for creative productive work are missed or neglected without cerebral integration (Samples, 1977; Torrance, 1978; Wittrock, 1980; Loye, 1982; Herrmann, 1986). Successful business people report using right brain processes with processes of the left brain; they use their hunches and synthesize; then they switch to logic to analyze and articulate (Herrmann, 1986).

Herrmann has developed an instrument for assessing cerebral preferences. His research indicates left cerebral hemisphere preference individuals prefer written directions and organized tasks, and they see the task in separate parts. Right cerebral preference people see the whole problem or situation, appreciate an artistic and aesthetic approach, and enjoy interpersonal situations. The implications for education are immense. Herrmann's Whole Brain Teaching and Learning Model is reproduced in Figure 12-1.

Ornstein and Brandwein (1977) identified teaching strategies to encourage development of both hemispheres of the brain, such as providing opportunities for gathering information in a holistic manner through music, art, dance, and field trips; broadening categories by using open-ended and ambiguous thinking; and using the inquiry method.

These ideas are complemented by Clark's (1983) suggestions of using an integrative education model based on brain/mind research. The Clark model includes four functions: (1) intuitive, (2) cognitive, (3) physical and sensing, and (4) feeling or emotional, and it is based on the early ideas of the psychologist Carl Jung. Teachers building integrative programs will plan curriculum experiences in each of the four areas and with integrated experiences, gifted students will use both cerebral hemispheres.

Brain Growth Periodization

Two individuals Toepfer and Epstein (1978) have made major contributions working on brain growth periodization. They report that the brain grows in definite periods or surges, as presented by Table 12-2, with corresponding Piagetian stages.

Epstein (1978) reports five periods of extra-brain growth, approximately in the age levels of 3 to 10 months; 2 to 4 years; 6 to 8 years; 10 to 12 years; and 14 to 16 years. Toepfer and Epstein (1978) report that there is virtually no growth in brain mass and that no significant increase in the neural complexity occurs during the intervening periods for 85 percent to 90 percent of the population. They also report a positive correlation between brain growth spurts and mental age with a large number of intelligence-associated tests, such as tests of memory, vocabulary, and language utilization. Epstein (1974, 1978) suggests that IQ may be related to the speed of learning while cognitive level may be related to learning style. This finding has implications for education, if brain growth periodization is associated with brain laterality and studies of cognitive style.

Implications of Brain Growth Research for Gifted

Toepfer and Epstein (1978) suggest that schools should stress the holistic needs of gifted students during their brain growth plateau periods and that the learning environment should be geared to the individual's cognitive level, emphasizing problem-solving information and skill development. An area of particular concern is the middle school, with the added stress of puberty and the brain growth

FIGURE 12-1 (on facing page)
Whole brain teaching and learning. (Ned Herrmann, "The Creative Brain II: A Revisit with Ned Herrmann," Training and Development Journal, December 1982. Reprinted by permission.)

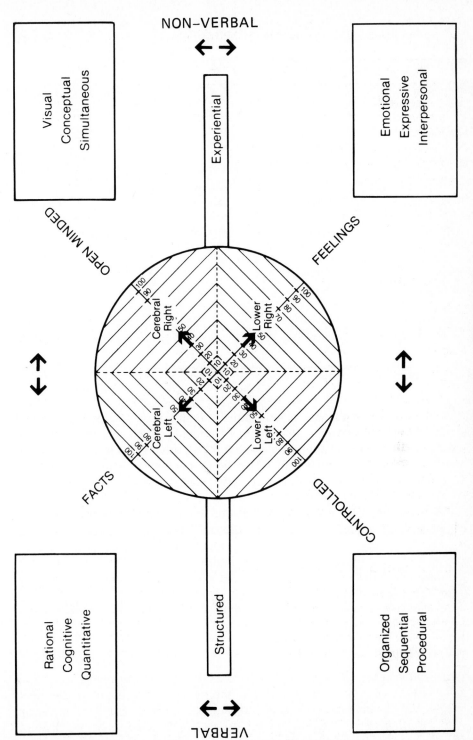

NON-VERBAL

VERBAL

Visual
Conceptual
Simultaneous

Emotional
Expressive
Interpersonal

Rational
Cognitive
Quantitative

Organized
Sequential
Procedural

OPEN MINDED

FEELINGS

FACTS

CONTROLLED

Experiential

Structured

Cerebral Right

Lower Right

Cerebral Left

Lower Left

TEACHING/LEARNING DESIGN MODEL

TABLE 12-2
BRAIN GROWTH PERIODS AS COMPARED TO PIAGETIAN
STAGES

Toepfer & Epstein		Piaget	
Periods of brain growth (BG)	Age	Age	Stages
1st Period	3–10 months	0 1	0–1 year, motor
2d Period	2–4 years	2 3 4	2–6 years, sensorimotor
Hiatus	4–6 years	5 6	
3d Period	6–8 years	6 7 8	6–7 years, concrete operations
Hiatus	8–10 years	9	
4th Period	10–12 years	10 11	10–11 years, final operations
Hiatus	12–14 years	12 13 14	

Adapted from Toepfer and Epstein (1978).

relaxation period. With many gifted middle school programs based on an acceleration model rather than on an enrichment model in which creativity is emphasized as well as practical applications and problem solving, Toepfer (1980) warns that this type of intellectual demand at the middle school level, dealing with increasingly complex input, may cause gifted students to reject all input and to develop negative neural networks.

The implication for education is that during positive brain growth periods, cognitive skill learning should be emphasized. The best time for skill instruction is when the brain is growing in mass and producing additional neural networks. During periods of negative brain growth, holistic learning can be increased with the assumption that right brain affective learning stimulates and aids cognitive growth during brain growth hiatus periods.

An effective learning tool for stimulating affective learning is visualization, which also aids consciousness and learning.

VISUALIZATION

Visualization, or visual imagery, is defined as seeing with the mind's eye. It is a different form of seeing than seeing with the retina; it is a sensing of the inner images. Visualization can be taught, and Samuels and Samuels (1975), in *Seeing With the Mind's Eye*, suggest using a prescribed, graduated series of activities. The teacher can start with visualization of two-dimensional objects; then visualization of distant memory images; visualization with movement; and visualization involving imagination memory.

When most people's eyes are closed and there is silence, images appear and they seem to be within the mind. In the "mind's eye," images are unlimited by time and space and people can see events from the past, situations in the future, and daydreams of what might have been. However, images are discounted and given little importance in Western society. Western society is more concerned with external reality and is continually bombarded by visual and auditory stimuli. When most people are given opportunities to visualize, they must make a conscious effort to shut out the outer world to become aware of inner images and experiences. Some people report difficulty in making the transition from outer reality to inner reality.

Some cultures do give credence to the inner world; an example is the American Indian. Neihardt (1961) reports that an Ogala Sioux chief told of a dream in which he was taken up into the sky with a herd of wild horses. The events of the dream greatly influenced his life, and they became the basis on which he later was made chief of the tribe.

Brief History of Visualization

Visualization, in the form of concentration on an image, has been employed since the ancient times of Patanjali, who wrote in approximately 200 B.C. (Campbell, 1960). Through focusing attention on a particular place, either outside or inside the body, a union between the object and the person is achieved (LeShan, 1975).

Most religions have used visualization as one of the basic techniques to help people realize spiritual goals. Visualization is particularly noted in the Christian communion service in which concrete objects, bread and wine, help the Christian to visualize the last supper (Jung, 1968).

Modern western medicine is also rediscovering visualization as a healing tool (Kamiya et al., 1975). Yet, as early as 1920, Schultz, a German doctor, reported using autogenic training involving relaxation, visualization, and autosuggestion to treat a variety of diseases (Luthe, 1969). In addition, psychologists and philosophers have accorded inner images and visualization great importance. Aristotle stated thought itself was composed of images, and images had the power to stimulate a person's emotions and motivations (Samuels & Samuels, 1975).

Throughout history, people have been exposed to the power of mental images and visualization has affected daily life. There are five types of visualization experiences: memory images, eidetic images, imagination, daydreams and fantasy, and dreams and visions). These will be discussed, along with visualization techniques to build personal awareness (consciousness) and to stimulate learning in gifted students.

Memory Images

Horowitz (1970) defines memory images as reconstructions of past perceptions. Memory images can be experienced spontaneously or summoned; for example, one can consciously recall where the car keys were left. Two concepts are used in describing images, vividness, and controllability, and images range from grey, vague, and fuzzy to clear, colorful, and detailed. Memory images are usually linked to particular events or occasions with personal references.

Eidetic Images

Eidetic images are images of especially vivid form, and are similar to photographic memory. Luria (1968) studied the individual's ability to remember random numbers, letters, and nonsense syllables arranged on a checkerboard. He found that many subjects accomplished the task by recalling the images, and eidetic imagers scanned the picture in their mind and reported precise details. Eidetic images are often experienced by young students. In fact, many child development researchers believe eidetic imagery is an underlying phenomenon of the learning process which diminishes in adolescence when abstract thought and higher verbal skills develop (Samuels & Samuels, 1975; Ahsen, 1977; Marks & McKellar, 1982).

Imagination

Another common visualization experience is that of imagination. An imaginary image contains elements of past perceptions, but the images are arranged in a different way. Some images in the imagination rely on past perceptions and others are made up of newly created material. Creative imagination imagery is the source material for writers, artists, poets, musicians, mathematicians, scientists, and other productive people (Khatena, 1984).

Daydreams and Fantasies

Daydreams and fantasies are still another type of imagery, made up of a combination of memory and imagination images. Daydreams are past and future oriented. Singer (1966) states that 96 percent of the subjects he studied reported having dreams about fear of failure, hostility, achieving success, sex, heroic activities, problem solving, and a sense of well-being.

Dreams and Visions

Dreams and visions are important categories of visual imagery. Dreams break the laws of causality, time, space, and rational thought. Dreamers can do anything. Gowan (1979) reports on the chemist F. Kekulé von Stradnitz, who dreamed of a snake holding its tail in its mouth. This dream gave Kekulé von Stradnitz the idea for understanding the structure of the benzene ring. This prophetic dream is an example of an inner image connected with outer reality. Memory, imagination, dreams, and visions share the common link of visual images and represent a continuum of the varieties of visualization. To develop visualization with gifted students, several techniques can be suggested.

Visualization Techniques

McKim (1972) suggests that the conscious mind be cleared of problems, if visualization is to be used as a tool for problem solving. He suggests meditation and relaxed attention. Guided fantasy can also achieve this relaxed, clear state. An example of a guided fantasy developed by a high school gifted student is:

> Relax, close your eyes. Everything is dark. All you see is a small spot of light ahead of you. You drift towards it. Slowly it grows larger and larger. You are entering a large cave. It is lit by eerie glowing fungus on all the walls. You look down towards the floor of the cave. You can see a plant growing. Slowly, it grows and grows and grows. A bud forms. It opens into a large flower. In the center of the flower is a swirl of clouds. They slowly part to reveal scenes from your life . . . hard times . . . fun times . . . warm, pleasant times . . . frightening times. The figure turns around, it is a loved one that you have yet to meet. The person reaches out a hand and you reach into the flower and float into the center of it with the figure. Its face fades away, as does its body. The flower starts to close, you step out. The flower dies before you and is gone. The cave becomes dark. There is no light. Slowly you open your eyes.*

Using a modulated voice to read it, this guided fantasy helps clear the mind, and offers rich images. Most people report positive feelings when they experience visualization. Gifted students, in particular, enjoy using visualization and sharing their images in discussions, creative writing, and artistic experiences.

Other examples of using visualization to stimulate learning are:

1 Visualizing settings for social studies using guided fantasies.

2 Visualizing success in taking tests to relieve pretest anxiety.

3 Visualizing solutions to problems dealing with classroom situations, as well as problems in social studies, science, and language arts.

4 Visualizing solutions to brief guided fantasies for stimulus material for creative writing or artistic production.

5 Visualizing particular parts of social studies or other factual material to increase memory.

Sources for classroom teachers include a book of creative activities for the use of imaging (Wayman & Plum, 1977), a tape and book by Bagley and Hess (1982), *200 Ways of Using Imaging in the Classroom*, and *Mind Sight* (Galyean, 1983), with coverage on the use of imagery in the areas of spelling, vocabulary, reading, language arts, social studies, mathematics, and science. Through the use of visualization, individuals are involved in total sensory experiences (McKim, 1980; Khatena, 1984). Visualization can stimulate intuitive responses with stimulation words such as those shown in Exhibit 12-1.

Using these words as guidelines, the teacher can involve the student in a guided fantasy using a chosen topic, such as the forest:

> Concentrate on your breathing. Breathe deeply. Close your eyes, and see yourself in a forest. Look around you. Listen. Be aware of what you are hearing. Reach out and touch the trees. Feel them. . . . Listen. Are there loud noises? Is it quiet? Be aware of your body, your feelings. Do you taste anything? Take your time in the forest. You have all the time you want. Slowly, give yourself permission to leave the forest. Open your eyes and share with someone.

* Reprinted by permission.

EXHIBIT 12-1

I hear _____

I touch _____

I feel _____

I see _____

I taste _____

I hear _____

I experience _____

Sisk and Shallcross (1985) share the following poem written by a 10-year-old gifted girl who experienced this guided fantasy and used the guide words in Exhibit 12-1.

I see the tall trees,
I hear the rustling leaves,
I feel the wet grass,
I see the rain coming down through the limbs,
I taste the water on my tongue,
I hear the drops on the leaves and
I experience coolness and quiet.

Visualization stimulates creativity as gifted students creatively visualize stimulus words like knight, prince, princess, guard, and wizard. The teacher can say:

Become aware of your breathing. Relax and take deep breaths. See a beautiful princess. Note as much about her as you can. Is she tall? What color is her hair? See her in detail. Now see a Knight. What does he look like? What is he doing? Add a prince to the visualization. Let your pictures flow. See a guard. What does he look like? What is he doing? Add a prince to the visualization. Let your pictures flow. See a guard. What does he look like? Enjoy the pictures in your mind. Now add a wizard. Give yourself time, and when you are ready, either write your story or go quietly to the recorder and share it with someone in the class.

Below is a product of gifted 6-year-old, after experiencing the visualization:

There once was a lovely princess with long blonde hair and big brown eyes. She lived in a castle. A Knight came to visit her on a big black horse. He came from far away, from a land where people were hungry. He needed food. The Princess gave him food. The Princess had a twin brother called Prince Paul. Prince Paul went home with the Knight. They saw a Wizard who was very smart. He helped them to learn to grow food. The people were not hungry anymore and they were happy. The Prince came home and everyone had a great festival.

This gifted student's creative response to the guided fantasy and stimulus words is evident in her writing. She dictated her story using a tape recorder, critically listened to it, and then wrote it. Gifted students' responses in creative writing are more elaborate when they are given opportunity to use visualization.

Other stimulus words are astronaut, Martian, robot, computer, soldier, hiker, explorer, and prospector.

Visualization can also stimulate creative thinking through having gifted students visualize specific incidents:

• You are on a mountain, climbing to the top. See yourself being very careful. Is it dangerous? How will you get to the top?
• See yourself lost in a desert. There is no food or water. How will you survive?

Visualizations encourage gifted students to experience emotions. After reading a descriptive passage teachers can offer gifted students opportunities to close their eyes, visualize scenes from the book, and thus vicariously experience the feelings of the characters. Through activities such as these, gifted students become more comfortable with themselves and others and more socially confident.

Another visualization activity to build self-confidence is one in which the teacher asks the gifted students to relax and to see themselves in a large room, with people milling about:

See yourself shaking middle fingers . . . See yourself shaking left hands . . . See yourself touching someone's right ear with your left hand . . . See yourself giggling . . . See yourself touching elbows . . . See yourself saying hello . . . See yourself grinning . . . See yourself touching left knees . . . See yourself feeling good . . . See yourself saying the first two lines of a poem you know . . . See yourself feeling proud . . . See yourself telling a joke . . . See yourself laughing . . . See yourself looking around feeling part of the group.

These activities encourage gifted students, particularly adolescents, to feel more secure about themselves. By experiencing visualization, gifted students rehearse their responses. After a session in which gifted ninth-grade students used visualization, the following comments were heard:

Student A   I always am so uptight when I have to do any kind of activity in which there is touching. By imagining myself doing the activity and enjoying it, I couldn't believe how easy it was, it really was!

Student B   I get good grades and I know I'm capable, but there are times when I feel so stupid. Activities like these really help. I don't know why I couldn't have done them when I was younger. It really would have helped.

Student C   My parents don't touch a lot and it really freaks me out when I feel I need to touch. But this was fun.

These activities are easy to integrate in the classroom, and they can be powerful in building awareness of self and others (Gowan, 1980). One last activity to stimulate awareness and creativity is called "I Want to Be." The teacher asks gifted students to close their eyes and see themselves in the role of the person or profession they wish to attain. They are asked to see themselves smiling, to see themselves in their professions, and to see themselves reaching their goals. After the visualization, the students are divided into small groups and each group creates a skit, using the characters in their group, and performing for one another.

The uses of visualization in the classroom are unlimited. In science and social studies, visualization can be used in predictive activities preliminary to writing scenarios; in language arts, to explore the meanings of poems, stories and students' own creative writing; and in social relations, to help understand self and others, to overcome stress and to focus attention. Two sources for teachers are *Directing the Movies in Your Mind* (Bry, 1978) and *The Relaxation and Stress Reduction Workbook* (Davis, 1982).

By using and exploring visual imagery, teachers help gifted students develop a growing consciousness and refine the skill of visualization to access total brain power. One researcher, attempting to encourage people to use total brain power is Lozanov (1977), a Bulgarian, who calls his technique "suggestopedia" or "suggestology." In psychology and education, it is also referred to as "superlearning."

SUGGESTOPEDIA

According to Lozanov, suggestopedia teaching uses the unconscious and the conscious parts of the brain to learn. Suggestology works on two levels. On the conscious level, the teacher makes a verbalized suggestion, and on the unconscious level impressions are received at a marginal level of perception.

Suggestology sessions begin with deep breathing exercises, and participants are encouraged to breathe rhythmically according to a precise count of eight (2 seconds for inhaling, 4 seconds for breath holding, and 2 seconds for exhaling). This rhythm coincides with baroque music which is played in the background. During the second phase of the session, the material to be remembered is read in accordance with the students' breathing. In a language lesson, the teacher reads the language materials in the following sequences: Bulgarian translation (2 seconds), foreign language phrase (4 seconds), pause (2 seconds). While the foreign language phrase is being read, the students retain their breath for 4 seconds; concentration is greatly improved by this device.

The technique has considerable potential for teaching gifted students basic facts or concepts, to enable them to work at higher levels of thinking. In the United States, several large corporations are investigating the use of suggestology and its adaptation to the needs of employees faced with an ever-growing knowledge base. In addition, many countries are researching suggestology, and the United Nations Educational Service (UNESCO) has published pamphlets and articles on the topic. The importance of suggestology is summarized by Roberts (1982), who states that human beings experience numerous states of waking consciousness without full awareness of the potentials and abilities unique to each. Education can help bring about awareness of these states. There are two Lozanov institutes in the United States, one in Baltimore and one in San Diego. In addition, there is a Society for Suggestive–Accelerative Learning and Teaching Incorporation (SALT) in Des Moines.

Suggestology can be used in every subject area to provide a restful atmosphere and immediate feedback on the degree of retention of information communicated.

Still another technique used to optimize learning and expand awareness and consciousness is biofeedback.

BIOFEEDBACK

Biofeedback has long been recognized as a tool for medicine, since nearly all parts of the human body generate electrical current and move and since more of this electrical activity is now within our control. The founder of the Biofeedback and Psycho-Physiology Center at Menniger Clinic states that to use biofeedback to aid the body, one must visualize what the body is to do; tell it to do it; and then relax and let it happen (Pew, 1979).

Many people, including Brown (1974) in *New Mind, New Body, Biofeedback: New Directions for the Mind* are convinced that the electrical power that each of us generates can be harnessed to power devices such as personal computers. Several exciting demonstrations have been conducted using bioenergy to light displays, power sound devices, and run electric trains. Individuals under stress, who are creating huge amounts of bioenergy, can witness evidence of it, as trains speed around a track powered by their stress-produced electrical energy. Through biofeedback, they learn about their bodies. Any object or material which gives information about the body's system is considered biofeedback. Biofeedback can be as simple as reading temperature cards or as complex as monitoring electronic devices.

Several individuals such as Kamiya et al. (1975) have used biofeedback to help students remove learning blocks. Holland (1984) uses biofeedback to manipulate and control behavior, reduce anxiety, and control hyperactive behavior. She uses feedback displays involving lights, beeps, and clicks to encourage students of all ages to learn to increase their production of alpha brain waves and to relax. Bagley (1983) uses biofeedback to build positive self-awareness, exploration, and self-control with gifted students and their teachers.

However, most educators are reluctant to use biofeedback except in serious cases, such as with students who have learning disabilities or emotional disorders. Yet biofeedback can help ensure better attention during learning, particularly when emotional states are blocking attention.

With biofeedback training, DeBoskey (1985) found that gifted students became aware of physiological states and learned to reduce anxiety, fear, and anger which impeded learning. The gifted students in DeBoskey's project enjoyed researching body data and shared it with other students. Other researchers who have worked with biofeedback are Shapiro et al. (1969) and Taylor and Bongar (1976). A helpful source of information is the *Brain/Mind Bulletin*, a research report published by Ferguson. Ferguson (1981), speaking on the importance of biofeedback, states:

. . . awareness is wider and deeper than anyone had guessed; intention, more powerful. Clearly, human beings have not begun to exploit their potential for change. . . .

Biofeedback phenomena can change the concept of brain, mind, and body as a continuum. In a world of increased technology, another important aspect to consider is the role of artificial intelligence and its impact on the human mind and the concept of giftedness. Artificial intelligence is a field where the state of the art is constantly changing. Today, it would be difficult to find many educators who do not have an opinion on the enterprise of constructing computer programs that model aspects of intelligent behavior or artificial intelligence.

ROLE OF TECHNOLOGY IN CONCEPTUALIZING INTELLIGENCE

Hunt (1982), in an amusing story in *The Universe Within* tells of a vice president entering a computer room to notice that the machine's teletype reads: TYPE ALL MESSAGES INTO THIS TELETYPE, AND END THEM WITH A PERIOD. The vice president, intending to demonstrate a system on the computer to prospective customers, decides to type out a message. He assumes the note was left by an employee who sometimes works at home using a teletype terminal. Assuming he is hooked into the computer, the vice president types a message to him, with the following results:

VP:	Do you think I can use the computer this morning?
Teletype:	Why do you ask?
VP:	I might be able to make some additional telecom sales.
T:	Why aren't you sure?
VP:	My prospective customers have never seen a demonstration of the system.
T:	Does this mean very much to you?
VP:	Of course it does.
T:	You seem very positive of that.
VP:	This is ridiculous.
T:	What do you mean this is ridiculous?
VP:	Is there any reason why I can't use the computer now?
T:	Tell me more about your prospective customers.

The vice president, in a fury, calls the employee to find he is not hooked up to the teletype and that the interaction just described was with a program left on the machine by another employee. The program is an adaptation of the famous ELIZA program (later known as DOCTOR) written by Weizenbaum of Massachusetts Institute of Technology (MIT) which simulates the responses of a Rogerian psychotherapist. Weizenbaum (1976) designed DOCTOR to use key words or punctuation marks in the patient's typed-in statements to trigger preprogrammed replies that appear to be understanding and responsive. When DOCTOR receives a series of words ending in a question mark, it replies, "Why do you ask?" It understands nothing, but Weizenbaum reports that people take the program seriously. The program assumes a life of its own, because people want it to do so.

For years, people have been interested in the idea of creating lifelike mechanisms, robots, androids, animated dolls, or thinking machines. The question of whether computers can be programmed to perform intelligent processes is an intriguing question. Many artificial intelligence researchers believe there is nothing the human mind can do that computers will not soon do as well and infinitely better. The views of two researchers who hold this opinion are reported by Hunt (1982).

> Marvin Minsky of MIT, computer scientist and artificial intelligence authority, believes in the foreseeable future a machine will reach the general intelligence of an average human being; the machine will educate itself and in a few months be at genius level.

> Edward Fredkin, professor of electrical engineering and computer science at MIT, says that eventually, no matter what we do, there'll be artificial intelligence with independent goals.

What Computers Can Do Better Than the Human Mind

Computers are clearly superior to the human mind in remembering immense masses of data and performing feats of swift calculation. These are superhuman tasks and are thought of as requiring superhuman intelligence. Yet speed of reckoning has little to do with the phenomena of higher intelligence or giftedness, such as the ability to understand, to organize experiences into new concepts, to reason, to create and test hypotheses about reality, and to solve problems.

In laboratories, universities, and companies such as Xerox, IBM, and Bell Labs, computers have been programmed to do advanced tasks such as formal logical reasoning, puzzle solving, game playing, and medical diagnosis. In these activities, computers match or outperform average human beings. This superiority is due primarily to their speed. Hunt (1982) reports on one program called "General Problem Solver." This program looks back on its own experience to generate possibilities for the next move, and tests them to see if they will advance it toward the goal; in short, it learns by experience.

A simple problem that "General Problem Solver" figured out is:

> A heavy father and two young sons have to cross a swift river in a deep wood. They find an abandoned boat which can be rowed across but sinks if overloaded. Each young son is 100 pounds. A double-weight son is just as heavy as the father and more than that is too much for the boat. How do the father and sons cross the river? (Hunt, 1982)

The answer is that both sons get in and row across; one debanks and the other rows back and debanks on the first shore; the father rows across and lands on the far shore; the son on that side rows back, picks up his brother, and the two of them row across to the far shore. Given the right rules and data concerning logic, computers prove theorems and other problems, including chess. Bell Labs has a chess program that can beat 99.5 percent of all competition chess players. Working with artificial intelligence, scientists are coming to a greater understanding of intelligence. Intelligence does involve adaptability and change, and therein lies part of what the human mind can do better than the computer.

What the Human Mind Can Do Better Than the Computer

The human mind can match incoming perception and words to meanings in a very different manner from the computer. The human mind can interpret, while the computer must match incoming data against templates or models. In addition, the human mind uses a wealth of knowledge linked through the associative networks of memory. Many researchers, including Weizenbaum (1976), state that computers simulate the logical processes of the left hemisphere of the brain, but there is no way that a linear, step-by-step artificial intelligence can simulate the intuitive and nonlogical processes of the right hemisphere. The human mind cannot simulate consciousness. People not only think, but they perceive themselves thinking. Hofstadter (1980) states, "the self comes into being at the moment it has the power to reflect upon itself, and as we contemplate our thoughts, the awareness of doing so is itself a thought and the foundation of consciousness."

Hunt (1982) further states that until artificial intelligence can duplicate human mental development from birth onward; absorb the intricacies and subtleties of cultural values; acquire consciousness of self; become capable of playfulness and curiosity; create new goals for itself; be motivated not by goals alone, but by some restless compulsion to do and explore; care about, and be pleased or annoyed by its own thoughts; and make wise moral judgment—not until all these conditions exist will the computer match or even imitate the most valuable aspects of human thinking.

To use the computer and computer technology wisely is an ongoing challenge. Weizenbaum (1976), in *Computer Power and Human Reason*, argues for humanity to beware of computers taking over decisions such as the functions of a psychotherapist or of military or judicial decisions. However, much more is known about the human intellect than a decade ago, through the use of information-processing models to understand human thinking.

Ennals (1984), a British historian, reports artificial intelligence researchers reflect dissatisfaction with conventional numerically oriented applications of computers. Their approach proposes a number of fields of application for the 1990s involving a change from machine-centered numerical computations to machines that can assess the meaning of information and understand problems. To accomplish this change, a number of developments are required. The 1982 report published by the Japanese Institute for New Generation Computer Technology predicts the following four developments, according to Ennals (1984):

1 To realize basic mechanisms for inference, association, and learning in hardware and make them the core functions of the fifth generation computers
2 To prepare basic artificial intelligence software to fully utilize the above functions
3 To take advantage of pattern recognition and artificial intelligence research achievements and realize man-made interfaces that are natural to man
4 To realize support systems for resolving the software crisis and enhancing software production

The focus in artificial intelligence has been the analysis of human learning. As Boden (1977) stated in *Artificial Intelligence and Natural Man*, artificial intelligence is not the study of computers but of intelligence in thought and action. Computers are its tools, because its theories are expressed as computer programs, which enable machines to perform in ways that would require intelligence if done by people.

A major theme of both recent classroom activity and artificial intelligence research has been the simulation of behavior to aid its understanding. An example from the artificial intelligence literature is reported by Abelson (1973), in an article entitled "The Structure of Belief Systems." He approached a familiar topic, the ideological conflict of the cold war, from an unusual perspective, that of the cognitive scientist. He analyzed the cognitive limitations faced by human agents in the face of transient, unfamiliar, noisy, and competitive information. In order to examine such limitations in action, he constructed what he called the "ideology machine." The ideology machine simulates responses to foreign policy questions by a right-wing ideologue. The simplified simulation of a cold war warrior has stored in it the vocabulary, conceptual categories, episodes, and master script appropriate to archconservatives. If the contents of memory were suitably changed, any other ideological system could be simulated with the same computer program.

There is considerable scope for educational application of such an approach to simulation. Ennals (1984) has also developed experience-centered classroom activities in which students take on the roles of historical agents in the Norman conquest, the Russian Revolution, and the European Parliament. The development of simulators to provide for higher-order thinking is limitless, but an equally exciting aspect of learning is studying how we think and process information. This study can lead to greater understanding of the complex concept of giftedness.

Computers can be partners in the home and the classroom. Doerr (1979), Papert (1980), Poirot (1980), Roberts (1985), and Dirkes (1985) recommend computers be used as problem-solving tools to enrich the classroom, and gifted students learn to program and direct the computer. Morrsund (1981) states that in learning how to program a computer, gifted students must tell the computer what to do, and they must know how to solve the problem. For the gifted student, the computer is a tool to save time and effort in carrying out necessary problem-solving steps (Schoman, 1979).

"Logo," developed by Papert and his staff at Massachusetts Institute of Technology, is a useful language for young gifted students (Papert, 1980). With "Logo," gifted students draw geometric figures and designs and they experience proportion and movement. "Logo" is an introduction to formal thought for the young gifted student. Papert suggests a computer-rich environment will shift the onset of "formal" thinking from approximately age 12, as suggested by Piaget, to an earlier age, because the computer makes formal operations concrete and personal. Upper elementary school level gifted students and secondary school level gifted students learn BASIC.

For the upper elementary gifted student, word processing is a tool for teaching composition. With a word processor, writing takes on a dimension of flexibility and fluidity. Gifted students learn to think by working with the computer, and their work improves in quality. As they become more adept at the computer, their prose becomes more fluent, clear, and more completely developed, teachers of the gifted report. However, word processing is not a substitute for rigorous thinking; it is a tool to facilitate composition. Three advantages to word processing, according to Trifiletti (1985) are that students learn (1) to type, (2) to edit compositions, and (3) to compose at the computer.

Computer simulations provide active investigations for gifted students. Some simulations are intended for groups, while others are intended for individuals.

One favorite with gifted students at the middle school level is SCRAM developed for Atari. This simulation is concerned with nuclear energy, and gifted students control a great number of variables, experiencing cause and effect and problem solving. Fantasy Land and Galaxy Search are examples of two programs that were developed for Apple II and use the adventure game format. Both games can be used with gifted students from kindergarten to third grade.

Another meaningful activity for gifted students is computer art or computer graphics. Computer graphics is a form of communication and a useful tool in technology. It helps gifted students learn to convey information and to organize material with minimal distortion. However, even as late as 1980 Taylor reports that experts (Dwyer, 1973; Luehrmann, 1980; Papert, 1980) have all noted that computer literacy and the use of computers as tools of education are not fully accepted as the common goals of parents, educators, and students.

In establishing programs for gifted with an emphasis on computer literacy, Tubb (1986) believes the focus of education in the classroom must shift from end-product to process, from acquiring facts to manipulating and understanding them. These goals are the stated goals of many planners in gifted education. Waurik (1980) emphasizes that work with computers is an appropriate and desirable area of study for gifted students, because many are perfectionistic and unwilling to make mistakes. Through computer programming, gifted students learn "debugging" and correcting errors as a major aspect of computer programming. Computer programmers say they learn more from mistakes than from successes, which is a valuable lesson for gifted students.

Technology, particularly the computer and its continued development, is awe inspiring in its impact on society. Each year as the transistor (the counterpart to the neuron in the human brain) is updated, technology comes closer to fully understanding the wonders of the human mind.

Trifiletti (1985) outlines teacher competencies for using computers with gifted students:

- Design and manage an instructional computer lab, including selection of hardware and software, curriculum design, and scheduling students.
- Describe the history of computer technology and outline present and future needs.
- Demonstrate familiarity and proficiency with computer terminology and language.
- Demonstrate familiarity with software directories.
- Subscribe to and read computer journals.
- Be a member of and participate in local, regional, or national computer users' group.
- Demonstrate familiarity with one or more teacher-authoring languages.
- Use computers and software to individualize instruction.
- Use computers and software to teach problem-solving skills.
- Use computers and software to teach programming skills.
- Use computers and software to teach graphics techniques.
- Demonstrate knowledge of local and regional networks.
- Secure information from commercial networks.
- Communicate with students, teachers, parents, and administrators about computerized education.

- Demonstrate familiarity with computer simulations and modeling techniques.
- Exercise grant-writing skills to secure funding for computerized instruction.
- Make data-based decisions on students' learning through computerized instruction.
- Evaluate software and hardware.
- Type and teach students to type.

Sources for classroom teachers include journals such as: *The Computing Teacher, Classroom Computer News, Electronic Education, Classroom Computing,* and *Electronic Learning.* Sources of information for courseware are the *Apple Blue Book,* the *TRS-80 Applications Software Source Book,* and Taylor's (1980) *The Computer in the School.*

Individuals who are committed to a better life and optimizing the future see the mission of educators becoming more and more complex (Papert, 1980; Triffiletti, 1985). In defining the concept of giftedness or in developing an approach to maximize giftedness, educators can use and direct computer technology. Computer technology will inevitably cause change in the traditional curriculum, and an essential point is that teachers of the gifted must initiate and direct that change.

SUMMARY

This chapter explored new concepts of learning including brain/mind research. Two areas of brain research have potential impact for educators of the gifted— brain growth laterality, (left-brain and right-brain research) and brain growth.

Implications from the brain laterality research were discussed in relation to the goal of total brain functioning. The problem of cerebral integration was covered, as well as the need for incorporating more right-brain activities into the educational program. Toepfer and Epstein's 1978 report on definite periods or surges of brain growth was reported, (Toepfer & Epstein, 1978) and the need for adapting school programs to accommodate these periods was emphasized.

Visualization was viewed as an aid to consciousness and learning, and a brief history of visualization and its impact on religion, psychology, and philosophy was discussed. In addition, types of visualization, such as memory images, eidetic images, imagination, daydreams and fantasy, dreams, and visions were covered. Specific visualization techniques for use in the classroom and the value of visualizing in social studies, science, language arts, and artistic production were noted.

Suggestology or suggestopedia, developed by the Bulgarian researcher, Lozanov, was examined. The Lozanov program is committed to the principles of the absence of tension; the fusion of the conscious and unconscious; and suggestive interaction.

Biofeedback was discussed as a technique to provide information about the body. Any object or material which provides information about the body's system is considered biofeedback. Biofeedback is as simple as reading temperature cards or as complex as monitoring electronic devices.

Lastly, artificial intelligence was covered as it relates to the role of computers in education and society. What the human mind can do better than the computer and what the computer can do better than the human mind was discussed. The challenge of using the computer wisely was stressed, and implications for the education of the gifted were noted.

EXTENDING ACTIVITIES

1 The Hopi Indians have a term for life out of focus. It is called *Koyanisquatsi*. Walk through your city, note the technology, the change, the impact of industrialization. Take pictures of your city and make a collage. Is it out of focus? If so, why? If not, why?
2 Find a copy of *The Aquarian Conspiracy* (Ferguson, 1980). Read one of the chapters dealing with transformation. Tell why you chose your chapter. Do you think we are in a great revolution?
3 Research the characteristics of right and left hemisphere functions. Make a list of the behavior such as left mode: logical, analytical, sequential; right mode: intuitive, non-linear, divergent.
4 Using selected behaviors from the above lists, design a teaching activity to develop right- and left-brain functioning.
5 Use the relaxation techniques suggested in this chapter before doing something creative. Try to be creative without the relaxation techniques. Were there any differences? Keep track of the changes in a journal.
6 Interview several young gifted students about their attitudes toward computers. Ask them if they think the computer keeps them from thinking or whether it helps them. Be prepared to record their responses for sharing with the class.

REFERENCES

Abelson, R. (1971). The structure of belief systems. In Shank (Ed.), *Computer models of thought and language.* San Francisco: W. H. Freeman.
Ahsen, A. (1977). Eidetics: An overview. *Journal of Mental Imagery, 1*(1), 5–38.
Bagley, M. (1983). The use of visual imagery and bio-feedback with gifted students. Presentation at the National Association for Gifted Children, Philadelphia.
Bagley, M. & Hess, K. (1982). *200 Ways of using imagery in the classroom.* Woodcliff Lakes, NJ: New Dimensions of the Eighties.
Boden, M. (1977). *Artificial intelligence and natural man.* London: Harvester.
Brown, C. (1974). *The Chippewa Indian identifies the gifted and talented.* Paper presented at a meeting of the Office of Gifted and Talented, Red Lake, MN.
Bry, A. (1978). *Directing the movies in your mind.* New York: Harper & Row.
Campbell, J. (1960). *Philosophies of India.* New York: Meridian Books.
Clark, B. (1983). *Growing up gifted.* Columbus, OH: Charles E. Merrill.
Davis, M. (1982). *The relaxation and stress reduction workbook.* Oakland, CA: New Harbinger Publishers.
DeBoskey, D. (1985). *Biofeedback experimentation with gifted students.* Paper presented in gifted seminar, University of South Florida, Tampa.
Dirkis, M. (1985). Problemsolving: The real purpose for computers in school. *GCT, 36,* 42–44.
Doerr, C. (1979). *Micro-computers and the three r's.* Rochelle Park, NJ: Hayden Press.
Dwyer, T. (1973). Heuristic strategies for using computers to enrich education. *International Journal of Man-Machine Studies, 6*(2), 137–154.

Ennals, J. (1984). *Artificial intelligence and educational computing*. Paper presented at an International Computer Conference, Sofia, Bulgaria.

Epstein, H. T. (1974). Phrenoblysis: Special brain and mind growth period in human brain and skill development. *Developmental Psychology, 7*, 212.

Epstein, H. T. (1978). Growth spurts during brain development: Implications for education policy and practice. In J. Chole & A. Mirstry (Eds.), *Education and the brain*. Chicago: University of Chicago Press.

Ferguson, M. (1981). *The aquarian conspiracy: Person and social transformation in the 1980's*. Los Angeles: J. P. Tarcher.

Ferguson, M. (1986). *Brain/mind update*. Presentation at the University of Massachusetts, Amherst.

Galyean, B. (1983). *Mind sight: Learning through imagery*. Long Beach, CA: Center for Integrative Learning.

Gowan, J. C. (1979). The production of creativity through right and left hemisphere functions. *Journal of Creative Behavior, 13*, 39–51.

Gowan, J. C. (1980). *Operation of increasing order*. Westlake Village, CA: Gowan.

Herrmann, N. (1981). The creative brain. *Training and Developmental Journal, 35*(10), 10–16.

Herrmann, N. (1986). *New frontiers of brain research*. Presentation at the Whole Brain Symposium, Key West, FL.

Hofstadter, D. (1980). *Gödel, Escher, Bach: An eternal golden braid*. New York: Vintage.

Holland, M. (1984). *The use of biofeedback to increase self-awareness*. Presentation to the Florida Governor's Honors Institute, Tampa, FL.

Horowitz, M. (1970). *Image formation and cognition*. New York: Appleton-Century-Crofts.

Hunt, M. (1982). *The universe within*. New York: Simon & Schuster.

Jung, C. G. (1968). *Man and symbols*. Garden City, NY: Doubleday.

Kamiya, J., Haight, M. & Jampolsky, G. (1975). A biofeedback study in high school. Paper presented at a meeting of the Biofeedback Society in Monterey, CA.

Khatena, J. (1984). *Imagery and creative imagination*. Buffalo, NY: Bearly Limited.

LeShan, L. (1975). *The medium, the mystic and the physicist*. New York: Ballantine Books.

Levy, J. (1977). The mammalian brain and the adoptive advantage of cerebral asymmetry. *Annals of New York Academy of Science, 299*, 264–277.

Levy, J. (1983). Human brain built to be challenged. *Brain/Mind Bulletin*.

Loye, D. (1982). People with balanced brains—better forecasters. *Brain/Mind Bulletin, 7*(3), 1.

Lozanov, G. (1977). A general theory of suggestion in the communication process and the activation of the total reserves of the learner's personality. *Suggestopedia, 1*, 1–4.

Luehrmann, A. (Ed.). (1980). *Computer and the school tutor—Tool and tutee*. New York: Columbia University Teachers College.

Luria, A. (1968). *The mind of a mnemonist*. New York: Basic Books.

Luthe, W. (1969). *Autogenic therapy*. New York: Grune and Stratton.

McKim, R. (1972). *Experience in visual thinking*. Monterey, CA: Brooks/Cole Publishing Co.

McKim, R. (1980). *Thinking visually*. Belmont, CA: Lifetime Learning.

Marks, D. & McKellar, P. (1982). The nature and function of eidetic imagery. *Journal of Mental Imagery, 6*(1), 1–28.

Morrsund, D. (1981). Introduction to computers in education for elementary and middle school teachers. *The Computing Teacher, 9*, 15–24.

Neihardt, J. (1961). *Black elk speaks*. Lincoln: University of Nebraska Press.

Ornstein, R. & Brandwein, P. (1977). The duality of the mind. *Instructor*, January, 54–58.

Papert, S. (1980). *Mindstorm: Children, computers and powerful ideas.* New York: Basic Books.

Pew, T. (1979). Biofeedback seeks new medical uses for concept of yoga. *Smithsonian, 10*(9), 106–114.

Poirot, J. (1980). *Computers and education.* Austin, TX: Sterling Swift.

Roberts, R. (1985). Curriculum guide for computer literacy. *GCT, 36,* 37–41.

Roberts, T. (1982). Consciousness meets education at UC Berkeley. *Brain/Mind Bulletin, 7*(12), 1.

Samples, B. (1977). Mind cycles and learning. *Phi Delta Kappan, 48,* 688–692.

Samuels, M. & Samuels, N. (1975). *Seeing with the mind's eye.* New York: Random House.

Schoman, K. E. (1979). *The basic workbook: Creative techniques for beginning programmers.* Rochelle Park, NJ: Hayden Press.

Shapiro, D., Tursky, B., Gershon, E. & Stern, M. (1969). Effects of feedback and reinforcement on the control of human systolic blood pressure. *Science, 163,* 588–590.

Singer, J. (1966). *Daydreaming.* New York: Random House.

Sisk, D. & Shallcross, D. (1982). *The growing person.* Englewood Cliffs, NJ: Prentice-Hall.

Sperry, R. W. (1974). Lateral specialization in the surgically separated hemisphere. In F. O. Schmidt & R. C. Warden (Eds.), *The neuroscience third study program.* Cambridge, MA: MIT Press.

Springer, S. & Deutsch, G. (1981). *Left brain, right brain.* San Francisco: W. H. Freeman.

Taylor, L. & Bongar, B. (1976). *Clinical applications in biofeedback therapy.* Los Angeles: Psychology Press.

Taylor, R. (1980). *The computer in the school: Tutor, tutee and tool.* New York: Columbia University Press.

Toepfer, C. (1980). Brain growth periodization data: Some suggestions for rethinking middle grades education. *High School Journal, 63*(6), 222–227.

Toepfer, C. F. & Epstein, H. (1978). A neuroscience basis for reorganizing middle grades education. *Educational Leadership, 35*(8), 656–660.

Torrance, E. (1978). Your style of learning: A right/left test. *The Gifted Child Quarterly. 21*(4), 563–585.

Torrance, E. P., Reynolds, C. R., Reigel, T. & Ball, O. (1977). Your style of learning: A right/left test. *Gifted Child Quarterly, 21*(4), 563–573.

Trifiletti, J. (1985). Using computers to teach the gifted. *Teaching Gifted Children and Adolescents.* Columbus, OH: Charles E. Merrill.

Tubb, G. (1986). *Computer: An intellectual tool for the gifted.* Presentation at leadership conference, University of South Florida, Tampa.

Waurik, J. (1980). Mathematics education for the gifted elementary student. *Gifted Child Quarterly, 24*(4), 69–173.

Wayman, J. & Plum, L. (1977). *Secrets and surprises.* Carthage, IL: Good Apple.

Weizenbaum, J. (1976). *Computer power and human reason.* San Francisco: W. H. Freeman.

Wittrock, M. (1980). *The brain and psychology.* New York: Academic Press.

CHAPTER 13

TRENDS AND ISSUES IN GIFTED EDUCATION

CHAPTER 13

TRENDS AND ISSUES IN GIFTED EDUCATION

No idea is so outlandish that it should not be considered with a searching but, at the same time, with a steady eye.

Winston Churchill

Few people disagree with the idea of learning being essential to societies that want to grow and offer their citizens opportunities for healthy, happy, and meaningful lives, and most people agree that in every society there are individuals who will be the creators and the leaders. Yet these individuals, the gifted, may or may not realize their potential depending on how the educational system values and serves them.

STATE OF THE ART

To gather the very latest information on the state of the art in gifted education, a survey of the state consultants was conducted (Sisk, 1984, 1985). The survey questions parallel the basic questions used in the 1972 report to Congress commissioned by Marland (Marland, 1972), the U.S. Commissioner of Education:

1 How many gifted children are currently being served?
2 How much state money is being spent on gifted education?
3 Is there legislation for the education of the gifted, and is the legislation permissive or mandatory?

Photograph on facing page courtesy of Elizabeth Crews, Berkeley, California.

4 Is there state certification for teachers of the gifted?

The overall query these basic questions addresses is: Are we meeting the challenge to the schools and society in providing an education for the gifted to develop their potential talent?

The answer to the above question is both yes and no. Since 1972, advocates for the gifted have attempted to convince individuals in power that financial and human resources must be invested in gifted children and youth. Their efforts are reflected in the 1984 survey findings.

In answer to the first question—How many gifted students are currently being served?—the states reported that 1.8 million gifted students received services. This figure represents a little over half of the 2.56 million gifted students hypothesized to exist (Marland, 1972). California leads the states in the number of gifted students being served, with a reported figure of 200,000. New York is second, with a reported 135,000. These numbers can be confusing and misleading in that they represent gifted students who attend full-time programs in special classes and special schools, as well as gifted students who receive enrichment services for varying amounts of time. This same condition prevailed in the original Marland survey conducted in 1972 and, in spite of the range in quantity and quality of service, the figures are interpretable, and they reflect considerable growth. The total percent of gifted being served in the Marland report was 40 percent, as compared to 57 percent in 1984.

To the second question—How much state money is being spent on gifted education?—the states reported spending approximately $175 million on gifted education. In examining the amount of state funds available to gifted programs in the various states, it was evident there exists a wide discrepancy in the financial support given to gifted education. Pennsylvania and Florida each reported spending $30 million on gifted education. California reported spending $17.8 million, and Georgia spent $18 million. The top ten states in funds expended for gifted programs for both 1984 and 1985 are listed in Table 13-1.

The figures indicate a wide variance in the numbers of gifted students served in relationship to funds expended on gifted programs. Part of this variance is explained by the different state reimbursement plans. The state of Florida, on the one hand, reimburses the salaries of teachers of the gifted, and therefore the funds expended do not reflect service to large numbers of gifted students. California, on the other hand, reimburses local education districts per gifted student served, so that funds are used primarily for materials and ancillary expenses. This funding method enables large numbers of gifted students to receive services.

In response to the question, Are you using federal block grant funds in gifted education?, several states reported the use of block grant funds, but, again, there was wide variance. Texas reported $1.56 million was funded in block grant money for gifted programs in 1984. This amount was atypical for the states, as most states reported spending token amounts or no expenditure. Priorities for the use of the federal block grant monies are established by the state educational agencies, and the reluctance to establish gifted as a state priority demonstrates the need for increased advocacy development for gifted students.

TABLE 13-1
FUNDS EXPENDED FOR GIFTED PROGRAMS
TOP TEN STATES

State	1984		1985	
	Amount of funds (million)	Gifted served (thousands)	Amount of funds (million)	Gifted served (thousands)
Florida	30	41	50.7	45
Pennsylvania	30	55		74
Georgia	18	47	21.3	40
California	17.8	200	20	211
North Carolina	14	60	17.7	65
Connecticut	8	60	17.7	65
Mississippi	8	12	12	12
Ohio	6	30	11.5	32
Illinois	6	82	6.3	85
Kentucky	5.2	15	5.2	15

In response to the questions, Is there legislation for the education of the gifted?, and Is legislation permissive or mandatory?, seventeen states reported mandatory legislation for the gifted; thirty-one reported no legislation. It is interesting to note that in the top five states, in terms of numbers of gifted students served and funds expended, three have mandatory legislation and two have permissive legislation. In states where gifted education is administered in special education or exceptional child education, legislation was more likely to be mandatory.

When the states were asked, Is there a full-time state consultant for the gifted?, the responses were that twenty-seven had a full-time state consultant for gifted education. Four states reported two individuals working with gifted students on a full-time basis—Georgia, Louisiana, New York, and Texas. Maryland and Oklahoma reported three individuals working full time for gifted education. Three states reported no one working on a full-time basis in gifted education—Wisconsin, Idaho, and Nevada. These three states did employ full-time state consultants when federal funds were available under Public Laws 93-380 and 95-561.

In comparing and contrasting the findings of the 1984 survey with the Marland Report of 1972, several conclusions can be drawn: (1) Where there is a full-time state consultant for gifted and available state funds for gifted programs, viable programs for the gifted do exist. This was true in 1984 and in 1972; (2) considerable growth has been made in total numbers of dollars expended and numbers of gifted students being served, but there remains a gap between the goal of providing for all gifted students in the public system and the current offerings for gifted students; and (3) a number of promising trends are emerging in gifted education.

TRENDS IN GIFTED EDUCATION

Increased Interest in Serving Specific Talent

This trend is reflected in the establishment of special schools, such as the Banneker

High School for Academically Gifted in the District of Columbia and the Fairfax County High School of Technology in Virginia, the latter for the specific area of mathematics and science. The Fairfax school has fifteen laboratories, including one in robotics, allowing gifted students the opportunity to use the latest equipment and work with professionals from the surrounding technological belt as mentors and part-time teachers. Another example of the interest in specific talent is the residential high school for gifted in mathematics and science established by Governor Hunt in North Carolina.

A Trend of Increased Interest in the Visual and Performing Arts

This trend was noted with many school districts which are already providing for gifted in the visual and performing arts or are planning and developing programs. The Duke Ellington High School in the District of Columbia, the Cincinnati School for the Performing Arts (serving fourth through twelfth grades), the School for Visual and Performing Arts in San Diego, and the St. Petersburg and Sarasota, Florida, Schools for the Performing Arts are all examples of this increased interest.

Increased Secondary School Programming for Gifted

Gifted students' needs are being accommodated at both the middle school and the high school levels. These programs include honors classes, advanced placement classes, specifically designated gifted courses, and the incorporation of international baccalaureate programs in many high schools. As gifted students progress through elementary gifted programs, parents' and teachers' demand for gifted programs to be extended in sequence and scope has stimulated development of secondary programs.

Increased Interest in Curriculum Development and Emphasis on Excellence

Another trend is increased interest in curriculum development. Many states reported working cooperatively with local school programs in developing curriculum guides in language arts, social studies, mathematics, and science. These efforts reflect two trends, the increased interest in secondary education for the gifted and an emphasis on excellence in the schools.

REPORTS ON EXCELLENCE IN THE SCHOOLS: IMPLICATIONS FOR THE GIFTED

A number of selected reports on excellence have implications for gifted education. Several important statements that pertain to curriculum content and the needs of gifted students were made in the National Commission on Excellence report: "gifted students . . . may need a curriculum enriched and accelerated beyond even the needs of other students of high ability . . . We must demand the best effort and performance from all students, whether destined for college, the farm, or industry." (National Commission on Excellence, 1983, p. 24.)

The National Commission on Excellence identified indicators of the nation's risk in terms of educational deficits and projected future needs. The deficits include a sizeable number of gifted students who are not achieving according to their potential. The report, *A Nation At Risk*, also addressed declining student literacy and achievement across a wide range of content and measures; costly remedial education; and the need for retraining in basic skills, which is currently being carried out by the military and business community. It stated that future needs center on providing personnel for the predicted acceleration of technology and extensive computerization.

The report *A Nation at Risk* calls for action in education. The goal is clear: ". . . to develop the talents of all to their fullest." (p. 13). Many of the recommendations to the National Commission on Excellence call for goals, curriculum, and types of instruction which are characteristic of current programs for the gifted. For example, the commission calls for English curriculum to emphasize skills of comprehension, interpretation, evaluation, writing in a well-organized manner, and discussion and understanding of literary heritage (p. 25). In mathematics the emphasis would be on understanding, applying, estimating, and use of higher levels of thinking skills (p. 25). In science the students would be working with concepts, laws, and processes of the physical and biological sciences and methods of scientific inquiry and reasoning. Lastly, the commission addressed the nature of the curriculum in computer science and foreign languages, stressing the higher level cognitive processes.

The commission proposed that funds be made available to develop special text materials to meet the needs of gifted and talented youth and other special populations (p. 28). It was suggested that these materials be rigorous, challenging, and that they present more complex and abstract concepts.

In recommendations related to age and placement, the commission proposed that the gifted be placed with their mental age-mates, stating, "Placement and grouping of students as well as promotion and graduation policies should be guided by the academic progress of students and their instructional needs, rather than by rigid adherence to age" (p. 34), and it suggested that additional time be found to meet the special needs of slow learners, the gifted, and others who need more instructional diversity than can be accommodated during a conventional school day or school year. Lastly, the National Commission on Excellence suggested that teachers be required to demonstrate an aptitude for teaching and competence in an academic discipline (p. 29).

Another selected report with relevance for noting trends and implications for gifted education is Goodlad's report, *A Place Called School* (1984). Goodlad states:

> American schools are in trouble. In fact, the problems of schools are of such crippling proportions that many schools may not survive. It is possible that our entire public system is nearing collapse. (p. 1)

Goodlad studied secondary schools (52 percent of the sample were high schools), and the study provides a sobering view of education. It reported that parents and professionals believe schools ought to be concerned with a wide range of goals. These goals include the development of love of learning; the ability to use and evaluate knowledge; the ability to solve problems; the development of aesthetic tastes and concerns; the development of qualities of curiosity and creativity; learning for the sake of learning; the effective use of leisure time; the development of satisfactory relations with others, which implies trust, respect, cooperation, and caring; and the understanding of differing value systems.

Despite this array of stated goals, the schools studied were found to be emphasizing a narrow, academic curriculum, largely ignoring broader goals. Goodlad reports that teachers teach to large groups in a relatively standardized manner, with textbooks, workbooks, and dittoed sheets. Teacher-oriented talk was the prime teaching technique. Many of the findings noted by Goodlad have been reported by various school districts designing secondary gifted programs.

Goodlad also recommended that early school entry should be made available (entry at age 4) to children who are capable of benefiting from early entrance, and completion of school at age 16 should be available on the same principle. This proposal would reduce the length of schooling for bright students and allow them to begin their professional education 2 years earlier. This recommendation is consistent with the trend in gifted education to use acceleration as a viable alternative. More specifically, Goodlad suggests both students and faculty participate in school problem solving and stresses the need for mentors. In addition, Goodlad mentions the inadequacy of test scores in fully measuring students' capabilities and interests, which may extend beyond academics.

Another report, *Action for Excellence*, chaired by Governor Hunt (1983), merits examination for implications for gifted education. It is a report authored by the Task Force on Education for Economic Growth, a subgroup of the Education Commission for the States (ECS). Governor Hunt describes the report as a blueprint for reform for mobilizing America's resources in the pursuit of education for economic growth. The chief recommendation of the report is for each governor to join with legislators, state and local boards of education, business and labor leaders, and others in the creation of state task forces. Each state task force would assess state and local needs to develop an action plan for improving the schools. Each plan would focus on education for jobs and economic growth and set forth specific objectives, timetables, and methods for measuring progress (p. 34). The report also recommends the creation of partnerships between education, business, and government to improve education for economic growth (p. 35). The central element in the plan is the involvement of business as a genuine partner with the schools to help determine what is taught, to assist in marshalling the resources needed to provide quality education, and to convey the skills needed in the workplace to educators. The task force report states:

> Because we are preparing young people for the jobs of tomorrow, we must make business a full partner in educating young people. We must tell the community that, if it wants better employees and higher profits, it must be involved in what the schools teach and how they teach it. (page 539)

Hunt's recommendations are consistent with an ongoing effort for gifted education directed by Jacqueline Meers (1985), the National Business Consortium for Gifted and Talented. This consortium recommends that selected governors appoint a state business leader to work with an executive committee and various subcommittees. Their goal is similar to Hunt's, but it is narrower in that it only addresses gifted education. The consortium has an active and influential board of directors, composed mostly of business leaders and the chairperson of the educational council. The National Business Consortium has the potential to be a constructive force for change. Its organization chart is shown in Figure 13-1.

The plan, *Action for Excellence*, addresses the needs of student populations that are currently unserved. Hunt (National Commission on Excellence, 1984) states, "we must investigate the needs of women, minorities, and the exceptionally gifted, to name a few, and we must invest more in developing their knowledge and skills." In addition, the report calls for a strong national leadership role and claims the cause for improving education will fail without national leadership: "The federal government need not assume full responsibility for all that needs to be accomplished, but appropriate federal support to complement state efforts is essential" (p. 541).

The Carnegie Foundation report (Boyer, 1983) studied the factors shaping the best high schools. Community support was found to be the major factor. Four priorities were named for education. They are:

1 Proficiency in oral and written English prior to high school
2 A core curriculum for all students containing foreign language, mathematics

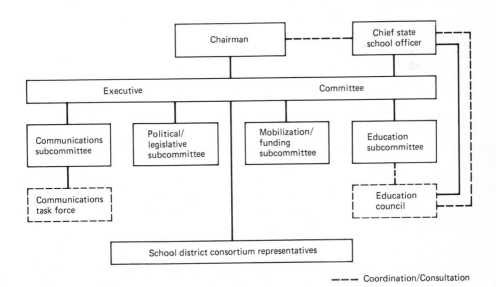

FIGURE 13-1
National business consortium for gifted: state consortium program organization chart.
(*Jacqueline Meers, Director of the National Business Consortium for Gifted and Talented, National Business Consortium, Washington, D.C., 1984. Reprinted by permission.*)

(3 years), English, science (4 years), social studies (3 years), courses on the arts, civics, nonwestern studies, and technology

3 Improvements for teachers in pay, recognition, and time to devote to professional tasks

4 More emphasis on responsible citizenship for students through volunteer work internships and a network for residential academics in mathematics and science for gifted students with federal funding and participation, as well as scholarships for top teacher involvement

One last report to be examined for implications for gifted education is the Twentieth Century Fund Task Force Report (Graham, 1983). This report on federal elementary secondary education policy calls for a core curriculum emphasizing basic skills (reading, writing, and calculating) and training in science and foreign languages. It emphasizes achieving technical capability in computers and increased knowledge in civics. This last recommendation by the Twentieth Century Fund Task Force is relevant to the current inequity of available funds for gifted students evidenced in the 1984 survey. A conclusion to be drawn from the various reports is that there exists strong support for a powerful drive for educational excellence. This drive for excellence is coming at a time when change is occurring rapidly and forces are impinging on society that can be viewed as major societal changes. In examining these forces, we may find other implications for teaching gifted students and for their learning processes.

Experts Respond to the Reports

Educators' interpretations of what the reports are suggesting, directing, or implying are varied. Several leaders in the movement for gifted education have addressed the reports, and their points of view and conclusions reflect the variety of opinions and beliefs in education in general and, specifically in the education of the gifted student.

Dyer (1984) stressed that the gifted will have to tackle a number of serious global problems and changes. He lists some of them: the world's population and poverty; the need to outline plans for settling new populations; and the need to provide employment and reduce the disparity of wealth that exists between the northern and southern hemispheres. Dyer's ideas echo Goodlad's recommendations (Goodlad, 1984) for solving problems; the need for understanding differing value systems; and the National Commission for Excellence recommendations for interpreting and evaluating. Dyer (1984) identifies social factors such as the search for national security and the destruction of natural resources as areas of concern. The ECS report noted the need for building job skills and defined the nation's task in education as preparing individuals for effective learning-to-learn skills. Dyer goes one step further and calls for education to help provide gifted students with the skills and opportunities to shape our global future.

Feldhusen and Hoover (1984) interpret the recommendations of the National Commission on Excellence as clearly leading to a need for special classes and differentiated instruction for gifted youth. They state that in the elementary grades this would mean special self-contained classes rather than pull-out programs. They also advocate continued acceleration of gifted students to provide the rigor and challenge called for by the National Commission on Excellence. They take issue with the commission's recommendation that the gifted and others who need more instructional diversity than can be accommodated during a conventional school day or school year should be given additional time. Their stated fear is that this might be interpreted to mean that gifted students will be responsible for the regular curriculum and will have their special needs met after school hours. For gifted students' needs to be considered as ancillary to the regular day runs counter to one of the basic beliefs stated in most policy statements for gifted education, that of gifted education being an integral part of the total school program.

Maker and Schiever (1984) discuss two of the educational reports, *A Nation At Risk* (National Commission on Excellence, 1983) and *Action for Excellence* (Task Force on Education for Economic Growth, 1983). The major difference between the two reports, according to Maker and Schiever, lies in the definition of new basic skills. In the report of the National Commission on Excellence, Maker and Schiever point out that the basics in the area of content are described in terms of time requirements, whereas the ECS report defines new basic skills in terms of competencies needed in the future. These competencies include basic as well as higher-order skills. For gifted students, there is a real danger in interpreting standards of quality or defining basic skills in terms of time requirements. If the majority of students were able to master 80 percent of material in some of their subject matter texts before they opened their books, as reported in *A Nation at Risk*, then these students should not be required to relearn or practice skills just to spend 4 years in a subject such as English or 3 years on mathematics.

Maker and Schiever (1984) praise the implications of the ECS report for emphasizing the use of competencies and proficiency tests or achievement tests to measure a gifted student's level and for stressing progress to higher levels to achieve depth of understanding. They see the focus being on principles and ideas.

Bruch (1984) states that *A Nation at Risk* fails to address several elements in gifted education—individualization, self-choice, autonomy, and learning styles. Her comments agree with Galyean (1983) who reports that *A Nation at Risk* did not treat differential learning styles, the interaction of intuitive and analytic modes, or the balance between rote memory and creative, exploratory activities. Another critique addresses the omission of self-understanding; the ability to guide one's own evolution; and the failure to deal with problem solving, current affairs, or curriculum reforms (Valett, 1983). Lastly, Weinstein (1983) noted the lack of cultural sensitivity or a cultural rationale for foreign language education.

Bruch (1984) takes a positive tone concerning Goodlad's statements in favor of mentors and the emphasis on faculty and student participation in problem solving. She states that education for gifted students must consider their potential futures:

This involves not only undetermined options for future careers but also their qualities as human beings capable of being sensitive to the needs of world humanity and of preventing problems as well as coping with change. A future perspective is called for: the next generation of gifted leaders cannot just let things happen.

In examining selected reports for their implications about gifted education, several statements were directed to the nature of curriculum content and the needs of gifted students, such as, "gifted students . . . may need a curriculum enriched and accelerated beyond even the needs of other students of high ability . . . We must demand the best effort and performance from all students, whether they are gifted or less able, affluent or disadvantaged, whether destined for college, the farm or industry" (National Commission on Excellence, 1983, p. 24).

Funds were recommended to support text development for the gifted and additional time was recommended beyond the conventional school day or calendar year to meet the needs of gifted students. Placement and grouping, promotion, and graduation policies were recommended to be determined by students' progress and instructional needs, not by rigid expectations. These generalizations call for individualization for gifted students, allowing each student the opportunity to ensure that this present trend of concern for excellence in education not become a temporary concern. Maker and Schiever (1984) summarize the urgency: "As a society, we will have only the kinds of excellence that we nourish, only the kinds of excellence we want and respect" (p. 6).

Specific issues in gifted education must be addressed to fully understand its expanding dimensions. Selected issues and their implications will be examined with emphasis on future education policy for the gifted student.

ISSUES IN GIFTED EDUCATION

One issue is the continuing gap between research and practice in gifted education. This is evident in the identification of and programming for gifted students. Equity is a critical issue in identification. Many students, such as the underachieving, the handicapped, the disadvantaged, the bilingual, and the creative are screened out of gifted programs. With education emphasizing excellence and specific academic aptitude, there is greater reliance on achievement scores and grades, and this keeps many students out of the gifted program.

Another issue is the considerable confusion over the definition of gifted and the nature and needs of the gifted. Giftedness is not a single phenomenon or a single score, and many gifted students and adults demonstrate multiple talents. This manifestation of multiple talents was noted by Fichter, the Ohio state consultant for gifted education, who related that the Cincinnati School for the Performing Arts won the district basketball championship and was second in academic rank in the city of Cincinnati (Sisk, 1984). Yet many school districts and state departments of education continue to address one type of giftedness, that of intellectual or academic talent, and ignore the multiple talents of gifted students.

Still another issue is that of potential versus achievement. As gifted programs move toward serving specific academic talent, they become more interested in grades and achievement, and they screen out gifted students who are not achieving in the regular classroom. These students are denied access to these new gifted programs.

In an attempt to use more than one criterion, many school districts have added several tests in which a student must demonstrate excellence. Hallahan and Kaufman (1982) suggest the multiple criterion of Renzulli (1978) (high ability, high creativity, and high task-commitment) as a definition, with modifications. They qualify Renzulli's definition in the following way: to the extent that a child has demonstrated that she/he is better than 85 percent (1 standard deviation above the mean) of his or her peers on all three Renzulli criteria and better than 98 percent on at least one criterion, he or she should be designated as gifted.

Most educators would not quarrel with a cut-off of 98 percent on high ability, as measured by standardized intelligence and achievement tests, or a 98 percent cut-off on creativity tests as criteria for a type of giftedness. In either case, educators would be identifying a gifted student with intellectual talent or one with creative talent. The problem comes when task-commitment is considered measurable on a rating scale or identifiable through judgements of teachers and parents, which are highly subjective. Many gifted students demonstrate task-commitment to individual interests, and schoolwork is not always an identified interest.

The concept of considering an 85 percent cut-off in all three areas as the criteria is an interesting idea for identifying gifted students. These students will be good "grade-getters" and achievers in the regular classroom, but they may not necessarily be gifted. One of the major problems in the notion of identifying achieving, contributing, creative adults and then projecting their characteristics onto children in an attempt to understand giftedness is simply that all intellectually gifted individuals are not creative. In fact, many creatively gifted individuals may not be intellectually gifted.

Long-term research is badly needed to study gifted students over a period of years or a lifetime. A great debt is owed to Terman and his associates (1925, 1947, 1959) and to Torrance (1970, 1981) for their long-term studies in creativity; however, a research project or study to follow gifted students who have been identified with one or more of the designated talents, such as intellectual, visual and performing arts, leadership, kinesthetic, or specific academic aptitude, throughout their lifetimes would contribute to greater understanding of the socioemotional and educational needs of gifted individuals.

In addition, there is a need to recognize gifted students' unique learning needs and differing learning styles. Too often gifted students experience the classroom as dull, frustrating, and removed from real life. This may be a result of education being too factually oriented, logical, and linear and failing to address the cerebral preferences of the gifted student.

Much has been learned in the last few years in brain research, as noted in Chapter 12, and technology has been improved to understand how one learns and how the brain functions. The concept of cerebral preference and the notion of learning using the whole brain need to be translated into educational practices. The key to these promising practices in gifted education is the classroom teacher, and there is continued interest and need to provide teachers with specialized training. Training in these new frontiers will assist the teacher of the gifted in individualizing the learning of gifted students. One laudable attempt is the foremat program of McCarthy (1984), which helps teachers build curriculum using a whole-brain approach. Progress is being made and several sustaining beliefs in gifted education have made this progress possible.

Sustaining Beliefs in Gifted Education

One sustaining belief is that change is possible. There have been changes in both the numbers of gifted being served and the funds expended by the states for gifted education. Another sustaining belief is that change can be equated with extended opportunity, removal of inequity, and affirmation of the gifted students' rights. As a direct consequence of this belief, there are more program offerings at the secondary and middle school levels that allow gifted students to move at their own pace and to have their educational rights affirmed. These rights need to be extended to the young gifted child. In fact, as Karnes (1979) states, "of all gifted, the young gifted and talented may well be the most neglected in terms of educational programming."

The earlier the gifts and talents of the young are nurtured, the better their chances for full development, but only recently have attempts been made to meet their needs. Five programs for gifted and talented children below the age of 5 were reported by Jenkins (1979). Karnes et al. (1982) report eighteen programs nationwide. Interest has increased in young gifted, but programming has so far failed to meet the need. There remains a pessimism that early identification may not withstand the test of time. That is, a young child who has been identified at age 3 or 4 may not continue to score high at age 8 or 9. We need research to refute this. Very few gifted preschoolers do not maintain their giftedness, unless there are intervening factors such as illness, frequent moves, or death or trauma in the family. These factors would affect any young child's school performance. The common age for identification and program development for gifted students is age 9. By then, many young gifted students have learned to conceal their talents and to react as average students because they are encouraged and expected to do so.

One last sustaining belief in gifted education is that alliances are helpful, and many states report successful attempts to reach out to community and private sectors. These efforts lead the private sector to greater understanding of and commitment to education of the gifted. One rewarding avenue for mutual cooperation is continued efforts with other countries. The World Council for Gifted and Talented, an international organization comprised of fifty-five countries, has sponsored a number of international conferences and cooperative efforts, notably the Banner of Peace festival which brings children from all over the world together to share creative activities. This conference is held annually in Bulgaria. Through continued efforts on behalf of gifted children and youth, enormous contributions and benefits will accrue to our global society and to gifted students.

SUMMARY

The chapter addressed the state of the art in gifted education. Findings from a national survey were examined. The questions directing the survey were:

1 How many gifted children are currently being served?
2 How much state money is being spent on gifted education?

3 Is there legislation for the education of the gifted and is that legislation permissive or mandatory?

4 Is there a full-time consultant for the gifted working on behalf of gifted children?

5 Is there state certification for teachers of the gifted?

The top ten states were identified in terms of funds expended, discrepancies in funds allocated for gifted students, and the numbers served. One conclusion from the survey is that when there is a full-time state consultant for gifted students and available state funds for gifted programs, there are viable programs for the gifted.

Trends in gifted education were discussed, such as increased interest in serving specific talent; increased interest in the visual and performing arts; increased secondary program offerings for gifted; and increased interest in curriculum development.

Reports on excellence in the schools were examined for implications for gifted education. Those selected included the National Commission on Excellence report, *A Nation at Risk*; Goodlad's report, *A Place Called School*; the Task Force on Education for Economic Growth report, *Action for Excellence*; The Carnegie Foundation report (Boyer, 1983), and the Twentieth Century Fund Task Force report (Graham, 1983).

A conclusion from these various reports is that there is a drive for educational excellence. Opinions of experts in gifted education concerning the reports were highlighted: funds were recommended to support text development for the gifted and talented; additional time was recommended beyond the conventional school day or calendar year to meet the needs of the gifted; and placement and grouping, promotion, and graduation policies were recommended to be determined by students' progress and instructional needs, not by rigid expectations. These recommendations call for individualization, affording each gifted student the opportunity to work at his or her own pace.

Issues in gifted education, such as the gap between research and practice and the equity issue in identification, were discussed. The ongoing confusion over the definition of giftedness and the concept of multiple talents was highlighted. Sustaining beliefs in gifted education were outlined, such as the belief that change is possible and that alliances are helpful.

Giftedness is the term used for multiple talents in our children and youth. Developing that giftedness is the challenge of education. Whether we meet that challenge or not may very well shape our future. For it is the gifted who will lead society to understand and optimally develop the human brain/mind system and, in turn, to develop society to its true fulfillment.

EXTENDING ACTIVITIES

1 Select one of the reports on excellence and summarize the findings. Concentrate on implications for gifted education. How realistic do you think the recommendations are for education in the 1980s?

2 You have been selected to give a talk on equity in gifted education to a group of parents. What would you tell them? Justify your position with as many facts as possible.

3 Increased interest in special schools is a trend in the education of the gifted student. Select a special school and report on its identification procedure, curriculum, and method of evaluation.
4 Read selected articles on experts' opinions about the reports on excellence. Sources are: Feldhusen and Hoover (1984); Dyer (1984); Maker and Schiever (1984); Bruch (1980); Galyean (1983); Weinstein (1983), and Valett (1983).

REFERENCES

Boyer, E. L. (1983). *High school: A report on secondary education in America.* The Carnegie Foundation for the Advancement of Teaching. New York: Harper & Row.

Bruch, C. (1984). Schooling for the gifted: Where do we go from here? *Gifted Child Quarterly, 28*(1), 19.

Dyer, J. (1984). Deterrents to change. *Education Canada*, Spring, 28.

Feldhusen, J. & Hoover, S. (1984). The gifted at risk in a place called school. *Gifted Child Quarterly, 28*(1), 9–11.

Galyean, B. (1983). AHP forum on education—comments. *AHP Newsletter*, October, 19.

Goodlad, J. (1984). *A place called school.* New York: McGraw-Hill.

Graham, P. A. (1983). The twentieth century fund task force report on federal elementary and secondary education policy. *Phi Delta Kappan*, September, 19–21.

Hallahan, D. & Kaufman, J. (1986). *Exceptional children: Introduction to special education* (3d ed.). Englewood Cliffs, NJ: Prentice-Hall.

Jenkins, R. A. (1979). *A resource guide to pre-schools and primary programs for the gifted and talented.* Mansfield, CT: Creative Learning Press.

Karnes, M., Shivedel, A. & Linnemeyer, S. (1982). The young gifted/talented child: Programs at the University of Illinois. *Elementary School Journal, 82*(3), 195–213.

Karnes, M. B. (1979). Young handicapped children can be gifted and talented. *Journal for the Education of the Gifted, 2*(3), 157–172.

Maker, C. J. & Schiever, S. (1984). Excellence for the future. *Gifted Child Quarterly, 28*(1), 6–8.

Marland, S. (1972). *Education of the gifted and talented.* Report to the Congress of the United States by the U.S. Commission of Education. Washington, DC: U.S. Government Printing Office.

McCarthy, B. (1984). *4MAT system: Teaching to learning styles with R/L mode techniques.* Oak Brook, IL: Excell.

National Commission on Excellence. (1983). *A nation at risk: The imperative for educational reform.* Washington, DC: U.S. Government Printing Office, April.

Renzulli, J. (1978). What makes giftedness? Re-examining a definition. *Phi Delta Kappan, 60*(3), 180–184, 261.

Sisk, D. (1984). *A national survey of the state consultants of gifted on state of the art in gifted education.* Report to the White House, Washington, DC.

Task Force on Education for Economic Growth (1983). *Action for excellence: A comprehensive plan to improve our nation's schools.* Report to the Education Commission of the United States, June.

Terman L. M. (1925). *Mental and physical traits of a thousand gifted children (Volume 1).* Stanford, CA: Stanford University Press.

Terman, L. M. (1947). *The gifted child grows up: Twenty-five year follow-up of a superior group.* Stanford, CA: Stanford University Press.

Terman, L. M. & Oden, M. (1959). *The gifted group at midlife: Thirty-five years follow-up of the superior child.* Stanford, CA: Stanford University Press.

Torrance, E. P. (1970). Broadening concepts of giftedness in the up's. *Gifted Child Quarterly, 14*, 199–208.

Torrance, E. P. (1981). Toward the more humane education of gifted children. In J. C. Gowan, J. Khatena & E. P. Torrance (Eds.), *Creativity: Its educational implications.* Dubuque, IA: Kendall/Hunt.

Valett, R. (1983). Human survival. *AHP Newsletter*, October, 16.

Weinstein, G. (1983). Education as an MX missile. *AHP Newsletter*, October, 19.

APPENDIX A

LIST OF COMPETENCES FOR CERTIFICATION OF THE TEACHERS OF THE GIFTED*

1 Candidate will be able to assess physical, intellectual, social, and emotional characteristics of both gifted and nongifted pupils.
2 Candidate will define the intellectual characteristics of gifted individuals according to both legal documents (education code) and psychological literature (research dealing with the construct, intelligence).
3 Candidate will demonstrate familiarity with the speculative literature dealing with the social, emotional, and physical characteristics of gifted individuals.
4 Candidate will recognize the speculated and empirically demonstrated differences between the intellectual characteristics of gifted and nongifted students.
5 Candidate will be able to assess learning abilities in relation to psychological, genetic, and physiological conditions.
6 Candidate will become familiar with the literature which deals with the relationship of cultural, ethnic, and socioeconomic factors of achievement.
7 Candidate will be able to effectively argue the point of varying assessment procedures depending upon the background of pupils.
8 Candidate will demonstrate the ability to assess the intellectual functioning of a pupil without referring to IQ.
9 Candidate will have knowledge of diagnostic and achievement tests useful to program development.
10 Candidate will demonstrate skill in generalizing from standardized achievement test data to the relative effectiveness of program elements for gifted pupils.
11 Candidate will demonstrate familiarity with the developmental stage generalizations

* Reprinted by permission, San Diego Unified School District, Supervisor Dave Hermanson.

of Piaget, Guilford's SOI, Bloom's Taxonomy, and other models relevant to gifted education.

12 Candidate will demonstrate the ability to informally assess general pupil attitudes relative to feelings of competence through group process exercises.

13 Candidate will be able to make reasonably confident statements about the relative motivational and attitudinal characteristics of pupils.

14 Candidate will be able to apply appropriate intervention to extend interaction among the pupil, his or her peers, and adults.

15 Candidate will demonstrate the ability to use appropriate standardized assessment instruments as tools for interpreting the learning characteristics of gifted individuals.

16 Candidate will be able to assess motivational and attitudinal differences including, but not limited to, self-control, anxiety, general attitudes toward learning, and the acceptance of success.

17 Candidate will recognize a range of behavioral characteristics of gifted individuals and ways of processing those characteristics in the classroom.

18 Candidate will self-select a structured system of motivation and attitude assessment.

19 Candidate will be able to describe and evaluate several theoretical instruction systems used to design programs for gifted pupils.

20 Candidate will demonstrate familiarity with programming characteristics to include, but not be limited to, segregation, enrichment, acceleration, and early school entrance.

21 Candidate will be able to utilize systematic observation, academic assessment, clinical teaching, or informal assessment procedures for individualizing instruction.

22 Candidate will generalize from evaluative procedures used in university preparation programs (as models) to procedures useful in school classrooms.

23 Given an observation format (or having designed the same), the candidate will plan instruction in light of observation.

24 Candidate will demonstrate the interacting relationship among individualized instruction, small group interaction, and whole class instruction.

25 Candidate will develop a file, the form of which will be of his/her own choosing, which will be a reference for bringing resource people into the classroom.

26 Candidate will, through in-class instruction, demonstrate the ability to look critically at oneself and see where professional growth should be directed.

27 Candidate will be able to initiate and pursue a program of self-assessment and professional improvement.

28 Candidate will become familiar with informal procedures for pupil assessment of teachers.

29 Candidate will become familiar with procedures for program and teacher effectiveness.

30 Candidate will demonstrate knowledge of San Diego Unified School District procedures relative to gifted education.

31 Candidate will be able to analyze and evaluate gifted program elements.

32 Candidate will formulate some useful ethical parameters in sharing pupil information with parents and sharing parental information with pupils.

34 Candidate will demonstrate skill in knowing what kinds of data are helpful in communicating about pupils and what kinds of data are likely to be merely prejudicial.

35 Candidate will have knowledge of the laws of the state relative to data collection and communication.

36 Candidate will use the literature in gifted education to become familiar with the general kinds of anxieties experienced by gifted pupils and/or their parents.

APPENDIX B

ELECTION OF A PRESIDENT

There are five individuals running for president of a country named Mercury. Mercury is a democratic country and the officials are voted in by popular vote. The problem is to choose the best candidate and to elect that individual as president. Magazines can be used to make pictures for candidates.

This election takes place in 1979 in a large democratic country. This country has two primary political parties, but there are also several smaller independent parties. There will be a primary election in which the number of candidates will be reduced to two or three. Campaigning will be conducted by each candidate in conjunction with his or her campaign and financial chairperson. Between the primary and general election there will be party conventions in which one candidate will be chosen by each party. However, the final decision as to who wins the presidency will be decided by popular vote. Secret ballot will be used for the final ballot.

Each individual candidate must assume a name and identity which she or he will not be able to alter during the campaign. The candidate will be allowed to change or alter his or her stand on some issues. Each candidate will choose a campaign chairperson and financial chairperson who will assist her or him in making political decisions and who will participate in all activities.

The game will be divided into phases and each phase will be timed. During these phases each candidate will be able to win points according to his or her identity, campaign efforts, financial resources, and ability to outwit fellow candidates. Points will be subtracted if each phase is not completed in the given time limit or if a major discrepancy in verification is found. Before anyone can win the presidency, she or he will have to be joined and supported by at least one other candidate, who will then withdraw from the election. The points of the candidate who is withdrawing will then be given to the candidate he or she supports.

In order for this game to run smoothly, a game director, a timer, and a score-keeper must be chosen before the game begins.

Each candidate will be given $100,000 at the beginning of the game to manage her or his campaign. Costs will be subtracted during the various phases of the game. If two candidates go together, the candidate who is withdrawing may decide to contribute part or all of his or her funds to the candidate she or he supports. If a candidate runs out of money, she or he cannot participate in those phases of the game that require money. Paper money can be used.

GAME PLAN

Phase I—Picking Your Candidate

This phase consists of choosing your candidate and giving him or her a name and an identity. This identity must include the name of the state she or he is from; what party he or she belongs to; and her or his basic and foreign policy, professional background, and character or personality traits. A time limit of 15 minutes is set for this section. Five points will be taken away if the assignment is not completed on time. Ten points are awarded for finishing. Before moving to phase II, a filing fee of $2000 will be required for each candidate.

Phase II—Facing the Issues

There is a 10-minute time limit for this section. Again, five points will be subtracted for not completing this phase in the time allowed.

Table B-1 shows the major issues and points scored for stand taken.

Look at these issues carefully, because no candidate can be for any two conflicting issues. Also remember that in order for a candidate to win the presidency, she or he will have to win the support of one of the other candidates. These two

TABLE B-1

Issue	Yes	No	No stand
1 Supports increase in government spending	8	6	3
2 Supports decrease in government spending	8	6	3
3 Supports strong ecological stand/laws	8	6	3
4 Supports increased manufacturing, even at expense of ecology	8	6	3
5 Supports federal aid to foreign countries	8	6	3
6 Supports cutting federal aid to foreign countries	8	6	3
7 Supports increased military expenditures	8	6	3
8 Supports aid to farmers	8	6	3

candidates must agree on at least three issues. A candidate cannot win the game if he or she refuses to take a stand on more than four issues.

If the candidate does not complete the assignment in 10 minutes, she or he loses 5 points.

Phase III—Campaigning for the Presidency

This phase will be handled primarily by both the campaign chairperson and the financial chairperson. They must decide how much money and in what type of campaign this money should be invested. Table B-2 shows that a candidate can invest more than once in any type of advertising.

Phase IV—Primary Election and Party Conventions

At this time, campaign chairpersons will present their candidates and barter with other candidates to win their support. By means of oral vote from the states, each party represented will choose one candidate. The states may divide their votes; however, if a candidate is from their state, they must stay with him or her during the first ballot. Should more than one candidate be from one state, that state's vote will be divided equally on the first ballot.

Each party will have its own convention, and the activities, presentation of each of its candidates, and voting will be conducted by that party chairperson. If any party should have only one candidate, then that candidate should automatically become her or his party's candidate. Any candidate who wishes to withdraw should say so at this time. The candidate in the race may change a stand on one issue in order to win the withdrawing candidate's support. If neither of the two conditions above is possible, then the two candidates who wish to join efforts must subtract 15 points from their total, because there will be a major verification discrepancy. The withdrawing candidate does not have to give his or her support or points to any other candidate. Three or more candidates may join together as long as the above rules are followed.

A 15-minute time limit will be set for each party convention, and 5 points will be subtracted if it is not met.

At the end of the convention, the candidate must pay her or his bills totaling $10,000 before he or she can go on to the general election.

TABLE B-2

Types of advertising and cost	Cost	Points
A Television commercials	$10,000	10
B Newspaper commercials	5,000	6
C Setting up campaign headquarters in key cities	40,000	15
D Billboards	3,000	4
E Travel expenses for the candidate to campaign in person	15,000	12

Phase V—The General Election

Points in this part of the game will be scored by matching the issues with the interests of the states. States may divide their vote in any way they wish, except that they may not vote for a candidate who clearly indicates that she or he does not support their best interest.

There will not be a time limit set for this phase, and one individual will be placed in charge of each state's votes. The voting will be done by secret ballot. If no candidate wins a majority of the vote on the first ballot, then subsequent ballots will be taken until one wins a majority of the vote. The voting will be conducted by the game director. Votes will count as points in this game. See Table B-3.

At this point in the game, the scorer will add up the points and a president will be elected.

It can be noted in the game *Election of a President* that the concept of a "reality-based activity" is the key part of the simulation. Gifted students who have experienced this game will have a fine grasp of the dynamics of selecting a president as well as what it entails to be a candidate. Sixth graders as well as secondary students can profitably experience *Election of a President*.

TABLE B-3

States	Votes or points
A Bountyland—a rural farming state with low population. Supports strongly decentralized federal government	18
B Picturesque—Primarily a tourist state with high density of population	26
C Metro—a highly populated state which depends on manufacturing and industry for income	28
D Inlet—a very small state primarily dependent on port trade and fishing for its income	4
E Potluck—large state with much industry and varied racial population	18
F Calabash—large farming and cattle-raising state; much of its produce must be exported	20
G Fairhill—medium-sized state that is underdeveloped and has no major industry. Primary means of support—small farms and tourist trade	16

APPENDIX C

RESOURCE LIST OF EDUCATORS IN GIFTED EDUCATION*

Alabama	Jonatha Vare, Education specialist Curriculm Alabama State Department of Education 111 Coliseum Blvd. Montgomery, AL 36193	(205) 261–2746
Alaska	Christine Niemi, Program Manager Office for Exceptional Children Department of Education Goldbelt Place 801 W. 10th St. Pouch F Juneau, AK 99811	(907) 465–2970 .20 FTE
American Samoa	Lui Tuitele Consultant Gifted/Talented Education Pago Pago, AS 96799	Deputy's #-Telea 011–684–633–5237 (Overseas operator)
Arizona	Dr. Lola Gross, State Coordinator Education Programs Specialist Arizona Department of Education 1535 West Jefferson Phoenix, AZ 85007	(602) 255–5008 unspecified—Special Projects

*In this appendix % is the percentage of time alloted for gifted education.

Arkanas	Dr. David Grapka Programs for Gifted/Talented Special Education Section Arch Ford Education Building Little Rock, AR 72201	(501) 371–2161 100%
	Martha Bass, Program Advisor Programs for Gifted/Talented Special Education Section Arch Ford Education Building Little Rock, AR 72201	(501) 371–2161 100%
	Paula Cummins, Program Advisor Programs for Gifted/Talented Special Education Section Arch Ford Education Building Little Rock, AR 72201	(501) 371–2161
California	Dr. Paul Plowman, Consultant Gifted and Talented Education 721 Capitol Mall Sacramento, CA 95814	(916) 323–4781 100%
	Linda Forsyth, Consultant Gifted and Talented Education 721 Capitol Mall Sacramento, CA 95814	100%
Colorado	Dr. Jerry Villars, State Coordinator Gifted and Talented Student Program Colorado Department of Education First Western Plaza 303 W. Colfax Denver, CO 80204	(303) 534–8871 ext. 354 1.0 FTE
Connecticut	Alan White, Consultant Gifted/Talented Programs State Department of Education 165 Capital Ave. Hartford, CT 06145	(203) 566–3695 100%
Delaware	Peggy Dee, State Supervisor Programs for Exceptional Children State Department of Public Instruction P. O. Box 1402 Dover, DE 19903	(302) 736–4667 .30 FTE P. L. 94-142
District of Columbia	Dr. Phyllis Hines Gifted and Talented Education Programs Bryan Elementary School 13th and Independence Ave., S.E. Washington, DC 20003	(202) 724–3894 100% (1 other—100%)

Florida	Program Specialist—Judy Miller Gifted Programs DOE/Bureau of Education for Exceptional Children Knott Building Tallahassee, FL 32301	(904) 488–1106 100%
Georgia	Christopher E. Nelson, Coordinator Programs for the Gifted Department of Education Twin Towers East, Suite 1970 Atlanta, GA 30334	(404) 656–2428 100%
	Mary Lillian White, Consultant Programs for the Gifted Department of Education Twin Towers, Suite 1970 Atlanta, GA 30334	(404) 656–2428 50%—Generalist Responsibilities in Education Services District 17
	Joyce E. Gay, Consultant Programs for the Gifted Twin Towers East, Suite 1970 Atlanta, GA 30334	(404) 656–2428 50%—Generalist Education Services District 1
Guam	Victoria T. Harper Associate Superintendent for Special Education Department of Education P. O. Box DE Agana, GU 96910	911-44-671-Local No.: 472–8906, 8702, 9802, or 9352
Hawaii	Margaret Donovan, Acting Ed. Specialist Gifted and Talented Special Needs Branch Department of Education 3430 Leahi Ave. Honolulu, HI 96815	(808) 737–2377 or 2166
Idaho	Martha Noffsinger Supervisor of Special Education State Department of Education Len B. Jordan Office Building 650 West State Boise, ID 83720	(208) 334–3940
Illinois	Wilma Lund Gifted Education Coordinator Education Innovation/Support Section State Department of Education 100 North First St. Springfield, IL 62777	(217) 782–3810 100% (2 others—100% and 50%)

Indiana	Walter Cory, State Coordinator Consultant Indiana Department of Education 229 State House Indianapolis, IN 46204	(317) 927–0111 100%
	Patricia B. Stafford Program Manager Gifted and Talented Education 229 State House Indianapolis, IN 46204	(317) 927–0111 100%
Iowa	Dr. LeLand Wolf Consultant, Gifted Education Department of Public Instruction Grimes State Office Building Des Moines, IA 50319	(515) 281–3198 about 75%
Kansas	Woody Houseman Education Program Specialist for Gifted State Department of Education 120 E. 10th Topeka, KS 66612	(913) 296–3743 60%—Homebound/ Hospital Programs and Special Education Compliance
Kentucky	Nijel Clayton, Program Manager Gifted/Talented Education Kentucky Department of Education 1831 Capitol Plaza Tower Frankfort, KY 40601	(502) 564–2106 100%
Louisiana	Patricia Dial, Supervisor Gifted and Talented Programs Louisiana Department of Education P. O. Box 94064 Baton Rouge, LA 70804-9064	(504) 342–3636 100%
Maine	Valerie Seaberg Consultant, Secondary Gifted/Talented State House Station #23 Augusta, ME 04333	(207) 289–3451 100%
	Patricia Kleine, Director Gifted and Talented Teacher Training Schibles Hall School of Education University of Maine at Orono Orono, ME 04469	(207) 581–2479 100%
Maryland	Lynn Cole Chief, Learning Improvement Section State Department of Education 200 W. Baltimore St. Baltimore, MD 21201	(301) 659–2000 100%

	Jay McTighe Specialist, Gifted/Talented State Department of Education 200 W. Baltimore St. Baltimore, MD 21201	(301) 659–2000 100%
	Toni Favazza-Wiegand Specialist, Gifted/Talented State Department of Education 200 W. Baltimore St. Baltimore, MD 21201	(301) 659–2000 100%
Massachusetts	Roselyn Frank, Director Office of Gifted and Talented Massachusetts Department of Education Bureau of Curriculum Services 1385 Hancock St. Quincy, MA 02169	(617) 770–7237 100%
Michigan	Nancy Mincemoyer, Consultant Programs for Gifted and Talented Michigan Department of Education P. O. Box 30008 Lansing, MI 48909	(517) 373–3279 50%—Specialist, Science and Environmental Education
	Eva Redwine, Specialist Programs for Gifted and Talented Michigan Department of Education P. O. Box 30008 Lansing, MI 48909	(517) 373–3279 100%
Minnesota	Lorraine Hertz, Program Specialist Gifted Education State Department of Education 641 Capitol Square St. Paul, MN 55101	(612) 296–4972 100%
Mississippi	Kelly Miller State Consultant for Gifted State Department of Education P. O. Box 771 Jackson, MS 39205	(601) 359–3488 or 3490 100%
Missouri	Robert Roach, Director Gifted Education Programs State Department of Elementary and Secondary Education P. O. Box 480 100 East Capital Jefferson City, MO	(314) 751–2453 100%

Montana	Nancy Lukenbill, Specialist
	Gifted and Talented Programs
	Office of Public Instruction
	State Capital
	Helena, MT 59601
		(406) 444–4422
		100%—Extra: Drug and
		   Alcohol Training,
		   Accreditation

Nebraska	Sheila Brown, Supervisor Programs for the Gifted State Department of Education P. O. Box 94987 300 Centennial Mall South Lincoln, NE 68509	(402) 471–2446 50%—Art Education
Nevada	Dr. Jane Early, Director Special Education Programs Nevada Department of Education 400 West King St. Carson City, NV	(702) 885–3140 0%—answers gifted mail; Education of the Handicapped
New Hampshire	Susan H. Newton, Consultant Special Education Section New Hampshire Department of Education State Office Park South 101 Pleasant St. Concord, NH 03301	(603) 271–3741 50%—Gifted, statewide 50%—Spe. Ed. northern NH
New Jersey	Jeanne Carlson Education Program Specialist Division of General Academic Education Department of Education 225 West State St. CN 500 Trenton, NJ 08625-0500	(609) 984–1971 100%
New Mexico	Mr. Elie S. Gutierrex, Director Special Education Education Building Santa Fe, MN 87501-2786	(505) 827–6541
New York	David Irvine, New York Gifted Education State Education Dept. Room 310-EB Albany, NY 12234	(518) 474-5966
North Carolina	Gail Smith, Chief Consultant Academically Gifted Programs Division for Exceptional Children State Department of Public Instruction Raleigh, NC 27611	(919) 733–3004 100%
	Ruby Murchison, Consultant for Academically Gifted South Central Regional Education Center P. O. Box 786 Carthage, NC 28327	(919) 947–5871 100%
North Dakota	Ida Schmitt, Assistant Director Special Education Department of Public Instruction State Capitol Bismarck, ND 58505	(701) 224–2277

Ohio	George Fichter Educational Consultant Programs for Gifted Division of Special Education 933 High St. Worthington, OH 43085	(614) 466–2650 100%—Adjunct Professor, Dept. of Human Services Education, Ohio State University
Oklahoma	Dorothy Dodd, Administrator Gifted/Talented Section State Department of Education 2500 N. Lincoln Blvd. Oklahoma City, OK 73105	(405) 521–4287 100%
	Anita Boone, Coordinator Gifted/Talented Section State Department of Education 2500 N. Lincoln Blvd. Oklahoma City, OK 73105	(405) 521–4287 100%
	Shirley Crawford, Coordinator Gifted/Talented Section State Department of Education 2500 N. Lincoln Blvd. Oklahoma City, OK 73105	(405) 521–4287 100%
Oregon	Robert J. Siewert Gifted/Talented Specialist 700 Pringle Parkway SE Salem, OR 97219	(503) 378–3879 .25 FTE
Pennsylvania	Dr. Gary Makuch, Director Bureau of Special Education Department of Education 333 Market St. Harrisburg, PA 17126-0333	(717) 783–6913
Puerto Rico	Consultant, Gifted Office of External Resources Department of Education Hato Rey, PR 99024	(809) 765–1475
Rhode Island	Judy Edsal, Education Specialist Gifted/Talented Education Department of Elementary/Secondary Education 22 Hayes St. Providence, RI 02908	(401) 277–6523 100%
South Carolina	Dr. Anne H. Elam, Coordinator Programs for the Gifted 802 Rutledge Building 1429 Senate St. Columbia, SC 29201	(803) 758–2652 100%

South Dakota	Programs for the Gifted Special Education Section Richard F. Kneip Building 700 N. Illinois Pierre, SD 57501	(605) 773–3678 50%—Title VI-B monitoring special education programs, state mediation/due process
Tennessee	Emily Stewert, Director Gifted/Talented Programs and Services 132-A Cordell Hull Building Nashville, TN 37219	(615) 741–2851 100%
Texas	Ann Shaw Director of Gifted/Talented Education Texas Education Agency 201 East 11th St. Austin, TX 78701	(512) 834–4451 100%
	Evelyn L. Hiatt Education Specialist II Gifted/Talented Education Texas Education Agency 201 East 11th St. Austin, TX 78701	(512) 834–4451 100%
Trust Territory	Harou Kuartei, Federal Programs Coordinator Office of Special Education Trust Territory Office of Education Office of the High Commissioner Saipan, CM 96950	160–671–Saipan 9312, 9428, or 9319
Utah	Dr. Keith D. Steck State Consultant for Gifted State Office of Education 250 E. 5th, South Salt Lake City, UT 84111	(801) 533–5572 100%
Vermont	Donna D. Brinkmeyer Arts/Gifted Consultant State Department of Education Montpelier, VT 05602	(802) 828–3111 ext. 33 50%
Virgin Islands	State Director of Special Education Department of Education Box 630, Charlotte Amalie St. Thomas, VI 00801	(809) 774–0100 ext. 271
Virginia	Dr. John D. Booth, Associate Director Programs for the Gifted Division of Special Education Virginia Department of Education P. O. Box 6Q Richmond, VA 23216	(804) 225–2070 100%

	Deborah Bellflower, Program Supervisor Programs for the Gifted Division of Special Education Virginia Department of Education P. O. Box 6Q Richmond, VA 23216	(804) 225–2070 100%
	Clyde Atkinson Office of Dependents School Department of Defense 2461 Eisenhower Blvd Alexandria, VA 22231	(804) 225–2070 100%
Washington	Gail Hanninen, Consultant Gifted Education Old Capitol Bldg. Olympia, WA 98501	(206) 753–6760 100%
West Virginia	Dr. Barbara Jones, Coordinator Programs for the Gifted 357 B, Capitol Complex Charleston, WV 25305	(304) 348–7010 100%
Wisconsin	Bob Gomoll Gifted/Talented Programs P. O. Box 7841 125 S. Webster Madison, WI 53701	(608) 266–3560
Wyoming	Susan Holt, Coordinator Language Arts/Gifted/Talented Wyoming Department of Education Hathaway Building Cheyenne, WY 82002	(307) 777–6238 50%

APPENDIX D

COGNITIVE AND THINKING SKILLS

Definition of cognitive skills	Program	Objectives	Methodology
Intelligence Education	S.O.I. Drs. Mary and Robert Meeker 343 Richmond St. El Segundo, CA 90245 (Based on J.P. Guilford's structure of Intellect model)	Improving the information processing skills of learners. Career counseling information available In figural, symbolic, and verbal form, skills include: Cognition Memory Divergent production (creative thinking) Convergent production Evaluation	Individual assessment of cognitive skills provides the basis for the preparation of a diagnostic/prescriptive remediation and enrichment plan. While exercises are extra-disciplinary, the use of the S.O.I. Learning Abilities Test provides valuable recommendations on student performance on content objectives. Intended audience: Pre-school to adult. Evaluation: retesting on the alternate form of the S.O.I. Learning Abilities Test.
Identifying and Modifying the Learning Process	Instrumental Enrichment Reuven Feuerstein, University Park Press, Baltimore Professional Training: Dr. Francis Link CDA Inc. 1211 Connecticut Ave., NW, Suite 414 Washington, DC 20036 David Hoffman Wester Center for Cognitive Education 15260 Ventura Blvd. Encino Medical Tower Encino, CA 91436	Developing student awareness of the learning/problem solving process and omissions which create errors or misconceptions. Instruments include: **Nonverbal** Organization of dots Analytic Perception Illustrations **Limited Vocabulary** Spatial Orientation Comparisons Family Relations Numerical Progressions Independent Reading Categorization Instructions Temporal Relations Transitive Relations Representation Stencil Design **Logical Reasoning**	Analysis of figural and verbal problems using discussion to describe the process. Extra-disciplinary exercises. Program designed for adolescents, but also used in upper elementary and middle school classrooms. Evaluation: Selection of commercial tests varies, but observation of student behavior is commonly practiced.

Definition of cognitive skills	Program	Objectives	Methodology
Piagetian or Experiential Methods (learning activities based on children's intellectual development, stressing experience and the use of concrete, semiconcrete, and abstract tasks)	Early Prevention of School Failure Lucille Warner Peotone School District 207-U 114 N. Second St. Peotone, IL 60468	Modality training for gross and fine motor development, visual & auditory discrimination, and language skill.	Diagnostic/prescriptive activities with screening instruments, management guides, classroom activities, and parent materials for students 4–6 years old. Prepost assessment instrument prepared by developer. J.D.R.P. validated.
	British Primary Schools materials Nuffield Mathematics John Wiley, N.Y. MacDonald Science Series Purnell Educational 850 Seventh Ave., New York, N.Y. 10019	Science and mathematics concepts relying on observation and measurement.	Teacher materials for conducting and organizing science and mathematics instruction in British Primary Schools. For students 5–13 years old. Evaluation by observation of student behavior.
	Alpha II Program 2425 Alamo SE Albuquerque, NM 87106	Piagetian skills: Conservation Classification Seriation Number and space perception.	Small-group administration of Piagetian assessment instrument allows small-group implementation of Piagetian tasks. Manipulatives lesson cards, a management plan, and questioning strategies are provided. Assessment by use of a diagnostic form and observation of student behavior.
	Comprehensive School Mathematics Program Claire Heidema 470 N. Kirkwood St. Louis, MO 63122	Classification, elementary logic and number theory.	Experiential, but not strictly Piagetian, approach to teaching mathematics by a spiral curriculum. J.D.R.P. validated for grades K-6. Pre-post assessment instrument prepared by developer, also evaluated by C.T.B.S. and Stanford Achievement Tests.

Definition of cognitive skills	Program	Objectives	Methodology
	Cognitive Level Matching Project Martin Brooks Shoreham Wading-River Central School District, Shoreham, NY 11786	Use of instructional methods appropriate to students' intellectual development as defined by Piaget. Extensive staff development was provided in recognizing and integrating Piagetian methods.	Implemented K-12 in academic subjects. Evaluated by teacher assessment of students' explanation of reasoning and by Piagetian tests.
Perceiving Relationships (Analysis Skills)	Strategic Reasoning Innovative Science Inc. Think Program Park Square Station, P.O. Box 15129, Stamford, CT 06901	Skills include: Thing making Qualification Classification Operation Analysis Component Analysis Analogy	Media kits and student workbook. Middle School through high school levels. THINK II is content related; other activities are extra-disciplinary. Assessment by cognitive abilities tests.
	Building Thinking Skills I, II, III Midwest Publications P.O. Box 448 Pacific Grove, CA 93950	In verbal and figural form, skills include: Similarities and Differences Sequencing Classification Analogy	Book I is designed for middle elementary grades; Book II, upper elementary grades; Book III, Junior high school. Items are drawn from content area vocabulary, hence seems content related. Teacher's manuals provide explanations of tasks, enrichment or preparatory activities, and guidelines for discussion. Assessment—Cognitive Abilities Test or DCAT. Criterion referenced tests can be designed by following references to corresponding items provided in the teacher's manual.

Definition of cognitive skills	Program	Objectives	Methodology
Formal Reasoning (Reasoning, with Principles)	Philosophy for Children Montclair State College Upper Montclair NJ 07043	Four courses include: Harry (Logic) Syllogisms Inferences Rules and generalizations Hypothesis Causes and reasons Contradictions Lisa (Ethics) Consistency Justifying beliefs Determinism Right, fair, true, will, natural	Students read special novels having inquisitive children as characters, followed structured discussions, as exercises, and games. New primary courses: Kio and Gus (reasoning about nature) Pixie (reasoning about language) These courses introduce young children to the definitions and processes of philosophical inquiry. Teaching method is dialog. Assessment: New Jersey Test of Reasoning Skills designed for evaluating Harry.
Formal Reasoning (Reasoning with Principles)	Philosophy for Children Montclair State College Upper Montclair NJ 07043	Suki (Aesthetics in writing) Expression Meaning Craftsmanship Experience Mark (Social institutions) Making judgements Social Theories Authority Justice and Freedom	

Definition of cognitive skills	Program	Objectives	Methodology
	Critical Thinking I and II Midwest Publications P.O. Box 448 Pacific Grove, CA 93950	Skills include: Formal (symbolic) and informal logic Language in reasoning Propaganda and persuasion Debate and decision making	Critical thinking course which can be integrated into the secondary English and social studies curriculum. Assessment by Watson-Glaser Test of Critical Thinking or Cornell Test of Critical Thinking.
	Critical Thinking In History Project Kevin O'Reilly Hamilton-Wenham Regional High School 775 Bay Rd. S. Hamilton, MA 01982	Skills include: Evaluation of evidence Evaluation of value statements Logical Thinking Types of Reasoning Fallacies in History Analyzing arguments	Supplemental logic course for U.S. history instruction (colonial period, new republic to Civil War period, and reconstruction to progressivism period). Each unit includes a student guide, worksheets, debate and analysis guide, and interpretations to history for student analysis. Evaluation includes the content and length of student essays, student attitude questionnaire, and the Cornell Test of Critical Thinking.
Implementing Thinking Skills Instruction in the Content Areas	Project Impact Orange County Superintendent of Schools Lee Winocur, Director P.O. Box 9050 Costa Mesa, CA 92626	Skills organized in a hierarchial sequence are presented in concrete and abstract learning units. Skills include: Classifying and Categorizing Ordering, Sequencing and Prioritizing Patterns and Relationships Fact and Opinion Relevant and Irrelevant Information Effective Questioning Understanding the Meaning of Statements Cause and Effect Making Generalizations Forming Predictions Making Assumptions Identifying Point-of-View Logical Reasoning	Designed for junior and senior high school students, lessons include direct instruction activities for students and thorough lesson plans for teachers. J.D.R.P. validated. Assessment: C.T.B.S. and Cornell Test for Critical Thinking.

Definition of cognitive skills	Program	Objectives	Methodology
	Learning to Learn Marcia Heiman Box 493 Cambridge, MA 02138	Skills common to the internal dialog of good learners: Raising and testing hypothesis Breaking complex ideas into manageable parts Feedback and correction Directed learning behavior to content.	Series of learning strategies designed to help students think actively while engaged in content learning. Used with junior high grades through college years. Assessment: G.P.A., course achievement, and content retention.
Creative ("Lateral") Thinking and Problem Solving	CORT Cognitive Research Trust Pergamon Press Fairview Park Elmsford, NY 10523	Problem solving strategies focus on: Breadth Organization Interaction Creativity Information and Feeling Action	Student exercises ("courts") with teacher's handbook containing methods, practice items, research results, teaching notes. Elementary, secondary, and college use; and ability level.
Developing Creative Thinking Skills (Activities based on E. Paul Torrance's definitions of skills)	Institute for Creative Education Educational Improvement Center Box 209, Rte 4 Sewell, NJ 08080	Skills include: Fluency Flexibility Originality Elaboration	Elementary and secondary manuals offer student exercises which are related to content objectives and may be used at any grade level and with any ability group. Assessment by the Torrance Tests of Creative Thinking, J.D.R.P. validated for grades 4–6.
Talent Development as a Content Learning Component	Talents Unlimited Title IV-C ESEA Florence Replogle 1107 Arlington St. Mobile, AL 36605 (Based on Calvin Taylor's multiple talent theory)	Skills include: Academic skills Productive thinking Planning Communication Forecasting Decision-making	Exercises are related to content objectives. Validated by J.D.R.P. Elementary grades; all ability levels.

Definition of cognitive skills	Program	Objectives	Methodology
Creative Problem Solving	CPS Creative Education Foundation, Signey Parnes, Director. Buffalo, NY (Materials are available from D.O.K. Publishers, P.O. Box 605, East Aurora, NY 14052	Students follow a process to solve personal, organizational, or hypothetical problems. Steps include: Sensing problems and challenges Fact finding Problem definition Idea-finding Solution-finding Acceptance-finding	Exercises are designed for all grades and ability levels. Applies to future studies, the Future Problem Solving competitions at the state and national levels are evaluated by an extensive review process.
Decision Making Programs	Critical Analysis and Thinking Skills Dr. Terry Applegate Salt Lake City, UT	Objectives include: Rational decision making Constructive criticism Identifying & solving problems Skills include: Clarification of terms Information gathering Discriminating fact from opinion Determining adequacy of authority Determining bias Identifying relevant information Testing consistency Criticism Developing questioning strategies	Instruction may be integrated into existing high school social studies courses for one semester or taught as a separate course. Validated by J.D.R.P. Curriculum package includes inservice materials, teacher manuals, and evaluation instruments.
	Guided Design Charles Wales Engineering Sciences West Virginia Univ. Morgantown, WV 26506	Solving Problems Finding a cause of a problem Anticipating potential problems Identifying & prioritizing problems	Materials are available at college level. Some field testing has been done for secondary use. Use of the model is district designed in content area.

Prepared by: Sandra Black, Cognitive Skills Development Associates, P.O. Box 468, St. Augustine, FL 32085, (904) 824-0648.

SURVEY OF THINKING SKILLS PROGRAMS

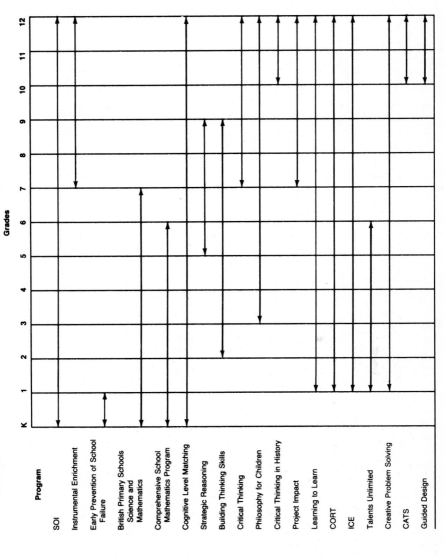

Grades

Program

SOI

Instrumental Enrichment

Early Prevention of School Failure

British Primary Schools Science and Mathematics

Comprehensive School Mathematics Program

Cognitive Level Matching

Strategic Reasoning

Building Thinking Skills

Critical Thinking

Philosophy for Children

Critical Thinking in History

Project Impact

Learning to Learn

CORT

ICE

Talents Unlimited

Creative Problem Solving

CATS

Guided Design

INDEX

Note: *Italic* letters following page numbers indicate: exhibits (*e.*), figures (*f.*), or tables (*t.*).